HISTORICAL SKETCHES

OF THE

TOWN OF LEICESTER,

MASSACHUSETTS,

DURING THE FIRST CENTURY FROM ITS SETTLEMENT.

BY EMORY WASHBURN.

BOSTON:
PRINTED BY JOHN WILSON AND SON,
22, SCHOOL STREET.
1860.

This unpretending Effort,

TO RESCUE FROM OBLIVION THE SIMPLE ANNALS OF MY NATIVE TOWN,

I Dedicate to those,

THE LIVING AND THE DEAD,

TO WHOSE KINDNESS AND AFFECTION I OWE SO MANY OF THE PLEASANT MEMORIES THAT CLUSTER AROUND THE HOME OF MY CHILDHOOD.

EMORY WASHBURN.

CAMBRIDGE, April, 1860.

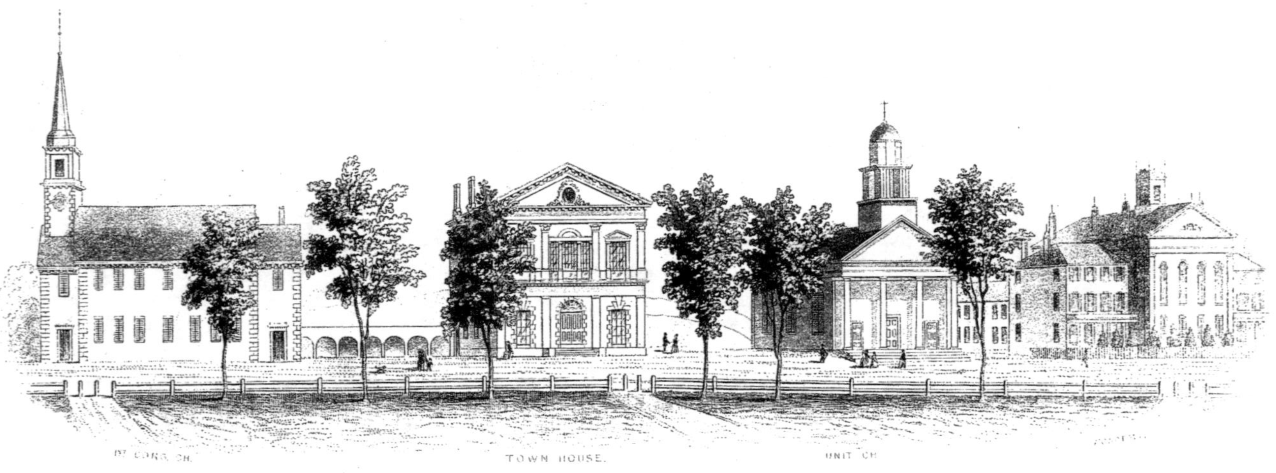

LEICESTER, MASS.

HISTORY OF LEICESTER.

INTRODUCTION.

IN attempting to embody the local incidents which go to make up the history of one of our municipal corporations called "Towns," it would be a matter of curious and interesting inquiry to trace the origin of these bodies politic. Nothing precisely like them had been known to the first settlers in New England, before their removal here; though the idea may have been borrowed from the early division of England into Hundreds, or Tithings. These had their origin in a rude state of society, for the purposes of civil and domestic police. But the division of a territory into local districts by geographical lines, and conferring upon their inhabitants corporate powers and duties like those with which the towns of New England are clothed, will, it is believed, be found to have been an institution originally peculiar to the Colonies planted there.

It was probably the result, in part, of accident at first; but was chiefly due, like so many of the measures which the founders of these Colonies inaugurated, to the singular wisdom and foresight with which they adapted their policy to the condition of the people. Without, at first, setting apart a prescribed portion of territory, and clothing it with corporate powers, the General Court conferred these upon such settlements as from their size, and remoteness from others, rendered a corporate organization a matter of safety and convenience. Thus it is said that the only Act of Incorporation of Boston, Dorchester, or Watertown, was an order of the General Court, "that Trimountain shall be called Boston; Mattapan, Dorchester; and the town on Charles River, Watertown."

The Colony, through its government, stood in two relations to the settlers upon the hitherto unoccupied lands; by one of which, a title to these lands was granted; and, by the other, the requisite powers were conferred and duties imposed upon them as bodies politic. Provision was thus made for the support of the gospel, the maintenance of highways, the management of their municipal affairs, and, at an early day, for the support of free schools. In process of time, grants of specific portions of territory were made in anticipation of settlements being formed thereon within prescribed periods; and, when formed, corporate powers were conferred upon them, generally by very brief Acts, which assumed that these powers and duties were understood and defined by the nature of the organization to which vitality was thereby given. This will be illustrated by the Act incorporating the town whose history it is now proposed to write.

But, whatever may have been the origin of these town organizations, it may be doubted whether the true New-England character which has distinguished the Northern Colonies, in their earlier and later history, may not be more directly traced to the existence of these than to any other single cause. While, as has been remarked, they were made the means of sustaining public religious worship and schools, and enforcing a salutary domestic police, they became the medium of accomplishing scarcely less important results in their social and political bearing. As little independent democracies, they gave to every citizen a part and share in the management of their concerns, and rendered him familiar with the forms and details of public business, as well as the nature and extent of popular rights and duties; and, by means of the discussions to which the meetings of the people of the several towns at stated intervals gave rise, every man learned how to give utterance to his own opinions, and to feel the dignity and responsibility of a free man among his equals.

Every man, moreover, felt that he was a part of one corporate whole. Its limits were the bounds of his home. Its very scenery became identified with his earliest and holiest associations and affections; and the church where his fathers had worshipped, and the churchyard where his fathers were sleeping, had for him a sanctified interest which no other spot could ever awaken. Its history became a part of his own. The burdens of taxation were relieved of half their weight by the consciousness that they were imposed by his own agents, for purposes connected with the honor, prosperity, and reputation of his own town; and, in this way, incidents in the domestic history of one of these little communities often acquired an interest for its members disproportioned to their intrinsic importance, and which it was difficult for a stranger to understand. They partook of the character which the mind spontaneously associates with the events that go to make up the inner life of one's own self and that of his family.

I hardly need to add, that it is with feelings like these that I have ventured upon a task of so much labor, — which can bring, in return, no reward of fame or money, — of gathering up the few and scattered materials which remain of the history of this now ancient town of Leicester, for the first century of its existence as a body politic. I cannot sufficiently express the regret I feel that some other hand had not undertaken the work, and that it had not been undertaken at a much earlier day. The brief and imperfect sketch of the history of the town, hastily prepared, now more than thirty years ago, was even then too late to be what it should have been. It is the more to be regretted, because, within the recollection of many now living, intelligent men and women were residing here who formed a part of the generation that succeeded the first settlement of the town, and possessed a rich fund of anecdote and local incident connected with its earliest history, which has been buried in their graves, and irretrievably lost.* Even of the events of the Revolution, in which the town took an early and active part, not a living witness remains.

But, much as we may lament the loss of these sources of her early history, I greatly miscalculate, or there will still be found, in the materials which have been preserved, enough to furnish a record of the fathers, which the sons may feel a generous pride in recalling. The very nature of the work of tracing out and collecting these bespeaks the indulgence which is due to him who undertakes it; and, if the following pages do no more, they will bear testimony to the grateful memories and associations of one, in whose mind they are connected with the spot of his birth, and, for twenty-eight years, the home of his affections.

---

* Among those I might mention, of the class here referred to, was Mrs. Mary Sargent, the widow of Nathan, and mother of the late John Sargent, sen. She was born in 1727, — a daughter of Daniel Denny, one of the first settlers in the town, — and survived till 1822; a period of ninety-five years, which went back within ten years of the planting of the town. She was a remarkably bright, intelligent lady. Her memory was stored with interesting local and personal anecdotes; and her recollections, if they had been noted down and treasured, would have furnished a most fruitful and interesting source of the history of the town. She retained her mental powers till a late period in her life; and is still remembered as a most agreeable, cheerful, and entertaining lady. I recollect a very pleasant journey, in her company, from Leicester into Vermont and back again, when she was eighty-four years old. Age had hardly dulled the quickness of her vivacity, or impaired the vigor of her mind or body.

CHAPTER I.

PURCHASE, INCORPORATION, AND SETTLEMENT OF THE TOWN.—NOTICES OF ITS ORIGINAL PROPRIETORS, ALLOTMENTS OF ITS TERRITORY, &c.

THE first notice we have of the place, afterwards called LEICESTER, is in 1686, when the territory was purchased of the Indian proprietors by a company of nine persons, most of whom belonged to Roxbury. Although the jurisdiction over and general property in the soil was conferred by their charter upon the Company of the Massachusetts Bay, the right of soil in the aborigines as occupants thereof was recognized by the government of the Colony, and was regarded in most instances by the colonists in making acquisitions of parts of the territory.

The usual course of proceeding in such cases was to obtain, from the head men or chiefs of the tribes inhabiting the portion of the territory which it was desired to acquire, a formal deed of release; for which some satisfactory, though often inconsiderable, compensation was paid. Upon application to the General Court, the title thus acquired was generally confirmed, but upon such conditions as they saw fit to prescribe.

Companies of private speculators early engaged in the business of thus buying up Indian titles to lands, which they secured to themselves by confirmatory acts of the General Court. There was, ordinarily, no difficulty in effecting these confirmatory grants, since the leading men in the Colony were largely concerned in these speculations. The spirit for such enterprises seems to have pervaded all classes, especially from the first to the middle of the eighteenth century; including, as the history of this town will show, officers the highest in authority, as well as ministers of the gospel. It would, in fact, be difficult to trace to its origin the rage and mania for speculation in lands with which our community is periodically afflicted. Without attempting it in this case, I have only to speak of the mode in which such enterprises were managed.

These companies became a kind of corporation known as a Proprietary; managing their affairs, even to the granting of their lands, by votes, of which they preserved records, and which, in many instances in Massachusetts, form the only evidence of the original titles to lands as acquired from the original proprietors. These books of "Proprietors' Records," therefore, have become valuable as muniments of title to lands; and, in most instances, have been carefully preserved.

Among other tracts which were purchased by the same company to whom the territory of Leicester was conveyed was the township of Hardwick, which, for a while, took the name of Lambstown from that of one of the company.

The township of Leicester lay in the heart of what was known as the Nipnet or Nipmuc country, which extended to a considerable distance to the south, embracing the ponds and streams in and around Oxford. The tribe seems to have been scattered over a pretty large territory, extending from Connecticut River, easterly, to the tribes along the coast, known as the Massachusetts Indians. The settlements of the tribe occurred at considerable intervals through this large territory; and over these were headmen, or sachems, who were nominally subordinate in authority to the principal chief or ruler of the tribe.*

* I find in the Secretary's office a letter from Col. Chandler to Lieut.-Gov. Dummer, dated July 7, 1724, wherein he says, "There is a tribe of Indians between Woodstock and Oxford; being women and children about forty, the men about seven or

The Indian name of the territory purchased by the Roxbury men was Towtaid, over which Oraskaso had been sachem. He had recently died, leaving two daughters, who, with their husbands, claimed title to the soil. Except by a rugged path called the New Connecticut Road, by which occasional intercourse was kept up between the settlements at Marlborough and east of that, and those on Connecticut River, this region was an inaccessible wilderness, and, at the time of the purchase, had no nearer white settlement than Marlborough. The settlements at Quaboog or Brookfield and Worcester had been broken up and dispersed by the war of King Philip in 1675. Indeed, the situation of the place and the circumstances of the country were so unpropitious to a settlement of the lands they had purchased, that the proprietors took no measures to accomplish this for nearly thirty years.

Their deed bears date Jan. 27, 1686,* and professes to convey eight miles square of territory for the consideration of "fifteen pounds current money of New England." A copy of this deed will be found in the Appendix to this work. It is executed by Philip Tray, with his wife Momokhue, and John Wampscon, and Waiwaynom his wife; the wives being the heirs of the late Sachem Oraskaso. It is also signed by Wandwoamag "the deacon," and Jonas his wife, though not named in the deed: from which I am inclined to suppose that they belonged to the "Praying Indians;" as there were, a few years prior to this, twenty families at Pagachoag, — a

---

eight." He suggests that they ought not to be permitted to live by themselves in the woods, and recommends that "they should be drawn in, and be allowed to hunt under conduct of an Englishman."

* This, by our present calendar, would be 1687; as, until 1752, the year was assumed to begin on the 25th March, or Lady Day, in the calendar of the Romish Church. At that time it began to be reckoned from the 1st January, which took the name of New Style to distinguish it from the Old; and it was common to give a double date for the year between the 1st January and 25th March. Thus a deed or event in January, after the year 1752, would be, for example, Jan. 25, 1755-6.

part of Worcester near to Towtaid, — and there were said to be one thousand converted Indians within the limits of the Nipmuc country.*

The description of the granted territory shows the wild and unsettled state of the region between Marlborough and the Connecticut River at that time. It is said to lie "near the new town of the English, called Worcester." It bounds southerly by lands which Joseph Dudley, Esq., afterwards Gov. Dudley, had lately bought of the Indians; which consisted of a gore of land, a part of which helped afterwards to form Charlton: a part was known as Oxford North Gore, and a part is embraced in the present town of Auburn. The western line cannot now be ascertained or identified; and the northern one is assumed to be known by its running "unto a great hill called Aspomsok," which is supposed to be the hill now called Hasnebumskit in Paxton; "and so on, easterly, upon a line, until it comes against Worcester bounds, and joins unto their bounds."

The war in which the colonists were involved with the French and Indians, known as King William's War, which had begun in 1690, was terminated by the peace of Ryswick in 1697. It was, however, followed by that of Queen Anne in 1702, which continued until the peace of Utrecht in 1713; and it was not until this time that the proprietors of Leicester, which they had till then called by the name of Strawberry Hill, began to take measures to avail themselves of the benefit of their purchase.

They caused their deed to be recorded, and applied to the Legislature for a confirmation of their title to the tract. This was granted upon condition, that, within seven years, fifty families settled themselves, in as defensible and regular a way as the circumstances of the place would allow, on part of said land;" and that a sufficient quantity thereof be

* Worcester Magazine, vol. i. p. 132.

reserved for the use of a gospel ministry there and a school, &c.

These were the usual conditions upon which the grants of townships were then made. By the same vote, "the town to be named LEICESTER, and to belong to the county of Middlesex." This vote was passed on the 15th of February, 1713. It does not profess to grant corporate powers, or to create a body politic for any purposes, except by implication; and yet it is the only Act of Incorporation ever granted to the town, and under which it has ever since executed full corporate powers and duties. The proprietors were limited in this legislative grant to a quantity not exceeding eight miles square of land.*

The persons named as grantees in the original Indian deed were Joshua Lamb, Nathaniel Page, Andrew Gardner, Benjamin Gamblin, Benjamin Tucker, John Curtice, Richard Draper, Samuel Ruggles, and Ralf Bradhurst. The grant of the General Court recites the former grant from the "heirs of Ouraskoe, the original sachem of a place called Towtaid;" and then goes on to confirm the title as above stated.

These proprietors had, probably, already associated others with them in the enterprise of settling the town and sharing in the speculation: for we find them executing a deed on the 23d of the same February, which was acknowledged before Penn Townsend, Esq., to thirteen other associates; dividing the same into twenty equal and undivided shares, of which two were equally divided, each between two, so as to make twenty-two proprietors of the twenty shares. The names of the persons who thus became interested with the original purchasers were Jeremiah Dummer, Paul Dudley, John Clark, Addington Davenport, Thomas Hutchinson, John White, William Hutchinson, Francis Wainwright, John Chan-

* In June, 1714, a survey of the town was made by John Chandler, by order of the General Court, in order to fix its bounds; and it is said by Whitney, that these were established by a special Act of the General Court in January, 1714.

dler and Thomas Howe as one, Daniel Allen and Samuel Sewall as one, and William Dudley.

Every one of these were men of influence in the Province; and, although none of the twenty-two proprietors ever became inhabitants of that portion of the town which retained the original name, it seems proper to give them a passing notice, from their early connection with its history. Many of them belonged to Roxbury, and others of their number were connected with these by family ties.

JOSHUA LAMB, distinguished as "colonel," was a magistrate of influence and respectability. He belonged to Roxbury, was extensively engaged in the land-negotiations of the day, and was a man of large wealth. It was from him, as already stated, that Hardwick took its first name of Lambstown.

SAMUEL RUGGLES also belonged to Roxbury. He was grandfather of the well-known "brigadier," Timothy Ruggles, whose loyalty to the crown made him an exile from his native Province; in which, while he remained, he had no superior.

BENJAMIN GAMBLIN, BENJAMIN TUCKER, and RALPH BRADHURST, belonged to Roxbury.

JOHN CURTICE, an original proprietor, had died, and was represented by Jonathan his son, who also belonged to Roxbury.

RICHARD DRAPER was a Boston merchant, and a deacon in one of its churches.

ANDREW GARDNER, of Roxbury, died about 1701, and was represented by his son Thomas, who died in Needham in 1757.

NATHANIEL PAGE, in 1691, was a resident of Bedford. He was the ancestor of the families of that name in Hardwick, and, among them, of the Rev. Lucius R. Page of Cambridge.

JEREMIAH DUMMER was a man of more consequence in the Province than any of the proprietors yet noticed. He belonged to Boston; was graduated at Harvard College in 1699, and afterwards received the degree of Doctor of Philosophy at the University of Utrecht. While in England, he shared the confidence and friendship of Bolingbroke. He resided there eleven years — from 1710 to 1721 — as Agent of the Province; which was one of the most honorable and responsible trusts in the gift of the General Court. Among his publications as an author was a "Defence of the New-England Charters;" a work of much ability. He died in England, at Plaistow, in 1739; leaving the reputation of a sound scholar.

Paul Dudley was Attorney-General of the Province at the time of his becoming a proprietor of Leicester. He was a son of Gov. Joseph Dudley, and was born in Roxbury. He was graduated at Harvard in 1690, and studied law at the Temple in London. In 1718, he was appointed to the bench of the Superior Court, and became Chief-Justice of that court in 1745. This office he held till his death, in 1751, at the age of seventy-eight. In addition to his acquirements as a lawyer and his services as an able judge, he published works upon theology and natural science, and was elected a member of the Royal Society in London; an honor conferred upon a few only of the residents of the Province.

John Clark belonged to Boston. He was born in 1668, and was graduated at Harvard in 1687. He became a leading politician in his day, and belonged to what was known as the "popular party," at the head of which were the Cookes, father and son, who were opposed to Gov. Shute. When, therefore, he was chosen to the Council in 1720, he was negatived by the Governor; but when he was chosen, the following year, Speaker of the House, the Governor was induced by prudential considerations to consent to the election, although strongly inclined to negative it. He afterwards was chosen to the Council, and admitted to his seat; and was a member of that body at the time of his death, Dec. 5, 1728. He was at that time sixty-one years of age. He is spoken of by Hutchinson as "a person of many valuable qualities."

Addington Davenport was connected by marriage with Paul and William Dudley and Francis Wainwright, all of them proprietors of the town; and, about the time of his becoming a proprietor, was associated with Thomas Hutchinson and John White, two others of the proprietors, as trustees of the Province loan of fifty thousand pounds, in bills, issued and let out at five per cent, upon mortgages of real estate, to the people of the Province, as a substitute for a bank, for which many were then striving. Judge Davenport was graduated at Harvard in 1689; and, in 1695, was appointed Clerk of the Superior Court. In 1714, he was elected to the Council; and, in the following year, appointed to the bench of the Superior Court; which office he held until his death, at the age of sixty-six, in 1736. His wife was the daughter of Col. John Wainwright of Ipswich, an influential citizen in the Province, whose brother Francis married the sister of Paul Dudley. His own daughter married William Dudley, above mentioned.

THOMAS HUTCHINSON was the father of Gov. Hutchinson, and belonged to Boston. He was a merchant, and possessed a leading influence in the political affairs of the Province. He was a member of the Council from 1714 to 1739, with the exception of two years. He died in the office, in 1739, at the age of sixty-five.

JOHN WHITE was, for many years, Clerk of the House of Representatives; and, as has been stated, was one of the trustees of the Province loan in 1714. He died of small-pox, taken by inoculation, in December, 1721; * leaving the repu-

* It should be recollected that inoculation for the small-pox was introduced into America in 1721. Notwithstanding the frightful ravages of this disease, — which carried off 884 out of 5,759 who were attacked with it in the natural way, in Boston alone, in 1721, — the proposition to apply inoculation, which was made by Cotton Mather from accounts which he had read in the Transactions of the Royal Society, was so violently opposed, that no physician but Dr. Zabdiel Boylston dared to adopt it, and he only in a secret manner. Mather's house was assaulted, and he mobbed, for his agency in promoting it. In the year 1721, 247 were secretly inoculated; of whom *six* only died, one of whom was Mr. White. So slowly, however, did it gain favor, that in 1730, while in Boston 3,600 had the disease in the natural way, of whom 488 died, 400 only were inoculated, and of these only 12 died. — *Mass. Hist. Soc. Coll.*, vol. iii. p. 292; *Holmes's Annals*, vol. i. p. 526.

tation, in the words of Hutchinson, of "a gentleman of unspotted character."

William Hutchinson belonged to Boston; which town he represented in the General Court in 1721. He is spoken of by the historian as "a gentleman of very fair character; sensible, virtuous, discreet, and of an independent fortune." He died young. He belonged to the popular party in politics.

Francis Wainwright belonged to Boston, and was the son of an influential man, — John Wainwright of Ipswich. He was a merchant, and married the daughter of Gov. Joseph and sister of Paul and William Dudley. His sister married Judge Davenport, as has been stated. He died in 1722.

John Chandler was born in Woodstock, then embraced in Massachusetts; his father having emigrated to that place from Roxbury in 1686. When the county of Worcester was organized in 1731, he was appointed Judge of Probate, and Chief-Justice of the Court of Common Pleas, for that county. Besides these offices, he held that of colonel of a regiment of militia, and was a member of the Council. He may be considered as the founder of the family of that name in the county; which for many years shared largely in the favor of the Royal Government, and held numerous offices of honor and trust, up to the time of the Revolution. Judge Chandler died in 1743.

Thomas Howe belonged to Marlborough; was a colonel of the militia; a leading and influential citizen; and was the son of the first white settler in that town.

Daniel Allen, of whom little is known, is said to have been a merchant of Boston.

Samuel Sewall belonged to Brookline. He was a son of Chief-Justice Sewall, and married a daughter of Gov. Dudley, and thereby became connected with Wainwright and the two Dudleys above named. He died at the age of seventy-two.

William Dudley, the last named in the deed before mentioned, was the youngest son of Gov. Dudley, and was graduated at Harvard in 1705. He resided in Roxbury. He held many important offices in the Province; was a member of the Council, a Colonel of the Suffolk Regiment, a Judge of the Court of Common Pleas, and, for several years, Speaker of the House of Representatives. As a military officer, he took part in the expedition against Port Royal in Nova Scotia, in 1710, which resulted in an easy conquest of the place. His wife was a daughter of Judge Davenport.

If it were proper, at this distance of time, to indulge in any conjectures in relation to the affairs of the proprietors, one would be led to remark upon the character and position of the men with whom the original purchasers shared the territory they had acquired. They embraced some of the most prominent and leading men of both political parties, some of them connected with the immediate government of the Province, and quite a proportion of them united by strong family ties; and if it could be supposed that by lapse of time, or defect in the original deed, or any other cause, it had become necessary to exert a combined influence over the government in order to obtain a confirmation of the title, it is pretty obvious that these were precisely the class of men through whose aid such a measure might be hoped to be accomplished.

Col. PENN TOWNSEND also, who certified the acknowledgment of the deed, was a leading man in the Province. He was connected by marriage with Judge Davenport; had been Speaker of the House of Representatives; Chief-Justice of the Court of Common Pleas for Suffolk; and had held other important offices.

But as we are bound to presume, in the absence of any positive proof to the contrary, that, in the "good old times" in which these events took place, every thing was properly done, we have only to follow out the action of these proprietors till the town was fully organized as a municipal corporation. The records of their proceedings, unfortunately, are somewhat mutilated; though enough remains to indicate the general course of their measures.

It will be recollected, that one condition upon which the grant of the Legislature was made was the settlement of fifty families within the township within seven years; and this the proprietors undertook at once to accomplish. The method they proposed was by holding out an inducement to a proper number of families to come and occupy their lands, by setting apart the easterly half of the township, and disposing of the same to actual settlers upon favorable terms, and thereby to save to themselves an absolute property in the other half.

A meeting was accordingly held in Boston on the same day with the date of their deed, at which John Chandler was chosen clerk. A vote was passed to dispose of one-half of the town to settlers, and to divide the remainder into twenty lots, of a thousand acres or less each, as a Committee appointed for the purpose "should judge best and most convenient, when on the spot." — "Col. Dudley, Capt. Lamb, Capt. Chandler, Capt. Howe, and Capt. Ruggles," were made the Committee to determine which half should be assigned to the settlers, and which retained for the proprietors, and to grant "lots, after-divisions, and rights, in that half to be settled."

On the 14th of May following this meeting, an allotment, in part, of the settlers' or eastern half, was made, but upon condition that the lots should be settled by May, 1717, or be forfeited. At the expiration of this time, however, several to whom allotments had been made had failed to perform the condition; and another term of one year was extended to them, upon their giving bonds conditioned to comply with the requirements. The vote of the Committee who had this matter in charge indicated a commendable spirit of liberality. Whatever sums might be forfeited were, thereby, to be employed for the purposes of a meeting-house, highways, bridges, and similar public uses.

One thing is observable in the making of these early allotments; and that is, the great value and importance which were attached to what were called "meadows." By these they understood the low and swampy tracts which were destitute of a forest growth, and in which natural grasses were found growing.

Most of these have, of late years, been esteemed of little value; partly, it may be, from having lost their original sources of fertility, and partly from a want of proper care and culture. But, as a means of supplying sustenance to the farming stock of the first settlers until they could till their uplands, these meadows were, indeed, invaluable. Provision was accordingly made, in respect to the western half, for dividing all the meadows of twenty acres or more among the proprietors in equal proportion; and it will be perceived hereafter that a similar policy was adopted in respect to the settlers' part of the town.

The "cedar-swamps," on the contrary, were at first suffered to lie in common for the personal use and accommodation of the owners of the other lands. There were two principal cedar-swamps in the settlers' half, — one of these in the north-west and the other in the south-west part of the town, — the latter of which was never partitioned, like the other lands in the town.

There were several meadows which were early distinguished by names; most of which can be still identified, though some of them have ceased to be improved as such. Among these were Town Meadow, about half a mile west of the meeting-house; now flowed for the purpose of carrying the works in the brick factory of Mr. Sargent. Another was Pond Meadow, lying south-west of Henshaw Pond, so called, through which the waters from that pond flow, and extending to the road leading to Auburn.

For the remainder of these, as well as for the localities of the allotments and many other points of geographical interest in the description of the town, I must refer the reader to the Map annexed to this work; for which he is indebted to the patient research, extended labor, and fondness for antiquarian lore, of Joseph A. Denny, Esq., for whose frequent aid in the prosecution of this work I am happy to acknowledge my indebtedness.

The allotment begun in May, 1714, to the settlers, was carried out by setting out to them fifty parcels, — some in quantities of thirty acres, some of forty, and some of fifty, — and appropriating a lot of a hundred acres for schools; reserving one forty-acre lot of the fifty for the ministry, and assigning three additional lots upon condition that mills should be erected thereon. These were considered as the original "house-lots;" and the proprietors of each were to receive, as "after-rights," a hundred acres in some other part of the town for every ten included in their respective house-lots. It was not, however, until the 23d July, 1722, that the conditions upon which these allotments had been made were sufficiently complied with to call for any action on the part of the original proprietors of the town, who as yet had made no formal deed of conveyance to the settlers of their lands. At that time, a meeting of these proprietors was held at the Green-Dragon Tavern in Boston.

To one who remembers the character of those famous meetings at that house, so well known in the history of the times, just before and during the Revolution, there may seem to have been something of unconscious appropriateness in the place in which this meeting was held, when he recalls, as this history will show, the early and persistent devotion of its people to the principles and cause of the American Revolution.

On that occasion, "it was voted that Col. William Dudley, Lieut.-Col. Joshua Lamb, Nathaniel Kanny, Samuel Green, and Samuel Tyley,* be a Committee and fully authorized and

* Samuel Tyley had become owner of a part of the share formerly belonging to Richard Draper. He was a notary public, and had his office in King Street, Boston. He became the clerk of the proprietors in 1726.

empowered to execute a good and sufficient deed or conveyance in the law, by order and in the name of the proprietors of Leicester, for the one-half of that township in the eastern half, to the first grantors and settlers thereon that performed the condition of their grant, or such persons as shall derive and make out title thereto from them to the satisfaction of said Committee, to them, their heirs and assigns, for ever." The Committee were directed to except out of their grant a forty-acre lot in contest between John Minzies and Samuel Prince.

The condition upon which the lots had been granted was, that one shilling per acre for each house-lot should be paid, and a family settled thereon within a prescribed time, or the same should revert to the grantors.

This vote was not, however, carried into effect until the 11th January, 1724, when a deed was executed of the several lots, designated by numbers, to thirty-seven different persons, some of whom, by procuring other families to settle upon their allotments, had acquired a right to more than a single lot each. A copy of this deed will be found in the Appendix;* and while it contains the names of persons who never removed to the town, and of others who, though once resident here, have long disappeared from its records, there will be found upon it the ancestors of many of the families which have constituted an important part of the prominent inhabitants of the town. Among them will readily occur the Dennys, the Greens, the Earles, the Henshaws, the Sargents, the Livermores, and the Southgates.

By the execution of this deed, the connection between the easterly and westerly portions of the town was, in a good measure, practically dissolved, although they continued to form one municipal corporation till 1753. At that time the westerly part was set off into a district, having most of the powers of

* The localities of the allotments may be traced upon the annexed Map.

a town except that of choosing a representative to the General Court, under the name of Spencer. It had been erected into a parish in 1744; and, at the breaking-out of the Revolution, the only distinction which remained between its character as a district and as a town was removed by the right it thereupon acquired of being represented in the Legislature. For this reason, and because the history of Spencer has already been so fully and faithfully given to the public by the Hon. James Draper of that town,* I shall confine what I shall have to say, chiefly, to that part of the original town which retained its original corporate name of Leicester.

* I am happy to acknowledge the use I have made of the history of Mr. Draper in the preparation of this work, to which reference has been frequently had.

CHAPTER II.

BOUNDARIES AND TOPOGRAPHICAL FEATURES OF THE TOWN. — STATISTICS OF ITS BUSINESS, POPULATION, &c. — HIGHWAYS. — STAGES. — TRADERS AND MANUFACTURERS. — SLAVERY.

THE latitude and longitude of the town are 42° 14′ 49″ north, and 71° 54′ 47″ west. Its distance from Boston is forty-three miles, geographically measured: by the travelled roads, it somewhat exceeds that admeasurement. From a survey of the town in 1855, its north line, bounding on Paxton, runs north 87°, west 1,237 rods; its west line, bounding upon Spencer, south ½°, east 2,064 rods; its south line, bounding upon Charlton, runs south 87°, east 370 rods,—then on Oxford, in the same course, 360 rods; its south-east line, bounding upon Auburn, runs north 40½°, east 583 rods, north 43°, east 288 rods, and east 156½ rods; its east line, bounding on Worcester, runs north 12°, west 1,338½ rods. It contains 13,453 acres.

This is what remains of the settlers' half of the original town, after having had two miles in width taken from its north side to help to form the town of Paxton in 1765, and about 2,500 acres from its south-east part in 1778 to help to form the town of Ward, now Auburn.

The town is situate upon the height of land between Connecticut River and the ocean, about a thousand feet above tide-water, sloping towards the south; so that the streams of water which flow from it find their way to the ocean by three principal channels,—one, towards the west, through Chicopee and Connecticut Rivers; one, towards the south, through French and Quinebaug Rivers; and one, towards the south-east, through Blackstone River. And so near are the sources of some of the branches of these streams in the town, that, at a point in the westerly part of it, the Great Road to Spencer separates the waters that flow into the Chicopee from those which flow into the Quinebaug; and at the foot of the Meeting-house Hill, east of the principal village, the waters upon the south side of the Great Road flow into the Quinebaug, while those upon its north side find their way into the Blackstone.

Though the face of the territory is generally uneven, and in parts hilly, it does not rise into any considerable peaks, nor are any of its hills rugged or abrupt. Some of these have received names, which, in some instances, they have borne from the first settlement of the town. Among them, I may mention that upon which the principal village is built. It was for many years, as one of the early deeds of the estates shows, called Strawberry Hill. It was here the first settlement was begun; and a house standing where that of Mr. May now stands was one of the first, and probably the first, erected in town, and was built upon the lot numbered "one" in the deed above referred to.

In the easterly part of the town, a little north-west from the village of Cherry Valley, is another eminence, called Bald Hill in the earliest records of the town, from the circumstance that it had been cleared and cultivated before the white men settled here.

The elevation east of this, adjoining the town of Worcester, was known as Chestnut Hill, and was first settled by Nathan Sargent.

Mount Pleasant lies about a mile west of the Meeting-house. There is an engraving, in one of the numbers of the "Massachusetts Magazine" published in 1794, representing what is called "Mount Pleasant in Leicester, the property of the late Thomas Stickney, as seen from the Academy." This estate was once a princely one, and was owned and occupied a while by the late Major Swan, formerly of Boston, who died a few years since in France. It had gone sadly to decay, however, when taken possession of by its late thrifty proprietor, Mr. Oliver Smith.

About three-quarters of a mile north of the Meeting-house is a considerable elevation, which has from an early date been called Carey Hill. Tradition has fixed it as the spot upon which the first settlers of the town found a hermit dwelling in a cave; but we are left to conjecture alone, as to who it was that had sought to escape from the troubles of life by burrowing in the earth here, amidst the primeval forest which then covered this region. The hill undoubtedly took its name from Arthur Carey, who was the first to settle upon it. It formed a part of lot No. 5, which bounded upon the north by lot 6, the one reserved for the ministry.

Moose Hill is one of the highest in the town, and lies at its north-west corner. For the remainder of these, I must again refer to the annexed Map.

From several of these elevations, wide and beautiful panoramic views of the surrounding country may be obtained. That from the mansion-house formerly standing upon the Denny Farm, so many years in that family,* formed the subject of a landscape by Ralph Earle, a distinguished native artist of the town, who is elsewhere noticed in this work; which was a production of much merit. It is still in possession of the family of the former proprietor of the estate, and, in its details as well as its outlines, is suggestive of the changes which the actual landscape has witnessed in the multiplied villages which have sprung up since the day of the artist's sketch of what then met the eye of an observer.

In respect to ponds and streams of water, the elevated situation of the town prevents either from being of any great

---

* This hill was formerly known as Nurse's, afterwards as Raccoon Hill.

magnitude, since it is chiefly the head-waters of the streams flowing from the town that are found here. Two of these natural ponds, only, have been distinguished by name, and these have been changed from time to time.

That collection of water, containing about forty-three acres, lying about a mile south-east from the Meeting-house, was formerly called the Judge's Pond, from being upon the farm of Judge Menzies, one of the early settlers of the town. It has been known as Henshaw Pond since the adjacent farm has been owned by the family of that name.

The other lies in the north-west part of the town, and was at one time known as North Pond; but afterwards took that of Shaw, from the owner of land upon its borders.

Several artificial ponds, of considerable magnitude, have been created for purposes of reservoirs for the operation of mills. One of these, called Burntcoat, contains over a hundred acres. Another, just below it, occupies the ground formerly one of the large cedar meadows of the town. The Town Meadow has been flowed for many years past; and a succession of reservoirs upon Kettle Brook, so called, has created a supply of water for that stream, sufficient to carry several important manufacturing establishments in the town.

The last-named brook takes its rise in Paxton, and, flowing through the easterly part of the town, discharges itself into Blackstone River, in Worcester.

The changes which have been made in this stream by these artificial reservoirs, and their effect upon the business and prosperity of the town, are some of the many illustrations, which are found all over New England, of what may be done for the country by a proper encouragement of her industrial interests. Within my own recollection, the only works upon Kettle Brook, within the town, were a little cheap sawmill, standing where the woollen mill of Mr. Hodges stands; a small gristmill belonging to the late Mr. John Sargent, where the woollen mill late of Mr. Capron stands; and a small clothier's shop, where Mr. Watson's woollen mill, which was burned, stood: and so small was the quantity of water flowing in it, that it was nearly dry most of the summer months. Since that, five woollen factories, three of them of a large size, besides several smaller mills, have been erected upon it, having an adequate supply of water, and giving employment to a large number of operatives, and, under proper encouragement, earning wealth for their owners, and contributing generally to the growth and prosperity and the enhanced value of property of the town.

This may be no place in which to discuss political economy; but the wisdom of that policy which protects home industry needs no better illustration than what is furnished in the history of the rise, progress, and results of manufactures in this town. The first attempt to introduce the manufacture of woollen cloth was made by Mr. Samuel Watson, at a little factory he erected upon the site of his clothier's works, on Kettle Brook, in 1814. The manufacture of cards had been carried on by hand for many years previous to that time: but the town had been chiefly an agricultural one; and its streams of water, in a great measure, had run to waste, though capable, as has been shown, of doing the labor of a hundred men. The effect of the changes which were from time to time introduced, by this means, into the industry of the town, will appear when we come to consider more minutely the history of these changes, and the progress of the statistics of its business.

To recur to the principal streams flowing from the town. The waters of Shaw Pond form one of the sources of the Chicopee. Those from Burntcoat and Henshaw Ponds unite, and form the source of French River, flowing through Oxford into the Quinebaug. The waters from the Town Meadow take the same direction, and unite with those from the Burntcoat above Greenville, in the southerly part of the town. The capacity of these streams, and the amount of business done upon them, will be spoken of in another connection.

As has already been observed, the early settlers of this town were farmers. The soil, though yielding good crops under proper cultivation and care, must have been rugged, and difficult to till; and does not seem to have been very attractive to new emigrants. It was thirty-eight years after the purchase from the Indians, and eleven after the erection of the territory into a township, before the requisite number of fifty families had been settled within the easterly half of the town.

The subsequent growth of the town was for many years slow. Indeed, such continued to be the case until the introduction of other employments than the cultivation of the soil.

A census was taken between the years 1763 and 1765; at which time, the town, which then included a part of Paxton and a part of Auburn, contained but 119 houses and 146 families, forming a total population of 763 souls. This was an increase of less than a hundred families in the space of forty years, and that within the first half-century of its settlement.

In 1776, the number of inhabitants had increased to 1,078; but — probably in consequence of the drain of the war, in part — there was no increase in numbers between that time and 1784. In 1786,* there had been a decrease of white inhabitants, though the blacks had increased from seven, in 1765, to twenty-four. The census of 1790 showed a total of 1,076, — two less than in 1776: and the successive censuses of 1800, when there were 1,103; 1810, when 1,181; and 1820, when 1,252, — indicated but a slow growth. The whole increase from 1776 to 1820 was only 174 in forty-four years, or a trifle over sixteen per cent; while that of the State as a whole, including Maine, was over ninety-nine per cent. From

* One contemporary statement mentions the number of white persons in 1786 as being only 814.

this time there was a much more satisfactory increase both of population and wealth. In 1830, the former had grown to 1,782: and, in 1850, the United-States Census showed a total of 2,269; viz., 1,169 white males, 1,099 white females, and only one colored person, — a female. The population of the town, by the State Census of 1855, was 2,589.*

The reports of the valuation of the property of the town, at different periods, is equally indicative of the causes of its wealth and prosperity; although, probably, some allowance is to be made for the difference in the standard of value of certain classes of property within the period referred to. In 1790, the valuation of the town was, in round numbers, $140,000; in 1800, $182,000; in 1810, $229,900; in 1830, $461,000; in 1840, $687,952; and in 1850, $1,219,330: showing an increase for twenty years — between 1790 and 1810 — of a little less than sixty-four per cent; while for twenty years — from 1810 to 1830 — the increase was more than a hundred per cent; and, from 1830 to 1855, more than two hundred and fifty per cent.

The relative growth and consideration of the town may be measured by comparing it with other towns in the county at different periods within the time which we have been considering.

In 1800 it stood, in the matter of population, the twenty-fifth town in the county, in 1810 the twenty-fifth, in 1820 the thirtieth, in 1830 the fifteenth, in 1850 the seventeenth, and in 1855 the fifteenth.†

---

* The increase of population for forty-four years before 1820 averaged, within a fraction, four a year. For thirty-five years before 1855, it was a fraction over thirty eight a year, upon an average.

† To apply the test of valuation at an earlier period: the town stood, in 1772, the twentieth in the county; in 1778, the thirty-third; so heavy had been the drain upon her resources during the war. In 1782 she had risen to the twenty-second place, in 1786 to the nineteenth, and in 1793 to the eighteenth, in polls and valuation. In 1801 in proportionate taxes, she remained the eighteenth; and the same in 1811: but in 1840 she had increased to the ninth, and in 1850 to the seventh, place in the scale of valuation of the towns in the county.

It was, as will appear, during the latter portion of the time covered by these statistics, that the manufacture of woollen cloths by water-power took its rise in the town. But, before entering upon that part of our subject, it may be pleasant to test, with such means as I have before me, the social condition of the people of the town at an earlier period of its history, compared with the present.

One means of doing this is by referring to a tax which was laid upon carriages in the years 1753 to 1757, inclusive, to promote the success of manufactures, especially of linen. In the first of these years, there were four "chairs" in town to be taxed; but before the next year these had disappeared, and, from that year until after 1757, there was no carriage of any description in town. Indeed, the use of carriages is practically a modern matter. There are persons alive who saw the first buggy-wagon that was owned in town, and pillions had not disappeared till some now upon the stage had grown into manhood.*

Something may be judged of the style in which the people of the town lived by recurring to the inventories of estates, as found in the Probate Office, at any given period. To two or three of these I refer for that purpose.

Dr. Lawton, a physician of respectable business and reputation in his profession, died here in 1761. His estate was appraised at £317. 8s. 6d. His books were appraised at £2. 4s. 6d., besides his law-books, which had probably come to him from his father, an attorney-at-law, and were appraised

* The first buggy-wagon that I ever saw, and I believe it to have been the first ever owned in town, belonged to Capt. William Sprague about 1810. There had been a few chaises in use in town at an earlier day. I have often heard a lady, now deceased, describe a journey which she made to Vermont from Leicester with her husband, on horseback. She rode and guided her horse, and carried a child two years old in her lap, who was born in 1788. It was the only mode of travelling then to be had in the country. It was one step in the progress of luxury when it became a matter of *haut ton* for a young gentleman to furnish a separate horse, instead of a pillion, for the use of the lady whom he should invite to be his partner to a ball or party.

at 5s. 3d. His silver plate was valued at £4. 15s. 4d.; and two looking-glasses, all he had, were valued at 12s. While he had an hour-glass and a pillion, he had neither watch, clock, nor carpet of any kind.

Israel Parsons died in 1767. He was the son of the Rev. Mr. Parsons, and a grantee of all his father's estate, real or personal. He was once a large landholder; and, at his death, his farm was appraised at £240. He left two looking-glasses among his household goods,—one valued at 32s., the other at 10s. 8d.; but he left neither watch, clock, nor carpet.

Dr. Larned, a young physician of considerable promise, died here in 1783; and his "physical authors," as they are called in his inventory, were appraised at 16s. 3d.*

Indeed, as may be remarked hereafter, the general use of carpets is of a modern date; while, in the matter of books, the change has been greater than in almost any other thing. I am authorized by a friend † to add, that the first carpets woven in Leicester were the handiwork of Mrs. David Briant, at the commencement of the present century.‡

---

* I might add to the above the inventory of Stewart Southgate, who died in 1765, and was a man of property, engaged largely as a surveyor and in public business. It contains no article of glass, china, or earthenware; a single silver spoon, valued at 11s.; three looking-glasses, valued altogether at 7s. 6d.; a clock; but no carpet. He had one Bailey's Dictionary, one Bible, and thirty-eight small pamphlets, for a library.

The inventory of Rev. Mr. Goddard shows the gratifying fact, that he left books valued at £32. 6s. 11d. in 1754, while all his other "in-door movables" were only £60. 3s. 3d.

† H. G. Henshaw, Esq.

‡ I know not how I can better illustrate the style of social life among what were regarded as comfortable, well-to-do farmers, in 1780, than by transcribing a memorandum, left by the father of a respectable family of that day, of what he furnished to a daughter on her marriage, with which to begin "to keep house:" "One cow; one low case of drawers; twelve chairs, one great one; one square table, and tea do.; one bed, bedstead, and cord; one coverlid; thirty yards of sheeting; one bed-quilt; twenty-four yards bed-ticking; one large kettle, and dish kettle, and tea do.; one set of tea-dishes; one teapot; three pewter platters; six pewter plates; one quart pot; one case knives and forks; six earthen plates; two quart basins; two pint do.; two porringers; one pot, spider, and skillet; two tubs; one churn; two pails; six wooden platters; one candlestick; one *slice* and tongs; one set flat-irons; six teaspoons; six large ones; one sieve; one bread trough; one pillion."

If we inquire into the state of the mechanic arts, and the arts as applied to manufactures, in various stages of the history of the town, we shall find that it was a long time before any beyond the most common and indispensable mechanics were to be found here.

Moses Stockbridge, for instance, was a carpenter, and was residing here in 1717; John Potter and Nathaniel Potter, carpenters, in 1722; Abiathar Vinton was a blacksmith here in 1723; Joshua Nichols was a tailor here as early as 1721; and Thomas Hopkins was a mason in 1724. Millwrights were employed here about the same time; and there were doubtless other mechanics, and in other departments, than those I have enumerated.

The first settlers were farmers; and, like others of that class generally in New England, the clothing of their families was principally of domestic manufacture. Probably no house was destitute of a spinning-wheel or a loom, and few families that did not understand more or less of the art of dyeing the fabrics which they wove. Cotton was unknown till a comparatively recent date; and few could indulge in the luxury of "India cotton" cloths, for which they must pay some four or five shillings the yard, though* they would not now sell for as many cents, if they would sell at all. They could clip from their own flocks the wool they consumed, and could raise the flax, which they understood how to work into linen of the purest white. It was from home-made fabrics wrought from these that the diligent housewife prepared the wardrobe of the family.

One of the early improvements upon this state of things was the substitution of carding the wool by machinery driven by water-power, for the former mode of doing it by hand; and a more fastidious taste in the coloring and finish-

* I find a bill of articles purchased in Boston for the use of a family in Leicester in November, 1788; and among them one pound of tea, 2s. 4d.; and *a pound of cotton*, 2s.

ing cloths led to the establishment of clothiers among the handicrafts of the town. But the progress of improvement in machinery, and the introduction of manufactures by means of this, long since expelled these household institutions of a former day, till a loom and a spinning-wheel have become the curious relics of rustic antiquity.*

As has already been stated, Mr. Samuel Watson had a clothier's shop, in which he carried on business, in what is now called Cherry Valley, previous to 1814. At this time he enlarged his works, and began the manufacture of woollen cloth. His weaving was done by hand; and the employment of men in what had been before regarded as within the peculiar province of females, in the arrangement of household affairs, was looked upon, by those who were not familiar with the processes of manufacture elsewhere, in something the same light in which people would now regard a man mantua-maker or milliner shaping and fitting ladies' dresses, or putting the finishing touch to a bonnet or a cap. By the revulsion of business which took place a few years after the war, Mr. Watson was led to lease his establishment to Mr. James Anderton, who had been bred a woollen manufacturer in Lancashire, England. He occupied the mill for a few years, and then disposed of his interest to a countryman of his own, — Mr. Thomas Bottomly, — who continued to carry on the business there until 1825.

While occupying this mill, Mr. Bottomly erected the works now owned by Samuel L. Hodges, Esq., upon the same stream, and just below the mill of Mr. Watson, upon land which he purchased of Capt. Darius Cutting.

* The first clothier in town was, I have reason to believe, Alexander Parkman, who came from Westborough in 1770. In 1771, he purchased the mill and privilege where Samuel Watson afterwards carried on the business, in Cherry Valley. He carried on the business till after 1776, and was succeeded by Asahel Washburn, jun., a son of a nephew of Seth, about 1794. Mr. Washburn left Leicester, and removed to Greensborough in Vermont, about 1797. He was succeeded by Mr. Samuel Watson. Mr. Washburn's son, of the same name, born in Leicester, is a clergyman in Suffield, Conn.

After a few years, an incorporated company, taking the name of the Bottomly Manufacturing Company, purchased this estate, and carried on business there for several years under the superintendence of the former owner.

Mr. Bottomly then purchased the site of a gristmill, formerly owned by Mr. John Sargent, and in 1837 proceeded to erect a manufacturing establishment, which was afterwards sold to Mr. Effingham L. Capron, who carried on the same for several years. Since his death it has passed into other hands, and is called the Manhattan Company.

Mr. Bottomly, in connection with his son Booth, in 1850, purchased a privilege something like half a mile above the Great Road, upon the same stream, and erected a brick factory thereon; in which the son has been carrying on the woollen business, and which now belongs to him.

Besides these, there is, at what is called Mannville, near the Quaker Meeting-house, upon the same stream, a considerable woollen mill belonging to Messrs. Mann and Marshall, giving an unwonted air of life and prosperity to that neighborhood; and, close by the Great Road in Cherry Valley, Mr. L. G. Dickson has a small woollen mill standing upon the site of a former one which he had erected and which was burned. These, with a sawmill about a mile above Mannville, another near the Quaker Meeting-house, and one about half a mile below, upon the farm of the late Capt. Daniel Kent, are operated by the waters of a stream once as inconsiderable as already stated.

Up to 1821, the only works upon the stream flowing from Burncoat Pond were a grist and saw mill near that pond, formerly belonging to Luke Converse; the tan-works of Mr. Jonathan Warren, a mile, more or less, below; a little sawmill belonging to Mr. Elkanah Haven, half a mile or more below that; a saw and grist mill at what is now Greenville; a scythe manufactory near to these, then called Wall's Mills; and a small cotton factory, which Mr. Thomas

Scott had erected near the turnpike, in what is now Clappville.

In that year, Mr. Anderton, above mentioned, purchased the mill and privilege of Mr. Scott, and began the business of woollen manufacture. It proved to be a valuable privilege; and a company was formed, which was incorporated as the Leicester Manufacturing Company, and enlarged the establishment and extended the business. This corporation became united with one in Framingham called the Saxon Manufactory, which took the joint name of the two; and the business was thus carried on for several years.

The works in Leicester were then purchased by Mr. Joshua Clapp of Boston, afterwards a public-spirited citizen of Leicester, who gave his name to the village which had grown up around these works, and which it still retains. Since the death of Mr. Clapp, the establishment has been owned and carried on until recently by Reuben S. Denny, Esq.; and, as a part of its history, it may be stated, that three of the mills belonging to it have been destroyed by fire and rebuilt within the last twelve or fifteen years.

There was a branch of manufacture commenced by Mr. Edmond Snow in the town, in 1785, consisting of making hand-cards, chiefly for the carding of wool for spinning for domestic use. It was, in fact, the dawn of a brightening day of prosperity to the town, to which it owes more of its growth and wealth than might at first be supposed.

The work, at first and for many years, was done by hand, by the aid of such improved machinery as ingenuity from time to time supplied. Mr. Pliny Earle, at an early day, engaged in the business; and it owed much of its success to his inventive skill.

Samuel Slater, the well-known father of the manufacture of cotton in America, was about commencing the experiment, but could not find machinery in the country suitable to his use, and was obliged to procure it to be made as best he could. This was about 1790. Among other things that he found it difficult to procure, were cards to clothe the machines by which he was to prepare his cotton for the spindle. After applying, without success, to several, he had an interview with Mr. Earle, who undertook to furnish the desired article; which he succeeded in doing. But, to accomplish this, he had to prick the holes in the leather, into which the teeth were to be inserted, by hand, with a couple of needles fitted and fastened into a handle. It was by cards thus manufactured that the first cotton ever spun in America by machinery was prepared for the spindle.

This led to the invention of the machine, long in use here, for pricking "twilled" cards, for which Mr. Pliny Earle obtained letters-patent. It is almost incredible, now that machines carried by water or other power for accomplishing the processes have become so common, that cards, in some years, to the value of two hundred thousand dollars, could have been produced in this town, in the manufacture of which every operation — from giving motion to the machines which pricked the leather and cut the teeth, to the setting of these, tooth by tooth, into the card — was performed by hand; and yet such is well known to have been the case. The importance of this branch of business to the town, and its connection with the growth and prosperity of the place, will, it is believed, justify, if it do not call for, a more minute account of its details, as well as of its recent condition, than might at first appear to be consistent with the plan of the work.

The manufacture, at first, was confined to hand-cards; and, as has been stated, was begun by Mr. Edmund Snow in 1785. That of machine-cards was added in 1790; and both were made in the same establishment, until the recent improvements in machinery which led to a separation of the business.

The manufacture of machine-cards was begun by Mr. Pliny

Earle. In 1791, he associated his brothers Jonah and Silas with him in business, under the firm of "Pliny Earle and Brothers." This continued till near his death in 1832. Silas Earle carried on business in his own name from 1815 till his death in 1842.

Col. Thomas Denny began the manufacture of hand-cards, in connection with William Earle, in the south-east part of the town, but removed to the village in 1802, and commenced manufacturing machine-cards in a building which stood where that occupied by the Bank now stands; where he also kept the Post Office, after the removal of Mr. Adams. He manufactured both kinds of cards extensively, with great success, till his death in 1814; and had thereby become the wealthiest individual in town.

Winthrop Earle occupied a part of the dwelling-house in which Col. Denny lived, and began the manufacture of machine-cards in the same in 1802. He afterwards built a factory in rear of Col. Denny's, and carried on business there till his death in 1807. The business was continued by Mr. John Woodcock, a very ingenious mechanic, who had removed into town from Rutland in 1805. He was born in Easton, Mass., in 1775. A machine which he invented, and for which he obtained letters-patent, for reducing the leather used in the manufacture of cards to a uniform thickness by a very simple and speedy process, was of immense advantage to the business generally; and the debt which the town owes to his ingenuity ought not to be forgotten.

In 1808, Mrs. Earle having married Alpheus Smith, he became a partner with Mr. Woodcock, under the firm of "Woodcock and Smith." The building in which they carried on business was removed to the west side of the Hotel,— where Capt. Cutting's hat-shop had formerly stood,— now occupied by the brick store standing there; and, in 1812, James Smith, Esq., who had come from Rutland a few years before, became a member of the firm. If I were at liberty to speak of living persons as I might wish, I could draw a ready illustration, from the private history of this gentleman, of the success with which a diligent and honorable pursuit of this department of industry has so often been crowned in this community. The business went on in the same name, though Mr. Woodcock had sold his interest in 1813, till the next year; when Alpheus Smith withdrew, and John A. Smith, Esq., and Rufus, his brothers, took his place, and the style of the firm became "James and John A. Smith and Company." Mr. Woodcock died about this time; leaving three sons and two daughters, and a handsome competence earned in his business. His son John, with Hiram Knight, Esq., and Emory Drury, joined the firm of "James and John A. Smith" in 1825. Rufus Smith having died in 1818, Mr. Drury left it in 1829, Mr. John A. Smith in 1830, and Mr. James Smith in 1833. In 1848, Messrs. Woodcock and Knight took in their sons, Theodore E. and Dexter; and the business is still continued in the name of "Woodcock, Knight, and Company."

Jonathan Earle commenced business at his residence on Mount Pleasant in 1804, and continued it till his death in 1813.

Isaac Southgate and Henry Sargent, whose names stand prominent among the men whose enterprise and public spirit have done so much for the town, began business in 1810, under the firm of "Southgate and Sargent." In 1812, Col. Sargent withdrew from the firm, and in 1814 took in his brother, Joseph D. Sargent, as a partner. The latter left in 1819, and the former continued the business till the time of his death in 1829.

From 1812 to 1826, Capt. Southgate was in business alone, but in that year formed a connection with Joshua Lamb, Dwight Bisco, Joseph A. Denny, Esq., and John Stone, under the firm of "Isaac Southgate and Company." Mr. Stone died in 1827. In 1828, the partners erected the large factory now standing in rear of the Meeting-house. Mr. Lamb left the firm in 1831, and Capt. Southgate in 1843. In 1857, Charles A., the son of Mr. Denny, and George, a son of Mr. Bisco, became, and still are, partners with their fathers, under the firm of "Bisco and Denny."

Col. Joseph D. Sargent continued in business until his death in 1849; Silas Jones, Esq., Nathan Ainsworth, and William Boggs, having been at different times associated with him.

After dissolving his connection with James Smith in 1830, Mr. John A. Smith continued business alone until 1844; when Mr. Samuel Southgate, jun., and his son John S. Smith, succeeded him under the name of "Southgate and Smith;" and in 1859 Mr. Southgate retired from the firm, and his place was taken by Horace Waite.

Cheney Hatch, Esq., began business in 1823, and continued it till 1836. He was then succeeded by Alden Bisco; who, in a few months, sold to Henry A. Denny; who carried it on till 1849, when he took in his sons Joseph W. and William S.: and the firm of "Henry A. Denny and Sons" continued till 1854, when they removed to Worcester, and their business passed into the hands of "White and Denny." This firm consists of Alonzo White and Christopher C. Denny.

Mr. White had been a partner with Mr. Josiah Q. Lamb from 1836 to 1846. After that, Mr. Lamb carried on business alone till his death in 1850.

Josephus Woodcock, son of the first Mr. John Woodcock; Benjamin Conklin, jun., who had married one of his daughters; and Austin Conklin, — began business under the firm of "Conklin, Woodcock, and Company," in 1828. In 1830, it was dissolved; and Josephus, with his brother Lucius, took the business, under the name of "J. and L. Woodcock." The next year they took in Danforth Rice, who left the firm in 1836; and William P. White joined it in 1848.

After dissolving with James Smith, Alpheus carried on business extensively in his own name, in the building now the dwelling-house of H. G. Henshaw, Esq., until 1823; when his brother Horace took the business, and carried it on till his death in 1828.

Joshua Murdock, jun., began business, in 1841, with Samuel Southgate, jun. On Mr. Southgate's withdrawing from the firm, Mr. Murdock took in his brother Joseph; and, in 1857, another brother, John N.: and they are still in business.

Reuben Meriam began business in 1821, and continued till 1831; having in the mean time had, as partners, Mr. George W. Morse and Henry A. Denny.

Harry Ward carried on business from 1810 till his death in 1824.

Samuel Hurd and Baylies Upham were in business, as partners, from 1825 to 1833. Then Mr. Upham carried it on alone until 1850, when he took in Erving Sprague. In 1855, Mr. Sprague left the firm; and, in 1857, Mr. Upham removed to Worcester.

John H. and William Whittemore began business in 1843. In 1851, the senior partner was accidentally killed upon the Western Railroad. His brother James had joined the firm in 1850; and it is still continued.

It is not in my power to mention all who have been engaged in the business of manufacturing hand-cards. Among them were Mr. Daniel Denny,— son of Col. Samuel, and father of the gentleman, of the same name, now President of the Hamilton Bank in Boston, — who carried on business in Cherry Valley, in the house opposite the Southgate Place, in 1792; Capt. William Sprague and Sons; Barnard Upham; Roswell Sprague, who, as is stated in another part of our work, was extensively engaged in the general manufacture of cards and merchandise, and afterwards removed to New York, where he has been a successful merchant; Samuel D. Watson, who was in prosperous business for several years at his place, lately owned by Silas Gleason, Esq.; Aaron Morse, who afterwards kept the hotel opposite the Meeting-house; Guy S. Newton; Timothy Earle; Samuel Southgate; and

William H. Scott. The largest establishment now engaged in this department of the business is Joseph B. Sargent and Edward Sargent, sons of Col. Joseph D. Sargent, in the brick factory west of the Meeting-house; who can manufacture more than two thousand dozen pairs of cards each week.

But, without going any further into details of the industry of the town, I will refer to statistics of the business done here at the several times, when, by order of the Legislature, returns were made from the several towns of the results of their productive industry.

In 1837, the woollen mills of the town employed three hundred and forty-four hands and a capital of $180,000, producing cloths valued at $319,450; there were seventeen manufactories of cards, employing a capital of $74,000, and producing $152,000 worth of cards annually; and the aggregate of the products of the several manufactures carried on in the town was $531,439 during that year.

The return for the year 1845 showed a much less favorable state of business. Only a hundred and eighty-four were employed in the woollen mills, and the product of their labor was but $250,500; eighteen card-manufactories produced $154,700 value of cards; and the sum total of the manufacturing products of the town was only $452,065.

The return of 1855 presents a much more gratifying result. The woollen mills were employing three hundred and forty-two hands, producing goods valued at $560,600; twelve card-manufactories produced $175,000; boots and shoes, the manufacture of which had been then recently introduced, amounted to $85,000: showing an aggregate product of the mechanical and manufacturing business of the town of over $900,000.

The amount of business in the town and vicinity induced the Legislature to charter a bank here in 1826, with a capital of $100,000; which has since been increased to $200,000. It has been in successful operation since June of that year.

John Clapp, Esq., was its first president; and John A. Smith, its cashier. Mr. Clapp was succeeded by Hon. N. P. Denny, and Mr. Smith by H. G. Henshaw, Esq. Joseph A. Denny, Esq., succeeded Hon. N. P. Denny as president, and D. E. Meriam, Esq., Mr. Henshaw as cashier, in 1845. Cheney Hatch, Esq., who succeeded Mr. Denny, has been its president for several years past. It is a well-managed and prosperous institution.

In connection with the facilities which they furnish for the transaction of business, it is proper to speak of the principal highways in the town. There are within the town probably more than seventy-five miles of ways, town and county, whose support is chargeable to the inhabitants; but, heavy as this charge is, few are more cheerfully borne. The laying-out of these, when done by the town, forms a part of its records; and, by the objects referred to for the purposes of description, one can often read the changes that have taken place in the face of the country, and the condition of the people, since the earlier stages of their history. These go back to the time when the Meeting-house was closely hemmed in by the primitive forest, and the scattered settlers were at war with the wild beasts that roamed through the wilderness.*

The present road to Paxton was laid out in 1721, and began at a "black-birch standing near a great red-oak, behind the Meeting-house and close by the same," and ran thence through the woods by marked trees.

In 1744, a road was laid out from the south line of the town, near the house of the late Mr. Thomas Parker, to Dr. Green's; one of its bounds being the "said Green's wolf-pit," which was, as recollected by the older inhabitants, a little to the north-east of Mr. Parker's house, and was dug for the purpose of taking wolves, by which the first settlers were much annoyed.

The principal road in the town has, from the first, been

---

* The location of several of these ways is given in the Appendix.

the great Post Road, formerly called the Country Road, from Boston to Albany.

There was a communication, by land, between the settlements around Boston, and those at Hartford and Springfield upon Connecticut River, from the time of the emigration of the Rev. Mr. Hooker with his flock from Newtown in 1635. This journey required a fortnight for its accomplishment. Their route, probably, was through what is now Leicester. But a new line of travel was afterwards adopted, leading through the southerly part of Northborough, Westborough, and Grafton, which was called the Connecticut Path; it being little more than a mere path which could be travelled on horseback. The principal communication, for a considerable time after the settlement at Hartford, was by water; and for many years after the destruction of Brookfield, and the dispersing of the settlement at Worcester, there were no inhabitants west of Marlborough, before reaching the settlements on the Connecticut. The direction of this line of communication was afterwards changed, so as to run through the centre of Northborough, Shrewsbury, Worcester, and Leicester, and was called the New Connecticut Road, though it still was but a rugged track through the forest.

In 1722, the town voted that the selectmen should apply to the Court of Sessions to have the Country Road laid out through this town. It had been previously laid out as a road; for, in a deed to the Rev. David Parsons, in March, 1721, it is called "the Country Road *formerly* laid out to Towtaid." But probably it had not been done by any competent body of men to constitute it a legal highway. The application to the County Commissioners in 1722 failed, and it was then laid out as a townway.* In a deed dated in 1727, the parcel granted bounds "northerly by the road as it was

---

* For a record of this location, see Appendix, which will give some idea of its condition for travel as late as 1723.

laid out by the selectmen of the town, but commonly called the Country Road." *

The direction of this road through the town has been changed, from time to time, within the recollection of the present generation. It formerly passed from New Worcester, over the summit of the hill, and near to the dwelling-house of Mr. John Sargent; and, from what is now Mr. Dickinson's factory, it passed up just above the house formerly of Matthew Watson, and along the brow of the hill to where the Waite Tavern used to stand. Another change was in its direction over Mount Pleasant. It passed directly up the hill, and along in front of the house formerly owned by Hon. N. P. Denny.

In 1806, the Worcester and Stafford Turnpike was laid out through the south part of the town; and, by a singular kind of civil engineering then in general use, it was laid as nearly as might be in a direct line; though, to do so, it had to surmount the longest hills and steepest acclivities, from the summits of which the wearied travelled might see the pleasant and convenient valleys, along which, without an increase of distance, the way might originally have been laid.

Before the location of this road, the travel from Charlton was by the road which led by the mills in Greenville; then on the road towards the Meeting-house, as far as the house of the late John King, Esq.; and then by the road leading by the Henshaw Place into the Great Road, at what is now Dickinson's woollen mill.† The travel from Sturbridge was by what was called the County Road; coming into the Great

* This road was originally laid out by the town, four rods wide. I infer from other circumstances that it was laid out by the county in 1728. It must have then been very steep in its passage over the Meeting-house Hill; for I find the town, in 1771, appropriating money "to *lower* the hill called Meeting-house Hill." And the extent to which it has been reduced within fifty years past, as many will remember, has changed its degree of elevation most essentially within that time.

† This road was laid out by the town, in 1739, through lands then of Southgate, Steele (Henshaw's), Bethune (Tainter's), William Green (late John King's), "into the way that leads through Green's land towards the Meeting-house."

Road at the house, afterwards, of Deacon Murdock, half a mile west of the Meeting-house.

There was a road early laid out from the Meeting-house to Green's Mills, — now Greenville, — for the purpose of providing access to these, for the accommodation of the people. It varied somewhat from the road as at present travelled.*

In the winter of 1826, the subject of adopting railroads as a mode of transportation began to attract attention. The system was then in its infancy. A short one had been put into operation at the Quincy quarries, for the transportation of stone; and, as no locomotive had then been invented, the only power applied was that of horses. In the June Session of the Legislature of that year, Abner Phelps, George W. Adams, and Emory Washburn, were appointed a Committee of the House, "to take into consideration the practicability and expediency of constructing a railway from Boston, on the most eligible route, to the western line of the county of Berkshire; in order that, if leave can be obtained of the government of New York, it may be extended to the most desirable point on the Hudson River at or near Albany."

As this was the first step ever taken in the inauguration of that enterprise which has been of such immeasurable advantage to the State, and as one of the Committee was then a representative from this town, it seemed a fit occasion to allude to the subject; since the conclusions to which the Committee came, that they were "satisfied of the practicability and convinced of the expediency of constructing a railway from Boston to the Hudson," though much ridiculed at the time, were successfully and triumphantly carried out and accomplished before the year 1841.

The Boston and Worcester Railroad was opened for use, July 6, 1835. In 1838, one of the Committee, whose judgment upon the subject had been so much sneered at in 1827,

---

* For the record of this location, see Appendix.

had the satisfaction, as chairman, on the part of the House, of a Committee in that year, to report in favor of a loan of the credit of the State to aid the Western Railroad to complete the same to Albany; and, by the confidence which the measure had then obtained, the same was carried by a decided vote through both branches. In 1841, Dec. 27, the road was formally opened for the public use. It runs through the south part of the town, and had been in use for some time before the entire work was completed.

The opening of this road wrought an entire revolution in the course of public travel through the town. It shortened the time of a passage to Boston from eight hours to three; but it put an end to the lines of stage-coaches, which, two or three times a day, used to keep alive the attention of the villagers by their arrival and departure, and made the bar-room of the hotel, for a few moments every day, a kind of public exchange, where friends met to greet each other, news was told, politics discussed, and a free intercourse kept up with the outside world.

Besides these, there was a large amount of travel through the town in pleasure-carriages, and especially by teams employed in transporting produce to Boston, and bringing supplies of goods for the country from that market.

Stage-coaches show a step in the progress of business in Massachusetts, as marked in its day as that by railroads in our own. The first line of these was designed to carry passengers between Boston and New York, by the way of Springfield and Hartford. It was established by Levi Pease, then of Somers, Conn., and Reuben Sikes, then of Hartford, Oct. 20, 1783, running *stage-wagons* between Hartford and Boston.* They

* In 1782, June 13, an advertisement was published in the "Spy:" —

"STAGE-COACH FROM WORCESTER TO BOSTON. — A gentleman in Boston, who is possessed of *a* genteel stage-coach and *a span of* good horses, would willingly be concerned with a trusty person, capable of driving said stage from Boston to Worcester and from Worcester to Boston, *weekly*, and transacting the business consequent thereon." But no one accepted the offer, and the scheme was abandoned.

left Hartford at eleven o'clock, A.M., on Monday; and reached Somers at night, stopping at Pease's Tavern: on Tuesday they reached Rice's, at Brookfield: on Wednesday they reached Northborough, at Martin's; and arrived at Boston on Thursday evening. The return stages left Boston on Monday, and reached Hartford on Thursday. The fare charged was fourpence per mile. This was the pioneer enterprise in the way of carrying passengers between these cities, and presents, in strong contrast, the time then occupied with that required by the present mode of travel, as well as the number of passengers to be carried. The traveller accomplishes now nearly as much in an hour as he was then able to do in a day.*

The mail between Boston and New York was carried on horseback; and a man, whom I knew, was living a few years ago in Charlemont, who used to "ride post" between these cities during the Revolution. It was afterwards carried by these stage-wagons. But the multiplication of post-offices is a thing of a much more recent date.

There was, I have reason to infer, a post-office established in Leicester in 1798; and, according to the recollection of an aged informant, Ebenezer Adams, Esq., was the first commissioned postmaster. Previous to that (in 1796), there was not, I believe, any post-office between Worcester and Springfield. He was succeeded in the office by Col. Thomas Denny; and, upon his death, Col. Henry Sargent was appointed to the place. Upon his death, Mr. John Sargent succeeded to the office; and the present incumbent (Mr. Henry D. Hatch), upon the death of Mr. Sargent, became his successor.

It would be of no practical utility to attempt to enumerate those who have at different times been engaged in the trade of merchandise in the town.

---

* I find the following memorandum in a private diary of a resident of Leicester: —

"1786, May 30. — Set out for Boston in the stage. Arrived at Boston that night. Paid for my ride in the stage, 13s. 6d.; spent a-going, 2s. 10½d."

I find the name of William Larkin in a process in court in 1735, in which he is styled "trader." He came from Boston, and owned the house which John Stebbings had built, where Mr. May's house now stands: and, if he carried on trade, it was probably in the same house; for I have reason to believe that the first building erected especially for a store in town was that built by a Mr. Fosgate in 1770. This was upon half an acre of land which he purchased of the Rev. Mr. Conklin, and stood nearly in front of the present Academy Building, close by the road. It was originally a small building, but was elongated from time to time, till it came into the occupation of Mr. Daniel McFarland in July, 1802.

Mr. Fosgate came from Bolton, and remained here but about a year. His immediate successor in trade was the Hon. Joseph Allen, who purchased the place in 1772, and soon after erected a dwelling-house upon the land. In 1777, Aaron Lopez purchased the estate, with an additional half-acre of land, and erected thereon the building which was afterwards occupied as the Academy, and in it carried on an extensive trade. He was a man of large wealth; and his stock of goods, at the time of his death, was appraised at twelve thousand dollars. His death took place in 1782.

Mr. Thomas Stickney removed from Newburyport to Leicester, and opened a store upon Mount Pleasant, about 1785. He owned the estate afterwards owned by Major Swan, — then of imposing elegance, — upon the south side of the Great Road; and his store adjoined his house. He died in July, 1791. John and Joseph Stickney, brothers of Thomas, carried on trade several years in the house, on Mount Pleasant, which afterwards belonged to Jonathan Earle, and subsequently to Hon. N. P. Denny. They both died in 1803: Joseph, Nov. 2; John, Dec. 5. Both were bachelors.

Col. Thomas Denny, about 1802, commenced and carried on business as a trader till his death, in a building which stood upon the spot where the brick store, next east of the Tavern, stands, now occupied by the Bank. In 1792, Messrs. Whitney and Hammond opened a store in this building, and continued business there a year or two. Mr. Phinehas Waite then occupied a part of it a while for the same purpose.

About 1792, William S. Harris, from Boston, opened a store in the Fosgate Building; which was occupied afterwards, a short time, by William Earle, a son of Mr. Thomas Earle, in 1795. Mr. Harris married Elizabeth Conklin, daughter of Rev. Mr. Conklin, and removed to the South. His brother Stephen, about the same time, engaged in the business of a bakery; which he carried on extensively in the basement of the west part of Mr. Swan's tavern-house, where Capt. Knight's house stands. He married Sally Denny, daughter of Col. Samuel, and removed to Norfolk, Va.

Mr. Daniel McFarland commenced trade in the building which had been occupied by Mr. Harris, in 1802; and continued there until the erection of a two-story brick store opposite the Academy, which has since been converted into a dwelling-house. He carried on business there until his death; and was succeeded by his brother, Mr. Horace McFarland, who continued the business for a few years.

Mr. Roswell Sprague erected a large store, in which he carried on merchandise and the manufacture of cards for several years, till his removal to New York. The same has since been owned, and occupied as a dwelling-house, by Mr. Reuben Meriam.

In later years, Mr. John Sargent, Mr. Danforth Rice, and, at a period contemporary with Mr. Daniel McFarland, Col. Ignatius Goulding, have been among those who were engaged in the business of trade in the town.*

The names which have by usage been attached to some of

---

* There were several small stores connected with the manufactories of cards; it being customary to employ numerous families in setting the teeth of the cards manufactured, and to pay them "out of the store," or in such goods as the manufacturer had on sale for such purposes.

the villages have already been mentioned. That of Cherry Valley, in the east part of the town, came into general use after 1820; that of Clappville, about 1830; and that of Mannville, in 1856.

The name of Greenville has been applied, within a few years, to the village around the Baptist Meeting-house, and mills near it; and is derived from Capt. Samuel Green, one of the first settlers of the town, who erected here the first sawmill in the town. He had also erected a gristmill upon the same privilege as early as 1724. The place was so favorable for such works, and their need to a new settlement so pressing, that three lots of thirty acres each, with the privilege of the stream, were granted, as has been stated, — two of them to Samuel Green, and one to Thomas Richardson, — upon the condition that they should erect mills thereon. It is believed that the condition was performed, and the land taken, wholly by Capt. Green; who became one of the founders of a numerous family, — a man of wealth, and of great influence in the town.

It may, however, be stated in this connection, that this was not the earliest gristmill in the town. That was erected, at the outlet of Town Meadow, about 1722; and parts of the original dam and raceway remained there until the erection of the present dam of the brick factory belonging to Messrs. J. B. and E. Sargent. This mill was erected by Joseph Parsons in pursuance of a vote of the town, exempting it from all taxes if he would proceed speedily to erect it. And yet there is reason to believe that it could only have run in the winter months; for the hay upon the meadow was too valuable to allow it to be destroyed by flowing the land in the summer season, and small parcels of the meadow continued to be regarded as valuable appendages to other lands many years after 1722.

The condition of the colored population of the town deserves a passing note in speaking of its local statistics.

The last vestige of the tribe of Indians that inhabited here has long ago disappeared. It was a place of consequence enough to have a distinctive name and a separate sachem; but, beyond its name, literally nothing remains of them. Their story was that of most of the tribes in New England: they disappeared; and the only memorials of the perished race are an arrowhead, a pipe, or a stone hatchet, occasionally turned up by the plough on the spots where they built their wigwams or planted their cornfields. The degenerate relics of a few of these tribes, here and there, still retain something of their color, and much of the habits of thriftlessness of the ancestors from whom they trace a questionable descent. One of these was the Hasnamisco or Grafton Tribe. One of the few remaining members of that tribe, by the name of Polly Johns, died here some fifty years ago. She was the last person in the town having Indian blood in her veins.

It is difficult to fix the number of negroes who have been residents here at different periods, from the want of proper censuses in the early history of the town. In that of 1754, there were six; in 1764–5, seven; in 1790, eight; in 1800, seven; 1810, twenty-three; 1820, two; 1830, four; 1840, six; and 1850, one. Their number at any time would not have called for any special notice, if with it there had not been connected, at one period, the question of the existence and extent of slavery in the town.

That slavery nominally existed here is undoubtedly true. The census of 1754 shows the number to be six. But, had they seen fit to test the question of their being held as such, it would probably have been found, that by the provisions of the Body of Liberties in Massachusetts, of 1640, most of them were free by reason of having been born in the Province.* But they

* The clause to which I refer, and which declares the law on the subject, was in these words: "There shall never be any bond-slaverie, villenage, or captivitie, unless it be lawful captives taken in just wars, and such strangers as willingly sell themselves

continued to be reckoned among the household property, partly from its being a traditional institution handed down to the people of the Colony from the mother-country, whose validity no one thought of questioning; and partly because the mildness with which they were treated, in the families in which they were domesticated, gave little occasion for dissatisfaction or discontent on the part of the slave. In the country, they were accounted of little value in the way of traffic; and we are told by Dr. Belknap that they were often given away in their infancy, like the young of many domestic animals, to those who were willing to take them, and rear them in their families. And what serves to show the character of their general treatment, and their own feelings in regard to it, better than any thing else, is the fact, that after it had been solemnly decided, in Quork Walker's case in this county, that, by the adoption of the Constitution in 1780, every slave in Massachusetts was declared free, a large proportion of them continued to reside in the families of their former masters as long as they lived.

Among the names of those known to have been held as slaves in Leicester were three belonging to Capt. Lyon, — Cæsar, Quashi, and Prince, — to whom he gave their freedom. Titus belonged to Col. Washburn, and was freed at the age of twenty, though he lived in the family till his death. Jenny, his mother, belonged to Mrs. Sergeant, who was a sister of Mr. Thomas Denny, and became the second wife of Col. Washburn in 1788. Jethro belonged to Mr. Joseph Sprague; but, after his death, remained in the family of his son, Capt. William Sprague, as long as he lived. Though deaf and dumb, he was bright and intelligent. At his death, he was laid in the old burying-ground behind the Meeting-house, — the last person buried there.

---

or are sold to us." Consequently, there never was a person, native-born, who could have been lawfully held as a slave in Massachusetts after 1640. — Vide *Mass. Hist. Soc. Collections*, Fourth Series, vol. iv. p. 334.

Aaron Lopez came from Newport, where slaves were more numerous than in the interior of Massachusetts, and brought with him three men, two women, and one boy. Mr. Rivera, who removed to Leicester with him, had three men and three women. All these, it is believed, went back with the families of their masters to Newport after the war.

Cain Bowman was the slave of Edward Bond, who had undoubtedly freed him before 1778: for I find him mustered that year, as a soldier in the army, by Col. Washburn; who would have violated the law, had he done so while he remained a slave. One who had been a slave before the war, and resided here after it, by the name of Peter Salem, will be noticed, in another connection, as one of the historical personages of the day.

I should need no further proof of the estimation in which slaves were held here, if I were not able to refer to the recollection of living witnesses, than the case of a slave which Samuel Denny of Maine * conveyed to his brother, Capt. Daniel Denny, — the first of that name in Leicester, — in 1752. The boy's name was Richard, and he was then five years of age. By the conveyance, he was to be held until he was thirty, with a power in the grantor to dispose of him after that time by will. But the grantee was restricted from selling or disposing of him to any one except one of his own children, and *never to sell him for gain or profit.* In his bill of gift, he charged his brother "that he and they deal kindly by and with the poor boy; that they look upon him as a poor orphan; and especially that they hold themselves engaged to bring him up in the fear of God, and do that to and for him that will bear a trial; knowing he has a precious soul as

---

* Samuel Denny came from England with his brother Daniel, and his sister Mrs. Prince, wife of Rev. Thomas Prince of the Old South Church, Boston. He settled in Maine about 1728, and became a leading man in Lincoln County; being "first Judge of the Court of Pleas" at the time of his death. Dennysville, in that State, was named from him.

well as we." Capt. Denny bequeathed the boy, by his last will, to his son Col. Samuel, for the balance of the time for which he was entitled to his service; and he died while a member of the family of the devisee.

It is hardly necessary to remark, that, with views and feelings like these on the part of masters, slavery is robbed of most of its odiousness, regarded as a personal relation of the parties. But there was a strong and growing sentiment in Massachusetts, before the war, adverse to the institution; and when the war broke out, for the professed purpose of securing their liberties, there was such an obvious inconsistency in holding slaves, that many formally emancipated them.* Col. Timothy Bigelow did but speak the public sentiment when he declared, that, "while fighting for liberty, he never would be guilty of selling slaves."†

Nor was it by profession only that the owners of these slaves, so long as they retained them, showed their disposition to ameliorate their condition. They worked with them in the same field, ate at the same table, and the master's children grew up with feelings towards them of almost fraternal regard.

Such was slavery, not only in Leicester, but in every other country town in Massachusetts.

There was one black man here, who, if ever a slave, had become free and a freeholder in 1754. His name upon the records, as well as by his contemporaries, was "Black Tom." He lived in a house remote from any neighbor, in the south-

---

* Such was the case with Seth Washburn, in respect to his man Titus; Edward Bond, with his man Cain; Capt. Lyon, with Cæsar, Quashi, and Prince. Others might be mentioned.

† In the instructions to their representative, Col. Thomas Denny, in May, 1773, which will be found in the Appendix, is this noble declaration: "As we have the highest regard for (so even as to revere the name of) liberty, we cannot behold but with the greatest abhorrence any of our fellow-creatures in a state of slavery. Therefore we strictly enjoin you to use your utmost influence, that a stop may be put to the slave-trade by the inhabitants of this Province."

west part of the town. With ready ingenuity, Tom was able to turn his hand to various kinds of handicraft, by which he gained a comfortable livelihood, and was thus enabled to cherish a happy temperament with which he was born. He became, in this way, a favorite among his lighter-complexioned neighbors. Tom was, withal, a sincere and humble Christian, and a careful observer of all his religious duties; but, as he kept neither watch nor almanac, he sometimes unwittingly suffered secular work to interfere with holy time.

One Sunday afternoon, a neighbor, passing by Tom's dwelling, was surprised to hear him singing, in a loud and unmistakable tone, a tune which had little of the psalm about it. Upon his going up to his door, he was still more surprised to find him, in his working-day garb and with his coat off, busily engaged upon an ox-yoke, which he had nearly completed. Upon the neighbor's expressing his astonishment in finding Tom thus employed, and reminding him that the day was Sunday, Tom threw down his tools, and, after a moment's reflection, exclaimed, "Well, massa, Lord knows I didn't mean to cheat him; and I won't: I'll keep to-morrow for Sunday instead." And he kept his promise.

Within the memory of some, there stood upon the County Road, so called, in the south-west part of the town, a small log-house, — the last of that pioneer class of dwellings in which the first settlers found shelter while they were erecting more comfortable habitations. The house, at the time of which I am speaking, was occupied by Rose Finnemore * and her son Cæsar Augustus. His brother Archelaus lived at that time at Harwood Place, about half a mile west of Mr. Eber Bond's. The family, as might be inferred from the names of the brothers, were much inclined to honor the memories of ancient worthies by adopting their names for family use. The scions of this illustrious stock became in time quite

* The family had emigrated here from Greenfield.

numerous; and, upon Mrs. Cæsar Augustus becoming a member of the church, it became proper that her household should be baptized. Some may remember — for, if they witnessed it, they would not readily forget it — the occasion when this goodly array of some half a score of children took their stand in the broad aisle, one in its father's arms, and approached the font. The eldest received the baptismal name of Romulus; the next, Remus; and the others, in turn, rejoiced in equally illustrious names of Roman emperors, and heroes of olden time, till it came the turn of the baby. Here patriotism had gotten the better of the parent's love of classic renown, and crowned the little *citizen* — it was before the day of Dred Scott — with the name of James Madison, the then President of the United States. As this little episode, in the usual Sunday services in the church, took place while the heat of excitement between the old Federal and Democratic parties was at its height, soon after the election of Mr. Madison, there was something approaching a smile upon some of the countenances of the congregation, when this last little hope of the house received the name of that distinguished patriot and statesman upon his family escutcheon.

But the log-house soon after disappeared; Rose was gathered to her fathers; and Cæsar and his numerous household, one after another, stricken down by the hand of consumption, so fatal to the colored race in this climate, soon followed to the land of forgetfulness.

CHAPTER III.

MUNICIPAL AFFAIRS. — FIRST SETTLERS. — PECUNIARY EMBARRASSMENTS. — CURRENCY AND PRICES. — REPRESENTATIVES. — SCHOOLS AND TEACHERS. — LIBRARY, &c.

THE first recorded town-meeting of the inhabitants of Leicester was held March 6, 1721–2; which, to correspond to the present style, would be March 17, 1722. But the record of that meeting shows that the town had already been organized, and provided with town-officers, by previous elections; for a Committee was raised on that occasion to settle with their treasurer. They had also then a meeting-house belonging to the town; for, at this meeting in March, a person was appointed to take charge of it, and measures were taken toward finishing pews and seats in it. We are, consequently, at a loss to fix the precise date when the town assumed the functions of a body politic by its first election of civil officers. From the number of families that we are able to trace as being here in 1717, it is probable that they began to have meetings as early as 1718. They were represented in the General Court, in 1721; as appears by a vote in May, 1722, to pay Judge Menzies, who had served them in that capacity in 1721. From supposed or real informality in the early action of the town, they felt it necessary to apply to the General Court for authority to assess and collect their taxes, in June, 1722. After this, their proceedings seem to have been regular and uninterrupted as a town.

Among the families whom we find here in 1717 were Richard and James Southgate and Daniel Denny, who came into town in July of that year; Capt. Samuel Green, and his son Thomas, afterwards Dr. Thomas; James Wilson; and, as the records render probable, Samuel Stebbins, the father of John and Joseph, who came here with him from England. Ralph Earle came here in 1718; and Arthur Carey was probably here at as early or an earlier period. Ebenezer Elliot was here in 1719; and Daniel Livermore, as early as 1720. The same was true of the families of John Armstrong, Edmond Taylor, and Hezekiah Russ. Thomas Newhall was still earlier in town, and Judge Menzies was carrying on his farm in July of 1719.

At the town-meeting in March, 1722, Samuel Green was chosen moderator, first selectman, first assessor, and grand juror, for the year. The other selectmen were John Smith, Nathaniel Richardson, James Southgate, and John Lynd. Nathaniel Richardson was chosen town-clerk; Hezekiah Russ and William Earle, constables; Richard Southgate, treasurer; Joshua Nichols, one of the assessors; William Brown, one of the surveyors of highways; Samuel Stebbins and Daniel Livermore, fence-viewers; and William Green and Rowland Taylor, tithing-men. I have given these names principally to show who, at that early day, were among the men of consideration in the town; and among them will be recognized the ancestors of families, some of whom were formerly well known in town, and some are remaining at the present time.

Among the subjects that troubled the inhabitants for many years after the settlement of the town was how to meet the expenses incident to a town-organization.

In the first place, they had to provide a minister, and support him; and this rendered it necessary to erect a meeting-house. Their highways were a heavy charge; and in 1725, and again in 1729, they were indicted for not having erected a bridge over Seven-mile River.* They were, as will be shown hereafter, in constant trouble with their minister.

* This stream is in the westerly part of Spencer, and crosses the Great Post Road; being one of the most considerable streams in that town.

In 1731, for the first time, they undertook to support a school, and contented themselves with a single one, kept, for the space of three months, in three different parts of the town. The total expense was £10. 10s. of the then depreciated currency: but even this trifle seems to have been felt as beyond their means; for they made no provision for a school in 1732; and the consequence was, the town was indicted at the Quarter Sessions for the neglect. Finding it a better expenditure of money to support a school than to pay fines, the inhabitants provided one, next year, for reading and writing, for the term of three months; and the same was kept at the house of Jonathan Sargent. He kept a public-house in a building, afterwards torn down, which stood opposite the Catholic Church.

But no measures were taken for procuring a schoolhouse before 1736; when it was voted to erect one, twenty by sixteen feet, and six and a half feet "between joynts,"—to be placed "about ten rods north of the Meeting-house, in the most *convenantest* place." The spot finally adopted seems to have been close by the road upon the Common, a few rods east of the then Meeting-house.

In 1741, the town had to raise a hundred pounds to cover and finish the Meeting-house, till then unfinished; and, in 1743, to enlarge it.

These were some of the sources of expense which weighed heavily upon the town. There was, moreover, a difficulty in raising money by taxation, from the lands of the town being held in such large quantities by single proprietors, and so large a proportion of them being not only unimproved, but, many of them, held by non-resident proprietors. Thus, in 1737, John Lynde owned eighteen hundred acres; Paul Dudley, five hundred; Thomas Steel, five hundred; Joseph Willard, a thousand; Richard Southgate, seven hundred and seventy; Jonathan Witt, four hundred; John Clark, four hundred and ninety; George Cradock, three hundred and forty-two; Jonas

Clark, five hundred; &c. Five of the above nine were non-residents of the town.

The whole Province was suffering from embarrassments incident to the condition of a young State, with a sparse agri cultural population in the interior, and a limited and feeble trade and commerce on the seaboard; while upon such a community rested the burdens of frequent wars, from which they were not fully relieved till the fall of Quebec in 1759. Various schemes were suggested for obtaining relief in the Province, which elicited much discussion, and gave rise to strong partisan feelings, that divided the counsels of the government for many years. I allude to these here because the fruits of some of the measures to which they led appear on the records of the proceedings of the town.

The ill-fated expedition against Canada in 1690 created an expense of fifty thousand pounds to the Province of Massachusetts; and, to meet this extraordinary demand, the Province issued bills of credit, designed to pass as currency, to the amount of forty thousand pounds. Another issue, of ten thousand pounds, was made in 1702; a third, of thirty thousand pounds, was made in 1709; and ten thousand more, in 1711; which last issue was made in view of a second expedition against Canada to dislodge the French. This, like the former, was unsuccessful.

In 1714, three parties grew up in the Province: one in favor of returning to a specie currency; one for establishing a land bank, as it was called, — being a private bank; and the third for a system of loaning its own bills by the Province to its inhabitants, on interest. The latter project prevailed; and fifty thousand pounds, in bills of the Province, were put into the hands of five trustees to loan at five per cent interest. Three of these trustees — Judge Davenport, Thomas Hutchinson, and John White — were proprietors of the town of Leicester. In 1716, a hundred thousand pounds was issued in government bills of credit, and put into the hands of county trustees, to be loaned on mortgage-security for ten years at five per cent. In 1720, the House voted another issue of a hundred thousand pounds; which, however, was stopped in the Council: but, the next year, a loan of fifty thousand pounds was granted, to be distributed among the towns in proportion to their respective taxes. In 1724, a new loan of thirty thousand pounds was issued; and, though they had been received, for taxes and the like, into the treasury, there were outstanding, in 1725, over two hundred thousand pounds of these bills of credit. But although, for currency, they had depreciated to less than half their nominal value, in 1728 a new emission was made of sixty thousand pounds. They were issued to towns in proportion to their taxes. These were authorized to let this substitute for money at six per cent; accounting to the Province for four, and paying one to the trustees, — thus saving one towards town-charges. Leicester had the folly to accept their share of this loan; and appointed trustees to take charge of it, with instructions not to let more than ten pounds, nor less than five, in any single loan.

Up to 1737, the purport of the bills issued had been, that they should "be in value equal to money, and be accordingly accepted by the treasurer, &c., in all public payments." In that year, an emission was made in the usual form; and another, of nine thousand pounds, in a different form, — the *tenor* and effect of which were, that they should "be in value equal to three ounces of coined silver, troy weight, of sterling alloy; or gold coin, at the rate of £4. 18s. per ounce;" &c. This new emission took the name of "new tenor," the former being known as "old tenor;" and the proportion of value between them was fixed at three to one. But the practical value, as allowed in business, was four to one: that is, one of the new was worth as much as four of the old tenor bills.*

* The facts stated above are derived from a very useful work, by the Rev. Mr. Felt, called an Historical Account of Massachusetts Currency, published in 1839.

There is a vote, on the records of the town in 1741, to take "manufactory bills" for all town-rates, except the minister's salary; and another for receiving "land-bank" bills, and turning them into "old money." These bills were issued by a private banking company in direct opposition to the government. The stockholders gave security, to the amount of their stock, upon *real estate,* — for which they received these bills, intended to pass as currency; and were to pay three per cent interest annually, in *manufactures* of a specified character, — such as hemp, flax, wool, &c., — at such prices as should be fixed by the directors. As these bills depended upon public favor alone for their currency, many of the towns adopted votes similar to that of Leicester in order to sustain them. There seems to have grown up a paper-banking mania in Massachusetts about 1740, which no effort of the government could repress. It appears that the people of Leicester shared the common mania in the Province to engage in the scheme of a bank of issue: and I find among its citizens who were held responsible as shareholders, and against whom legal process was issued in 1744, the names of James Jackson, assessed eighty pounds; Benjamin Johnson, forty pounds; and Ichabod Merritt, Joseph Shaw, and Josiah Robinson, the amounts of whose assessments are not stated.

Without taking up any more time upon this subject, — which has been introduced by way of explanation, — I may remark, that the substitution of such a currency in the Province led to the sending abroad of all the gold and silver to pay debts and make purchases, where those bills would not pass: and the consequence was, they went on depreciating; so that when the Province received from the mother-country, in part of the expenses incurred in the Louisburg expedition in 1745, £183,649 in gold and silver, it was employed in redeeming these bills, at the rate of one specie dollar for forty-five shillings old-tenor bills; and, for new tenor, eleven shillings and threepence. The amount redeemed was the incredible sum of £1,792,236. This was in 1750; and all debts contracted after that were payable in silver at 6s. 8d. per ounce, which took the name of "lawful money." The effect of this depreciation in the currency was one of the causes of the unhappy controversies that grew up between the town and their minister (the Rev. Mr. Parsons), which will be spoken of more at length hereafter.

To recur to the subject of schools. I have little more to add than what may be found in an able and interesting report upon the subject, from the pen of Joseph A. Denny, Esq., which I have ventured to add as an Appendix to this work.

John Lynde, jun., the first schoolmaster, was the son of John Lynde of Malden; was born in 1710, and removed to Leicester with his father. The family were connected with the Greens by the marriage of Dr. Thomas with a sister of the father. From the son being but twenty-one years old when he first kept the school, and his father, though a large landholder, having been a farmer, it is not probable that he could have had many advantages for an education; since he probably came to Leicester when he was less than ten years old, and there had never been a school there which he could have attended. He settled and became a substantial citizen in Leicester, where he married, and raised up a family. As he was, by the vote of the town, a schoolmaster "to reed and wright" merely, the want of a finished education seems not to have stood in the way of his being employed as such two or three subsequent years.

Joshua Nichols, the second schoolmaster in order, was employed to keep a school in two places, in 1736, for one month each; but, for some reason, completed only a single month. He was a tailor by trade, and came from Malden. He married a daughter of Capt. Samuel Green, — sister of Dr. Thomas, — and probably was in mature life when he removed; for we find him elected an assessor at the first recorded town-meeting, in 1722. He had a family of six children, the oldest of whom was born in March, 1721. He was employed in many town-offices, and appears to have been a man of influence in its affairs.

I do not find that Mr. Cooledge, Mr. Gibbons, or Mr. Bullard, — who were early schoolmasters here, — were ever residents in town, except to keep the school for shorter or longer periods, as stated in the report referred to; nor have I been able to learn any thing of their personal history.

After these, Pliny Lawton, who will be noticed among the physicians of the town, was employed during 1747 and a part of 1748. Solomon Parsons, who will be noticed in the same connection, was employed in 1751; and Dr. John Honeywood, in 1753.*

There was an organization of the town into school-districts, in 1776; which I shall have occasion to notice in another connection, for the purpose of giving the names and residences of the families then dwelling in the town.

I am able to give quite a complete list of the Representa-

* I have mentioned the time of erection and the locality of the first schoolhouse. The second was built upon the north side of the Great Road, where the brick factory stands, formerly of Col. J. D. Sargent. This was some time before 1762. The next schoolhouse in the Centre District was erected in 1791, and was placed about six rods east of the house of J. A. Smith, Esq., opposite what was called the Crossman Road, where it enters the Great Post Road. So long as I attended school there, — though it was improved afterwards, — it was the perfection of discomfort, and of ill adaptation for its purpose. The outside had originally been painted with Spanish brown, much of which had been washed off by the weather. The outer door opened into an entry that ran along the west side of the house, — wholly unfinished, — in which wood was stored for the fire, and into which the chimney for warming the house projected its bare brick walls. The house was warmed — so far as such a thing was possible — by a huge wood-fire, built in an immense fireplace; around which some of the scholars were always gathered to warm their feet, which grew cold again the moment they had taken their seats. This kept up a constant circulation between the seats and the fire in cold weather. These seats, or benches, were narrow, and intolerably hard; and extended the whole length of the building, with the exception of passage-ways in the middle and at each end. In these cramped-up, crowded pens, the pupil wrote, ciphered, and studied, without ever associating any thing but aching limbs and stiffened joints with the acquisition of a schoolboy's knowledge. The condition of what were called the "little scholars" was even worse. They were ranged around the open area in front of the fire, — upon low, narrow seats, the backs of which were the fronts of the desks above them, — with nothing to lean upon. My bones still ache at the recollection.

tives to the General Court that have been chosen by the town. It should be remembered, that, until a late period, each town paid its own representative. The consequence was, that towns often refused to be represented, and were occasionally fined by the General Court for the neglect. Sometimes a hard and sharp bargain was driven with a candidate, to reduce the price at which he was to serve them.

Their first representative (in 1721) was Judge Menzies, who will be mentioned hereafter. When, the following year, the town voted to pay him for the service, he declined accepting compensation; and they thereupon voted him to be their representative for the year 1722. He was again elected, in 1723; and was paid by a vote of thanks, as he declined any pecuniary satisfaction.

The town then voted, that whoever should be chosen the year 1724 should be paid the same as Judge Menzies; and Lieut. Thomas Newhall was elected to serve "on the conditions aforesaid."

The next year (1725), Judge Menzies was again chosen; but from that time to 1733 they were not represented. This covered the time while the town was subjected to constant annoyance and expense in consequence of their difficulties with their minister, which may account for their being unwilling to incur any additional expense.

In 1733, Josiah Converse was chosen for a single year. He was the son of John Converse, a blacksmith; and came with his father from Woburn. He lived in the westerly part of the town, upon a farm which he exchanged with Christopher J. Lawton, Esq., in 1735; and removed to Brookfield, where he afterwards lived.

The order in which the town was subsequently represented was as follows: 1736, '40, and '41, by Christopher J. Lawton (who will be noticed hereafter); 1745, '46, '47, Daniel Denny; 1749, '50, '56, '57, '58, '59, '61, '62, '64, '65, '67, '68, John

Brown;* 1752, '53, '54, '55, Thomas Steel; 1770, '71, '72, '73, '74, Thomas Denny; 1774, balance of term; 1775, delegate, Joseph Henshaw; 1775, Hezekiah Ward, delegate; 1776, Seth Washburn; 1777, Seth Washburn and Samuel Green; 1778, '79, Seth Washburn; 1780, Seth Washburn and William Henshaw; 1781, '82, '83, '88, Seth Washburn; 1786, John Lyon; 1787, Col. Samuel Denny; 1791, '92, '94, 1800, 1801, Thomas Denny; 1796, '98, William Henshaw; 1803, '4, '5, '6, '8, '11, '25, '28, '41, Nathaniel P. Denny; 1809, '10, '21, '22, '29, John Hobart; 1812, '13, '14, '15, '16, '17, Austin Flint; 1819–20, John King; 1826, '27, Emory Washburn; 1830, Nathaniel P. Denny, Waldo Flint; 1831 and '32, John Hobart and John King; 1833, Waldo Flint and Joshua Murdoch; 1834, Reuben Meriam and Joshua Murdoch; 1835, Silas Earle and Cheney Hatch; 1836, Cheney Hatch and Thomas Sprague; 1837, Thomas Sprague and Isaac Southgate; 1838, Samuel Watson and Joseph D. Sargent; 1839, Isaac Southgate and Samuel Watson; 1840, Isaac Southgate and David Henshaw; 1842–43, John Sargent; 1844, '45, John Woodcock; 1847, Henry A. Denny; 1848–49, Dwight Bisco; 1850–51, Samuel Watson; 1852, Abram Firth; 1855, John D. Cogswell; 1856, Lucius Woodcock; 1857, Hanson L. Reed; 1858, Joseph A. Denny; 1860, John D. Cogswell.

The following persons have been members of the Senate of Massachusetts while residents in this town: viz., Seth Washburn, 1780 and '81–'84, '85, '86, and '87; Nathaniel P. Denny, 1823 and '24; Waldo Flint, 1835–6.

---

* Capt. Brown is more than once mentioned in this work. He had held a captain's commission in the French War; took part in the taking of Louisburg, and, at that time, paid a large tax for his property; represented the town twelve years with great acceptance; took a leading part during the Revolution, and had three sons in the service. It is painful, therefore, to read the record of a meeting of the town, called in 1778 to see if they would redeem a certain mortgage, in order to "indemnify themselves from the maintenance of Capt. John Brown." He was then eighty-five years old. His wife was the aunt of Hon. John Coffin Jones; but probably, like many of his contemporaries, he had devoted heart and hand to win a nation's independence at the sacrifice of his own.

The delegates from the town to the Convention which formed the Constitution in 1779 were Seth Washburn and William Henshaw. Col. Samuel Denny was their delegate to the Convention that met to consider the question of adopting the Constitution of the United States, in January, 1788. Col. Henry Sargent was their delegate to the Convention which met in 1821 for revising the State Constitution; and Hiram Knight, Esq., of that for its second revision, in 1853.

As the proprietors' half of the town was much more slowly settled than the eastern half, though they continued to form one corporation, great complaint was made that the settlers' half enjoyed more than a fair share of the offices, while a full proportion of burdens fell upon the western half.

But, though the majority appear not to have hesitated in exercising their legal powers, there does not seem to have been any disposition to retain this power; for, in 1741, the town voted to consent to the westerly half being set off into a new town. A petition was accordingly presented to the General Court, who passed a Bill to that effect; but the Governor (Shirley) refused his assent to the Bill, and the measure failed. It was renewed in 1744, and resulted in the incorporation of the western half into a *precinct.*

There still remained sources of difference between the two parts; one of which was a complaint on the western part, that the town would not lay out roads for the accommodation of the people residing there. The eastern half answered, that, when the lands in that part of the town were laid out, sufficient of these had been appropriated for roads; whereas no such reserve had been made by the proprietors of the other half when it was divided among them. The matter came before the Legislature in 1749, and a new Act, incorporating the western half, was passed; but was again vetoed by Lieut.-Gov. Spencer Phipps, because the effect of it would be to increase the number of representatives in the General

Court. Nor was the separation effected between the two parts of the town until 1753, when an Act was passed, creating the second precinct into a district; which was, in effect, a town to all intents, except having the privilege of sending a representative to the General Court, for which purpose it still remained united with Leicester.

But the attempts to dismember the town did not meet with the same favor, when, in 1743, a petition was presented by several to have a town set off from Worcester and Leicester, substantially as Ward (now Auburn) subsequently was; and another, to set off a part of the town to Rutland as a precinct. The town voted to oppose these, and were successful in so doing.

In 1761, an attempt was made to have a new town — Paxton — created out of the north part of Leicester, and the south part of Rutland, upon the petition of John Smith; and the same thing was moved again the following year, upon the petition of Oliver Witt. Both of these petitions were resisted by Leicester, and, for a while, with success. But, the following year, the town favored the movement; and it resulted in the incorporation of Paxton in 1765.

Ward (afterwards called Auburn) was incorporated as a town in 1778.

A vote of the town in 1754 is not very intelligible without some explanation; for which I avail myself of the first volume of the Collections of the American Statistical Association, prepared by Mr. Felt. The vote was "unanimously to disapprove of the Excise Bill passed by the Assembly at their last sitting."

The taxes at this time had become heavy; and the House were desirous of relieving, as far as they could, the polls and estates from this burden; and, to do this, contrived a plan for laying an excise upon wines and spirituous liquors consumed by the people. The Council refused to approve of it. Gov. Shirley sent for the House into the Council Chamber, and there stated his objection to the measure, that it would be inconsistent with the natural rights of every private family to be subjected to keep and render an account of the quantity of excise liquors which they consumed in their private houses.

The House immediately ordered the objectionable part of the Bill to be printed, and sent to every town for consideration; which led to the above vote of this town. The towns voted, — some, that it was contrary to their liberties; and some, that it was not. The measure, however, was dropped for a short time; but passed, with some amendments, in December, 1754.

Out of this grew a memorable pamphlet, styled "The Monster of Monsters," attacking the Bill and the House. The latter voted it a scandalous libel, and imprisoned the publisher, after having ordered the pamphlet to be burned by the common hangman. For this imprisonment, the speaker, the messenger of the House, and the jailer, were sued; and the Province employed Edmund Trowbridge, James Otis, and Jeremy Gridley, — three of the best and most learned lawyers in the country, — to defend them; and the suit resulted in the acquittal of the parties charged.

The prices which certain things bear at different periods are a subject of curious and interesting inquiry, as serving to test the comparative value of the circulating medium in cases where the relation of supply and demand shall be the same. Laws have, for this purpose, been passed at times, fixing arbitrary prices to labor, wheat, corn, wool, and the like; as if legislation were as strong as the imperative laws of trade. But still they may serve as an approximate test of the value of the common medium of exchange, — whether gold and silver, or issues of paper promises; and, at the same time, the comparative value of the same things at different periods of time. A few only of these, however, can I give; and, such as they are, they may not be very satisfactory.

In 1726, four shillings per day were allowed for work on the garrison.

In 1733, the pay of the schoolmaster was four pounds ten shillings per month. This was in a depreciated currency; and, in 1737, the price was six pounds per month: which, at the rate of calculation between new and old tenor money, would be, in the former year, about twenty shillings — nominally three dollars and a third — per month, though considerably less, in fact, in silver money.

In 1720, the town paid Mr. Parsons, their minister, seventy-five pounds per annum, salary. In 1736, they were to pay Mr. Goddard three hundred pounds, with one hundred pounds settlement; which was but about the same as that paid Mr. Parsons, allowing for depreciation, if the salary of the latter was calculated upon money at par. In 1753, they fixed the salary of Mr. Roberts at £133. 6s. 3d., silver money, at 6s. 8d. per ounce; whereas, when Mr. Goddard was settled, silver was worth 27s. 6d. per ounce, and had risen, at the time of his death, to 60s., — or, what is the same, the paper currency had depreciated in that time more than a hundred per cent. Mr. Conklin's salary, in 1763, was fixed at the same as that of Mr. Roberts ten years before. Dr. Moore's salary, in 1797, was fixed at four hundred dollars. But, to show, somewhat, the rate of depreciation in the paper money in the mean time, the town added, in 1779, five hundred pounds to Mr. Conklin's salary for a single year; which was, in fact, but a hundred dollars in value.

In 1779, a convention of delegates from the towns met at Concord, — of which Mr. Henry King was a member from Leicester, — for fixing the prices which might be charged for the common necessaries of life. Among these were corn, £3. 12s. per bushel; labor in husbandry, £2. 14s. per day; beef, per pound, 2s. 6d.; wool, £1. 4s.; and men's shoes, £6 per pair.*

---

* In 1777, Massachusetts passed what was called a Monopoly Bill, fixing the prices above which no man should charge for the articles specified. Among these were beef,

I have before me a bill for time and expense of an officer "in getting along the six-months' men" in 1780; and among the items are seventy dollars for an advertisement in the Worcester paper, and thirty dollars for *two* dinners.

In 1776, the town allowed their delegate to the Provincial Congress five shillings per day; and the same price was paid to their representative in 1786.*

But I forbear entering into further detail upon this part of our subject, and pass to other topics.

In 1793, a Social Library was formed in town; and its proprietors held their first meeting, Dec. 10 of that year, at the house of Dr. Austin Flint. The number of volumes in this library, however, has never done justice to the character of the town as a reading people.

In 1812, the members of the Fire-engine Company, then recently formed, commenced a new library with much spirit, and for a while with good success; but it was soon after merged in the old organization.

In 1829, another library was commenced, consisting of more modern works. For many years it was used by its proprietors; but, in 1858, it was, like the former one, merged in the

---

3d. and 4d. per pound; wheat, 7s. 6d. per bushel; cotton, 3s. per pound by the bag, — 3s. 8d. per single pound, — at the port where first landed from the *West Indies;* English hay, 5s. per hundredweight; West-India rum, 6s. 8d. per gallon by the hogshead, — 7s. 8d. single gallon; wool, 2s. per pound. The scale of depreciation in 1779 was based upon assuming the prices of some of these articles as the par, upon which the depreciation should be calculated.

* I have memoranda of the travelling expenses of the member of the convention in 1779 from Leicester, and of the representative from that town in 1788; which I give for several purposes: first, to show the nominal value of money at these times; secondly, the mode of performing the journey; and, thirdly, the habits of the most temperate men of that day.

"Set out for Cambridge to the convention, Oct. 27, 1779. An account of what I spent: To oats, 5s.; to dinner, 18s.; to flip, 9s.; to supper and lodging and horsekeeping, £1. 10s.; to breakfast, 12s.; to shaving, 6s.; to flip, 9s.; paid board 15 days, £46. 4s."

The pay per day of the representative in 1788 was four shillings. "May 27, 1788, set out from Leicester to Boston to Court. Got down by six o'clock that day. Spent a-going down: To sling in the morning, 5d.; to half a bowl of toddy, 5d.; to a mess of oats, 4d.; to dinner, 1s.; to bating my horse, 4d.; to toddy, 6d.; to oats, 4d.; to grog, 3d."

original Social Library. The latter now contains about nine hundred volumes.

I should be glad to speak in this connection, if I had proper data, of a Literary Association, which was organized, and pursued its purposes for many years with admirable spirit and brilliant success, among the younger ladies of the town. It had its origin some fifty years since. It was what it professed to be, — a literary association; holding meetings at regular brief intervals, in which the amenities of kindly social intercourse were united with the fruits of a refined taste and a cultivated intellect; and tradition has done no more than justice to the high rank to which, in its day, it helped to elevate the female society of the town. The records of the Association have shared the fate of the many bright thoughts and sage reflections to which its social hours gave utterance; and both are irrecoverably lost. History can only now record the fact that it once existed, flourished many years, and disappeared.

CHAPTER IV.

ECCLESIASTICAL HISTORY.

MEETING-HOUSE. — MR. PARSONS. — MR. GODDARD. — MR. ROBERTS. — MR. CONKLIN. — MR. MOORE. — MR. NELSON. — MR. DENISON. — MR. COOLEDGE. — SECOND MEETING-HOUSE. — SACRED MUSIC. — BAPTISTS. — QUAKERS. — METHODISTS. — UNITARIAN SOCIETY. — JEWS. — CATHOLICS.

THERE are no records preserved of the early condition of the church connected with the Congregational Society, or First Parish, in Leicester; and it is, therefore, impossible to fix the precise period of its organization. From the known custom, however, which so generally prevailed in settling and incorporating towns in Massachusetts at that period, we may safely assume that a church was organized as early, at least, as the town itself. Every town, in fact, constituted a parish, though it managed its parochial affairs by means of its municipal organization; so that, as soon as a church had been gathered agreeably to the usages of the early New-England churches, the town was ready to call and settle a minister, if of ability to afford him the necessary support. Although, as has been stated, the first recorded meeting of the town was held on the 6th (17th) of March, 1722, a church, as well as the town, had been organized some time previous to that date.

A meeting-house had been erected, such as it was, in 1719; and was undoubtedly done by the town, — for its records after that time show, that it was a frequent subject of action on the part of the town. From the accounts which are gathered, chiefly from records, but partly from personal narration of living witnesses, the house must have been of the most primitive, plain, and cheap character imaginable. It stood nearly in front of the present one, and close to the Great Road. It had three outside doors, one upon the front and one at each end of the house, but no door-steps. It had neither porch nor belfry on the outside, nor pews nor gallery in the inside. What pews it ever had, were built by individuals, to whom the town sold "pew-ground" from time to time; and it was not till several years after the erection of the house, that all these "pew-grounds" were disposed of.* It had small windows, made of diamond-shaped glass; and these swung upon hinges, instead of the modern mode of sliding sashes. The outside was clapboarded, but was never painted. The finishing of the interior consisted of being "sealed" with boards, from the floor to what was called, in the votes of the town, "the great girt" of the house. But it is pretty certain that the ceiling over the body of the house was never completed; so that it is not difficult to conceive, that going to meeting upon a sharp winter's day, in those times of long sermons, before stoves had been invented, was a pretty serious operation.

The general style of the work in the interior of the house may be judged of by the sum which was paid, in 1725, to Jonathan Watson "for building the deacon's pew," — which, by the way, had never been built before. This sum was *twelve shillings*. A considerable proportion of the interior of the house was appropriated to "body" seats, or seats which were public. Those west of the centre line of the house were occupied by the men; those upon the east side, by the women.

The name of the architect of this singular temple, whose order of architecture history has not preserved, was, there is reason to believe, Capt. Eleazer Howe. He at least furnished

---

* As late as 1743, only fourteen pews had been built, and all these were along the walls of the house.

the frame, as appears by a vote in 1725, "that Capt. William Wood be allowed the sum of two pounds one shilling and ten-pence; being in full of all Capt. Eleazer Howe's account for the Meeting-house frame."* The bill for the underpinning of the house amounted to four pounds twelve shillings.

In 1725, the town began to take measures for the erection of galleries in the house. Nothing was accomplished then upon the subject, and it came up again for discussion in 1728. But it does not appear when they were built.† The access to these galleries was by means of stairs within the body of the house, leading to them at the south-east and south-west corners of the same; and we may judge of the dimensions of the whole structure from the fact that there was only space enough for one pew, between the door at the west end and the stairs that led into the gallery. This pew at one time belonged to Christopher J. Lawton, Esq.; and I learn the facts I have above stated, as to the size of the church, from the records of a lawsuit which grew out of a controversy, between him and Joshua Nichols, in regard to the ownership of that pew.

The house continued in this condition until 1741: it had never been finished, and by that time needed to be newly covered. The town, that year, accordingly levied a tax of a hundred and fifty pounds for the purpose of finishing and covering the Meeting-house. As this was undoubtedly "old-tenor" money, which was not worth more than one-quarter as much as gold or silver, the amount probably did not exceed a hundred dollars of our decimal currency.

The galleries, like the body of the house, were provided

---

* Besides, the records show that Capt. Howe was absolved from the forfeiture of a certain lot of land from not having settled upon it by a certain day in 1719; it having been "by reason the said Howe was building the meeting-house."

† A vote was adopted, in 1728, "to buy a thousand boards to build galleries, and build our part." At the same time, certain persons were authorized to build stables upon the town's land.

with seats; the eastern side of the dividing-line of the house being occupied by the women, and the western side by the men: the one sex making use of one pair of the stairs; the other, of the other pair. In 1741, it was proposed to erect one or more pews in the front gallery: and it was accordingly voted, "that Noah Jones, Israel Parsons, Thomas Richardson, jun., James Lawton, jun., and Nathan Sargent [who, in the warrant calling the meeting, had been called 'sume young men'], have, and it is hereby granted to them, liberty to build a pew in the hind-seats on the women's side in the front-gallery; and that they, and each of them, shall take it for their seat in the Meeting-house." Peter Silvester, jun., Benjamin Wheaton, Joshua Silvester, Benjamin Gilson, and William Green, jun., had a like permission to build a pew in the hind-seats on the men's side in the front-gallery.

It will be borne in mind, that this was many years before any part of the house had been assigned for the singers. We shall see, as we proceed, that what served as singing was of a congregational character at that time.

There seems to have been little done in the way of repairing the house until 1743, though the subject was frequently agitated. In that year, it was voted "to make an addition to the back-side of the Meeting-house, twelve feet the whole length of said Meeting-house," and "to have a new *ruff* upon the Meeting-house." It was also voted "to move the pulpit to the back-side of the Meeting-house; that the body of the Meeting-house be repaired with the old clapboards that come off the back-side of the Meeting-house; and also to have steps at the door of the Meeting-house:" leaving the back-side, probably, without clapboards. It was also voted "that the inside of the Meeting-house be *sealed* all around, up to the plates, with good white-pine boards;" and a hundred pounds, old tenor, was granted towards finishing the house. The difficulty, if not impossibility, of procuring lime at that time, was doubtless the reason for making use of the style of inside finish which it was voted to adopt. The town still continued to sell "pew-grounds" for the erection of new pews, and fixed the prices to be paid for the same; the highest being twelve pounds, old tenor, — something less than ten dollars of our currency.

In 1754, the town voted to put up a "sounding-board" over the pulpit. It must have been, however, because a meeting-house, at that day, was not deemed complete without this appendage, — or because, as I suppose was the case, the interior was open to the rafters of the roof, — that the town incurred the charge of such a structure in a house of no larger dimensions; and the impressions we thus derive from the records of the town, as to the character of this house, were more than confirmed by the statements of one who had been familiar with it in childhood.

The contemplated enlargement was made; but most of the principal upright timbers which had supported the north side of the house remained standing and exposed to view in its new arrangement, and formed striking objects of notice, if they did not add to the architectural symmetry of the design.* Rough, uncouth, and uncomfortable as this structure must have been, it was the only meeting-house belonging to the town until 1784, when the present one was erected.

It was, moreover, the scene of gatherings and discussions of the deepest local interest; and, in later days, of high-toned eloquence and patriotism, that would have honored a nobler temple and a wider sphere.

It was here that the people met to elect and settle their first minister; it was here that they came together so often afterwards to adopt measures to rid themselves of their "bondage" to him; and it was here that the fickle tide of favor ebbed and rose in the popular mind towards one who

* In 1768, it was voted that Joseph Sargent, Benjamin Richardson, and Edward Bond, be a Committee "to see northerly part of the roof of the Meeting-house decently repaired."

stood towards them at one time as the pastor of a Christian flock; and, at another, as the bitter and vindictive adversary, who again and again put at nought the instructions of the apostle, as to going to law with his own church and his own people.

The man selected by this church and people for their first minister was the Rev. DAVID PARSONS. He then belonged to Malden, and had been settled there as a minister for twelve years. He was brother of Rev. Joseph Parsons, who had been a considerable landholder in Leicester; and he had himself become a proprietor of the town.* His attention had thus been directed towards it; and his interest in its people had been excited by the removal of several families from Malden, and their settling in the town. A difficulty, moreover, had grown up between him and the society over which he was settled; and when, therefore, by the recommendation probably of his former townsmen, he was invited to settle over the church and people of Leicester, he readily accepted the call.

For the history of his connection with the society, I propose to confine myself almost exclusively to the recorded proceedings of the town. I shall, in that way, be in less danger of doing injustice to his memory, than by depending upon traditions in respect to the unhappy controversies which

---

* Joseph and David were the grandsons of Joseph, the first of the name in the country. He was in Springfield in 1636, and removed to Northampton in 1655, where the Joseph here referred to was born in 1671. He was graduated at Harvard, 1697; and was probably brought into connection with the Leicester proprietors by marrying Elizabeth Thompson of Roxbury. He was settled as a minister in Lebanon, Conn.; but left his parish before 1714, and removed to Boston, where he engaged extensively in land speculations, was a grantee of Rutland, and puchased Richard Draper's share in Leicester. He was one of the grantees in the settlers' half of the town, as proprietor of lot No. 23. He was the owner of several other lots, on one of which he caused a gristmill to be erected, — the first built in town, — upon the outlet of Townmeadow Brook. He never resided in Leicester. About 1718, he was again settled as a minister in Salisbury, Mass., where he remained till his death, in 1739, at the age of sixty-nine. His son of the same name was the minister of North Brookfield.—*Hist. Geneal. Register*.

imbittered the relation between them. These controversies were chiefly of a personal character, and do not seem to have partaken in the least of differences in religious opinions, in imputations upon his moral character, his ability as a preacher, or of the strife of political party. It would be singular if there were not faults on both sides.

At the time of his removal to Leicester, he was about forty years of age. He came there under the most flattering auspices; and there seems to have been no misgiving upon the part of the people in settling him, as was the usual mode at that time, for life.

The first vote on the subject is recorded upon the first page of the town-records, in choosing a Committee "to lay out the vacant land, lying northerly from Mr. Carey's, to Mr. Parsons, if he settles among us." This land was upon the North Road, leading over Carey Hill, and north of that hill, next to land laid out to Arthur Carey; and was afterwards the ministerial land of the town.

There had been, as the vote implies, a previous action on the part of the town upon the subject of settling Mr. Parsons; and in the History of Spencer, by Mr. Draper, we find the copies of two letters addressed to Mr. Parsons, which contain a statement of the votes which had been adopted at a meeting of the town, Nov. 28, 1720, about three months prior to the vote above mentioned. It had been then "voted that the Rev. David Parsons be our gospel minister; that Mr. Parsons have the forty-acre lot next the Meeting-house, and the right, in quantity and quality, as other forty-acre lots drawn in after division; that Mr. Parsons have sixty pounds' settlement; that Mr. Parsons have sixty pounds' salary."

The second of these letters was addressed to him two days after the passage of the above votes by six of the principal men of the town, — Thomas Newhall, William Brown, James Southgate, Ralf Earle, Daniel Denny, and Nathaniel Richardson, — and contrasts singularly with the sentiments which, at a later period, were entertained towards him by some of these men, and the people of the town generally.

"REV. SIR, — We, with our heart and consent, do call and invite you to be our settled minister in the work of the gospel amongst us, if you see cause to accept, and see your way clear to remove. But, alas! if we reflect back upon ourselves, we cannot but see we are unworthy of *so great a blessing*. But, if you have such a blessing to bestow on us as we hope you will be, we desire for ever to praise His name for his goodness to usward."

This "blessing" was "bestowed" upon the town. Let its own records tell how they enjoyed it. In 1732, this same Ralf Earle stands at the head of the list recorded as "of the persuasion of those commonly called Quakers."

Mr. Parsons replied to the call of the town; but his letter, though it encouraged the hope that he might be induced to accept, suggested such difficulties in the way, that thirty individuals of the town addressed him a letter, in January, 1721, wherein they engaged to add forty pounds to his settlement, and fifteen pounds a year to his salary; and conclude their appeal to him by saying, "We do humbly beg a brief and speedy relief under the difficulties which we have labored under a long time." This seems to have overcome any remaining scruples in Mr. Parsons's mind; for a meeting was had, upon the 30th of March following, "to come to an agreement with the Rev. Mr. David Parsons as to his settling in the work of the ministry among us, having formerly had a call to it."

Mr. Parsons, it appears, was then in waiting at the public-house kept by Nathaniel Richardson, which stood where Capt. Hiram Knight's house now stands. The meeting was, accordingly, adjourned from the Meeting-house to that place, "to discuss and agree with Mr. Parsons." — "It was proposed, whether the town be of the mind now to come to an agreement with the Rev. Mr. Parsons, *you* having formerly voted him to be *your* minister. It passed in the affirmative." — "Mr. Parsons being called in, it was desired that he would show

how far his way was clear to leave Malden; upon which he produced and read the judgment of a council of clerks favoring his remove." — "It was proposed to Mr. Parsons, whether he was ready to give his answer. Mr. Parsons did then show his resolution, God assisting in giving opportunity, to serve the town in the work of the ministry here at Leicester." The town then proceeded to vote him the proposed forty-acre lot "behind the Meeting-house," seventy-five pounds' salary, and a hundred pounds "gratis," and to be at the expense of removing his family and goods to Leicester. Every thing seems to have passed harmoniously, and in the most hopeful and contented spirit.

Soon after this, at Mr. Parsons's request, the town changed the direction of the road leading north from the Meeting-house, — which at first lay through the middle of his lot, — so as to run along the west end of it, where it now is. This lot he continued to own till just before his death; and, by his own direction, he was buried near the middle of it. His house stood upon the south-east part of it.

But the town was poor, a considerable portion of the land belonged to people residing abroad, and it was no easy matter to provide for its current expenses. They applied to the General Court to abate their share of the county-tax; and every thing in their history, at that time, goes to show that they found great difficulty in keeping up their town-organization and meeting their engagements. It is not to be wondered at, therefore, that they suffered their minister's salary, at times, to be in arrear.* In 1726, it had been suffered to be

---

* To show that Mr. Parsons himself so understood the delays on the part of the town in the payment of his salary, I transcribe a petition of his to the Legislature, which is found in the printed journal of its proceedings under date of Dec. 7, 1725: —

"A petition of Mr. David Parsons of Leicester, in behalf of himself and family, showing that, by reason of the present Indian war, the said town of Leicester is reduced to low circumstances, and unable to make provision for him for his support in the ministry, which they would be able as well as willing, otherwise, to do; praying that this Court would please to make him such allowance for his support, out of the

two years in arrear; and they then proposed to give him a bond for his salary for the year 1724. Among the extraordinary expenses which they had been obliged to incur for his protection and their own, was to erect a "garrison" around his and some other houses, to guard against the threatened attack of the Indians upon the town.

But the salary did not come. Hard feelings, and doubtless hard words, ere long ensued between the parties; and in January, 1727, the town had a meeting "to see if the town will raise Mr. Parsons's salary, or otherwise to see if they will be willing that he should remove out of this town." It was voted, "that the town be willing that Mr. Parsons should remove and remain out of this town."* But Sinbad, in the story, might as well have attempted to rid himself of the Old Man of the Sea by a vote, as the people of Leicester to free themselves from the burden they had assumed, by a hint like this. Mr. Parsons had no idea of quitting either the town or the ministry, or even relaxing his claim upon them for the means of continuing both.

He accordingly memorialized the Legislature upon the subject, though it is not easy to see what they could do in the matter. The town, on their part, in 1727, voted to raise his salary; appointed a Committee to answer his memorial; and applied, themselves, to the General Court for authority to assess a tax of a penny an acre upon all the lands in the

---

public treasury, as to their wise compassion shall seem meet for the reasons therein mentioned."

An allowance of ten pounds was made out of the public treasury to the petitioner, "the better to enable him to carry on the work of the ministry, and support his family, in Leicester."

* This was in consequence of a new memorial of Mr. Parsons to the Legislature, — presented Dec. 2, 1726, — praying that the money heretofore raised for the ministry there might be applied for the use for which it was granted, and that he might have present support granted. The town was notified to show cause why the money granted had not been paid. A hearing was had before a Committee; who reported, in June, 1727, that there was a sum in arrear from the town to Mr. Parsons, but that he had a sufficient remedy for that by law; and recommended that the petition should be dismissed.

eastern part of the town, divided and undivided, towards defraying the town's charges. They proposed, moreover, to Mr. Parsons, by way of settlement, to pay one-half his arrearages (thirty-seven pounds ten shillings) in two months, and the other half in four. Of these arrears, forty pounds were for the years 1724 and 1725; and they proposed to prosecute the collector for his neglect in not having collected the tax of 1726.

Nothing, however, seems to have come of Mr. Parsons's memorial, or this offer of compromise; and the next step was a complaint to the Quarter Sessions by Mr. Parsons against the town for neglecting his support. It was attended with the ordinary fruits of most lawsuits, — ill blood and retaliatory measures. The town met in January, 1729, to see if they would any longer continue to support Mr. Parsons in the work of the ministry in the town; and, if not, "then to see if the town will concur with the church in deposing Mr. Parsons from the ministry in this place; and to see what steps and method the town will take for the upholding, supporting, and the *orderly* and *peaceable* dispensation, of the gospel ministry in this place." They thereupon voted not to support him any longer, and that they would concur with the church in deposing him; and they voted to take measures to supply the pulpit. But Mr. Parsons does not seem to have been any more moved by their vote not to support him, than he had been by so long a practical neglect to supply him the means; and he seems, moreover, to have been one of those spirits which it is not easy to lay. This vote to depose him produced no effect.

They next tried more peaceable and persuasive measures; and, in March of that year, met "to see what steps they should take to settle and *make up* with Mr. Parsons." But he would neither be deposed, settled with, nor "made up with," by them; but, instead of that, brought a civil action for the recovery of his salary, and attached the property of Lieut.

Newhall (whose name stood first upon the letter above quoted, asking for "so great a blessing") to respond the judgment he should recover. This was followed by a second complaint (in 1730) against the town to the Quarter Sessions.

The town, at last, grew nearly desperate. They met in February, 1731, "to see if the town will take into their further consideration the complaints of *Mr.* [the *Rev.* is carefully omitted] David Parsons, exhibited to the Quarter Sessions, against this town; who and which have caused a great deal of disturbances, and have been greatly prejudicial to the peace of this town, and very hurtful both to the civil and religious interests thereof." Nothing seemed to be left for them to do but to appeal for relief to the General Court, "under the difficult circumstances which we labor under at this time."*

One source of embarrassment, however, grew out of a schism that was growing up in the town itself. No quarrel, in which considerable numbers are concerned, can be carried on, any great length of time, all on one side. A part of the inhabitants took sides with the minister: and, that it might appear how they stood numerically upon the subject, it was voted that a list should be prepared in two columns, to be sub-

* In March, 1731, they accordingly petitioned the Legislature; and Mr. Parsons made an answer. The Council voted, in June, to dismiss the petition: but the House voted to hear the parties; and a hearing was accordingly had before that body, and the consideration of the petition postponed. At a subsequent time, they heard the parties again upon the same subject, and then referred the matter to a Committee of which Mr. Lynde (afterwards Chief-Justice Lynde) was chairman. On the 23d June, 1731, the Committee reported a resolve; upon which the House adopted a vote with a long preamble, reciting that difficulties had arisen of long standing, and had "proceeded to such a degree as greatly to prejudice the interest of religion, and *disserve* the ends of the gospel ministry," &c.; and that application had been made in the name of the town, and of a great number — if not a major part — of the brethren of the church, for relief. The vote provided for permitting any who conscientiously dissented from Mr. Parsons's ministry, respecting points either of doctrine or discipline, to signify the same to Joseph Wilder, Esq.,* and be exempt from taxation on his account when they should have provided an orthodox minister, or diligently attended public worship in neighboring towns, — saving Mr. Parsons's right to two hundred acres of land; &c.

* He was Judge of the Court of Common Pleas, and belonged to Lancaster.

scribed by all the inhabitants,—indicating whether they were for or against "his continuing in the work of the ministry,"—"to be laid before his excellency, to inform him how many in this town *is* for Mr. Parsons's continuing in the work of the ministry, and how many against it;" and Daniel Denny and Samuel Green were to be despatched to the Governor for that purpose. The subscription-paper was begun upon the spot: and, as the record shows, "after all persons that signed against Mr. Parsons, the moderator made proclamation to desire any person, that had been persuaded to sign to the subscription contrary to their judgment and conscience, if any there were, to come and take their names out again; but they refused, for they said they had acted conscientiously in the matter."

But the fates were singularly against the town in their struggle to escape from the persevering pursuit of their uncompromising pastor. The General Court passed a resolution relieving them from any longer supporting Mr. Parsons; but the Governor refused to approve it, and a Committee of the town was appointed to address him upon the subject. But it was nothing new for Gov. Belcher to differ from the popular branch of the Legislature, and Mr. Parsons probably felt himself safe beneath the shelter of prerogative.

These events took place in 1731; and Mr. Parsons had, in the mean time, obtained a judgment against the town upon his complaint before the Quarter Sessions; but the town, instead of submitting, held a meeting to consider whether they should apply to the General Court to allow them to appeal from this judgment, "that so the town may have the privilege of a trial in the common law."*

The Court of Quarter Sessions was one having criminal jurisdiction, held by all the justices of the peace in the several counties,—every second man not being then a justice; and trials took place before a jury, with a right of appeal to a

---

* Draper's History, p. 81.

higher court. It had also civil powers, — such as laying out highways and taking charge of the financial matters of the county; wherein it did not act as a common-law court. By the law as it then existed, if a town neglected to support their minister, he might apply, by complaint, to this court, who had authority to provide an effectual remedy, and impose a fine upon the selectmen for this neglect; and there was no provision for any appeal, or trial by jury, in such a case.*

The General Court, however, had been prorogued before the petition of the town reached them. But another meeting was held by the town, in December of the same year, "to see if the town would put in a memorial to the General Court for to revive a petition which the town had put in, in hope of being relieved from *Mr. Parsons's bondage;* or to see if the town would proceed in any other way to put an end to the differences which we are under in all our affairs."†

By one of those sudden revolutions in public sentiment so common under democracies, whether small or large, — where the man most berated to-day becomes the idol of to-morrow, and *vice versâ*, without, quite as often as with, cause, — the whole tone of the votes of the town was changed. They voted "not to send a memorial to revive said petition;" "that the former vote concerning Mr. Parsons's salary be reconsidered;" "that the former vote concerning Mr. Parsons's not being paid should be null and void," and "that the vote passed Jan. 21, 1728–9, that the town would no longer support Mr. Parsons in the work of the ministry, be null and void;" that

---

* Ancient Charters, p. 256.

† This petition was presented 28th July, 1731. It was in the name of the selectmen, asking the Legislature to explain the Act as to supporting ministers; and that the petitioners might have leave to appeal from a judgment obtained by the Rev. Mr. Parsons against them, or that they might "have a hearing and trial *de novo* in a process at common law," or any way by which they could have the benefit of a trial by jury; and that the execution against them might be stayed. The House fixed a time for hearing the petition, and ordered the execution to be stayed. On the 18th of the following August, the petition was dismissed. — *Journal of House of Rep.*

"the arrears of his salary be paid with all convenient speed;" and that, "notwithstanding the vote passed the 25th January, 1728–9, Mr. Parsons is esteemed to be the regular settled gospel minister in this town." They further voted to raise money to satisfy the execution against the selectmen for neglecting to pay Mr. Parsons's salary; but, being unwilling to countenance those who had opposed Mr. Parsons, they excepted from this appropriation "the fine laid upon said selectmen for their neglect." The selectmen were accordingly left to pay out of their own moneys the penalty for carrying out the votes of their constituents.

It might be more satisfactory to witness this retrocession of the town, in their controversy with their minister, if there was not pretty strong evidence that his friends and partisans took his opponents by surprise in carrying this measure.

The meeting was adjourned; and, when it was again convened, there seems to have been a general rally of the forces on both sides. The record says, that, upon the foregoing votes being read, "there appeared a number of men, and desired to know how those votes came to be passed, and desired to hear the warrant read. Some of them said they never had been warned to such a meeting. The warrant being read publicly, Capt. Green said he had not been warned to the meeting, and that they had voted that that was not set forth in the warrant; and he, with several other men, desired that the moderator would see if the town would not reconsider of those votes that were acted contrary to warrant, as Capt. Green declared that he would enter his dissent against the meeting as illegal. But the moderator wholly refused, and said he would not put no such thing to vote, without giving any other reason than 'I will not.' Then the moderator, with other of the inhabitants, desired some particular men to draw up some proposals to lay before the town, and they would adjourn the meeting to hear these proposals and consider on them."

An adjournment was accordingly had; and then, "the town being convened and the proposals being read, Mr. Moderator and Mr. Parsons, with some others of *their company*, made some unhandsome reflections, by reason that the proposals did not suit them; and so the moderator dissolved the meeting."

These certainly look like rather high-handed measures. The moderator who thus played the part of autocrat over this little republic was Mr. Josiah Converse, and the triumph of "*their* company" was short-lived. In April, 1732, the town voted that they would not raise any money to pay Mr. Parsons's salary for the year 1731." But within a few months the scale turned, and Mr. Converse was again chosen moderator of a meeting, called, among other things, "to see what method the town will take to call in the town's money, so that Mr. Parsons's arrears may be paid."

Before reading this article, the meeting was adjourned; and the town-clerk, who had made so full and circumstantial a record of the action of the moderator at the former meeting, probably anticipating what would be the action of the adjourned meeting, staid away from it, and withheld his book of records.

The people came together at ten o'clock; and, in the words of the record, "they tarried until about one of the clock: and the town-clerk, who was Mr. Joshua Nichols, neglecting his duty in bringing or sending the town book and papers that was then in his hands, there could be nothing further done in their affairs; and so the moderator dissolved this meeting."

But Mr. Nichols staid away to no purpose. Mr. Converse's star was more than ever in the ascendant, and his popularity was well-nigh unbounded; for at the March meeting, in 1733, he was chosen moderator, first selectman, town-clerk (thereby superseding Mr. Nichols), town-treasurer, first assessor, and a hog-reeve.

In April, they "voted not to allow any part of the money assessed upon the land for the five years past to be disposed of to any other use than to pay Mr. Parsons, until all his arrears are paid."

In May, Mr. Converse's cup of honor was made full by his election to the General Court. But though there was an armistice, so far as Mr. Parsons was concerned, there seemed to have grown up a bad state of feeling in the town, which showed itself by the multiplied lawsuits which were commenced about this time (1733). Thomas Newhall had one suit against the town, Thomas Richardson and Steward Southgate had three; and the town was indicted again for the want of a schoolmaster.

The quarrel between Mr. Parsons and the town had been so long continued, and had become so scandalous in the public mind, that the people of the neighboring towns were inclined to interpose to put a stop to them; and "six Worcester gentlemen, appointed to come into Leicester to see if they can reconcile the differences between Mr. Parsons and the town," paid a visit to the town for that purpose. This led to the appointment of a Committee on the part of Leicester, who waited upon Mr. Parsons, "and had discourse with him concerning his laying down the gospel ministry amongst us."

The proposition was favorably received, and mutual proposals for a settlement were adopted, which were ratified on the part of the town, and resulted in calling a mutual council to dissolve the connection between Mr. Parsons and his people. This action took place in January, 1735; and in March the council met, and came to a result which was accepted on the part of the town; and Mr. Parsons thereupon ceased to be their pastor. But he did not cease to make his presence known and felt in that community.

In May following, the town were called together "to see if they would come into some effectual measures to prevent Mr. Parsons encroaching upon the ministry lot or town land, or making strip or waste on the timber that groweth thereon." The next year, the town raised thirty pounds to "pay Mr. Lynde the court-charges which he had been put to by Mr. Parsons, about the way that went over Cary's Hill;" though what Mr. Lynde had done which had aggrieved Mr. Parsons does not appear.

Though we shall have occasion to recur to Mr. Parsons again, it is a relief to bring to an end the narrative of these protracted details of strife and bitterness.* The contrast which will appear in their personal and official characteristics, between him and his successor, might serve as an interesting study in the science of human nature.

Where the blame lay, in the origin of the feelings of alienation which gave rise to such disreputable transactions, it is unnecessary now to attempt to settle; nor is there any occasion to impute bad motives or dishonest intentions to either party. It is but an instance and an illustration of what is witnessed every day, in every age, of passion and will unconsciously putting on the guise of conscience and duty; and the man, be he minister or be he layman, really thinking he is battling for truth and right, when, in fact, intent only upon a party success, or a personal triumph over an enemy.

The whole history of Mr. Parsons's connection with this people, up to his death in 1743, is a sad one. He carried to the grave the feelings of bitterness which had been engen-

---

* By records discovered since the above was written, it would appear, that, soon after his dismissal, Mr. Parsons removed to Belchertown, then called Cold Spring, and resided there a few years, and where a son of his settled permanently. While there, in 1737, he commenced two actions against the town; I suppose, for arrears of salary. What the result of these was does not appear. The town made a defence, and, as appears by their records, paid their agents ten shillings per day for their time and expenses in attending court, and "forty shillings which they paid the attorneys."

I find a deed from "David Parsons, formerly of Leicester, now of Cold Spring, clerk," to James Lawton, jun., of Leicester, saddler, dated November, 1739, of "forty acres of land, lying on both sides of the brook where the said David Parsons built a mill, with the said mill (being a gristmill) and the appurtenances." This mill stood at the outlet of the Town Meadow. Mr. Parsons, however, soon chose to return to the battle-ground he had so long occupied, where he continued to reside till his death.

dered in his controversy with the town; and was buried, by his special direction, on his own land, apart from the graves of his people. He was unwilling that his ashes should repose by the side of those with whom he had worshipped in the sanctuary, and to whom he had broken the consecrated bread. His grave, once visible in a mowing-field, about thirty rods north of the present Meeting-house, has been levelled by the ploughshare; and the headstone, with his name inscribed upon it, no longer serves, as it did for more than a century, as a monument of human frailty.*

It is pleasant, therefore, to turn to the brief history of his successor, — the Rev. David Goddard.

There was, however, an interval of more than a year between the dismission of Mr. Parsons and the settlement of Mr. Goddard. It required some time, in fact, to overcome the state of things, in respect to the religious interest of the town, which had been produced by these protracted difficulties and disputes with Mr. Parsons. The Meeting-house, never in complete order, had been suffered to fall into such general dilapidation, that it required an expenditure of ten pounds merely to repair the glass in its windows, before it could be considered fit for the use of a new minister.

---

* Since the above was written, a question arose, which could not be settled by record, when Mr. Parsons died. The published genealogy of the family states the time as 1737; but a deed was found, bearing date 1743, signed by him. I induced the friend who has aided me so much in preparing this work to make search for his headstone. It was ascertained that it had been used, in building a chimney in a house erected several years since, as a covering-stone for the ash-pit; and it was concluded to look into this, and see if the name might not be legible. I copy the note I received on the subject. "I sent a man's head into the ash-hole of the house, &c., the other day, for his shoulders could not be admitted; and, as good luck would have it, the Rev. Mr. Parsons's gravestone happened to be right-side *downward*, and the following inscription could be read: 'In memory of Rev. Mr. David Parsons, who, after many years of hard labor and suffering, was laid here, Oct. 12, 1743, aged sixty-three.'

"'Sarah Parsons died June y[e] 17, 1759, aged seventy-three.'"

It may be no place to moralize on a subject like this; but it is certainly enough to cause one to pause and ask, "What is fame?" when the only record of the decease of a man who filled so important a sphere, and was the founder of so widely spread and honorably distinguished a family, is found in such a place, and devoted to such a service.

In this interval, preaching was supported by contributions taken up from sabbath to sabbath; and the pulpit was supplied a part of the time by a Mr. Rice. The church and society, during that time, set apart a day of fasting and prayer for direction from on high, in regard to a successor to Mr. Parsons; and on the 30th January, 1736, they gave Mr. Goddard a call to settle. They offered him three hundred pounds as a settlement, and a hundred pounds per year as a salary *so long as he should remain their minister.* The form of the vote indicated an intention to avoid the life obligation, which they would have been understood as assuming towards him if the offer had been unlimited or unqualified in its terms. They had learned from their recent experience to be chary in forming life alliances even in so sacred a relation.

He accepted the invitation in a brief and pertinent answer, wherein, among other things, he expressed a wish that the church might be governed by the rules adopted by the New-England churches in the Cambridge Platform of 1648. He was ordained June 30, 1736; and remained their pastor until his death, Jan. 19, 1754. He lived in a house belonging to him, upon the east side of the Charlton Road, near, and as is supposed in front of, the house where Mrs. Hobart lives, but which disappeared before the memory of any one now alive.* His salary was often in arrear; but a spirit of Christian forbearance on his part led to a corresponding concession upon the part of the town, who repeatedly added fifty pounds to his salary, in the way of an appreciation of his claims upon their consideration, for these delays and the great depreciation of the currency. His connection with his people was uniformly kindly and happy on both sides; and his sudden and early death, at the age of forty-seven, was deeply lamented as the loss of a faithful minister and good man.

---

* He bought this of John Curtice of Leicester, in March, 1736. The parcel contained fifty acres, a *small house* and barn thereon, bounded south by lands formerly of James Jackson and Benjamin Johnson.

Mr. Goddard was born in Framingham, Sept. 26, 1706. He was the son of Hon. Edward Goddard, who, at one time, was a member of the Council. He was graduated at Harvard in 1731, and married Mrs. Mary Stone of Watertown for his first wife, in 1736; and, for his second, Mrs. Martha Nichols of Framingham, in 1753, less than one month before his death. His death occurred while he was upon a visit at Framingham, during what was known there as the "great sickness." It prevailed with great mortality in that and the neighboring towns of Holliston and Sherborn, and carried off the father and mother of Mr. Goddard within a month after his death. His widow married again, and removed to Framingham; and I am not aware that he left any family in Leicester.

After the death of Mr. Goddard, the pulpit was supplied by occasional preachers, who seem to have visited the town on horseback. I find £17. 10s. appropriated to pay for the entertainment of these ministers, and £18 for that of their horses.

The Rev. Joseph Roberts was invited in July, after Mr. Goddard's death, to settle over the church and society; and in his answer accepting the call, which is too long to copy here, that sordid love of money, which became his ruling passion, is strangely mixed up with professions of a devotedness to God and his service.

The town voted him a settlement of £133. 6s. 3d. silver money, and £66. 13s. 8d. per annum salary, in silver money at 6s. 8d. per ounce. Though nominally a less sum than that paid to his predecessor, it must have been considerably more in value, by reason of the difference between silver and Province bills, which constituted almost the entire currency of the Province at the time of Mr. Goddard's settlement. At that time, silver was worth 27s. 6d. per ounce; though it rose at one time before his death to 60s. per ounce.

Provision was made by the town for the entertainment, at the ordination of Mr. Roberts, of "ministers, messengers, and scholars."

Ordinations were made, in fact, at that time and for more than half a century afterwards, occasions for a general festivity and unbounded hospitality on the part of the people of the town where it was to occur. Ministers were settled for life; and it was a great marriage-feast, to which every door, however humble, was opened. It became a holiday for all the surrounding country; and no man, though he were a stranger, was suffered to depart from the town, without having shared at the hospitable board of some of its people.

For some reason, the ordination was postponed until Oct. 23, 1754.

Though a bachelor, he purchased, and at first lived upon, a large tract of land in the westerly part of the town, where Mr. Robert Watson resided: but, in 1760, he purchased the estate where Rev. Mr. May lives; which was afterwards owned and occupied by Rev. Mr. Conklin, his successor.

He was settled under favorable auspices; was a man of good natural powers of mind, and of respectable attainments in scholarship. But there were inherent defects in his moral and mental organization, which soon brought him into differences with his people. He was grasping and avaricious, and manifested far more eagerness to gain and save money than to win the favor of those over whom he was settled. The consequence was, that, as early as 1762, a council was called to settle the difficulties which had grown up in the society. The only part taken in the measure, by the town, was to make provision for the entertainment of the council; while the church prepared, and laid before the council, a statement of their grievances. In view of these, a dissolution of the connection between them and their pastor was recommended; and he was accordingly dismissed Dec. 14, 1762, though very much against his will. He very soon after sold his estate in Leicester, and removed to Weston; where he lived to the age of ninety-one, and died April 30, 1811.

Mr. Roberts was born in very humble life, in Boston, in 1720. He was graduated at Cambridge in 1741. In a class of twenty-five, he ranked, in dignity of family, the twenty-second of the number. The struggles to which he was probably subjected while obtaining his education might perhaps have developed that sordid love of hoarding which characterized him in the latter part of his life.

After his removal to Weston, he preached occasionally, but was never settled. The difficulties with the mother-country coming on, he took an active part in the political agitations of the day; and was, at one time, a member of the Committee of the town for the purpose of enlisting and providing soldiers for the army. He was a member, and took an active part in the deliberations, of the convention which framed our State Constitution in 1779. He was frequently, afterwards, a representative from Weston in the General Court.

He engaged in business with a cunning and unscrupulous speculator; whereby he became involved in several expensive and harassing lawsuits, and lost a considerable part of his estate. This soured his temper and imbittered his life: he became a miser and a misanthrope. He suffered himself to be imprisoned for a debt growing out of his connection with the speculator above mentioned, and remained in prison two or three years, until his creditor was glad to compromise the debt. He had, at the same time, bags of money lying in his house; which were found after his death, and had been so long hoarded there, that they were too much decayed to hold their contents upon being raised from the place of their deposit. He died, as he had lived, like a beggar. He had for years denied himself the necessaries of life, and not an article of his wardrobe was fit for the tenant of an alms-house. Such was the sequel of the life of a man who was possessed of more than ordinary natural powers, educated to a liberal profession, once the pastor of a respectable religious society, and who, with nobody but himself to care for, sacrificed his reputation, his influence, and his comfort, to a sordid love of useless and unused gold.

The successor of Mr. Roberts was the Rev. Benjamin Conklin. He was invited to become the pastor of the church and society, in August, 1763; and was ordained Nov. 23 of that year. At his ordination, the Rev. Mr. Forbes of Brookfield made the introductory prayer, Rev. Mr. Maccarty of Worcester preached the sermon, Rev. Mr. Buckminster of Rutland gave the charge, and the Rev. Mr. Davis of Holden gave the right hand of fellowship. His salary was fixed at the same sum as Mr. Roberts's had been; and provision was made for the entertainment of "ministers, scholars, and *gentlemen*," at the ordination.

A connection thus formed continued with mutual satisfaction for thirty years; and was another illustration of a familiar observation, that a man may be useful and influential without being great. He was never distinguished for brilliancy or originality as a preacher, but always maintained a respectable rank in his profession, and exercised a marked and salutary influence among his people.

Mr. Conklin was a native of Southhold, L.I.; and was born in 1732. He was graduated at Princeton, N.J., in 1755. His manners were easy and familiar, and his conversation was enlivened with humor and pleasant anecdote. In one respect, he was fortunate: his sympathies were all in favor of the movements which resulted in the Revolution, and the ardor of his temperament harmonized with the popular enthusiasm that prevailed in the community in which he moved. A dissatisfaction had grown up in one of the neighboring towns, with their minister, on account of his want of fervor and animation; and some one gravely advised that he should exchange with Mr. Conklin, that the people might be supplied with all they wanted of either.*

---

* The following illustrative anecdote of Mr. Conklin has been recently told me. He was of that class of ministers who are called liberal in their views, because they

It was a time when all ranks and professions were engrossed by the calls of patriotism; and none lent a more willing ear to these than Mr. Conklin. At one time, he was a member of a patriotic convention; at another, one of the Committee of Correspondence of the town; and, at all times, he was an active and zealous advocate of the popular cause. This might have arisen partly from the character of the parishioners by whom he was surrounded. Among them was an unusually large number of prominent and leading men upon the same side in politics. The names of Henshaw, Denny, Allen, Washburn, Brown, and Newhall, will at once occur to any one at all familiar with the history of the town. On the other hand, with the exception of Judge Steel, I doubt if there was a loyalist to be found in the town.

When the State Government had been established, Mr. Conklin was found an equally decided advocate for its support. This rendered him so much an object of jealousy and disfavor on the part of the insurgents, at the time of "Shay's Rebellion," that he was repeatedly obliged to fly from his own house, and conceal himself, in order to escape the violence with which he was threatened.

He married Mrs. Lucretia Lawton, the widow of Dr. Pliny Lawton of Leicester, in 1769; by whom he had three children, — two sons and one daughter.

In his person he was large, and rather inclined to corpulency. For many years before his death, he was afflicted with a painful and incurable disease; which induced him to accept a proposition from his people to pay him a gratuity of a hundred and seventy pounds, exempt his property from taxation, and have his connection as their pastor dissolved.

---

are willing to think they should not harm the people of another society by preaching in their pulpit. One who differed from him in this sentiment remonstrated with him upon his error, and closed by saying, "Mr. Conklin, would you preach in Mr. ——'s pulpit?" — "Yes," was the ready reply: "I would preach on Mars' Hill, if I could get a chance."

The arrangement was carried out by a council, consisting of Drs. Sumner of Shrewsbury, and Austin and Bancroft of Worcester; who bore testimony to his high character as a clergyman and a citizen. This took place in June, 1794. The separation was with kindly feelings on both sides; and the town, in a vote expressive of their sentiments towards him, tendered him their thanks for his useful and arduous services, and their sympathies for his declining health and increasing infirmities.

He lost his wife, who died of dropsy, in March, 1793; and his own death took place Jan. 30, 1798, in the sixty-seventh year of his age. A part of the epitaph inscribed upon his headstone had been selected by himself, and is as follows: —

"Hic jacet Benjamin Conklin M., in expectatione diei supremi. Qualis erat, dies iste indicabit."

Mr. Conklin lived in a house which stood where the Rev. Mr. May now lives. His land extended westward as far as the Common, and the lane leading to the house formerly occupied by Mr. Parsons. The house was, I presume, as old as any in town, if not the oldest; and was probably erected by Mr. Samuel Stebbings, to whom lot No. 1 — on which it stood — was allotted in the first division of the town. It was afterwards owned by Mr. Larkin, from whom it passed to Mr. Roberts, and from him to Mr. Conklin. Ebenezer Adams, Esq., next owned the house: he moved into it in 1800, and thoroughly repaired it. Mr. Luther Wilson purchased the place of Mr. Adams. Mr. Alpheus Smith owned it, and lived there many years after Mr. Wilson's removal, and enlarged and repaired it; and, at last, the house was removed by the Rev. Mr. May to make room for his present much more elegant mansion.

After the dismission of Mr. Conklin, Mr. James Tufts was employed to preach for the society, and was invited to settle as their minister. But, there being some opposed to his settlement, he declined the call, and was afterwards, in 1795, settled over a society in Wardsborough, Vt.; where he long sustained the character of a useful and faithful minister, until his death a few years since.

After this, the Rev. Dr. Appleton, afterwards President of Bowdoin College, preached here, and received a unanimous invitation to become the pastor of the society; and it was a matter of great regret on the part of the people that he declined their invitation.

After Dr. Appleton, the Rev. Zephaniah Swift Moore was employed to supply the pulpit; and, by a unanimous vote of the society, was invited to settle as their minister, in October, 1797, upon a salary of four hundred dollars a year. He accepted the call, and was ordained Jan. 10, 1798. The Rev. Mr. Pope of Spencer made the introductory prayer; Rev. Dr. Backus of Somers, with whom he had studied divinity, preached the sermon; Rev. Dr. Sumner of Shrewsbury made the consecrating prayer; Rev. Dr. Fiske of Brookfield gave the charge; Dr. Austin of Worcester, the right hand of fellowship; and the Rev. Mr. Mills of Sutton, the concluding prayer.

He married Miss Phebe Drury,— daughter of Thomas Drury, Esq., of Ward, now Auburn,— Feb. 27, 1799; and lived in the house, now of Mr. Edward Knowles, at the corner of Charlton and Great Post Road, which had been erected a few years before by Joseph Washburn.

He remained the minister of the town until Oct. 28, 1811; when, having been appointed Professor of Languages in Dartmouth College, he asked and obtained a dismission from his people, to their universal regret. In his position as minister of this people, he exerted an influence and commanded a respect, which every one was ready to acknowledge, and which has rarely been surpassed. He left town on the 1st November, 1811, attended by a large number of

J. Grozelier's Lith. Boston.

Zeph. Swift Moore.

his parishioners and friends in carriages, who escorted him several miles from the town; while the children of the schools, ranged by the side of the road along which he was to pass, paid their simple testimony of respect, and of sorrow at his departure, by standing with saddened countenances and uncovered heads as the procession passed slowly by them.

Dr. Moore filled too many important stations, besides that of pastor of this church, to be passed over with a mere mention of his connection with the town.

He was born in Palmer, Nov. 20, 1770. His mother was a Swift, from Sandwich, from whom he took his name; she having been the daughter of Zephaniah Swift. His father was a farmer; and, being in somewhat straitened circumstances, removed to Wilmington, Vt., then a new settlement, when this son was about seven or eight years old. Here the son was employed upon the farm until he was about eighteen years of age, with only limited means of cultivating his mind. At that time, he began to attend the Academy at Bennington; and, the next year, offered himself for admission to Dartmouth College. He took at once a prominent rank in his class, and maintained it by strong natural powers of mind, improved by close and constant devotion to study. He was graduated in 1793, with a high reputation for sound learning and scholarship.

After leaving college, he taught an academy in Londonderry, N.H., for one year. He then commenced the study of theology with the Rev. Dr. Backus of Somers, Conn.; for, it will be recollected, this was before the days of theological seminaries in our country. He was licensed to preach, Feb. 3, 1796.

Passing over his connection with the people of Leicester,—except to say, that one year, while minister there, he filled the place of Preceptor of the Academy with great acceptance,—he remained connected with Dartmouth College until the autumn of 1815; when he was elected to the presidency of Williams College, made vacant by the resignation of Dr. Fitch. He remained at the head of that college until 1821; when he accepted the place of President of Amherst Collegiate Institution, which, after his death, was incorporated as a college. In 1816, he received the degree of Doctor of Divinity from his Alma Mater. In 1818, he preached the Election Sermon before the government of the State; and was, for several years before his death, a member of the Board of Commissioners for Foreign Missions.

He died June 30, 1823, at the age of fifty-two, in the midst of his vigor, usefulness, and honors. His wife survived until 1857.

Dr. Moore left but few publications, and these were principally occasional sermons. Like most of the public men in New England, he built up his success by his own exertions. He sometimes amused his friends by tracing what he pleasantly called the causes of his success.

His sister had married the Rev. Mr. Mills of Sutton. Soon after being licensed, he made a journey to Sutton to visit her. This was extended several days beyond its intended limit, by reason of his horse becoming lame and unable to travel. It was during this delay that Miss Drury, who was a friend of the family of Mrs. Mills, came there upon a visit. This accidental interview led to a visit on his part to the young lady, at her father's: and, while there, the people of Leicester invited him to preach for them; and, being pleased with, settled him. Here he formed an intimate acquaintance with Mr. (afterwards Professor) Adams, which grew into a strong and ardent friendship. Mr. Adams, after residing a while at Exeter and Portland, became a professor in Dartmouth College in 1809; and when, by the death of Professor Hubbard, and Mr. Adams's appointment to succeed him, there was a vacancy in the office which he had been filling for the year then past, he recommended and induced the trustees to elect Mr. Moore to the professorship. And thus, in the order of sequences as traced by himself, he owed his election to the presidency of a college to the opportune sickness of the animal he rode.

In whatever situation Dr. Moore was placed, he showed that he had a fitness and capacity for filling it with honor and usefulness. Though he was a profound thinker, and his turn of mind was decidedly metaphysical, his style was remarkably simple and clear, and his sermons were adapted to the taste and comprehension of his hearers. His manner was dignified, calm, and self-possessed. The tones of his voice were clear and pleasant, but not loud; nor did he in the pulpit ever attempt to play the orator, although he invariably commanded the attention of his hearers. There was a great sweetness of manner in his intercourse with others, especially towards the young; but underlying this was a firmness of purpose, an indomitable resolution of spirit, which no discouragement could daunt or defeat. He was eminently fitted for the office of a teacher and manager of a literary institution: the accuracy of his knowledge, the clearness of his apprehension, the plain and simple manner of communicating his ideas to others, his great tact in understanding character, with his uniform urbanity of manner, were qualities which he possessed, as a college-officer, to a degree rarely excelled. However others might have differed from him in respect to measures, no man could deny his eminent claims for consistent piety, great executive talent, and profound sagacity; nor hesitate to accord to him the qualities of a gentleman, a companion, and a friend, as well as a faithful servant of the Master he professed to serve. He left no children; and the results of a life of prudence and industry were devoted to the college to whose early success he gave the best energies of his life.

It is now near half a century since Dr. Moore's connection with Leicester ceased; but the silent, indirect influence of such a man's teachings and example might have been traced, in the moral and intellectual tone of that community, for many years after his voice had ceased to be heard in their pulpit, their schools, and their social circles. His memory is still one of the historical treasures of which the town has so goodly a store in the recollections of the past.

The Rev. John Nelson was invited to preach as a candidate, by the society, the week following Dr. Moore's departure from town. An invitation to settle there was soon tendered to him; and on the 4th March, 1812, he was ordained, upon a salary of four hundred and fifty dollars per annum. The ordination-services were performed by the Rev. Dr. Bancroft; Dr. Austin, who preached the sermon; Mr. Avery of Holden; Mr. Pope of Spencer; Mr. Whipple of Charlton; and Mr. Mills of Sutton, who, it will be recollected, had taken part with Dr. Austin and Mr. Pope in the ordination of his predecessor.

Happily, the time has not yet come, — and long may it be delayed! — when it is proper to speak of Mr. Nelson with the fulness of detail in which the living may indulge when recalling the virtues and excellences of one upon whose character Death has set his seal.

He was born in Hopkinton. He removed at an early age, with his father, to Worcester. He was graduated at Williams College in 1807, and was afterwards a tutor in that college for the year 1809–10. He studied theology with the Rev. Dr. Austin of Worcester. He married Zebiah, daughter of Abijah Bigelow, Esq., of Barre, May 4, 1812. From 1826 to 1833, he was a trustee of Williams College; and, in 1843, received the honorary degree of Doctor of Divinity from that college.

The amount of salary paid to Dr. Nelson was increased from time to time, in order to meet in some measure the rapidly increasing expenses of living; which, within the period since he was settled, have more than doubled, by a comparison of prices paid, and the style demanded by the customs of social life.

In consequence of impaired health, the society of Dr. Nelson

L. Grozelier [illegible]

Very truly yours
John Nelson

thought proper to call, as a colleague to his aid, the Rev. Andrew Clark Denison, who accepted the invitation; and on the 4th March, 1851, — on the thirty-ninth anniversary of Dr. Nelson's ordination, — he was ordained as such. He was to receive six hundred dollars as salary, while Dr. Nelson was to be paid the sum of four hundred dollars; each of which was afterwards increased by an additional hundred dollars a year.

Though the vigor of his early manhood and middle life had been spent, and enfeebled health had diminished his capacity for labor, the society would have done great injustice to themselves, as well as to him, if they could have suffered him to be left unprovided for in his age. The instances, however, are not rare, where the claims of an old and faithful servant have been forgotten by the generation that have taken the place of those upon whose invitation he united his fortunes with a parish whose interests he had labored to advance. The harmony that has prevailed, hitherto, in the society, is the best guaranty that a life of usefulness and devotion to the cause of his Master will be cheered to its close by the reciprocal regard of an appreciative people. Whoever shall complete this work will speak of one, who, for almost fifty years, has ministered to this people as the faithful pastor, the useful citizen, and the Christian gentleman.

Mr. Denison was born in Hampton, Conn.; was graduated at Yale College in 1847; and studied theology at the seminaries in East Winsor, Conn., and New York. He remained the colleague-pastor with Dr. Nelson until March, 1856; when, at his own request, he was dismissed. His connection with the society was mutually pleasant and agreeable; and the dissolution of their connection was upon satisfactory terms, and with harmonious feelings.

Mr. Denison was succeeded by the Rev. Amos H. Cooledge, who was ordained as colleague with Dr. Nelson, April 21, 1857. He was born in Sherburn, Mass., Aug. 17, 1827;

graduated at Amherst College, 1853; and at Andover Theological Seminary in 1856. He is still the associate-pastor of the society.

As the law stood for a hundred years or more after the incorporation of the town, its parochial affairs were managed by the town, under its municipal organization, although there was a society of Friends, and also of Baptists, which had early withdrawn from the original religious society of the town. The town held its meetings in the Meeting-house. The society's meetings were called by officers of the town, and the record of its proceedings was preserved as part of those of the town.

In 1826, however, the town took measures to provide themselves with a public hall. It was dedicated on the 1st January, 1827; on which occasion a public address was delivered by Emory Washburn. It was built in connection with the Leicester Bank; occupying the upper story of a building which stood, substantially, where the present Town Hall stands.

This, having become inadequate for the accommodation of the town, was removed to its present position, a little south of the public-house; and, in 1854, the present commodious and expensive structure was erected in its place.

In the mean time, the members of Dr. Nelson's society, as the First Parish, applied to Emory Washburn, Esq., as a justice of the peace, to call a meeting of the same, for the purpose of organizing them as a parish; and upon the 9th of February, 1833, a meeting was held, by virtue of a warrant issued upon this application, and a body corporate was, accordingly, organized as the First Parish in Leicester, who have since had their own records and managed their own affairs.

A history of the first meeting-house in town was attempted in the first part of the present chapter; and it seems proper, in this connection, to give some account of the edifice that succeeded it.

It is hardly necessary to repeat to what extent the first house had become unsuited to the convenience, comfort, and taste of the people. The burdens assumed by and imposed upon the town during the war precluded the idea of voluntarily incurring that of erecting a new meeting-house; but, immediately on the return of peace, the attention of the inhabitants was turned to supplying so urgent a want.

The building was raised in the first week of July, 1784; and was placed a little in the rear of the former one. In size it was substantially the same as it now is, except that it had no belfry or steeple. These were added four or five years afterwards. The main entrance was upon the south; the doors opening directly into the body of the church. There were also doors at the east and west end of the building. A broad aisle ran from the front-door to the pulpit; and a narrow one diverged from this to the right and left, and, running around the interior of the house, came into the broad aisle again in front of the pulpit; leaving a row of square pews next to the wall, extending from the front-door around to the pulpit on each side, with a space between them for the opening of the east and west doors.

There were fifty square pews, in all, upon the lower floor, and twenty-three in the gallery; those in the gallery being constructed along and adjoining to the east, south, and west sides of the house. To reach these fifty pews from the principal doors and avenues, sundry narrow passage-ways were necessary; and the movements of the people, in order to reach their several localities in the house, seemed to a looker-on very like the moves of the pieces upon a chess-board.

Upon each side of the broad aisle, in front of the pulpit, were sundry long seats, or benches, with upright backs, called "body-seats;" which were free to all, though generally occupied only by the aged and the poor, — the women sitting upon one side of the aisle, and the men upon the other.

This arrangement of "body-seats" continued up to 1807; when they were all removed but one upon each side, and their places supplied by four new pews.

The pulpit was of rather a unique order, though not uncommon at the time it was built. Its front was a section of an octagon, projecting from the general panelled front of the structure, terminated below by the sides being curved and brought to a point. Below this was an oblong box, called the "deacon's seat." The access to the pulpit was by a single flight of stairs turning at right angles about half the distance from the floor to the pulpit-door; forming a "broad stair," which it was very common for some large dog, that had accompanied his master to church, to select for a place of repose while the services were going on. Over the pulpit hung a formidable sounding-board, which corresponded in shape somewhat with the projecting front of the pulpit; its upper surface converging to a point at the top, and looking as if fitted to serve for an extinguisher for the pulpit.

The galleries were square, extending upon three sides of the house. The square pillars that supported these, the base and cornice of the fronts of the galleries, of the deacon's seat and pulpit, and the cornice running around the sounding-board, were painted in a kind of pointed block-work of shaded marble, unlike any thing ever seen in nature, and rarely if ever in art anywhere else.

The pews, as has been stated, were square, and were furnished with narrow seats all around, except at the entrance by the door, and the side next the pulpit; and, consequently, a considerable proportion of the audience presented only a profile-view to the preacher while addressing them. The pews were finished with panelled sides; above which was a wide rail, supported by little turned balusters, some six or eight inches long, the chief use of which, next to their beauty, was to give employment to the ever-busy hands of the little children who attended church, in finding out which of them could be turned around, and occasionally disturbing their more sedate mammas by the unmistakable creak which some of these balusters would give if forced to move. Scarce a single seat in the church was furnished with any thing like a cushion.

But the most remarkable arrangement in respect to these pews — though it is believed to have been universal in meeting-houses of that date — was that all these seats were hung upon hinges, and were so divided as to be easily raised when the worshippers stood up, as was always done, during prayer-time. Each pew, therefore, had about five or six separate seats to be raised or let fall; and as it was the universal custom to raise these whenever the congregation stood in service, and as universal to let them fall without regard to the noise thereby made, and as this was always done pretty nearly in unison, the effect can be imagined upon one unused to such a singular fusilade, — as this process seemed to be, to an unaccustomed ear. Some may remember the alarm manifested, on one occasion, by a gentleman from Philadelphia, who attended church here with a friend whom he was visiting, whose pew was upon the western side of the meeting-house, under the gallery. At so sudden and unlooked-for a termination of a solemn devotional exercise, he was persuaded, for a moment, that the gallery was cracking, and coming down around his ears; and, seizing his hat, he was about to rush for the door, when the undisturbed aspect of his neighbors dispelled his apprehension.

No material change in the condition of the house, beyond the erection of a belfry and steeple, took place until 1826; when it was removed back to its present position, — thereby occupying a portion of the original burying-ground of the town, and covering the graves of several persons who had been early laid there. In 1829, there was a complete change and renovation of the interior of the church. Its old pulpit, with its sounding-board and its deacon's seat, and the old square pews and the galleries, disappeared; and it assumed its present form. It was dedicated anew on the 13th December of that year. It may boast a better observance of the laws of symmetry, and a greater convenience of arrangement; but it has lost, for the few remaining representatives of a former generation, the associations which hallowed even its ugliness in architectural proportions, and its violations of good taste.

The first bell and clock which had ever belonged to the town were manufactured by Mr. George Holbrook of Brookfield, and placed upon this meeting-house, Jan. 13, 1803. There had previously been placed on the Academy a small bell, which is said to have been a gift to that institution; but, with this exception, there seems to have been no means of calling the people together by any thing like a bell, till the year 1803. The first bell was recast in 1810, and again in 1834. About the same time, a valuable clock was presented to the town by Joshua Clapp, Esq., and became a substitute for the original one, which had become somewhat irregular in its movements by thirty years' use.

No history of the society that has worshipped in these houses can be deemed complete, without some allusion to the changes through which its sacred music has passed. Although the practice of psalmody, in some form, has been adopted by the New-England churches from the earliest planting of the Colonies, few are entirely familiar with the history of the changes through which it has passed. Two or three works, professing to give these changes, have been published within a few years;* to which I shall take the liberty to refer, as explaining some of the proceedings of the town which appear in its records, and some which have come down to us from authentic sources in the form of anecdote and personal incident.

According to the universal custom of these churches, the singing, such as it was, was strictly congregational. The tunes were exceedingly few: some of them, by omitting or

* One by George Hood, Esq.; the other by Nathaniel D. Gould, Esq.

inserting a syllable in certain lines, were made to serve the double purpose of long or common metre. The consequence was, that not only were the whole congregation at liberty to unite in the exercise, but they did so, often to the sacrifice of accent and time, and not unfrequently of tune also. From the want of books, it was customary to sing from dictation; the deacon reading one, and after a few years two lines, which were sung; and then followed a suspense, until another line or two was "deaconed out" and the tune resumed.

The Pilgrims brought with them Ainsworth's version of the Psalms. This gave place to the "Bay Psalm-book," which was the first book printed in America. It went through many editions in this country and England, — more than seventy in all; and, in 1758, it was revised and published by Rev. Thomas Prince of Boston, who had married a sister of Daniel Denny, the first of the name in Leicester.

If space permitted, it might be amusing to refer to some of the matters upon which the public mind was agitated at different times in the Colony and Province: such as, whether one person alone should sing, — the congregation joining in spirit, as in prayer; whether women should be allowed to sing in public; whether "carnal men" and pagans, or only Christians, should be allowed to sing; and whether singing should be practised "in tunes invented;" and whether it might be done by reading from a book, and the like.

An edition of Tate and Brady's version of the Psalms was published in 1741; and, from the recollection of an informant, it was used in this society some time before and after 1765; though from the greater popularity, in its day, of Dr. Prince's edition of the "Bay Psalm-book," and his connection with some of the principal families in town, I should have supposed it more probable that the latter was the one then in use here. However that may be, the condition of the singing, as above described, is by no means exaggerated.

Before 1720, a singing-school was an unknown thing in the Province. In 1690, there were only five or six tunes known here.* In 1714 was issued an edition of the "Bay Psalm-book," in which were printed thirty-seven tunes, *all of which but one were common metre.* The first book of music, ever printed by itself in the country, was by the Rev. Mr. Walter in 1721; and this was the first music with bars ever printed in America. This, it will be recollected, was a few years after the settlement of this town. The singing of psalms was regarded, like prayer, as a sacred exercise, in the performance of which people uncovered their heads. An edition of Watts was published in Philadelphia in 1741, but when it was adopted here I have no means of ascertaining; though it was not till after the war of the Revolution that it was generally adopted, and then only after a long and violent struggle.

Before 1764, music had been printed with three parts; but a work published in that year was printed with four parts, giving the principal melody to the tenor.

Before, — from 1765 to 1770, — there were few or no choirs in the churches in the country. As these were formed, the custom of "lining," or "deaconing," the psalm, grew into disuse; but, like every other change in the fashion of church music, it was only after a most violent and determined struggle that it was given up. It had been recommended by the Westminster Assembly of Divines, "as many could not read;" and, having come down to them from their ancestors, the custom had become sanctified in their minds, and was not to be surrendered.

The first singing-book typographically printed, as distinguished from engraved scale and notes, was published in Worcester in 1786.

---

* These were Oxford, Litchfield, York, Windsor, St. David's, and Martyrs. The introduction of a new tune was a rare and grave matter, acted upon by the church, and often submitted to a vote of the parish.

It is, therefore, not surprising that a reform in the matter of singing gained ground slowly in Leicester.

The first singing-school ever taught in the town was about 1767 or '8. In the latter year, they were called together "to see if the town will grant a number of young men, who have attained the rules of singing, the hindermost seat in the front gallery." Upon grave deliberation, that seat was appropriated to "those who have learnt the rules of singing, until the further pleasure of the town."

This was not accomplished, however, without serious opposition, as has already been observed; but a far more violent and determined resistance was offered to the more serious innovation of singing without "lining."

This took place in 1780. The singers had applied for permission to occupy the front seat in the gallery; with a view, doubtless, of performing the service of singing as a choir, as a substitute for the general and promiscuous singing by the congregation. The permission was granted: and the choir, not stopping for the deacon to read the line, drowned his voice when he attempted it; greatly scandalizing him in his sacred office, and giving mortal offence to many by such an unholy usurpation. Many persons left the meeting-house in disgust: good Mr. K. and his wife were among the number; and they consoled themselves in the assurance, which they pretty audibly expressed in the hearing of the congregation, that, "when Col. W. got home from the General Court, he would put a stop to such scandalous doings." Unfortunately for them, the gentleman referred to had become familiar with the change in Boston, and approved it; and it was found that revolutions in psalm-singing, any more than in more worldly affairs, never go backwards.

Since that time, nothing of an historic interest has occurred in this department of public worship here, beyond the occasional outcropping of that sensitiveness and those petty jealousies which form an essential element in every singing choir.

About 1827, a few members of the society purchased by contribution, and placed in the meeting-house, a cheap church organ; which, in a few years, gave place to the one now in the church. This was the first church organ ever owned in town; and it may be stated in this connection, that the first piano-forte, ever in town, was purchased by the late Col. Thomas Denny, for his daughter, about 1809. It was several years before there was a second one; and this was owned by Miss Southgate, daughter of the late John Southgate.

In concluding what I propose to say of the First Congregational Society, I may add, that the idea of warming the meeting-house by artificial heat seems never to have occurred as a practicable thing until about 1812.

The good lady of the family was supplied with a tin foot-stove, upon which the children were occasionally permitted to warm their aching fingers. At the interval between the forenoon and afternoon services, the houses of those living near the meeting-house were warmed and opened, and generally crowded by those who lived more remote from the meeting-house. Especially was this the case with the two public-houses, in the bar-rooms of which the affairs and topics and news of the week sometimes intruded upon holy time. At last, it having been ascertained by the public that the same means by which a shop or factory could be warmed of a week-day might be applied to render a meeting-house comfortable of a Sunday, a few individuals — though not without opposition on the part of others — contributed the necessary means; and, about 1812, stoves were placed in the meeting-house. The physical comfort of the congregation has since been cared for, without, as it is hoped, detracting from the spiritual well-being of those who worship there.

BAPTISTS.

A society of Anabaptists were worshipping here as early as 1736. It had been gathered by Dr. Thomas Green; and their place of worship was in the south part of the town, in what is now Greenville, in the vicinity of Dr. Green's residence. He was the first minister of the society; and, through his instrumentality, a meeting-house was early erected, which remained without any considerable change until 1825; when it was enlarged and repaired, and rendered a comfortable and convenient house of worship.

I am unable to give the names of those who constituted the society at its commencement; but I find among its members, in 1744, William Wicker, Benjamin Pudney, Thomas Jones, Joseph Trumbull, Nathaniel Jones, Josiah Powers, Jonathan Pudney, and Ebenezer Tolman.

Dr. Green, the first minister of this society, was the son of Capt. Samuel Green, and was born in Malden in 1699. His father came to Leicester as early as 1717, and was one of its earliest settlers. While he was preparing to remove his family, he visited the town, bringing his son with him; and left him there to look after some cattle, which he had driven from Malden, and turned out upon his lands in Leicester. It was summer; and, as he expected to return in a short time, no danger was apprehended in leaving the young man — then seventeen or eighteen years old — thus alone in the wilderness. He, however, was soon attacked with a fever; and his father was unexpectedly prevented from returning as he had intended, and he was left to battle with the disease as he best could. His only shelter was a kind of cave under a rock, near the stream on which his father afterwards erected his mills. His only sustenance consisted of the milk of one of the cows, which he contrived to obtain by tying her calf to a tree near his cave; which led her to visit the spot several times a day, and brought her within his reach. The water he used, he obtained by creeping upon the ground to the stream. In this deplorable condition, some of his former neighbors who were landholders, and about to remove to Leicester, and had come there to look after their cattle, found him. He appealed to them for aid to return home; but they were unable to afford it, and left him. On their return to Malden, they informed his father of his condition; and he immediately came to his relief. But he had no other means of removing his sick son through the new and (a considerable part of the way) wilderness country between Leicester and Malden, except on horseback; and, after four days' travelling, he accomplished the journey.

He removed to Leicester with his father, and continued to reside in the same immediate vicinity as long as he lived. He became an eminent and successful physician; having, by somewhat peculiar circumstances, been enabled to acquire a medical education much superior to that of neighboring physicians. It is said that two English surgeons, who had been engaged in the half-piratical character of buccaneers, and had surrendered themselves to the government under a promise of pardon, became the inmates of Capt. Green's house, and boarded in his family for several years. Finding the son tractable, and inclined to cultivate a natural taste for medical science, they readily undertook his instruction; and supplied him, moreover, with such few books as they could command. With an education thus begun, and a vigorous and discriminating mind, — by which he wrought the facts that fell under his observation into the materials of science, — he soon attained eminence in his profession; and was called into all the region around, and often into Rhode Island and Connecticut, in the course of his wide and successful practice. A notice of his death, in the "Boston Evening Post," speaks of him as "a very noted physician."

But, as already mentioned, it was not in the medical profession alone that he took an active and prominent place. He became a distinguished divine as well as doctor. The church and society which he helped to organize and build up, was, at first, composed of persons in Sutton and Leicester. He was ordained its pastor, in Leicester, in 1736; the society having erected a meeting-house near his father's, where the Baptist Meeting-house now stands. This lot of land he gave to the society, together with a farm and house for a parsonage which lie a little west of the Charlton Road, upon the road leading by the house now of Charles Barton. The house in which he himself lived was next beyond the river, on the Charlton Road; in which his grandson Samuel afterwards kept a tavern. He was a faithful, zealous, and devoted pastor, and a popular preacher. It is hardly necessary to add, that his life was one of great activity and usefulness.

He married Martha, daughter of Capt. John Lynde of Malden, the father of one of the settlers of Leicester, who was here as early as 1721. His wife died June 20, 1780. The doctor died Aug. 19, 1773, at the age of seventy-four. They were buried in the cemetery around the church in which he ministered, where their remains reposed until the consecration of the Rural Cemetery in Worcester; when a distinguished descendant, who has sustained the reputation of the ancestor as a physician, removed them to that beautiful repository of the dead. Dr. Green had seven children: Samuel; Martha, who married Dr. Robert Craige; Isaac; Thomas; John, who removed to Worcester; Solomon; and Elizabeth, who married her father's successor, the Rev. Dr. Foster.

Rev. Benjamin Foster, D.D., was settled over this society in 1772. He was born in Danvers in 1750, and was graduated at Yale College in 1771. He studied theology with the distinguished Dr. Stillman of Boston; having become a convert, it is said, to the opinions which he afterwards maintained, by having, while in college, been appointed to defend infant-baptism by sprinkling.

After remaining at Leicester about eight years, the society being unable to provide him a suitable maintenance, he was dismissed, and preached about two years in Danvers. From thence he removed to Newport, where he was settled over a society, and remained until 1788; when he removed to New York, where he became the minister of the First Baptist Society in that city. Here he remained till his death, in 1798, in the forty-ninth year of his age. His death was as heroic as his life had been eminent for piety and usefulness. He was residing in the city when the yellow-fever broke out in 1798. While others fled in consternation from the power of the destroyer, he stood at his post undismayed: he shrunk from no call of duty; and fell a martyr to a devotion, in his ministrations, to the dying and the dead. He died Aug. 26, 1798.

He was a learned scholar and an eminent divine. He was honored with the degree of Doctor of Divinity, from Brown University, in 1792. While in Leicester, he published a work on polemical divinity, and subequently a dissertation upon the seventy weeks of Daniel. He was well acquainted with the Greek, Hebrew, and Chaldaic languages; and had achieved a high reputation for learning and ability, when cut down in the midst of his usefulness and growing reputation.

He married, for his first wife, Elizabeth Green, daughter of Dr. Thomas Green; and, for his second, a lady of New York.

Dr. Foster was succeeded by the Rev. Isaac Beals; and the Rev. Nathan Dana became his successor. The Rev. Peter Rogers succeeded Mr. Dana: he lived where Mr. Charles Whittemore lately lived; and, after a few years, removed, and was settled over a society in Leyden.

I regret my inability to speak more fully of these gentlemen. The society, never numerous or rich, has been at times embarrassed and feeble; and, consequently, unable to retain settled pastors for any considerable length of time. Their supply has, therefore, often been temporary.

Among those who, at times, have supplied the pulpit, was

Rev. Nathaniel Green. He was the son of Capt. Nathaniel Green, who is elsewhere mentioned in this work; and was born in Stoneham in 1721. He removed to Leicester, and resided there more than twenty years; after which he removed to Charlton, where he continued till his death, in 1791, at the age of seventy. He was ordained as a Baptist minister at the mature age of forty-three; and preached at various times in Leicester, Spencer, and Charlton. He had ten children, — all born in Leicester between the years 1749 and 1770.

In 1818, the society was divided in consequence of the remoteness of several of its members from their place of worship; and a new society was formed in the north-east part of Spencer. Since that time, the Rev. Mr. Hill, Rev. Benjamin N. Harris, Rev. John Green (a descendant from the primitive stock of the name), and Rev. Moses Harrington, have preached at different periods to this people. It is pleasant to know that the society are about to erect a better house of worship, upon the site of the one hitherto occupied by them.

Besides the Baptist society above mentioned, there was, for many years, a society of that denomination in town, to which Elder Richard Southgate was preacher. They met in the schoolhouse which stood opposite the house then of Judge Steele. It was never organized as a corporate religious society; and, after the death of Elder Southgate, seems to have been merged in other societies.

Elder Southgate was a son of Richard Southgate, who came here from England at the first settlement of the town. He was born in England, July 13, 1714. He married Eunice Brown of Leicester; and lived in a house (where there is now a cellar) near the west line of the town, upon the north side of the road leading by the house of the late Thomas Sprague. He died in 1798, at the age of eighty-five. Among his descendants is a well-known gentleman, who is elsewhere noticed; who has been, for many years, a prominent and enterprising citizen of Leicester.

QUAKERS.

There was an association or society of Friends, in Leicester, from a period as early as 1732 till recently; when, in consequence of the removal of so large a proportion of its members, its place of meeting was transferred to Worcester.

One of the earliest of these was Ralph Earle,—the ancestor of the once numerous, and always respectable, families of that name in town. He became an owner of lands in the town, and removed there from Tiverton, R.I., in 1718. At what time he associated himself with the Friends, I am unable to determine; though, from the active part which he took in the settlement of Mr. Parsons, I infer that at that time, and for some time after, he was a member of his society and church. In 1732, however, he, with seven others, certified to the clerk of the town, that they belonged to what the clerk, with evidently little regard to the spelling of the king's English, calls "those people called Quackers." The names of his associates were William Earle, Thomas Smith, Robert Earle, Daniel Hill, Nathaniel Potter, Joseph Potter, and Benjamin Earle.*

I have not been able to trace more fully the origin of the society which, soon afterwards, was in possession of a house of worship that stood where their present meeting-house stands.† The present house was erected in 1791. As most

* Steward Southgate, who had been a member of the church of the First Society, joined the Quakers about 1745. I find a copy of the following vote of the church:—

"At a meeting of the First Church of Christ in Leicester, May 23, 1745, the following vote was put to the brethren: 'Verily, brethren, if it be your minds to choose a Committee to deal with Brother Steward Southgate, and inquire into the reasons of his withdrawing himself from communion with us, both in word and ordinances, you are desired to manifest.' It passed in ye affirmative; and Deacon Southgate and Brother John Brown were chosen to be a Committee for the above-mentioned end, and to make return at our next meeting. D. GODDARD, *Pastor*."

"Deacon Southgate" was James, uncle of Stewart.

† I find it mentioned as standing in 1742. A friend describes it as a low, one-story building, twenty by twenty-two feet. It was sold, in 1791, to Luther Ward; who

of the society resided in the northerly part of the town, their house was naturally located in that neighborhood. The spot is one of much beauty; and if, as Whitney (in his History of the county) says, the house "is a very good one for their way of worship," — taken with its surroundings, it is singularly attractive to persons of a contemplative turn of mind. Few things in nature could be better fitted to soothe and harmonize the tired spirits of a busy week than the solemn stillness that reigns there of a calm sabbath morning in early summer, when nothing is heard but the rustling leaves of the forest-trees by which it is surrounded, and the pleasant notes of the birds that nestle in their branches.

The society was never numerous, but always embraced a large proportion of thriving, intelligent, order-loving members. In 1826, their number was about a hundred and thirty; but, as already stated, so many have since that time removed from the town, especially to Worcester, that meetings are no longer held in their meeting-house. It stands as an historical monument; and the ashes of some of the best citizens of the town, in their day, repose within the enclosure which surrounds it.

EPISCOPAL SOCIETY.

In 1823, a Protestant-Episcopal church and society were formed, in that part of the town now called Clappville, of families belonging to Leicester and Oxford (then called Oxford North Gore). Among these, Samuel Hartwell, Esq., James Anderton, Francis Wilby, and Hezekiah Stone, were the most active. A church was erected upon land given by the last-mentioned gentleman; which was consecrated by Bishop Griswold on the last Wednesday of May, 1824.

The first rector inducted into office was the Rev. Joseph Muenscher. He was born in Providence; was graduated at

---

removed it to the place where it now stands, upon the Rutland Road, south of where Barnard Upham formerly lived, at the intersection of what was once called Tea Lane with that road. It was fitted and occupied as a dwelling-house by Mr. Ward.

Brown University in 1821; studied theology at Andover; and was admitted to orders by Bishop Griswold, in March, 1824. He married Ruth, a daughter of Joseph Washburn, Nov. 21, 1825; and their marriage was the first ever solemnized in a church, in the county, according to the forms of Episcopal service. He left Leicester in 1827; and was subsequently rector of a church at Northampton, and in Saco, Me.; afterwards a professor in Kenyon College, O.; and, for many years, rector of a church in Mount Vernon, O. He received the honorary degree of Doctor of Divinity from Kenyon College.

Upon his removal from Leicester, the Rev. William Horton succeeded him in the ministry for two years. The Rev. Lot Jones was then rector for four years; Rev. Stephen Millet, one year; and Rev. Mr. Blackaller, four years. In 1838, Rev. Eleazer Greenleaf became rector for one year; when Rev. John T. Sabine succeeded him. After six months, Rev. William Withington became the rector, and remained nearly two years. In 1841, Rev. F. C. Putnam was rector for one year. In 1843, the Rev. Orange Clark, D.D., was rector for one year. The next five years, the Rev. James L. Scott filled the office; and, since that time, the present incumbent, the Rev. J. Hill Rouse, has been the rector.

UNITARIAN SOCIETY.

In the autumn and winter of 1832–3, several families in the town formed a Unitarian religious society, which was organized on the 13th April, 1833. The following year, they erected a neat and convenient house of worship. Aug. 13, 1834, the Rev. Samuel May was ordained over the church and society, and remained their pastor until July 12, 1846. Mr. May was a native of Boston; was graduated at Harvard in 1829. He married a daughter of the Hon. Nathaniel P. Russell of Boston.

The society has at no time been numerous, and has been for a considerable part of the time, since the dismission of Mr. May, without any permanent preacher. Among those who have supplied its pulpit has been the Rev. Dr. Thompson, formerly settled in Barre.

METHODISTS.

Previous to 1828, there were very few, if any, Methodists in the town. With a pretty general acquaintance with the people, I am now unable to recall a single one. About 1841 and 2, an interest was awakened in the minds of many in favor of the views entertained by that denomination of Christians; and, in October of the latter year, they began to hold meetings in the Town Hall. After this they continued to increase till they were able to erect (in 1846) two meeting-houses, — one in Cherry Valley, the other in the village of Leicester: the first being a Methodist-Episcopal society; the other, a Wesleyan-Methodist society. That in Cherry Valley was burned down in February, 1856; but soon after rebuilt. The ministers of the Methodist-Episcopal society have been — George Dunbar, J. T. Pettee, G. F. Pool, T. W. Lewis, D. Z. Kilgore, W. B. Olds, Daniel Atkins, G. E. Chapman, J. W. P. Jordan, Albert Gould. Those of the Wesleyan-Methodist society: William C. Clark, Christopher C. Mason, David Mason, Simon E. Pike, J. A. Gibson, Thomas Williams, and Benjamin R. Bullock.

CATHOLICS.

A still more remarkable innovation upon the early religious notions and habits of the people was made by the erection of a Roman-Catholic church on the Great Post Road, about half a mile east of the village, in 1855.

My own memory goes back to a time, when, with the exception of an amusing and ingenious Scotch tailor, there was scarcely a single person of foreign birth in town. It is believed there was not one. The establishment of manufactories in town led to the introduction of a few (chiefly English) families, between 1815 and 1821; but I cannot recall a single Catholic resident of the town till many years after the period last mentioned.

The influx of a Catholic population of foreign birth within a few years past, many of whom are now freeholders in the town, led to the erection of the church above mentioned for their accommodation.*

If we could imagine some of the early inhabitants of the town returning to their former homesteads, we could easily conjecture their surprise at hearing the shibboleth of a strange tongue around the very hearthstones where they once gathered their now scattered and almost forgotten households.

Happily, there seems to have been a disposition to yield without complaint to what, in our country, is regarded by many as the law of progress; while the chief evil of these multiplied sects consists in weakening the disposition and ability to sustain either, in a manner suitable to the dignity and importance of the religious institutions of a people.

JEWS.

Perhaps no more proper connection than the present will present itself in which to introduce an interesting episode in the history of the town, — the residence here, for some years, of several families of Jews. It has not, however, any thing properly to do with the ecclesiastical affairs of the town; though these families brought with them, and scrupulously maintained while here, their peculiar forms of faith and worship.

They came here from Newport, in 1777, to find a refuge from the invasion of the island by the British troops, as did

---

* It is stated upon reliable authority, that, for a few years past, a majority of the births in town have been of foreign parents.

several other families from the same neighborhood; this being regarded a retired and healthy locality, where they might find a safe and hospitable retreat. I have heard the late venerable Thomas Rotch, jun., of New Bedford, — whose wife, then a young woman, had removed with her family from Newport to Leicester, — speak with an interest, which nearly seventy years had not subdued, of the character of the town for hospitality and public spirit during the period of which I am speaking, and during which he more than once visited it. He spoke in terms of affectionate recollection of families with whom he then became acquainted, whose names, even, have now become matters of history only; but to some of whom I shall have occasion to allude again, when I come to speak of the general history of the town.

Including their servants and slaves, of whom I have spoken in another place, the number of persons embraced in these families of Jews was about seventy. They were of Portuguese descent, as might be inferred from their names, — Lopez, Rivera, and Mendez.

Abraham Mendez lived, a part of the time, in the house opposite to where Mrs. Samuel Newhall now lives; and a part of the time in the old house which stood at the foot of the Meeting-house Hill, where the house of the late Capt. Joshua Sprague now stands.

Jacob Rod Rivera lived in the house, which forms a part of the Hotel, opposite the Meeting-house. He purchased this estate, consisting of thirty-one acres of land, of Nathan Waite, in September, 1777; and, in his deed, is described as a merchant.

Five of the number bore the name of Lopez. The principal and head of the families of this name was Aaron Lopez, a man universally esteemed and respected by a wide circle of personal and business friends. He was a merchant of great wealth, and engaged extensively in trade while he resided in Leicester. He purchased the estate, afterwards occupied by the Academy, of Henry Bass of Boston, and Joseph Allen, Esq., of Leicester, Feb. 1, 1777; and erected thereon what was called in that day "a large and elegant mansion," designed for a store as well as a dwelling-house. His stock of goods on hand, at the time of his death, exceeded twelve thousand dollars; while his entire estate was valued at more than a hundred thousand dollars.

I give the boundaries of his estate, which are described in his deed, as partly depicting the condition then of that portion of the village. It is said to be "on the north side of the Country Road, eastward of and near to the Meeting-house: bounded southerly by the Country Road, six rods; eastwardly, to a heap of stones; then by the land of the Rev. Benjamin Conklin, &c., to a heap of stones on a rock; then turning, &c., to a stake, and heap of stones, by the *lane* leading from the Meeting-house to the *remains* of a house formerly possessed by Israel Parsons, deceased; from thence bounded westerly by said lane in part, and partly by the *training-field*, to the south-east corner of the place whereon the *old* school-house stood, — and containeth half an acre by measure, together with a dwelling-house and shop situate thereon." He afterwards added a half-acre adjoining it, upon the east; and these two constituted the estate which Col. Crafts and Col. Jacob Davis afterwards purchased, and gave to the Academy.

Mr. Lopez also owned other lands in Leicester; but none of these families engaged in agriculture as a business. Mendez and Rivera, as well as Aaron Lopez, were traders, though to a much smaller extent. Moses Lopez and Jacob Lopez were clerks of Aaron; as well as Joseph, his son, who was also a member of his family.

Though without a place of assembling for worship here, they rigidly observed the rites and requirements of their own laws, keeping Saturday as holy time; but, out of regard to the sentiments of the people among whom they were settled, carefully keeping their stores closed from Friday evening until Monday morning of each week.*

Though differing from their neighbors in matters of religious faith, they won the confidence and esteem of all by their upright and honorable dealing, the kindliness and courtesy of their intercourse, and the liberality and public spirit which they evinced as citizens.

They remained here until the ratification of peace in 1783; when, with the exception of Mr. Lopez, they returned to Newport, carrying with them the respect and kind regard of a community with which they had been intimately associated for six years.

No one of their contemporaries here survives; but their residence was always spoken of, by such as had personally known them, as a matter of pleasant memory, which it is believed was reciprocated by those who had found here a pleasant home.†

The fate of Mr. Aaron Lopez was a melancholy one. I have spoken of him as a man of wealth and liberal views. He had been one of the merchant-princes of Newport, when that city commanded the foreign commerce of the country. After his removal to Leicester, his style of living was generous and hospitable; and the furniture of his house, the plate upon his table, and the retinue of his servants, wore an air of magnificence among his less-endowed neighbors: but the cordiality of his manners and his liberal hospitality disarmed all cavil and envy on their part.

On the 20th May, 1782, he started with his wife and some members of his family for Providence. His family were in a

---

* I cannot forbear noticing a very small, though rather important, typographical mistake of the printer, in publishing a brief history of the town in 1826. The writer had spoken of the return of these families of Jews to Newport, and of their synagogue *there* being unoccupied, &c. By some accident, the "*t*" was dropped from the word *there*, so as to fix the locality of the synagogue "*here;*" and inquiries have often been made by the curious to ascertain in what part of Leicester it was to be found.

† Mr. Rivera died at Newport in February, 1789.

carriage; he in a "sulky," driven, of course, by himself. In Smithfield, the road passed close by the edge of Scott's Pond, so called, the shore of which is very abrupt, and the water, at a short distance, deep. Mr. Lopez, probably being unaware of the fact, allowed his horse to enter the water in order to drink; but, perceiving he was getting beyond his depth, sprung from the sulky into the water, and, being unable to swim, sank and perished, in view of his agonized and affrighted wife and children.

The following just tribute I copy from a paper of the day; which, after noticing the circumstances of his death, adds, "He was a merchant of eminence, of polite and amiable manners. Hospitality and benevolence were his true characteristics. An ornament and a valuable pillar in the Jewish society of which he was a member. His knowledge in commerce was unbounded; and his integrity, irreproachable. Thus he lived, and thus he died; much regretted, esteemed, and loved by all."

CHAPTER V.

LOCAL HISTORY.

GARRISONS. — INDIAN WARS. — CASUALTIES. — JOHN SOUTHGATE, JUN. — VILLAGE OF LEICESTER. — THE LAST SPINNER. — AUNT HANNAH. — SOCIAL HABITS. — CELEBRATION OF FOURTH JULY. — WASHINGTON. — LAFAYETTE. — CEMETERIES. — MOUNT PLEASANT, &c. — PUBLIC-HOUSES. — CELLARS. — EMIGRATION.

By local history, which is the subject of the present chapter, is intended those incidents and events which are supposed to have a sufficient interest to be preserved by their local association and relation, but have no immediate connection with the persons or events which are treated of in the general history of the state or country. In all candor, therefore, to the reader, it should be observed, that, without the attraction of local attachment or personal associations, he can hope to find little to repay him for the time its perusal might cost him.

Besides the difficulties inherent in the very attempt to record such events, there are in the present case many peculiar to the undertaking. The time for writing such a chapter has gone by. A thousand incidents worthy of being preserved have been lost or forgotten, or have ceased to be of interest, because few or none are left to narrate them, or to appreciate their value if made accessible by the labors of others.

Of the groups who, fifty years ago, might be gathered in any part of the town, with memories teeming with recollections and traditions of the days prior to and during the Revolution, not one remains.

This circumstance has before been alluded to; and it is again recalled, because it is chiefly to memory and tradition that any community is indebted for much of the material of its own proper local history. From the immediate descendants of a generation which shared in the hardships and dangers of the Indian and French wars, the boy of fifty years ago often listened to the tales which the fathers of that generation had told their children of their trials and sufferings. Some of the first settlers were alive when the war of the Revolution broke out, and could have told of the felling of the first tree by the white man, while the smoke yet rose from the wigwam in the forest. They could have pointed out where they had seen the beaver building his dam in the meadow, and told how the wolf and the bear and the wild-cat had divided with the settler the mastery of the wilderness in which he reared his lonely log-cabin.

Traditions derived from such sources would have found credence and been read with satisfaction by the children of those who shared in the scenes they described. But the children as well as the actors are gone; and, if these traditions are gathered up at all, it must be for a generation who can feel little personal interest in their preservation.

I have already spoken of the hermit of Carey's Hill, whom, it is said, our fathers found dwelling all alone among the denizens of the forest. Who he was, or why he had chosen this retreat from a world by no means overcrowded, has not come down to the present age; and even a belief in the tradition at all is somewhat of a tax upon modern credulity.

That our fathers found here the Indian, and the wild beast which he hunted, there have been proofs preserved to the present generation, besides the records of the settlers. The arrowhead, the rude stone axe and chisel, of the aborigines, have been occasionally dug up in the places of their former haunts. The dam which the beaver constructed, and the deep, well-like holes which he dug, in connection with the half-human habitation in which he dwelt, have been visible in various parts of the town within a few years; and might, I doubt not, still be seen in the Town Meadow, if objects, which were once the subject of curious research, have not been obliterated by having been overflowed in the process of converting it into a mill-pond.

The outline of Judge Menzies' garrison, that stood near the Henshaw Place, as a refuge from the Indians, might, till recently, have been easily traced by the eye; and the erection of a garrison around Mr. Parson's house was one of the first corporate acts of the town which are contained in its records. Another garrison stood near the house of the late Jonah Earle; and the house of the late John King, Esq., which was among the earliest built, is said to have been a garrison, and, till within a few years, to have shown marks of musket-balls, which must have been received at that early period.*

It will be recollected, that, till 1725, this was a frontier town. A war began with the eastern Indians in 1722, and continued till December, 1726; in which the frontier settle-

---

* Since the above was written, I have found in the Secretary's office the following allusion to two of these garrisons: Aug. 3, 1724, Thomas Newhall wrote to Lieut.-Gov. Dummer, that, in pursuance of orders from Col. Chandler, he had received nineteen soldiers into his majesty's service, and, by advice of the Shrewsbury officers, had posted ten of them in that town. Nine, with himself, were posted satisfactorily to the inhabitants. But, understanding that Judge Menzies complained that he was abused in posting the men, he goes on to explain, that, as the judge's tenant had no suitable provision to accommodate a soldier, he had ordered him to board at the next neighbor's, who was ordered, as well as the soldier, "to the judge's garrison." Capt. Wright had been there, and did not see any cause to make any alteration; but to oblige the judge, "there being now an honorable family removed into the judge's garrison," he had "billeted him out there."

May 31, 1725, the Rev. Mr. Parsons writes to the Lieut.-Governor, in which he says he is under great obligation, &c., — "1st, About my garrison; 2d, As to the two soldiers, by Capt. Wright, posted by your honor's order. But they have been a considerable time without avocation. I meet with some difficulty with one of them, who is not pleased with my family orders, and, his captain being at a distance, takes more liberty than is very pleasing to me." He says he does not mean to complain, but suggests some one, fifty miles distant, to take his place. The reverend gentleman seems to have been unfortunate in his associates in his garrison as well as his church.

ments in Massachusetts were often threatened, and sometimes attacked, though no general engagement took place in Massachusetts during that period. At the east, the memorable engagement at what was afterwards Fryeburg, known as Lovewell Fight, took place in May, 1725. In 1724, three persons were killed by the Indians in Rutland. Worcester was threatened; and, whenever its inhabitants had occasion to go into the meadows to gather hay, they went guarded by armed scouts or soldiers.

From Mr. Lincoln's model "History of the Town of Worcester," and other reliable sources, we find that a detail of two men was made from the company of scouts under Major John Chandler, belonging to Worcester, for the protection of Leicester. These, with others from the same company, of which Thomas Newhall of Leicester was a sergeant, were posted at Leicester, doubtless at one of the garrisons above mentioned.

In 1724, in consequence of the more threatening aspect of the war, twenty-nine men were detailed from the company of Capt. William Chandler, and posted at Leicester for the protection of its inhabitants.*

The state of apprehension in which its inhabitants then lived may be learned from a letter which is preserved in the Secretary's office in Boston. It was signed, as will be perceived, by most of the principal inhabitants of the town; and was in these words: —

"LEICESTER, April 30, 1725.

"*To his Honor the Lieut.-Governor.*

"With all dutiful respect, these are to acquaint your honor, that, just now, there came news to us of two companies of Indians dis-

---

* This was probably on account, among other things, of the letter of Thomas Newhall, of Aug. 3, 1724; a part of which has already been given. In that he goes on to say, "By order of Col. Chandler, I understand I had command of the soldiers (the nineteen before mentioned). If otherwise, I pray your honor to signify it. We have not as yet made any remarkable discovery. Only, last Friday, one of our inhabitants, a very credible man, reaping near here, informs us that an Indian had got within seven rods of him, and, looking up, he had a certain discovery of him; and, stepping a few rods for his gun, he saw him no more, but hastened home."

covered between us and the Wachusetts; which is very surprising, considering our inability for our own safeguard. As to the truth of the report, with the circumstances, we are altogether at a loss; but we hear there is a post gone down to your honor about it. Your honor having always been ready to keep us, and we having had some encouragement upon our late petition, we are encouraged to beseech your honor, if it may be, that we have some speedy assistance of soldiers to defend us.

"Our number of inhabitants is very small, and several were much discouraged. It was so late the last summer before we had soldiers, that we were exceedingly behind with our business.

"So, wishing your honor all happiness, and confiding in your honor, and rather from our experience, we are your honor's in all gratitude and obedience.

"THOMAS NEWHALL.
RICHARD SOUTHGATE.
BENJA. JOHNSON.
RALPH EARLE.
JOHN LYNDE.
WILLIAM BROWN.
JOHN SMITH.
JAMES SOUTHGATE.
NATHL. RICHARDSON."

The same year, the town presented a petition to the General Court to be relieved from the Province-tax, by reason of having been so much exposed and reduced to very low circumstances by the late Indian war; and their petition was accordingly granted.

Their condition in the year 1724 was thus referred to in a letter addressed by Gershom Rice, of Worcester, to Col. Chandler: "We are informed that it is objected against our having assistance, that Brookfield, Rutland, and Leicester defend us. As to Leicester, the people there more need help from us than they are able to render us any; as likewise do Shrewsbury and Hassanamisco."

Of the particular sufferings to which the people of Leicester were subjected during this war, no record is preserved. Amidst the general state of alarm which pervaded the scattered population of the interior, perhaps nothing occurred that was worthy of being recorded. The spread of civilization operated like an act of extermination upon the once hostile tribes; so that the early settlers were, in a few years, beyond the immediate danger of attack.

The annoyance from noxious animals and venomous reptiles continued to a later period. Their records show, as late as 1740, the employment of pitfalls and other means for destroying wolves, and the payment of bounties for the killing of rattlesnakes.

The town has had its share, too, of the ordinary and extraordinary casualties to life and property. A few only of these have been preserved, and fewer still can now have any particular interest in their detail.

In 1738, Mr. John Henshaw lost his dwelling-house by fire;* and a second house, in the same manner, the following winter.

The public-house of Edward Bond, situate where the house of Capt. Hiram Knight now stands, was burned, with all its contents of provisions and furniture, on Sunday, the 18th January, 1767.

In 1779, May 13, a valuable house of Phineas Newhall, together with most of his furniture, and a quantity of grain and liquors, were burned.†

About 1811, the house of Stephen Sadler, once the house of Jonathan Newhall, in the south-west part of the town, was burned on Sunday.

In 1822, the house of Capt. Amasa Whittemore, in the south part of the town, was burned. In 1824, the house of Calvin Hersey, in the west part, was burned.

In 1825, the tan-house of Jonathan Warren, with its contents, was burned.

---

* The house stood where, or near where, Mr. Edwin Waite's stands. It was set on fire by a female slave in his family, who had come with them from Boston, and, being homesick, adopted this as a means of compelling her master to return to that place.

† This house stood upon the North County Road, where Col. Newhall kept a tavern, and where Mr. Eddy now lives.

In 1829, the barn of Edwin Waite was struck by lightning, and consumed.

In 1833, the dwelling-house of the late Col. Henry Sargent, with its barn and wood-shed, and the barn, shed, and wood-house of Capt. Isaac Southgate, were destroyed by fire.

In 1835, the dwelling-house of Josiah Kingsbury, in the south-west part of the town, was burned.

In 1841, the house of Asa M'Callum, in the south-west part of the town, was destroyed by fire, on Sunday, June 20.

Feb. 9, 1846. In Clappville, the woollen factory of Messrs. Barnes and Denny, with its machinery, was destroyed by fire.

Feb. 11, 1848. The woollen factory of Mr. Samuel Watson, in Cherry Valley, was consumed, with its contents.

March 24, 1848. The woollen factory of Mr. Loyal G. Dickenson, on the same stream, and just above Mr. Watson's, was destroyed by fire.

Oct. 19, 1848. Mr. Henry E. Warren's tan-house was burned, — situate half a mile north of the Great Road, in the west part of the town.

April 17, 1850. The large brick woollen factory of Reuben S. Denny, Esq., in Clappville, was burned, with its contents: the loss estimated at $65,000, mostly insured.

Nov. 3, 1853. The barn attached to the hotel of Mr. William Hatch, opposite the Meeting-house, was destroyed by fire in the night, together with eight horses and a large quantity of hay.

Feb. 12, 1854. Another factory belonging to R. S. Denny, Esq., in Clappville, was consumed, with most of its contents: valued at $20,000, principally insured.

April 26, same year. Mrs. Newhall's barn, about half a mile north of the Meeting-house, was struck by lightning, and consumed, with three cows.

June 17, same year. The barn of Mrs. Dr. Holmes, in the village, was burned in the night-time.

July 1, same year. A part of the store of Mr. Danforth Rice was destroyed by fire.

Feb. 21, 1855. The barn of Michael Kane, about a mile north of the Meeting-house, was burned.

Feb. 3, 1856. The Methodist Meeting-house in Cherry Valley was destroyed on Sunday, about noon; the day being intensely cold.

On the 11th of April, 1856, a barn upon the Bridges Farm, in the south part of the town, and on the 7th of February, 1827, a barn of Mr. Kibbe, were burned, the latter with seven head of cattle.

In 1756, as stated in the "Boston Evening Post," Joshua Smith and son were killed in Leicester by the falling of a tree, which was blown down by the wind.

In 1759, there occurred a remarkable hurricane, which passed over the westerly part of the town. Its direction was from the south-west to the north-east. In its course, it struck the house of Mr. Samuel Lynde, which stood where the house of Mr. Robert Watson now stands, upon the north side of the Great Post Road. Ten or twelve persons were in the house at the time. The force of the wind was such, that the house was removed to a considerable distance, and torn into atoms. A barn and corn-barn, standing near the house, were entirely demolished; and a horse in the barn was killed. The trees and fences in the track of the hurricane were prostrated; and nails that had been in the house were found driven into trees by force of the wind, so firmly that they could not be withdrawn by hand.

After passing some distance from the house, the wind took a course upward from the earth, so that the extent of its ravages was small. But of its force, where it was felt, some judgment can be formed from the fact, that a negro man, standing at the door, was taken up, carried near ten rods, and thrown with such violence upon the ground as to break both his legs and several of his ribs, causing his death.

A little girl, also standing at the door, was carried through the air forty rods, and had an arm broken. Four women, who had been in the house, were found in the cellar, greatly bruised, but unconscious how they came there. A little boy was found completely covered by the rubbish of the buildings, and rescued. A watch, hanging in the house, was found at a distance of more than a mile from the place where it had stood; and articles, that were in it when struck by the wind, were afterwards found in Holden, more than ten miles distant.

I have copied the foregoing facts from a contemporary statement published in the newspapers of the day; and borrow from the article its closing paragraph, to show the danger of even attempting to describe so fearful a tempest: "A pile of boards, 'tis said seven thousand feet, being near the house, was shivered to splinters, and carried to a great distance, so that there were not pieces large enough left to make a coffin to bury the negro in!" Where the materials of the unfortunate negro's coffin were obtained, history does not tell; though, as the track of the hurricane was both short and narrow, it is to be presumed there were enough left elsewhere in the town to serve the purpose.

An incident connected with two of the inhabitants has an interest beyond its being connected with the history of the town.

Francis and Isaac Choate were, in November, 1790, taken prisoners by the Indians, at a block-house upon the Muskingum River in Ohio, about forty miles above Marietta. Isaac was carried to Detroit, and there sold; while Francis was given away to a Mingo chief. They were redeemed, and returned home in May following. There might be little worthy of remark in the mere fact that a citizen was taken prisoner in a war with the Indians; but there is something calculated to awaken a train of interesting reflections in the circumstance, that it should have happened within the memory of living witnesses, in the very heart of a State, then a wilderness, which now counts its population by millions. It serves to mark the extent and rapidity of the progress of a country, where the ordinary work of ages is accomplished in a single generation.

One incident, the authenticity of which is beyond doubt, occurred in 1804, and had an interest beyond the neighborhood where it happened, from its partaking of the character of one of those mysteries which often puzzle the philosophy of the wisest.

John Southgate (a wealthy and respectable gentleman of the town, often employed in the transaction of business which required intelligence and experience, and who is noticed in another connection) had a son of the same name, then some twenty-five years of age. The father was an extensive landowner at Stillwater, between Bangor and Orino, in Maine. The son, though unmarried, was residing there for the purpose of taking charge of the property. His health was generally good, the employment was a pleasant one, and his temperament not otherwise than hopeful and cheerful, though his habits were at times somewhat unsteady. In June of that year, his father received a letter from him requesting him to come and bring him home, as he had but a short time to live.

His father, supposing he was sick, hastened to him; but, on arriving, found him apparently in usual health. The son seemed to be greatly relieved that he had come; re-iterated his wish to return home, and to hasten his departure, because on such a day (naming it) he was to die, and was desirous of some time in which to make previous arrangements.

The father, willing to humor what he regarded as a strange fancy, but without the slightest apprehension that it had any foundation, left Stillwater after a short delay, taking his son with him. He stopped in Boston: but the son seemed very anxious to hasten his journey; and, as soon as he had transacted some business, he started, and reached home the next day.

Here the son appeared to be in good health; was cheerful, communicative, and calm in his manner and conversation, though often reminding them that such a day was to be his last. In the mean time, he was busy making arrangements, as if sure that the term of his life was measured and extremely brief.

The time fixed for the event of his death was the night of a certain day which he named. During that day, he visited and bade adieu to several families in the neighborhood, and repaired to various familiar and favorite spots upon his father's farm, which he seemed to be looking upon for the last time. In the evening he sat with the family, and conversed freely and cheerfully with them upon different topics. At the usual hour, the family made the customary preparations for retiring; but he urgently requested them not to do so, as he had but a few more hours to spend with them.

They, however, regarded this as a mere idle fancy; and were confident in the belief, that, if he were to fall asleep, he would awake in the morning, relieved by finding that he had outlived the period suggested in his brain. They accordingly urged his retiring; which he did, occupying a bed with his younger brother. The other members of the family also retired; but the earnestness of his conviction left so strong an impression upon their minds, that they could not readily sleep.

John wished his brother not to fall asleep: but, acting upon the prevailing idea of the family, he affected to do so, and actually fell into a slumber; and, as he thought, John did the same. In a short time, however, he was startled and aroused by the peculiar breathing of his brother. He immediately called the family, who tried in vain to arouse him from what they supposed was sleep. It was the convulsive breathing of a dying man; and at the age of twenty-six, on the 12th July, 1804, at the very hour which he had more than two weeks before told his father was to be his last, he died.

No cause for this impression or for his death could be traced. His health gave no signs of being seriously impaired. Nothing indicated that death was occasioned by any thing he had taken. It was a mystery which was never solved; and now that every witness of the scene, who could have been old enough to know its character, is gone, it would be worse than idle to speculate upon theories to explain it.

I have had occasion to speak of the destruction of the house of Edward Bond, by fire, in 1767. A description of this house, and its style of finish, may serve as a sample of the houses of the early settlers; though it had been always kept as a public-house, and was undoubtedly erected for one, and, consequently, somewhat more elaborate in its character than the private dwellings in the neighborhood.

The house was small, I apprehend, from the description, — only a single story in height. There was not a handle upon a single door in the house, inside or out. The latch was of wood, to which a string was attached; and, passing through a hole in the door, was taken hold of and pulled by any one on the outside who wished to raise it in order to enter. This contrivance, then universally in use, served as a very simple and handy lock; for, by drawing in the latch-string, no outsider could gain admittance except by the aid of some one inside of the house.

In this connection, I shall venture to give, from the narrative of one who was familiar with the condition of the town at the time of this house being destroyed, a description of what formed the only village then existing in the town.

Beginning at the west, near the Town-meadow Brook, on the south side of the road, stood a one-story house, which has been standing within the recollection of some persons now living, and was then occupied by Judge Steele. Next east of that, and on the north side of the road, was the house of Seth Washburn, where Mr. Joseph Denny more recently lived, about half-way from Judge Steele's to the Bond Tavern. It was one story in height, and consisted of three rooms, — a front room, bed-room, and kitchen. Opposite this, the woods came up to the road, without any fence along its side; and the children of the family made their play-ground among the trees that stood there. The next house east of that was the Bond Tavern. Then came the Meeting-house, such as has been elsewhere described in this work. Opposite the Meeting-house stood an old house, with one room and a shoemaker's shop attached to it, in which Deacon Fletcher lived, and carried on his trade of making and repairing shoes. It was afterwards sold to Nathan Waite, who erected a tavern upon the spot, which forms a part of the present Tavern House.

A few rods east of the Meeting-house, at the corner of the Training-field, or Common, stood the old schoolhouse which I have before described, and which was then little better than "an old shell." Some twenty or thirty rods to the north-east of the schoolhouse stood an old house formerly belonging to Mr. Parsons, which was approached by a "lane" leading from the Training-field. Ten years later, it was spoken of as "the remains of a house." In rear of the Meeting-house was the Burying-ground, belonging to the town; which was surrounded by a brush fence, beginning at the north-west corner of the Meeting-house, and running around, enclosing it from Mr. Parsons's land on the north, and the Training-field on the east and south.

The only house between the Meeting-house and the Meeting-house Hill was one at its top, built by Mr. Stebbins, and afterwards owned by Mr. Conklin. Part-way down the hill, where a cellar-hole now remains, upon the north side of the road, stood a house owned by Peter Silvester. Next east, upon the same side of the road, stood a house at the corner of Flip Road, as the records early called the road that once led from the Great Road to Carey Hill. Nearly opposite the last-mentioned house was a one-storied "gambrel-roofed" house, which stood upon a high bank on the south side of the road, where Benjamin Vickery afterwards lived from 1777 till after 1800.

These half-dozen houses constituted the entire village, so far as it was built upon or near the Great Road. The present house, upon the east side of the Rutland Road, half a mile from the Meeting-house, was then standing; and a small house upon the South Road, about half a mile from the Great Road, in which Mr. Goddard had lived. Not one of these, it is believed, had any paint upon them, inside or out; and they were all of humble dimensions, without any pretensions to architectural ornament or proportion. Probably that upon the North Road, with a front-room, kitchen, and bed-room, was quite as imposing in style and magnitude as any of these.

There were one or two appendages to the Common, near the Meeting-house, which are not familiar in our day. One of these was an immense horse-block, or stone, at each end of the Meeting-house, upon which the women mounted in order to seat themselves on their side-saddles, or more commonly on pillions behind their husbands or some male member of the family, before the days of carriages. This appendage had not entirely disappeared, though it had been mostly disused, within the last forty or fifty years. But the other appendage, it is believed, had yielded to the progress of civilization before the commencement of the present century; and that was the "public stocks." They were in use for the punishment of petty offences; while those guilty of more serious ones were subjected to whipping or the pillory, or branding or cropping. They were borrowed from England, and have been too often described by writers, from Hudibras to M'Fingal, to need any further account of their form or construction. The last of those in Leicester were erected in

1763, by Benjamin Tucker, at the cost of thirteen shillings; and stood near the Meeting-house.

It may not, perhaps, be deemed a matter too minute for a purely local history like this, to note, so far as I am able to ascertain, by whom and when some of the other houses now standing were erected. Beginning on Mount Pleasant, the house upon the south side of the road was built by Col. Joseph Henshaw, in 1772, from lumber brought from Boston. That on the north side was erected by Mr. John Stickney in 1789; that at the corner of the Silvester Road, by David and Jonathan Trask, about 1811. Their blacksmith-shop stood where the brick factory was built by Messrs. James and John A. Smith and Co. in 1827. The house opposite this was built by Mr. John Hobbs, about 1818, upon the site of an ancient house formerly occupied by Judge Steele. The gambrel-roofed house, which Deacon Murdock altered and enlarged and occupied, was built by Col. Seth Washburn, and finished in 1784. It was first occupied by his son-in-law, Samuel Sargent. The large house nearly opposite this was erected by Col. Joseph D. Sargent. The house now occupied by Mr. John Loring was enlarged, and made into a two-story structure, by Col. Washburn, in 1782; and was further enlarged by Mr. Joseph Denny. Col. Washburn's blacksmith's shop was a little west of this house. The house opposite was built by Col. John Worcester about 1804. The building occupied by the Leicester Boot Company was built by Joseph Denny, for a dwelling-house and card-factory, in 1812; and occupied by Harry Ward. The house formerly of Matthew Jackson was built by him about 1790: his shoemaker's shop stood a little east of it. The house of J. A. Denny, Esq., was erected by him in 1838. A part of the factory of Denny and Bisco was erected by Earle and Walter, hatters, as a dwelling-house and shop, about 1812. The house next east of that was erected by John Wilder, about the same time, for a saddler's shop; and the double dwelling-house next to that was erected by him, for himself and Mrs. Ruth Washburn, in 1814. The house opposite this, occupied by Mr. Warren, was erected by N. P. Denny, Esq., about 1808. That of J. A. Smith, Esq., was erected by Reuben Swan about 1801; that opposite to it, occupied by Mr. Knowles, was built by Joseph Washburn about 1789. Capt. Isaac Southgate built his house in 1826, and Capt. Knight his in 1843. Mr. John Whittemore built his dwelling-house, about 1820, upon the site of a small house, one story in height, once owned by Martin Rice, whose blacksmith's shop stood near where Capt. Southgate's house stands. The house east of Mr. Whittemore's was built by Capt. Darius Cutting in 1789. The two brick dwelling-houses opposite the Academy were built by Daniel M'Farland, — one for his store, about 1809 or '10; and the other for his own dwelling-house, in 1813. Nearly opposite these stood a long, low, one-story building, before mentioned, which Mr. M'Farland had used for a store, which was removed when he erected his new store. Next to this was a one-story house, in which Mr. Joseph Sargent lived at the time of his death in 1784, but had disappeared before the store was removed. East of this, Dr. Austin Flint erected his house in 1784: it was removed by Mr. Joshua Clapp to give place to the much more imposing structure which he erected in 1832–3. The two houses opposite this were erected by Roswell Sprague — one for a card factory and store, the other for a dwelling-house — about the same time that the house of Mr. M'Farland was erected. Dr. Edward Flint erected the house in which he lives about 1820. That in which Mr. John Woodcock lives was built by Waldo Flint, Esq., in 1830; and that next to it was erected by Alpheus Smith, for a card factory, about 1813. Dr. Nelson built his cottage in 1828.

From fear, however, of being wearisome, I will only add, that a man now of the age of sixty years might readily recall the village when the whole number of its dwelling-houses would not have exceeded twenty; when there was no house upon the south side of the road east of Col. Denny's; when there was none between Col. Worcester's and Mr. Moore's; when the only buildings between Capt. Cutting's and the Charlton Road were the small house I have spoken of, where Mr. Whittemore's house stands; the blacksmith-shop above mentioned; another little shop west of it, with a single room, in which Mr. Denny at one time kept his law-office; and a small, low building, at the corner of the Charlton Road, in which Widow Dunbar carried on her trade as a tailoress. At that time, I apprehend there was not a single house upon the south, or Charlton Road between the Great Road and Mr. Richard Bond's.

MISCELLANEOUS.

The local history of the town would be incomplete if I failed to notice some of those personal institutions, which, in the progress of the age, have become obsolete, though once forming an important element in its social structure.

I have spoken of the substitution of machinery for the simpler implements of domestic manufacture, — the spinning-wheel and the loom. With these has disappeared a class of labor to which the families of the town resorted, to a greater or less extent, to aid the housewife in working up the wool, flax, and tow, which had been raised upon the farm, into bed and other linen and clothing for the family.

There were in most of the country towns more or less of these useful personages, who went from one family to another to "do up" their spinning. The implement chiefly in use was the large spinning-wheel, whose hum, now no longer heard, was familiar to the ear of every household of that day. The last of this class in Leicester was Sally Bradish; and as a representative of a race, which, like the Dodo among the birds, has disappeared, never to be revived, she deserves to be preserved as an historical personage.

The records of the town furnish no clue to her age; but

she was obviously on the shady side of forty. She had breadth enough to have been a Juno; but from having worn off her nether extremities by following her thread back and forth so many years, or from some other cause, her height would not justify the comparison. What her beauty might once have been, this history does not go back far enough to determine. When he, who is now to be her chronicler, first saw her round, good-natured face, furrowed here and there by a deep wrinkle, it had been so often twisted into shapes to fit the expression of countenance suited to the actors in the stories she was accustomed to tell, that it was difficult to infer what had been its original configuration. Her annual revolution to that point in her orbit — where, like a comet, she was visible for a few weeks at a time — was an event of no inconsiderable moment. To see her in her glory, however, one must have followed the hum of her wheel into some back chamber heated to a summer glow, or the more spacious precincts of the kitchen, where she plied her task, and sat and listened in the gloaming of the evening, lighted only by a bright fire on the hearth, to the songs she used to sing as she paced backwards and forwards, and gave her wheel a fresh buzz and a louder hum at each return; or gathered around the hearth of glowing coals, after her day's work had been "reeled off," and she was at liberty to luxuriate in some of the exhaustless supply of stories she possessed, of witches, ghosts, robbers, and Indians, with an occasional interlude showing the fate of some faithless swain, or the crowning recompense of constancy and love.

Sally was an undoubting believer in witches and ghosts, omens and warnings; and was possessed of a perfect encyclopædia of facts, known to herself to be true, which she detailed with great circumstantiality, when her clue run in that direction. And so deep and vivid were the impressions made on her groups of listeners, that I have no doubt, though nearly threescore years have passed by, were a ghost to show itself to any one of that number, it would be recognized at once as an old and familiar acquaintance.

Sometimes her fancy took a facetious turn; and then the manner in which she put her face into forms to suit the action of her story, seen in the dimly reflected light of the fading fire, was as irresistible for mirth as her ghosts were for terror.

She was, I believe, the only Methodist in the town till I was full grown; and the tunes with which she regaled the listeners as well as herself, in her devotional frames of mind, uttered with a peculiar emphasis and tone, with which she poured out verse after verse of her favorite hymns of interminable length, have not yet lost their echo on the ear.

But this was not the only field for her genius. The tea-table, when the older members of the family were gathered around it, furnished new topics of equal interest and importance. She was a perfect budget of the gossip and news of the town. She was an entire believer in the power of foretelling events; and could read, in the tea-grounds in her neighbor's cup, the future, especially so far as it related to funerals, weddings, and riding in coaches. In this round of duties, toils, and pleasures, Sally was entirely content, nor ever dreamed that anybody was plotting to impair her usefulness or importance. But the power-loom and the spinning-jenny came, and they found Sally in the wane of life. It required no ghost or omen to foretell the fate of the old-fashioned spinning-wheel, and, with it, the old-fashioned spinsters who had gladdened the hearts of the children of many a neighborhood, while they supplied the yarns that were to be wrought into stockings and jackets for their outside comfort.

Here and there may be found in some old garret a spinning-wheel, which creaks, instead of hums, when it is turned; but no page records, no stone marks the spot, where the last spinner of Leicester was laid, by the hand of charity, in her final resting-place.

The revolution of public sentiment upon the subject of popular education has converted another of the former social institutions of towns into a matter of history; and that is the natural "school-mams," — they who, without ever having heard of a normal school or of the machinery now in use for fitting men and women to teach the uneducated, contrived by their own mother-wit, and an intuitive power of guiding and developing young minds, to attain to the highest art of the teacher. Every town had its "aunt" this or that, who had the training of successive generations, and coaxed and urged the lagging powers of the grandchild, just as she had done the once curly-headed urchin, who, as a venerable grandfather, had long since outgrown being her contemporary.

Leicester had her "Aunt Hannah," — she was everybody's aunt, — who exercised too marked an influence, in shaping the moral and intellectual character of its rising generations, to be silently passed over in a history of its social condition. She could have counted her pupils by thousands, and found them in almost every rank, condition, and employment in life. Merchants, physicians, lawyers, ministers, and women who have been the honored wives and mothers of the great and useful men of the land, were, at one time or another, her pupils; and would have borne testimony to her skill, fidelity, and success in the life-business of primary education.

What was the secret of her power and success, a stranger could never have understood. She was unconscious of it herself. But she had a power to which every child instinctively yielded as to that of a superior being. It was not the attraction of beauty or grace, or the over-awing of her pupils by any display of dignity or command.

"Aunt Hannah" was by no means a beauty. She was tall, muscular, and awkward. Her voice, though not harsh, had but little music in its tones; and her exterior, as a whole, indicated what was true, — that she had a good supply of the elements of masculine strength in her physical as well as intellectual composition. But, though the casket was a rough one, it contained the jewel of one of the kindest and softest hearts that ever looked into the loving face of a child, and gave back the sympathy of a kindred affection. If the children of her school looked upon her with something like awe the first half-day of their attendance, they had forgotten the next day that she was plain; and, before a week was out, she had grown into a standard of grace and beauty, as well as the embodiment of knowledge and wisdom. The whole secret of her success lay in this, — her heart was in the work; and the enthusiasm of her own nature infused itself into that of the children, who were beguiled into learning the dullest lesson by the pleasure they were thereby giving to one whose approbation was the highest of rewards. Men may talk about the genius of the poet and of the painter, as well as that of the orator and the mechanician. If there is any calling or department of life in which genius manifests itself in a peculiar and unmistakable form, it is in that of "keeping school."

The circumstances of the schools in the several towns, and the demand for competent teachers, formerly served to develop this genius where it existed; and, when developed, its fruits were seen in the improved condition of successive generations within the region where it had been exerted. Such were the character and qualifications of the humble individual of whom I am speaking; and there is here and there one who still lives to remember what he owes of his after-success in life to the impressions he received from her influence and early teachings.

It is the life of such an individual that serves to show the springs of action which give motion to society, while they lie hid from the eye of casual observers; and while we speak of the patriotic devotion of the men of a former generation, in the struggle of a nation for political freedom, it would be doing injustice to our subject, had we forgotten the devoted labors of those of the same generation, and educated in the same school of hardship and difficulty, who, in teaching little children their duty to God and the world, were fitting a generation to take its place among the actors on the stage of life, upon whose character and energy the maintenance of the social fabric was to depend.

The changes in the fashions and social habits of a people are so constantly going on, and yet are so gradual, that it is only by contrasting periods somewhat remote from each other that the differences are perceptible to an ordinary observer; and whoever undertakes to record these is generally at a loss when he goes behind the memory of living persons for his facts, as few think of noting down what is passing on, every day, around them. And yet no history of one of these little communities could be complete which should omit these altogether.

Every age has about the same tastes and passions to be supplied and gratified, although the form in which this is done varies most essentially at different periods. Our fathers sought their amusements at home, and within their own neighborhoods, far more than is done in our day. A visit to the city was an event of a life; and, as for watering-places and pleasure-excursions to a distance, they had not found a place in their vocabulary. Lyceums and lectures and societies of a hundred sorts, to reform everybody and every thing, and give employment and pay to a set of agents who thrive upon strife and excitement, had never then been dreamed of.

Many of their social gatherings partook of the useful as well as the pleasant. They joined together to help their neighbor to husk his corn, or raise the frame of his building; or the good housewives gave up an afternoon, every now and then, to the *quilting* of a covering for a bed for a neighboring housewife.

They made these and similar meetings occasions of pleasure and amusement to both young and old, and not unfrequently for both sexes. Not that the women did much of the work of stripping the husks from the ears of corn, nor that the men understood the knack of laying stitches in fantastic lines in a bed-quilt; but it was an easy thing to find sources of amusement, if not of useful employment, when once together. And a walk home under the light of the broad harvest-moon had its poetry in that day, though they had never read Bryant or Longfellow. They had balls too, — not where they went at eight or nine o'clock, and got home in the small hours after midnight; but where they went in broad daylight, in the middle of the afternoon, and staid till broad daylight of the next morning: not whirling and shuffling in dizzy waltzes or indescribable polkas or schottisches, to the music of a regimental band; but luxuriating in sober reels, and good, honest "country dances," at the inspiration of a fiddle, and, perchance, a bass-viol or a tambourine as an accompaniment.

Though, as is elsewhere remarked, in the progress of luxury, in the absence of all carriages, it became better *ton* to substitute a second horse for a pillion, the more common mode of transportation to balls and merry-makings, as well as meetings of a Sunday, was by the lady seating herself upon a pillion behind the gentleman who attended her.*

Athletic exercises too, among the men, especially the young and middle-aged, were commonly practised at all gatherings for social labor or amusements; and the championship of the

---

* Accidents would happen in the processes of locomotion, even in those days of primitive simplicity of conveyance; though the luxury of being smashed up, a dozen at a time, was reserved to our own days of railroads. I may, perhaps, be pardoned for narrating here an incident of this kind, which was related to me by an eye-witness, in which Mr. R. and Miss S. participated. Several of the houses in Cherry Valley stand so high, that they have a steep bank between them and the road. Mr. R. called at one of these, prepared to give Miss S. an airing on horseback. The animal was rather small, the lady of goodly size, and the gentleman no pigmy. Standing upon the bank wall in front of the house, the lady seated herself behind the gentleman, and the little horse made a desperate effort to start: but the load being unequally balanced, and the bank steep, his legs upon the lower side gave way under the weight; and the consequence was, that the horse and his riders rolled down the bank into the road together. Fortunately, no serious harm followed; and a better starting-point was selected the next time.

wrestling-ring was an honor which could be gained or held only by a decided pre-eminence in muscle and skill.

It has been customary, occasionally, for the people of the town to commemorate the anniversary of the declaration of independence by orations, public dinners, and a reasonable amount of patriotic uproar. There has been a less-marked exhibition of the latter, since the days of punch before dinner and wine after, than formerly; though, taking the average patriotism of a given number of days, including the "glorious Fourth," the balance is believed by many to be quite in favor of the modern mode of observing this great national holiday.

The last considerable demonstration upon such an occasion was in 1849; when, in pursuance of an invitation, of which a copy is appended,* there was a large attendance of the people of the ancient town; and many from distant homes came back to indulge in the pleasant memories of the past, while they renewed the ties that bound them to a spot once dear to them. The Hon. James Draper presided. Four were present who had taken part as soldiers in the scenes of the Revolution. One of them was Mr. Craige, who had been in the battle of the 17th June, '75. Dr. Flint was too ill to

---

* May 23, 1849.

Dear Sir, — The citizens of the towns of Leicester, Spencer, and Paxton, with a portion of Auburn, which were originally incorporated in one town under the name of Leicester, propose to unite in a celebration of the ensuing Fourth of July in the present town of Leicester; for the purpose, principally, of refreshing our minds by the early reminiscences of our history, and recalling the interesting events of the Revolutionary War, and the part which the citizens of these towns, then acting together, took in achieving our independence, and laying the foundation of our present form of government.

The Hon. Emory Washburn, a descendant of this town, but now a resident of Lowell, will deliver an historical address in the First Congregational Meeting-house in Leicester, at half-past ten o'clock, A.M., on that day.

A dinner will be provided for such ladies and gentlemen as may be present on the occasion, at as low a price as can be afforded.

To increase the interest of this celebration, it is to be hoped that many of the absent sons and daughters of the towns once composing this district will return on that day to join in its festivities, and review, with their friends and relatives here, the interesting events of past times.

The Committee of Arrangements hereby invite you, with your family, to be

be present.* The day was fine; no accident detracted from the pleasure of the gathering; and after a bountiful dinner, a variety of patriotic sentiments and interesting speeches from sundry gentlemen, the assembly separated with a feeling that the memory of the fathers ought not to be lost.

Instead of attempting to give, in this place, an original account of the celebration, I have preferred to copy from a newspaper article of the day the detailed statement, which was prepared by one who took a very active part in the arrangements for the occasion, and whose aid in the present work I have more than once acknowledged. As an incident in the local history of the town, it is hoped it will not be deemed too unimportant or minute for insertion.

HISTORICAL CELEBRATION AT LEICESTER.

Mr. Editor, — Presuming that a more particular account than has yet been given of the recent celebration of the Fourth in this place, by

---

present with us on that day; and, for the purpose of ascertaining as nearly as possible what preparations may be necessary for the accommodation of our friends, we request you, if it is convenient for you to attend, to notify us, by mail or otherwise, as early as the *twentieth day of June next*, by addressing your communication to John Sargent, Esq., Postmaster, Leicester, Mass.

Respectfully yours,

Edward Flint,	James Draper,
Isaac Southgate,	William Pope,
Henry A. Denny,	Thomas Pierce,
John Sargent,	Foster Bisco,
Jos. A. Denny,	Harvey Prouty,
Jos. D. Sargent,	William Baldwin,
Sewall Sargent,	Jeremiah Grout,
Horace Knight,	William Henshaw,
Samuel Watson,	Geo. W. Morse,
John Woodcock,	Alonzo Temple,
Reuben S. Denny,	*Spencer.*
Henry E. Warren,	
John King,	Geo. S. Lakin,
H. G. Henshaw,	Simeon Anthony,
Silas Gleason,	David Harrington,
Joseph Whittemore,	Solon G. Howe,
Hiram Knight,	David Manning,
Joshua Lamb,	*Paxton.*
Billings Swan,	
Leicester.	

* The names of the others were Asahel Matthews, Joel How, and Phineas Jones, — the two last of Spencer.

the united towns of Spencer, Paxton, Auburn, and Leicester (once composing the original town of Leicester), might be interesting to the hundreds of absent sons and daughters of those towns who were unable to be present on the occasion, I send you a sketch of the transactions of that interesting day.

A circular having previously been sent out to the former residents of these towns to meet together on that occasion, "for the purpose of refreshing their minds by the early reminiscences of their history, recalling the interesting events of the Revolutionary War, and the part which the citizens of these towns, then acting together, took in achieving our independence, and laying the foundation of our present form of government," the quiet village of Leicester, where the celebration was to take place, was enlivened during the previous day and evening by the arrival, from various quarters of the land, of the friends and relatives of its present citizens, and the absent sons and daughters of the town from a distance; and the many happy meetings which took place among former friends and acquaintances were only a prelude to the enjoyments of the following day.

The morning of the Fourth, which was bright and beautiful, was ushered in by the ringing of bells, and the discharge of a national salute on the Common. The refreshing showers in the early part of the week had prepared for us just such a day as would have been chosen for the occasion; and, previous to the hour assigned for the services, the gathering throng from the neighboring towns manifested the deep interest they felt in this novel celebration of our nation's birthday.

At about ten o'clock, a long procession of the citizens of Spencer in carriages, preceded by their Fire-engine Company in full uniform, with an elegant engine drawn by two horses, were met on their way, and escorted into the village by the Leicester Fire-engine Company, accompanied by the Northbridge Band, which, by its rich music, enlivened the performances of the day.

At half-past ten, A.M., the multitude assembled at the grove, — about eighty rods south-west of the Common, — where seats were prepared to accommodate two thousand persons, which were all filled; and some hundreds of others stood around, and sat in carriages near the stand erected for the orator of the day.

Music from the band announced the time for the commencement of the services, which were introduced by an earnest and appropriate prayer from the Rev. Dr. Nelson, the venerable minister, who has for nearly forty years past been settled over the First Congregational Society in this place.

The following hymn, by HENRY S. WASHBURN, Esq., of Worcester, was then sung by the audience, to the tune of Old Hundred: —

We gather, from a thousand homes,
Around the old ancestral tree,
From rural vales and city domes,
The favored children of the free.

We tread in olden paths to-day;
We muse on hallowed memories here;
And linger fondly by the way
With friends we've missed for many a year.

And spirits of the just and true,
Of men who spurned the tyrant's power,
Whose names are fragrant as the dew, —
They, too, are with us at this hour.

Their graves are with us, green and fair;
The cold sod lies upon their breasts;
And Freedom breathes no holier air
Than where the patriot sweetly rests.

And, Father, while with filial love
We kneel around this ancient shrine,
Oh, may thy Spirit from above
Renew and sanctify us thine!

And, strengthened by these rites to-day
For harder toil, for sterner strife,
May we press on Life's checkered way
Till we have won the crown of life!

Of the oration by Hon. EMORY WASHBURN we shall attempt no description. Its subject was, in accordance with the design of the celebration, a history of the part which our citizens took in the events of the Revolutionary War; and the intense interest with which the audience listened during the hour and a half occupied by the orator gave strong evidence of the power of his eloquence and the interest of his details.

We trust that, in accordance with a request of the hearers, this interesting address will be given to the public.

During the delivery of the address, quite a sensation was produced in the audience by the arrival of the venerable Lieut. Nathan Craige from Spencer, the only survivor of the Leicester Minute Company; who was in the battle of Bunker Hill, in the company of Capt. Seth Washburn; and who now, at the age of ninety-five, was introduced to the assembly by the President of the day. On the same platform also sat three other venerable Revolutionary soldiers belonging to the original town of Leicester.

After the services at the Grove, a procession was formed, under the direction of HENRY A. DENNY, Esq., Chief-Marshal, and escorted by the fire companies, and band of music, to the table, which was spread under a spacious tent on the Common.

Among the flags that were floating around this spot was one erected by the students of Leicester Academy, and surmounting the cupola of that venerable institution; bearing as its motto, *Libertas et Doctrina sorores germanæ.*

Of the dinner, which was provided by John Wright, Esq., of Boston, it is but justice to say, that every thing was arranged in the most perfect order, and in a style unequalled by any public table we have ever before seen.

The bountiful bill of fare, tastefully arranged, was apparently satisfactory to every guest; and, what was somewhat remarkable in so extensive a celebration, every seat was occupied, and every one who desired a seat was provided for. Between nine and ten hundred persons of both sexes partook of the dinner.

During the three or four hours which passed at the table, the most perfect order prevailed, while a general hilarity seemed to pervade the company. Not a gun was heard in the village around, not a cheer was raised, with one exception, throughout the tent, during their long sitting; and the only demonstration of applause which followed the many toasts, poems, speeches, and songs, which were said and sung by the assembled multitude, were the clapping of hands and the suppressed laughter of the guests.

The order and decorum which prevailed throughout the day was worthy of remark, as showing the favorable change for a few years past in the celebration of this anniversary, by the banishment of wine, and the introduction of our wives and daughters to the festivities of the occasion.

The Hon. JAMES DRAPER of Spencer presided at the table, assisted by five vice-presidents; and among the many toasts which were read, and the *many more* which were omitted for want of time, a few only can be given.

"*The Massachusetts Delegation in Congress.* — Though they have cut down her proportion from an *eighth* to less than a *twenty-second* part, they will find that Massachusetts can be, and will be, the Old Bay State still."

This sentiment called up the Hon. CHARLES ALLEN, who, in his usual felicitous manner, interested the audience by his appropriate remarks, and, in conclusion, offered the following sentiment: —

"*The Fathers of the Revolutionary Age.* — Living for the future, they live in that future. May the priceless inheritance acquired by their privations and sacrifices be augmented and enriched by each succeeding generation!"

"*The Clergy of New England.* — They rendered their country good service in times that tried men's souls. May they ever be found at the post of duty, laboring to *save* men's souls."

To this sentiment, Rev. Dr. NELSON, the Chaplain of the day, responded in a few interesting remarks.

"*The Orator of the Day,* — who, improving upon the liberality exhibited by his honored ancestor * on Charlestown Neck, has not only permitted us to 'go back,' but has actually *led* us back, to the *beginning of our history.*"

"*Worcester.* — When a plain *country matron,* she lent our fathers muskets in the War of Independence, which spoke well if they were only charged well. Now that she is a *city lady,* she has done better. She has lent us *men* to help celebrate that independence, who not only can *speak* well, but are *always well charged.*"

This sentiment called up his Honor the Mayor of our neighboring city, HENRY CHAPIN, Esq., who, as usual, was not only *charged,* but *primed,* and *went off,* with a speech full of wit, fun, and poetry, which kept his audience in a roar of laughter, and left them all in great good-humor. He closed with offering the following sentiment: —

"*The Scattered Families of the Tribe of Leicester.* — Whether they dwell on hill-top or in valley, may peace be their offering, plenty their inheritance, and virtue the crowning glory of their character!"

---

* Capt. Seth Washburn of Leicester, grandfather of Judge Washburn, while crossing Charlestown Neck to Bunker Hill on the memorable 17th of June, '75, exposed to the raking fire of the British, halted his company, and gave leave to any one, who chose, TO GO BACK. Not a man in the company accepted the offer.

The following song, written for the occasion by HENRY S. WASHBURN, Esq., was then sung by the Glee Club: —

'Twas pleasant, in the ancient days,
To gather snugly round
The fireside, in a merry mood,
And let the nuts abound.
The nuts and cider, gentlemen, —
Ye well remember how
They disappeared before the ken
Of some who are with us now.

But such refreshments, gentlemen,
We bring you not to-day;
For nuts and cider, as you know,
Have long since passed away.
But as the cup flows merrily,
With sparkling waters bright,
We'll gently hint, our boards are spread
A little nearer *Wright*.

Our mothers, too — in olden times
They had their quilting-bees;
But little thought that they should live
To see such times as these.
Nor did we dream, a year ago,
That friends so far away
Would bring their wives and children here
To dine with us to-day.

Then let the song flow merrily,
And heart with heart commune:
'Tis very easy now to sing
In almost any tune.
And very long this partial hour
Will memory retain;
And often shall we breathe a wish
To meet you here again.

"*Our Forefathers*, whose characters have been so graphically portrayed this day: their sepulchres are with us. May their rigid adherence to civil and religious freedom be embalmed in the hearts of a grateful posterity!"

"*Our Patriotic Grandmothers of* '76. — Although they could not cause the sun and moon to stand still, yet, by converting their clock-weights into bullets, they did what they could to cause *time to stop*, until their sons had 'avenged themselves upon their enemies.' " *

"*Lieut. Nathan Craige, our venerable Guest*, who in his youth, like Cincinnatus, left his plough to serve his country. Like that worthy old Roman, he is permitted, after a long and virtuous life, to spend the evening of his days in the peaceful enjoyment of a quiet home, a good conscience, and the respect of a grateful community."

"*The Ladies.* — Crowns of our rejoicing in prosperity; angels of consolation in adversity: Without them, the earth would be a desolation; with them, it may become a paradise."

The following song, by Hon. CHARLES THURBER, was sung by the audience in the tune of Auld Lang Syne: —

With buoyant hearts and merry feet,
The young go out to roam;
But, ah! 'tis bliss again to meet
Within the bowers of home.
How sweet to think we've come away,
From Business' giddy whirls,
With such a host of boys to-day,
And such a lot of girls!

Old Mrs. Leicester, t'other day,
Was thinking at her home
About her children far away,
And wrote to have them come;
And so, this morn, with merry voice,
And proud as any earls,
There came a host of Leicester boys,
And lots of Leicester girls.

The cannon roared, that proudly tells
The brave are on the way;
The bells were rung to show that belles
Are "all the go" to-day.
No sound is heard but Freedom's voice,
No flag but hers unfurls,
'Midst such a host of Freedom's boys,
And such a lot of girls.

---

* When word came that the British were marching out to Lexington and Concord, Mrs. Sargent, grandmother to the present Postmaster, during the brief hour in which her two sons prepared for their march to join the patriot forces, took off her clock-weights, and run them up into bullets for them to carry.

Not those alone to-day we view,
We used to greet before;
For many a *one* is changed to *two*,
And many a two to — more.
So Leicester, like Cornelia, stands,
And calls her children pearls;
While o'er her boys she waves her hands,
And also o'er her girls.

Old bachelors enjoy the scene,
Who never laughed before;
And simpering girls, but just sixteen,
For forty years and more:
The smiles around their faces play,
The zephyrs round their curls;
For here are hosts of boys to-day,
And lots of merry girls.

The farmer lets his weary team
O'er hill and valley stray;
The frugal housewife leaves her cream
To churn another day.
We have no time for such employs;
We're prouder now than earls;
For here are almost all the boys,
And nearly all the girls.

The merchant puts his ledger back;
The banker locks his chest;
The doctor drops his ipecac,
And lets the weary rest:
For Care may find no harbor near,
Where Freedom's flag unfurls;
For almost all the boys are here,
And nearly all the girls.

The anxious lawyer, bruised and scarred
By many a legal thump,
And boys that nicely work the *card*
Till cash becomes the trump,
Have come to-day to taste of joys
That rival all the world's,
Amidst a host of Leicester boys,
And lots of Leicester girls.

The parson from his sermon comes,
  With Freedom's spirit gay;
And e'en the Judge has left his looms,
  To spin *our* yarn to-day.
Oh! such the time, and such the cheer,
  And such the string of pearls! —
Why, almost all the boys are here,
  And nearly all the girls.

And, while the hours go merrily,
  A prayer shall end the lay:
May Madam Leicester ever be
  As happy as to-day!
And, when the ransomed spirits wear
  Their glorious crowns of pearls,
May all the Leicester boys be there,
  And all the Leicester girls!

By the President of the day: —

"*The First Settlers of Leicester.*—They had a *King* and an *Earl;* yet they had respect to no other nobility than that of the soul. They had one *Frier;* but they abjured the *Pope* and his doctrine. With a *Sargeant* to aid in driving out the enemy, and two *Southgates* to shut him out; with their Dennys, their Henshaws, their Greens, and 'John Smith,' — they proved themselves efficient pioneers for establishing a new settlement."

By Amos Warren, Esq., of Woodstock, Vt.: —

"*Leicester, our Early Home.* — Though *progress* is the rallying-word of the times, and *onward* and *forward* the labor of the *head* and the *hands;* yet the *heart* calls us *backward,* and the pilgrim of nearly a half-century's absence finds his youth renewed in the homes and haunts of his childhood."

The following glee, contributed by a friend, was also sung by the Glee Club: —

Come, come, come,
Come to this festal board,
Ye who have wandered long,
Ye old friends tried and true;
Oh! come in a phalanx strong.
Not often thus we mingle
In Life's uncertain way;
Not often thus we gather
As we have met to-day.

Come, come, come,
Come to this festal board,
Ye who have wandered long,
Ye old friends tried and true;
Oh! come in a phalanx strong.

Come, come, come,
Come to this festal board;
With kindred hearts draw near;
Come to this feast of love,
With a hearty welcome here.
Oh! many a weary hour
Shall we tread Life's rugged way,
Ere we shall meet again
As we have met to-day.
Come, come, come,
Come to this festal board;
With kindred hearts draw near;
Come to this feast of love,
With a hearty welcome here.

By JOHN PARTRIDGE, Esq., Paxton: —

"*The Seeds of the American Revolution*, sown broadcast over Europe. — May all the nations of that continent soon be able to sing the Harvest Home!"

By ABRAHAM FIRTH, Esq.: —

"*The Permanent Residents of the Town.* — May their private and public virtues be so pre-eminent, that the sons of Leicester everywhere, and in all time, may never feel ashamed of their birthplace!"

By a Citizen: —

"*Our Fire-engine Companies*, the *minute-men* of modern times. — Like their Revolutionary fathers, they conquer the enemy by the use of their *arms*."

By a Fireman: —

"*The Ladies.* — Their eyes kindle the only flame we dare not encounter, and which our *arms* cannot conquer."

By SAMUEL ALLEN, Esq.: —

"*The Memory of the late Col. William Henshaw*, — a man without fear and without reproach."

By H. G. Henshaw, Esq.: —

"*The Memory of the late Hon. Joseph Allen,* once a prominent and favorite citizen of Leicester. — His memory is 'fragrant as the dew.'"

Among the sentiments received from our absent friends were the following: —

By Andrew H. Ward, Esq., Newton: —

"*The Town of Leicester,* the home of our ancestors. — While her *farm has decreased,* her *children have increased.* When we visit the hearthstone again on a like occasion, may we, *as now,* find her *Sargeants* in the line of promotion, her *Flints* well picked, *Kings* and *Knights* among her sons, her *Woodcocks* and *Swans* unmolested by sportsmen, and herself choice of her *Lambs!*"

By Hon. Waldo Flint, Boston: —

"*Our Ancestors of the Revolution.* — We shall prove ourselves ungrateful sons, and unworthy of the blessings we inherit, if we ever fail to rise up and call them blessed."

By Hon. Nathan Sargeant, Washington, D.C.: —

"*The School-houses and the Meeting-houses of New England,* — the brightest jewels in her diadem."

By Rev. George Allen: —

"*Liberty,* the right of *all.* — God speed to all the *fruition* of that right!"

Among the speakers at the table was Hon. Joseph Sprague, Ex-Mayor of Brooklyn, N.Y.; who, in responding to a sentiment, gave some sketches of the campaign on Long Island, during the Revolutionary War, while our troops were stationed there.

Letters and sentiments were received from many invited guests who were unable to be present; some of which were read, but many were necessarily omitted. They showed, however, the deep interest felt by all the descendants of the place in the object of the celebration.

Among the interesting events of the day was the welcome meeting, at this table, of many former friends, and the greeting of those who had for many years been separated, and had now again come together from all parts of the country to renew their acquaintance, and, perhaps for the last time, to look upon the associates of their childhood.

Many a hearty welcome was exchanged, and many a silent tear was shed, as the guests moved about from friend to friend during the time occupied by the speakers at the table.

From our cities and towns came together the loved and honored sons of old Leicester, some with gray hairs, who went out from us in early youth; and we were pleased to see among the happy group many who left us in early life, penniless and alone, to seek their fortune in other climes, return with their families to visit us on this occasion, blessed with prosperity, and enjoying the fruits of their industry and enterprise.

Long will the fathers and mothers, the sons and daughters, of old Leicester, remember this happy meeting, and the interesting incidents which occurred on the occasion; and may the success which attended our efforts in this novel and interesting enterprise be the cause of many such happy gatherings of the descendants of the Pilgrims, in years to come, on the hills and in the valleys of New England!

J. A. D.

LEICESTER, July 10, 1849.

In Washington's diary, recently published, he speaks of the towns he passed through, and the places at which he stopped, on his journey to Boston. He spent the night of the 22d October, 1789, at Mr. Jenks's tavern, in Spencer. On Friday, the 23d, "we commenced our course with the sun; and, passing through Leicester, met some gentlemen of the town of Worcester, on the line between it and the former, to escort us."

The circumstance is also noticed in the diary of a citizen of Leicester, now before me; and was long recalled as a memorable event, although there does not appear to have been any public demonstration on the part of the town. A scarcely less interesting occurrence of the kind was the passing through the south part of the town, by Gen. La Fayette, Sept. 3, 1824. The people crowded to greet him; and all along the roadside, and at every village, they were seen cheering him with shouts and the waving of hats and handkerchiefs; and, wherever he stopped, his carriage was surrounded by people pressing for a chance to shake the hand of this early and noble friend of America. He was attended by a troop of horse, and an escort of carriages, military officers, citizens, &c., — the free ovation of a grateful people.

CEMETERIES.

While we are thus indulging in the recollection of what men did, and where they lived, while filling up the incidents of the local history of the town, we ought not to pass unnoticed the spots where they are reposing, — the cemeteries of the town. As a test and standard of refined sentiment in selecting and adorning the last resting-place of the dead, the early cemeteries of this town, like those all over New England at the time, would be of the most humble pretension. Indeed, there have been few more decided marks of a growing refinement in the public taste than the selection of beautiful and becoming spots, where art and affection combine to rob the externals of the grave of all that is repulsive, and to add the attractions of the lovely in nature to the associations of love and affection which consecrate the mound beneath which the wife, the child, or the friend, is reposing.

Beginning with Mount Auburn, the beautiful idea has found a type in the recent rural cemeteries of many of the towns in the Commonwealth; and will, ere long, be copied in every one. Such has been the case with Leicester. A new cemetery, in a sequestered spot, amidst the spreading shades of the pine and other forest trees, was consecrated by suitable and appropriate ceremonies in 1841. It is about half a mile south-west of the Meeting-house. But, before noticing this further, I recur to the earlier burying-places in the town. One of these was in rear of the Congregational Meeting-house; probably occupied as such from the very first settlement of the town. Here, borrowing the language of poetry, without meaning to do injustice to their character, "the rude forefathers of the hamlet sleep."

It ceased to be used, except occasionally, as a burial-place, after about 1765 (at least, for new families), when the one, half a mile west of the Meeting-house, was opened; and, when it was thought desirable to extend the Common in rear of the Meeting-house, the headstones were removed, the graves levelled, and every mark and vestige of the spots where some two or three generations had successively been laid were effectually obliterated. Jethro, elsewhere noticed, was the last person buried within the original cemetery; and this must have been about 1810.

The second cemetery, in point of time, was that around the Baptist Meeting-house in Greenville. Capt. Samuel Green was, as is supposed, the first person buried there; which was in January, 1736.

The burying-ground around the Friends' Meeting-house was begun to be occupied about 1739, and formed originally a part of the farms of Nathaniel Potter and Robert Earle.

About 1750, a cemetery was begun upon the farm in the north part of the town, then owned by John Lynde, Esq., afterwards by Isaac Choate, and more recently by Deacon Joseph Elliot. Mrs. Benjamin Wheaton, a daughter of John Lynde, was among the first persons interred there, after the burial of her father, which took place in 1756.

Another collection of graves may be seen, in the south-westerly part of the town, upon the farm formerly belonging to Elder Richard Southgate. The grave of the Elder is among them. The last interment there was that of Judah Southgate in 1799.

There is a cemetery in Cherry Valley, originally begun by Benjamin Studley in 1816, which is laid out with much taste as a public burial-place for the people in that part of the town.

Several small clusters of graves, and single graves, are scattered in various parts of the town. Those of the Rev. Mr. Parsons and Dr. Lawton are mentioned elsewhere. Several of these are memorials of the time, when it was thought necessary to resort to "pest-houses," as they were called, in which the patient submitted to inoculation as a protection from the small-pox, before the days of vaccination. Although this was found to be comparatively far more safe than being subjected to that loathsome disease in the "natural way," it was attended with much hazard; as was attested by more or less graves found near the localities of most of those hospitals. One of them was the house formerly of Joseph Shaw, near the "Shaw Pond," so called; it being, as all such hospitals were, remote from any road or any other dwelling-house. One inscription upon one of these headstones is still legible: "In memory of Miss Ruth Paine, daughter of Mr. Jabez and Mrs. Elizabeth Paine, who died April 10, 1778, in the 24th year of her age. This stone was set up by a *sencear morner*." But no headstone records to whom the sleeper there was indebted for this simple tribute of affection.

The proprietor of the Mount-Pleasant Estate (Mr. Lewis Allen) was, by his direction, buried in the garden in 1780. He died at the age of thirty-five. In the conveyance of his estate after his death, this spot was reserved; but, some forty years since, it shared the lot of most such private graves. The estate had fallen into the hands of a stranger; and, regardless of the uses to which the spot had been consecrated, every vestige of it was levelled beneath the ploughshare; and it is no longer to be distinguished.

MOUNT PLEASANT.

The estate which has long been known by this name, was, at one time, of sufficient magnitude and importance to be the subject of particular notice. The mansion-house stands on what was originally lot No. 33; at first laid out to Joseph Parsons, who is mentioned in this work. From him it passed to Nathaniel Kanney of Boston; and belonged to William Brown in 1724, when the deed of the proprietors of the town was made to the settlers of the east half of the township. After that, it belonged to Ralph Inman, who sold it to Darby

Ryan. He sold one-half of the farm to John Ryan, his father, in 1767. He sold to Jonathan Sargent, jun., in 1771. The same year, Mr. Sargent sold it to Joseph Henshaw, then called of Boston. He owned it seven years, and, during that time, erected the mansion-house now standing upon it, as has already been mentioned, from materials brought from Boston. Col. Henshaw is noticed in another part of this work.

In March, 1778, he sold to Lewis Allen, of Shrewsbury, called a goldsmith. He had, in the mean time, become the owner of some adjacent land, making a hundred and thirty-six acres in all; and the sum paid for it at that time was two thousand five hundred pounds. Mr. Allen was a man of peculiar habits and notions; and, in the early part of the Revolution, had been a royalist. He gave the estate the name it has since borne; and, when he died, was buried, by his direction, in the garden, as has been stated. The reason for this, as related in Ward's History of Shrewsbury, and as given by Mr. Allen, was, that he might hear the news from Boston when the stage came along. A little grove of maples, growing close by the road near the avenue to the house, was planted by him. He died there in 1780. His administrators sold the estate, together with an additional seventy acres which he had purchased of Darby Ryan, to Samuel Brooks of Worcester, in 1783, for nine hundred and twenty-six pounds, reserving a rod of land where said Allen had been buried. Thomas Stickney, who had removed here from Newburyport, then became the owner, and carried on business as a merchant there until his death in August, 1791.* In September, 1795, Capt. John

* I have been enabled, by the favor of J. Henry Stickney, Esq., an eminent merchant of Baltimore, and a grandson of Mr. Stickney, to present to the reader a view of this estate as it appeared in 1794; it being a copy of a print published in the Massachusetts Magazine of that year. I give below the account which accompanied the original print. As a memorial of the primitive condition of the estate, the print has much interest; while the source from which it has been derived, gives it additional value.

"*Description of Mount Pleasant, accompanied with a striking View.* — The annexed plate exhibits a view of Mount Pleasant, in Leicester, Mass., — the real estate of the late

J. H. BUFFORD'S LITH. 313 WASH. BOSTON.

MOUNT PLEASANT in LEICESTER,

Lyon, then called of Worcester, who had married the widow of Mr. Stickney, sold the homestead, then containing two hundred acres, with the "mansion-house, barn, potash, farm-house, and all other buildings thereon," to James Swan, then called of Boston, for five thousand two hundred and sixty-seven dollars. In other contemporary deeds he is called of Dorchester, where he had an elegant seat.

The extent of his estates, and the style of magnificence in which he lived, rendered the removal of Major Swan to Leicester a memorable event in its history. In all these, he so far exceeded any thing which had been before familiar to the people, that he was the object of general interest and attention; and fabulous stories of the wealth he displayed were told for many years after his brief reign of magnificence and admiration had passed by. He had been a major of a regiment of artillery in the Continental service, commanded by Col. Crafts, in which Capts. Todd and Henshaw, and Lieut. John Southgate, of Leicester, had held commissions. He may have been led to think of this as a place of residence from his acquaintance with these gentlemen, but more probably from the attractiveness of the estate. He at one time must have owned some seven or eight hundred acres of land in a body; embracing, besides the homestead, the farms known as the Calvin Hersey Estate; the John A. Denny Estate; the Moore Farm, afterwards of Col. Henry Sargent; the William Silvester Farm, and parts of several other farms. There are persons living who remember the marks of a liberal culture and tasteful arrangement which this estate presented in many of its parts, enclosed by firm and substantial walls and gates,

---

Mr. Thomas Stickney, deceased. This elegant seat is fifty-five miles from Boston, on the post-road to New York. It commands an extensive prospect of the neighboring country; and, for salubrity of air, is perhaps unequalled: a situation equally favorable for philosophical retirement and manly improvement. The gentleman of agricultural taste on this farm of two hundred and twenty acres may amuse himself with various experiments in the most useful science of husbandry, and the sportsman from its forests and streams may find salutary exercise and varied pleasure."

but whose productive mowing-fields and tillage-lands, after a few years of neglect, were changed into rough and unsavory pastures, covered with brush, and rendered little better than unprofitable wastes. I speak principally of the homestead; the buildings and fences of which were, after the removal of Major Swan, suffered to go to decay; and remained in that condition till its late proprietor, by judicious skill and labor, did much to restore the soil to its productiveness, and the dwelling-house to a pleasant and comfortable homestead.

I am unable to state how long Major Swan occupied this estate; but I apprehend it was for a few years only. He seems to have been a man who lived in a style beyond his actual wealth, or, by some revulsion of fortune, was induced to retire to France, where his creditors endeavored in vain to coerce the payment of their debts. I find the following notice in the "Worcester Spy" of the 18th September, 1830: "A letter from Dr. Niles, now at Paris, mentions, that, on July 22, St. Pelagie (the Debtor's Prison in Paris) was opened, and that among the liberated was Mr. Swan, an American citizen (formerly of Leicester), who has occupied the same room thirty-two years and one day."

The papers have since mentioned his death in Paris; he never having returned to America. His social position and family connections in this country were of the most respectable rank in life. But this work has properly little connection with his personal history, except so far as it was connected with that of the town.

If we were to trace the history of other estates here, it would be found remarkable that so few have remained in the line of any one family. Of the few that have any claim to being paternal acres, may be mentioned that of Mr. Sewall Sargent; whose ancestor, Nathan, purchased it, and moved upon it in 1742. Lyman Waite, Esq., lives upon a part of the estate which his grandfather cleared of the primitive forest, and owned as early as 1735, and perhaps earlier; and which came to the present owner by descent from his father. Mr. Daniel Livermore owns and lives upon a part of the estate which was conveyed to his ancestor, Daniel Livermore, as one of the settlers of the town in 1724. There is one other estate which has been held by the same family since previous to 1728; and that is the one on which Joseph Whittemore lived at the time of his recent death. It was purchased by Deacon John, his grandfather; and was afterwards owned by his father, Lieut. James. But, beyond these, I do not recall one which has passed by descent in any one family for the term of a hundred years, or even approximating to that length of time.

Mr. William Henshaw lives upon a part of the original farm of his ancestor, Daniel Henshaw; and Dr. Pliny Earle lives upon part of that of his ancestor, Ralf Earle. The place on which Mr. Henry E. Warren lives belonged to his grandfather; and the place owned by Mr. Eber Bond was owned by his ancestor, Benjamin, before 1747.

PUBLIC-HOUSES.

Among the houses in town which have been occupied as inns, or taverns, are the following; though I am unable to give all the occupants, or to mention them in their order where they have been ascertained.

The first in order of time was one standing where Capt. Knight's house is, at the corner of the Great and the Rutland Road. It was early built, and occupied as a public-house from the first. The first occupant was Nathaniel Richardson, as early as 1721. John Taylor owned and occupied it in 1746. He sold to John Taylor, jun., in 1755. In 1756, it was kept a short time by Seth Washburn. He appears to have been succeeded by Mr. Taylor again. Benjamin Tucker occupied it in 1761, and, by permission of the town, dug a well upon the Common, now remaining, — "a little west of the sign-post." The house then belonged to the estate of Mr. Taylor, who had died. It was soon purchased by Edward Bond; and while in his possession, in 1767, was burned, as stated in another part of this work. The house was rebuilt and occupied by Mr. Bond until 1775, when he sold it to Isaac Kibbe; but I apprehend he never lived upon it. It was kept by Elijah Lathrop from 1776 to 1778; when Peter Taft, from Uxbridge, who had purchased of Kibbe, occupied it till 1781. He then sold it to Reuben Swan, who enlarged it, and continued to occupy it until 1801; when William Denny purchased and occupied it till about 1810. He was succeeded by Aaron Morse, who occupied it until he removed into the tavern opposite the Meeting-house.

The next house in order of time was that of Jonathan Sargent, which stood opposite the Catholic Church. It was built and occupied as a tavern as early as 1727. Mr. Sargent occupied it till his death. He was succeeded by his son Phinehas, who occupied it till his death in 1776. Upon his death, the estate was purchased by Nathan Waite, who owned it till his death, but discontinued it as a tavern several years before that time.

The house standing where Mr. Robert Watson lately lived was kept as a public-house in 1740 by James Smith. It was afterwards kept as such by Samuel Lynde in 1755; and, in 1759, was destroyed by a hurricane, as has been stated.

As early as 1776, Col. Phinehas Newhall kept a public-house upon the North County Road, where Mr. Eddy lives. It was kept by him as such for many years, and continued to be so occupied into the present century. It was a large and commodious house; but has, within a few years, been replaced by one of smaller dimensions.

The house opposite the Meeting-house, which has been so long kept as a hotel, was built for that purpose by Nathan Waite in 1776. The following year, he removed to the place where he afterwards lived, and sold the estate to Jacob Rod

Rivera. Mr. Rivera traded there until his removal to Newport in 1783.

From that time, the house has been kept as a hotel by various persons, among whom were Mr. George Bruce and Mr. Bugbee; Abner Dunbar; Johnson Lynde, in 1797–8; Arad Lynde, his son, and Nathan Felton, 1799; when John Hobart purchased it, and carried it on with great success till about 1817. When he first took it, it contained but two front-rooms and a kitchen and bedroom in the body of the house. He enlarged it from time to time to its present size. He sold the estate to Alpheus Smith; under whom Aaron Morse occupied as a tenant until his removal to New Haven about 1822.

Mr. George Bruce kept a tavern in the Mount-Pleasant House after the removal of Major Swan; and, during the Revolution, Abner Dunbar kept as a tavern the house standing opposite the Mower Place on Mount Pleasant.

Samuel Green kept a tavern many years in Greenville, in the house next west of the river.

Mr. Hezekiah Stone built, and for several years kept, a hotel in what is Clappville, upon the Stafford and Worcester Turnpike.*

There is one class of memorials often met with, connected with the history of the town, which I ought not to pass over unnoticed, — the cellars of dwelling-houses, which, with their occupants, have long since disappeared. Many of these were constructed before the highways of the town had been laid out, and are now remote from other settlements or travelled ways.

The quiet and sequestered spots in which some of them

---

* When speaking of Clappville, it should have been stated that a post-office was established there in 1824, and the Rev. Mr. Muenscher was appointed the first postmaster. After him was Edward L. Stone; then Horace M'Farland; and, in succession, Butler Goodridge, Abraham Firth, Reuben S. Denny, George Roberts, and the present incumbent (Samuel L. Stone).

There was a post-office established in Cherry Valley in 1859; and Harvey Tainter, Esq., appointed postmaster.

are found, indicate much taste in their original selection; and outlines of gardens and enclosures by which they were surrounded, with occasionally an aged tree that shaded the cottage or supplied its inmates with fruit, remind one, that, however humble they may have been, they were once the abodes of men to whom life had its attractions. Even if one took no interest in tracing the name of him who built or occupied it, he could not come upon the site of one of these early dwellings, nestled in some sheltered valley or looking out from some lonely hillside, without being reminded that it was once a human habitation and a home; that here some one had shared in what makes up life's common experience in every age. Some young man had brought hither, in the flush of hope and pride, the happy bride he had chosen: they had here begun life together. Here children had played and grown up, and gone forth to their several spheres of action; and here, too, death had entered, and taken away the infant in the morn, and the old man in the evening, of life.

If thoughts and emotions like these might be awakened by such an object, when only excited by the associations of a common nature, it surely cannot be foreign from a work like this to give these objects a passing notice, when they are associated, many of them, with the names and events which make up the town's history.

They are interesting in another point of view. They indicate, by the very humble dimensions of the houses, the condition of the first settlers of the town, in respect to comfort and convenience. The names of their occupants and the numbers of their children, as shown in the genealogies of their families, present a singular disproportion between the capacity of their houses and the number of persons they were made to accommodate.

Most of these houses were a single story in height, and few of them contained more than a couple of rooms, and perhaps a projecting bed-room, in this story; and the inventories of the furniture they contained were as meagre as the proportions of their rooms were small.

They illustrate the social history of the first and succeeding generation which planted and subdued the soil of Leicester. One of these is on Dix Hill, so called, in the north-west part of the town, where Benjamin Dix lived from previous to 1744 till after 1759. On the west side of Shaw Pond is another, where Joseph Shaw lived, which was built about 1748. It was used as a hospital or pest-house about the time of the Revolution.

There are two on the east side of Shaw Pond. In one of these, John Cummings lived. He married Rachel Snow, 1752. In the other, which is about a quarter of a mile east from the first, Robert Woodward lived in 1740. There is one west of George S. Bond's house, where John Converse lived in 1729, as I suppose; and, after him, his son Joshua, who was living there in 1776.

At the corner of the Eddy Road, so called, near the North-west Schoolhouse, is the cellar of the house in which Robert, the father of Sally Bradish, mentioned in this work, lived; and afterwards Seth Washburn, jun., son of Col. Seth, just before the Revolution. His blacksmith-shop stood near it.

In 1755, Benjamin Woodward built a house, the cellar of which remains, about thirty rods east from the road leading to Zolva Green's, and about a quarter of a mile from the Whittemore Road, as it is called. His son Jesse lived there after him; and, in 1776 it was occupied by a Widow Sawin. Deacon John Whittemore built his first house, about 1730, some sixty rods south-west from that which he afterwards built, where his son Joseph lived. A house once stood on the west side of the road leading to the Whittemore Sawmill, in which Hiram Newhall was living about 1764. Joseph Sprague, the first of the name in town, built a house which stood near the one in which his son, Capt. William, lived. The house of

Dudley Wade Swan, in 1736, stood near the present house of Mr. Sturtevant, in the north-east part of the town. Reuben Swan lived there in 1776. John Potter, as early as 1730, lived in a house that stood on the south side of the road, a little west of where Jonah Earle lived. Joseph Trumbull's house, in 1737, stood a little south of the house of the late Daniel Kent. Nathaniel Waite built his house, about that time, where his son Samuel afterwards built the house in which he lived. The house of Deacon James Southgate was standing, in 1730, on the knoll a little north of the house of David Morton; and the house of his brother Richard stood upon the upper side of the old Country Road, a little north-west of where Capt. John lived and died. On the knoll west of the brick factory and of the pond, the house of Nathaniel Sargent stood, about 1750. The cellar on the west side of the Sylvester Road, about sixty rods from the Great Road, was the residence of Joseph, and afterwards of his son Seth Washburn. A cellar, upon what is called Ballard Hill, about half a mile south of William Silvester's, was built by George Cradock, Esq., for the tenant of his farm, and afterwards occupied by Zaccheus Ballard, who came from Framingham in 1770. The house was burned before the Revolution.

Capt. Isaac Southgate was born in a house occupied by his father, which stood in the pasture about sixty rods north-west from the house of the late Peter Silvester. Where Benjamin Earle's house now stands, there was once a house, in which Mr. Lynde lived, and after him Abner Dunbar kept a tavern. It was occupied by Elijah Howe in 1776. On the Oxford Road, nearly in front of Mrs. Hobart's, stood a small house, formerly occupied by the Rev. Mr. Goddard; afterwards by Joshua Crossman in 1776. A Mr. Kane had a small house where Ira Bond's now stands; and a little farther south stood the house of Mr. Bowker, on the same side of the road. In a lot west of Eber Bond's house was the house of Mr. Barnes, occupied by James Graton in 1776. Matthew Watson's house, built by him in 1720, stood about sixty rods north-east of Deacon Lyon's, on land now of Joseph A. Denny, Esq. Samuel Watson's house was built early, and stood on the hill south of that of his son Benjamin, in the south-east part of the town.

None of these, it is believed, have been standing within the recollection of any person now living. In some cases, they have given place to more commodious and convenient dwellings; in others, they were suffered to go to decay, and were abandoned. It was by the diligence and research of the one who prepared the map of the town, which accompanies this work, that I trace their history.

I add, from the same authority, a few of the houses which have disappeared within the recollection of living witnesses. Among these was the house of Col. Samuel Denny, on Moose Hill, built in 1756, and taken down about 1817. The house occupied by Robert Woodward in 1750, by Benjamin Livingston in 1776, and by sundry others prior to Joel Marsh, its last occupant, stood about half a mile north-west from Joseph Whittemore's. The house of Azariah Eddy, near the North-west Schoolhouse, was originally built by Benjamin Converse, and was occupied by him in 1776. Capt. John Holden's house stood on the east side of the Rutland Road, about a mile and a quarter from the Meeting-house. It was built by Joseph Sprague, and occupied by his son Timothy in 1776. The house in which Peter Silvester lived in 1776, and afterwards occupied by Adam Gilmore, was upon the eastern slope of the Meeting-house Hill, upon the north side of the road, where there is still a cellar. Benjamin Vickery's house was below that, upon the opposite side of the road.

The house of Daniel Denny, which he built about 1725, stood upon the top of Denny Hill, then called Nurse's, upon the east side of the road, where a barn now stands. He died there in 1765. Capt. Nathaniel Harwood lived in a house opposite the house of William Silvester. The house of James Harwood stood about half a mile west of Eber Bond's.

Jonas Livermore built a house, before the Revolution, upon the west side of the road, at the southerly foot of the Livermore Hill. It was afterwards occupied by Isaac Livermore, and subsequently by Joseph Washburn.

The house of Elder Richard Southgate, in which he was living in 1776, and in which he died, stood upon the north side of the road leading by William Silvester's, and near the line of Spencer. There are several other spots, once occupied by dwelling-houses, which are noticed in other connections in this work.

I have had occasion, more than once, to allude to the changes which have taken place in the families that have at some time formed a part of the inhabitants of the town, and the great numbers who have disappeared from it by removal. Some of these I can now trace, though their number is small; and it seems in keeping with the rest of the work to mention them here.

John Brown, and Francis and Isaac Choate, removed to Ohio early in its history. Quite a number emigrated to Vermont when it was settled. Among them, Jabez Paine went to Westminster; Asa Washburn (son of Col. Seth), Samuel Sargent (who had married his sister), John Hodgkins (who had married another sister), Ebenezer Saunderson, Israel Saunderson, and Abijah Stowers, went to Putney; Hezekiah Saunderson, to Westminster; Richard Southgate, son of "Elder Richard," and his three sons, with Thomas, Willard, and Aaron, sons of Nathan Lamb, went to Bridgewater; the father went to Corinth; Isaac, son of Dr. Thomas Green, went to Windsor; Dr. Edward Lamb, to Montpelier; Thomas Hammond, to Orwell; Samuel Upham, to Calais; Benjamin Livingston went to Townsend, and James to Peacham; Gen. Lyman Mower and Amos Warren went to Woodstock; William, Elias, and Ezra Kent, sons of Ebenezer, and John Earle, Daniel Hubbard, and his son Jonathan, went to Wallingford; Joseph Cerley, to Whitingham; and Elias Greene and family, to Cambridge.* Most of these had families, who removed with them.

Robert Henry and family, and Ezra Silvester, went to Charleston, N.H. Among those who removed to Maine were Asa Green and family, to Deer Isle, in 1797; and William Paine, Benjamin Watson, jun., and Clark Works, with their families, to Mercer.

Reuben Earle, son of William, went to German Flats, N.Y.; John, another son, to Herkimer; and Oliver, his brother, to Vermont; so did Nathan, George, and Esek, sons of Robert Earle; Sylvanus, son of Thomas Earle, and his family, went to Ohio in 1816; so did Daniel, Reuben, and Homer, sons of James Earle; Joseph Sprague went to Brooklyn, N.Y.; Otis, his brother, to Indiana, afterwards to Wisconsin; John and Otis, sons of John Hobart, and Theodore V., son of Joseph Denny, went to Indianapolis; Ebenezer D. Washburn, to Alabama; Joseph, his brother, to Georgia; Joshua, son of David Henshaw, went to Ohio, but returned late in life to Leicester; Andrew went to Alabama; Jonathan Bond, to the western part of New York; James, son of Thomas Mower, went to New York in 1792; Dr. Andrew Denny, son of Nathaniel P., to Alabama; and Samuel and Bloomfield Parsons, sons of Solomon, to Louisiana; Samuel Whittemore, son of James, with his family, removed to the State of New York; John Sprague, son of Timothy, with his family, went to the State

* For the account of the emigrants to Vermont, I am much indebted to Hon. Reuben Washburn, who is noticed among the native graduates of college. Upon his authority, I am happy to state that the emigrants to Vermont from Leicester were generally a hardy, robust, industrious, frugal, and enterprising set of men; and they and their descendants have contributed their full share to the prosperity of the State, and to its character for general intelligence and a spirit of independence. I might mention among them Thomas Hammond, Judge of Rutland County; Gen. Mower, first President of the Woodstock Bank,—a man distinguished for enterprise and public spirit; and Dr. Lamb, who attained great eminence in his profession. William Upham is mentioned in another place, a senator in Congress.

The contemporaries of these emigrants, as many may now remember, always spoke of Vermont as the "new State;" such being the term by which it had once been known to them.

of New York; Dr. Robert Southgate went to Scarborough, Me.; David and Isaac, sons of Samuel Denny, settled in Vermont; Billings Hobart now lives in Charleston, Va.; Thomas Denny, son of Col. Thomas, in the city of New York; Elijah Washburn and Joseph, sons of Elijah, and nephews of Col. Seth, removed to Hancock, N.H.; Seth, son of Seth, and grandson of Col. Washburn, went to Lansingburg, N.Y.; Asahel Washburn, nephew of Col. Seth, and family, went to Greensborough, Vt., in 1801. Among others who removed to Vermont were Joseph and John Lynde; William, son of Richard Bond, and Stephen Sargent; William Sargent, son of Jonathan, jun., went to Canada; Capt. William Todd, to Keene, N.H.; Hartwell and Denny Hayward, sons of John, went to New York; so did Edward Westly, Phinehas Barton, jun., Samuel Sargent, and his son Samuel, jun., with their families; Benjamin Tucker removed to New Hampshire in 1765; James Scott, with his father Andrew, went to Pennsylvania; Charles and Z. S. M. Hersey, to Canada.

I have not attempted to enumerate those who have removed from Leicester to other towns in Massachusetts. Many of them have made their mark in the places in which they have settled, in the several departments of business and pursuits in life in which they have been engaged, and reflected credit upon their native home. And it may not be inappropriate to remark in this connection, that, of the presidents of banks in Boston, Henry B. Stone, Esq., late of the Suffolk; Hon. Waldo Flint, of the Eagle; and Daniel Denny, Esq., of the Hamilton, — were natives of the town; while one of the collectors of that port (Hon. David Henshaw) was also born there.

CHAPTER VI.

PERSONAL NOTICES.

PROFESSIONAL MEN. — GRADUATES AT COLLEGE. — PUBLIC MEN. — ARTISTS.

In attempting to present personal notices of individuals who have been connected with the town, it cannot be expected that I should confine myself to such only as have been known in eminent and distinguished positions, and in the relations of public office or place. My aim is free from all such pretence; as the sketches I shall attempt to offer are designed only to illustrate the proper local history which I am attempting to embody. Among these are the public and professional men; exclusive, of course, of the clergymen, who have already been spoken of.

Of those who have been judges of courts, the first in order of time was John Minzies. He removed here from Roxbury in 1720, and became a large landed proprietor in the town. He lived in, and undoubtedly built, the house upon the Henshaw Place which recently belonged to the Hon. David Henshaw. He was a Scotch gentleman, educated for the bar, and a member of the Faculty of Advocates in Edinburgh. He was appointed, by the crown, Judge of the Court of Admiralty for Massachusetts, New Hampshire, and Rhode Island; and arrived in Boston, in the ship "Samuel," in December, 1715, bringing with him his commission. He settled in Roxbury; where he probably became associated with some of the leading proprietors of Leicester, and was induced to take up his residence in this then almost unbroken wilderness.

The next year, he was chosen to represent the town in the General Court, receiving the cordial thanks of his constituents as the compensation for his services; and was re-elected, upon the like advantageous terms, in 1722, '23, and '25.

His political career was brought to a sudden and untimely end by the action of the House in expelling him from that body. The reason of this harsh measure was his having written home letters to the Lords Commissioners, in which he complained of the manner in which the courts of the Province interfered with the jurisdiction of his own court by issuing prohibitions to suitors from prosecuting their claims before him; and saying it was impossible to get a jury of the country to do justice to the king in trials involving the rights and authority of the crown.

This coming to the ears of the Legislature, he was arraigned before the House to answer to the charge; but, so far from denying it, he re-iterated the charge, and insisted that it was fully justified by the facts, and that he had done no more than his duty required of him. As he declined to apologize, the House voted to expel him.

The following year, he removed to Boston; where he died, in September, 1728, in the seventy-eighth year of his age.

He was a friend of Dr. Douglass the historian, from whom he borrowed money; and had pecuniary dealings with Gov. Shute, and the Hon. Robert Byng, the Receiver-General of the Admiralty in England. Like so many of his contemporaries, he seems to have entered largely into the land speculations of the day.

He was interested in other new townships besides Leicester. In the settlers' deed of the latter he is named as a grantee; having purchased Lot No. 25, which had been originally assigned to Thomas Hollioke. By virtue of this right, he became the owner of four hundred acres, where he lived; and afterwards purchased the rights of Capt. Baker in Lot No. 34; and of Samuel Prince, father of Rev. Mr. Prince the annalist, in Lot No. 37; which, with other purchases, made him, at one time, owner of more than sixteen hundred acres in the town.

His speculations did not turn out successful. He was obliged to mortgage his estates heavily; and, after his death, his widow Katherine, as his administratrix, sold his lands for the payment of his debts.

The body of water adjoining his estate was designated, in the early plans of the town, "*the* Judge's Pond," from the title of honor with which he was always spoken of by his contemporaries.

He left no children; and, upon the death of his widow, the family became extinct in Massachusetts.

THOMAS STEELE was the son of Thomas Steele, who purchased Judge Menzies' estate after his death. He was born in Boston: graduated at Harvard in 1730, ranking fourth in the class, on the score of family dignity; Chief-Justice Oliver standing at the head of the class. He was bred a merchant, and pursued the business of trade before and after his removal to Leicester.

In 1756, he was appointed Judge of the Court of Common Pleas for the County of Worcester; and held that office until the Revolution.

In 1752, he was chosen to represent the town in the General Court; and was re-elected in the years '53, '54, and '55.

In 1761, he was elected town-clerk, and, by annual election, held the office till 1769; and the records of the town furnish evidence of the beauty of his chirography, and the fidelity with which he recorded the transactions of the town, many of which must have been very little in unison with his own political sentiments.

He was a firm loyalist in his feelings and opinions, though he was probably prudent enough not to provoke censure by the too free expression of them. Besides this, his daughter having married so thorough and tried a patriot as Joseph

Allen, and another having married Dr. John Honywood (who early entered into the army), would have formed a pledge of fidelity to his country, which must have gone far to disarm the jealousy of his neighbors.

He lived in various places in town; probably, for some time, at first at the Henshaw Place. At one time, he lived and did business in the large old house which he built, and which stood at the foot of the Meeting-house Hill, at the intersection of Flip Lane with the Great Road. For some time before and after 1776, he lived in the Rawson House, so called, upon the Great Road, just east of the Town-meadow Brook.*

Every thing we can gather relative to Judge Steele leads us to believe that he was a man of high respectability of character, who possessed the confidence of his fellow-citizens, though differing from them in his political sentiments.

His father, who was a merchant in Boston, was also, at times, called upon to act in a judicial capacity, though never appointed to the bench. I find one case, where, with Thomas Hutchinson, Thomas Fitch, and Anthony Stoddard, he was appointed Special Justice of the Common Pleas for Suffolk, to try an action wherein Chief-Justice Byfield of that court was a party. This was in 1732.

Though possessed of a considerable estate when he removed to Leicester, Judge Steele was not a successful business-man, and had lost much of his property before he died.

One of his daughters, as already mentioned, married Hon. Joseph Allen; another, Dr. John Honeywood; another, Dr. Edward Rawson; another, a Mr. Hitchcock of Brookfield; and one (Mary) survived them all, and died unmarried. He had two sons, — Thomas and Samuel; but no branch of the family has been connected with the town since the death of his daughter Mary. Thomas died in 1768, unmarried.

---

* He died there, of apoplexy.

Hon. JOSEPH DORR resided some years in Leicester, and, a part or all the time, occupied the house built by Judge Steele at the foot of the Meeting-house Hill. He was a son of the Rev. Joseph Dorr of Mendon; born May 24, 1730; graduated at Harvard in 1752, and studied divinity. He preached occasionally for several years, but does not appear to have ever been settled as a minister. He was an active and devoted friend to the cause of the Colonies in the struggle with the mother-country, and took an early and leading part in the measures which resulted in their independence.*

While residing in Mendon, he was a magistrate, a member of the Committee of Safety, a member of the Legislature, and a part of the time, Judge of Probate and of the Court of Common Pleas. He was one of the first senators chosen under the Constitution from the county of Worcester; having been elected in 1780–81 and '82.

In 1776, he was commissioned as Judge of the Court of Common Pleas for the county of Worcester; which office he resigned in 1801. In 1782, he was appointed Judge of Probate to succeed Judge Lincoln, and held the office till November, 1800; when he resigned, and was succeeded by Judge Paine. He removed to Ward (now Auburn) between 1784 and 1790, and resided there a while.

I am unable to state the time of his removing to Leicester, or of his leaving there. He was there in 1797 and 1798; and, as the records indicate, removed to Brookfield in 1802, where he continued to reside till his death, Oct. 31, 1808, at the age of seventy-eight.

The offices which Judge Dorr was called to fill, and the general respect in which he was held, furnish the strongest evidence of his character and abilities as a citizen, and as a man of intelligence, energy, and integrity.

---

* He was one of the commissioners chosen by the people to wait on the Mandamus Councillors for the county of Worcester to demand a surrender of their commissions.

He left several children; among whom were the late Hon. Samuel Dorr, and Joseph H. Dorr, Esq., eminent and respectable merchants in Boston.

Besides the above, WILLIAM WARD of Southborough, in 1731, was appointed a Judge of the Court of Common Pleas. He was a resident here in 1721; was a surveyor, and removed here from Marlborough. He afterwards lived in Southborough; and is spoken of in the "History of Northborough," by the Rev. Mr. Allen.

Of the *Lawyers* who have resided in the town, the first in order of time was CHRISTOPHER J. LAWTON. He took up his residence here in 1735;* and, from the best information I can gain of him, was a native of Suffield in Connecticut.

A writer in the "American Quarterly Register," No. 15, speaks of a person of this name in this manner: "As early as 1720, John Higgins and Christopher J. Lawton were noted lawyers in Connecticut; and, by their knowledge and worthy example, gave early and honorable character to their Provincial bar."

As the subject of this notice could hardly have been old enough in 1720 to have attained such distinguished consideration, and as the name is somewhat peculiar and probably a family one, I am led to suppose that the person above mentioned was the father of the one of whom I am speaking. In fact, I find that he was admitted to the bar of Hampshire County in 1726, and was practising his profession in Suffield in 1733. In 1734, he was appointed a coroner for the county of Hampshire, though still residing in Suffield; and continued to reside there until his removal to Leicester in 1735.

Had he removed from Connecticut into Hampshire County,

---

* Before that time, the town certainly had been made familiar with some departments of the law by the suits and complaints to which they were subjected by their minister; and I find, besides, the following article in a warrant for a town-meeting in 1724: "To see if the town will have *the law-book* belonging to the town filled with those laws that are wanting in the same."

the date of his admission to the bar there would not have been conclusive as to the time of his beginning practice. But this apparent discrepancy between his place of residence and the county in which he did business is readily explained, when it is remembered, that, from 1713 to 1747, a tier of towns now belonging to Connecticut, embracing Suffield, Enfield, Somers, and Woodstock, were regarded as within the jurisdiction of Massachusetts; and it may be recollected, that some of the most important offices in Worcester County, at its organization, were held by persons residing in Woodstock, which was then a part of the county.

In 1735, Mr. Lawton purchased a farm in the westerly part of the town, upon both sides of the Great Road, of Josiah Converse, and Josiah Converse, jun., who both, that year, removed to Brookfield. He afterwards resided upon that farm.

In 1736, '40, and '41, he was a representative in the General Court.

After removing to Leicester, he resumed the practice of his profession; which he continued until 1751, though with what success I have no means of forming a judgment. He conveyed his farm to his son, Dr. Pliny Lawton, in 1753; and I infer, from his discontinuing his profession and thus disposing of his estate, that he had become aged or infirm, and did not long survive, though I am unable to fix the period of his death.

He had a brother James, a saddler, who removed with him into town from Suffield, and lived on what used to be called the Mower Place, on Mount Pleasant.

The son will be noticed hereafter, among the physicians.

The next counsellor and attorney at law in town was the Hon. Nathaniel Paine Denny. He was a son of Col. Samuel Denny, and was born July, 1771. He graduated at Harvard in 1797, and studied his profession with the Hon. Nathaniel Paine of Worcester; whose name he assumed, by Act of the

Legislature, in exchange for that of Thomas, which he had received in his infancy. He was admitted to the bar in 1800, and opened an office at once in Leicester. He married Sally, daughter of Reuben Swan, in November, 1798.

Though never eminent as a lawyer, he practised the profession with good success for about twenty years, when he withdrew from it altogether. For five or six years — from 1813 — he was a partner in business with Bradford Sumner, Esq. He removed to Norwich, Conn., in 1845, where he resided until about 1854; when he removed to Barre, in the county of Worcester, where he died in 1856. While a citizen of Leicester, he shared liberally in the public favor, and was often called to fill places of public and private trust.

From 1803 to 1808, he represented the town in the General Court; and was elected to the same place in 1811, 1825, 1828, 1830, and 1841. In 1823, he was chosen to the Senate, and held the place two years by re-election. From 1815 to 1845, he was a member of the Board of Trust of Leicester Academy; and in 1830 was chosen, and for some time held, the office of President of Leicester Bank.

He was a man of a strong and vigorous mind, great shrewdness and good sense; of agreeable and convivial manners; and a pleasant companion.

He built, and for many years occupied, the house now owned by Mr. Charles W. Warren. He afterwards lived a few years in the house next east of Mr. Joseph Whittemore's; then owned and occupied the house where Mr. Knowles lives, formerly occupied by the Rev. Mr. Moore; but, for some time before his removal from town, he owned and occupied the house on the north side of the Great Road, on Mount Pleasant, formerly owned by Jonathan Earle.

He left three sons and two daughters. One of the former is among the active and enterprising business-men of the place. The other children have removed from the town, —

one son residing in Alabama, one daughter in Indiana, and another in Cambridge.

BRADFORD SUMNER removed to Leicester from Spencer, where he had been a short time in business, in 1813. Soon after his removal here, he married Miss Amelia Bertody of Wrentham, July, 1813. He remained here until October, 1820, when he removed to Boston, where he continued in the practice of his profession until his death; though, for several years, his residence was in Cambridge.

He was born in Taunton, 1783; was graduated at Brown University in 1808; was two years a tutor in that institution; and admitted to the bar in 1812. He died Sept. 25, 1855, aged seventy-three; and, in the published notice of his death, is spoken of as "an honorable and upright lawyer of the Suffolk Bar."

He was a diligent student in his profession, and obtained a very respectable rank at a bar which has always been eminent for men of distinguished ability; was a good manager of causes, a neat speaker, and an effective advocate, without pretending to the higher powers of eloquence. He was a courteous and agreeable gentleman in manners, and an intelligent and pleasant companion in social life; a man of literary taste, and a good degree of literary culture; and for a short time was principal of the Academy, while residing in Leicester.

DAVID BRIGHAM was in practice here a little more than two years; having removed here from New Braintree in 1817. He was a native of Shrewsbury; born Aug. 15, 1786; and was graduated at Harvard in 1810. While fitting for college at the Academy, he taught the Centre School in Leicester one winter, in 1805–6.

He commenced the practice of law in New Braintree. Thence he came to Leicester; and, after remaining here something over two years, removed to Greenfield. While in Leicester, he was employed for a single term as a teacher in the Academy. In Greenfield, he was a partner in business with the Hon. Samuel C. Allen; and there married a daughter of Jerome Ripley, Esq.

After several years' residence in that town, he removed to Shrewsbury, and practised his profession there a while. From thence he removed to Fitchburg, where he was in business for several years. He was then induced to remove to Iowa; where he died, in 1843, at the age of fifty-seven.

Though never successful in his profession to an extent that his talents and industry would have seemed to warrant, he was a good scholar, with literary tastes, amusing and agreeable qualities; and is pleasantly remembered by those who knew him during his brief sojourn here.

Daniel Knight took up his residence here in the autumn of 1821. His health was feeble, and a pulmonary consumption had begun to develop itself in his system before his removal here. He was a native of Worcester; was graduated at Brown University in 1813; studied law with Gov. Lincoln; and commenced business in Spencer in 1817. He was unable to attend to business after a year or two after his removal to Leicester; and died, unmarried, Aug. 30, 1826.

He was an amiable, upright man, of refined taste and respectable attainments, but too early a victim of disease to develop his powers by study or by the practice of his profession.

Emory Washburn was in practice here from Sept. 29, 1821, to March 28, 1828; when he removed to Worcester. He was born here, Feb. 14, 1800; graduated at Williams College in 1817; and was admitted to the bar in March, 1821.

Waldo Flint succeeded Mr. Washburn in the practice of the law, in Leicester, in 1828. He was a native of the town, a son of Dr. Austin Flint; was graduated at Harvard in 1814. He was employed one year as a preceptor in the Academy. He studied his profession principally with the Hon. Lewis

Strong of Northampton; and commenced business in Boston in 1818, where he remained until his removal to Leicester. He was a member of the Senate, and, a part of the time, president of that body. He afterwards held the office of bank-commissioner for one year, when he was induced to accept a lucrative and responsible position in the Eagle Bank in Boston; of which institution he afterwards became and is now president. This led to his removal to Boston in 1839, where he still resides.

In June, 1828, he married Miss Katherine Dean of Charleston, N.H.; and lived in the house now belonging to Mr. John Woodcock, which he erected. He represented the town in the Legislature in the years 1830 and 1833.

SILAS JONES was, for a while, in the practice of the law in town, after Mr. Flint had given it up; but the change in respect to professional business generally in the county, after the year 1820, was such as to be gradually withdrawing itself from the towns bordering upon Worcester to that as a focal point, and to render its practice less and less lucrative. The effect was, that the emoluments of the business in Leicester ceased to be sufficient to support a lawyer there; and, after a brief period, Mr. Jones removed to New York. He was a son of Mr. Phineas Jones of Spencer. He was never graduated at college. He studied his profession chiefly with Mr. Sumner, before mentioned; and had been in business in Connecticut before removing to Leicester.

PHYSICIANS.

The first person who settled in Leicester as a physician was Dr. THOMAS GREEN; whom I have already mentioned in another part of this work.

JOHN HONEYWOOD was here before 1753. He was born in England; but at what time he came to this country, I am unable to determine. He taught a school here three and a half quarters in 1753. In 1761, he was married to Elizabeth, daughter of Judge Steele. He lived about half a mile west of the Meeting-house, in a house formerly Judge Steele's, afterwards that of Edward Rawson, Esq. His reputation has come down to us as having been a learned and skilful physician, and, although somewhat irregular in his habits, as having held a high rank in his profession. His early education and associations (although there was a mystery in regard to the circumstances under which he left England, and it was generally supposed he had been there involved in some political difficulties) led him at first to regard the resistance of the Colonies to the mother-country as rash and unadvised; and these impressions were strengthened by the influence of Judge Steele, his father-in-law. But, it is said, when he saw the spirit with which the people of the Colony rushed to arms at the time of the Lexington alarm, he was convinced that he had been mistaken, and, in language rather strong to be repeated, expressed his belief that they would fight, and, what was more, that they would not be conquered. At any rate, he evinced his devotion to the cause by entering the army as a surgeon; and died while in the service, at Ticonderoga, in November, 1776. He had four children; one of whom was St. John Honeywood, who is hereafter noticed; one (Mary) married Mr. Nathaniel Lyon of Woodstock, formerly of Leicester; and one (Elizabeth) married Samuel Allen, Esq., of Worcester, in 1810, — for many years the worthy and most estimable treasurer of the county. With her the name disappeared, and the family became extinct.

Pliny Lawton was the son of Christopher J. Lawton, Esq., already mentioned; was born in Suffield, Conn., and removed with his father to Leicester in 1735. In 1748–9, he was employed fifteen months in teaching school, though then called "doctor."

In 1753, he married Lucretia, daughter of Jonathan Sargent; and, in the same year, purchased the farm on which his father had lived, in the westerly part of the town. But he afterwards removed to the house which Judge Steele built, at the corner of Flip Lane; where he was residing at the time of his death. This, it is supposed, took place, from the fact that his inventory was returned in February, 1761, about the close of the year 1760. He died of the small-pox; and so great was the terror which that disease created at that period, that he was not allowed to be buried in the general cemetery, but in his own field, on the east side of Flip Lane, about twenty rods from the Great Road, where his head-stone was standing till within a few years, though it has now wholly disappeared. He had two sons, — James and William. He died in the vigor of manhood. His widow married the Rev. Mr. Conklin in 1769. His son William became a physician.

SOLOMON PARSONS was the son of the Rev. David Parsons; and was born April 18, 1726. He taught the school in town, nearly a year, in 1751. In 1752, he married Elizabeth Taylor, who was born in 1734.* At one time, he lived in the house opposite Mrs. Newhall's, half a mile north of the Meeting-house; but, in 1776, was living in what was called the Gage House, on the road leading by Joseph Whittemore's, opposite where the road turns to go to the Jabez Green Place. He was a deacon of the church, as well as a practising physician; though the remoteness of his residence from the centre of the town did not indicate that his practice was an extensive one. He had three children; one of whom (Elizabeth) married Jonathan Hubbard, Esq., of Paxton; at whose house he died, March 20, 1807, at the age of eighty-one. His son Solomon is mentioned in another part of this work. His wife died the same year as Dr. Lawton (1761), and of the same disease; and her husband was obliged, from the terror that

---

* I am led, by the inspection of the rolls, to infer that he was a surgeon in the army in the year 1761.

it created, to bury her by the aid of a single assistant, and in the night-time.

Isaac Green was a son of the Dr. Thomas Green already mentioned. He was born in 1741, and studied medicine with his father. He married Sarah Howe, and built and occupied the house where Charles Barton lives, in the south part of the town. His professional practice was not extensive, nor did he attain any particular eminence as a physician. He was a surgeon in Col. Samuel Denny's regiment in 1777; and marched to Saratoga, and was in the service at the time Burgoyne was taken. He was much respected as a citizen of the town; and died at the age of seventy-one, in November, 1812. He left two daughters, but no son.

Edward Rawson was born in Mendon in 1754, and was the son of Edward Rawson, Esq. He commenced practice in Leicester in 1782. He married Margaret, a daughter of Judge Steele; and was a successor to Dr. Honeywood, who had married her oldest sister. He lived in the house which Judge Steele had occupied, and in which his father afterwards lived, west of the Meeting-house. He had three children, — two daughters and a son (Benjamin Pemberton). His wife died in September, 1784; and he in 1786, at the early age of thirty-two, just as his character, and skill in his profession, were developing themselves.

Absalom Russell was in practice here in 1777 and in 1781; and, in the former year, purchased of Aaron Lopez the house formerly of Peter Silvester, on the east side of Meeting-house Hill, where there is now a cellar. How long he was in business in the town, I have been unable to ascertain. He was a surgeon in Col. Doolittle's twenty-fourth regiment of Massachusetts troops, in the "eight months' service," in 1775. He married Sarah, a daughter of Dr. Frink of Rutland; and his daughter Elizabeth was born here in December, 1778. She married the Hon. Lovell Walker of Templeton. He removed to Paxton from Leicester after

L. Grozelier's Lith Boston.

Austin Flint

1781; but at what precise time, I have not ascertained. His wife died at Rutland, December, 1801. Her husband had died a short time previous. He left two sons, — Salario and Absalom.

Robert Craige studied medicine with Dr. Thomas Green, whose daughter Martha he married in 1753. He was the father of Nathan, mentioned in this work. He lived in the south part of the town. How actively he was engaged in his profession, I am unable to state. For many years before his death, he lived upon his farm.

Jeremiah Larned was a practising physician here a few years. He was born in Oxford; settled here; and died of a consumption, at an early age, in the spring of 1783.

William Lawton, a son of Dr. Pliny, studied medicine, and commenced business here as a contemporary with Dr. Larned. He did not remain long in town. He occasionally visited it afterwards with his family, and was here in 1788 and 1792; but I am unable to state where his residence was after leaving Leicester. He was born April 9, 1759; but I have not ascertained the time of his death.

Thomas Hersey was in practice here in 1794. His wife Esther died that year, at the age of twenty-two; but I am unable to give any further account of him, except that he lived in the west part of the town.*

From the brief notices we have given above of the physicians who have been residents in the town, it will be perceived, that, after the time of Dr. Thomas Green, there were, occasionally at least, three in practice here at the same time. A practical change in this respect was wrought under the administration of Austin Flint. He removed in April, 1783, to Leicester from Westmoreland, N.H., where he began practice, and lived for a short time.

---

* There was a Dr. Thaddeus Brown and wife who moved into town from Paxton in 1785, and lived in a house belonging to Col. Thomas Denny. But how long he remained here, I have not ascertained.

He was the son of Dr. Edward Flint of Shrewsbury, a physician of eminence and extensive practice, who had been a surgeon in Col. Ruggles's regiment in the Canada expedition in 1758, and afterwards in the Massachusetts troops at Cambridge in 1775.

He was born in January, 1760; and was, consequently, twenty-three years old when he came into town. He had, however, gone through some of the experiences peculiar to the young men of that day. At the age of seventeen, he shouldered his musket, and marched to join the Northern Army at Stillwater. He served for the term of three months, and was present at the battle of the 7th October, 1777, and witnessed the surrender of Burgoyne. In that expedition he belonged to Capt. Ingolsby's company, in Col. Job Cushing's regiment. In 1781, at the age of twenty-one, he was surgeon of Col. Luke Drury's regiment; and was in the service, stationed at West Point, from July to December of that year.

In June, 1785, he married Elizabeth, the daughter of Col. William Henshaw; and, the same year, erected the house in which he lived till 1831; when he removed into the house upon the opposite side of the street, in which he died. His former house was taken down, and a new one erected in its place, by Mr. Joshua Clapp. But the spirit he manifested in earlier life never faltered or failed him. Wherever public duty called, he never hesitated to follow. In the unhappy outbreak of the people of the interior of Massachusetts in 1786–7, he was a firm and fearless supporter of the government; and in February, 1787, joined Col. Newhall's regiment at Hadley, in the words of his journal of that date, "to help drive the mobites home;" and was in the memorable night-march, under Gen. Lincoln, from Hadley to Petersham, which resulted in dispersing and crushing out that ill-advised enterprise.

He commanded such confidence in his profession, that, for many years, he was not only without a competitor in his own town, but was often called into the neighboring towns in the way of his business.

As an intelligent, well-informed man, of strong will and indomitable courage, he could hardly fail to exercise a commanding influence in the community around him. Not only was that the case, but he shared very generally the personal confidence of his townsmen: so that, during the active period of his life, he was, almost constantly, in places of public and private trust, — clerk of the town; moderator of its meetings; representative in the Legislature; appraiser, executor, administrator, guardian, and the like; in which, it is believed, his fidelity or honesty was never called in question.

From 1812 to 1817, he was a representative in the General Court. For twenty successive years, he was the moderator of the town-meetings; and for fifteen, I believe, town-clerk. From 1815 to 1831, he was a member of the Board of Trustees of the Academy; and, for some thirty years, an acting magistrate.

In the sick-room he was always a welcome visitant, by his quiet and pleasant cheerfulness and humor. While exerting an acknowledged influence over all classes, no child ever passed him in the street without a kindly recognition; and, in his social intercourse, he was everywhere welcome by his free and affable manners, and his fund of anecdote and good sense.

He survived till the 29th of August, 1850; retaining his mental faculties, and, when not suffering from a most painful disease, his cheerfulness, to the last. His last entry in his journal, a few days before his death was, "Appetite is gone, and I am running down quite fast."

His wife died in July, 1827, aged sixty-three; but the declining years of his life were cheered by filial devotion. His son, Joseph H., an eminent and skilful physician, died four years before him. Dr. Flint was succeeded in his business by his son, —

Edward Flint. He commenced business here in 1811. He was born in 1789, Nov. 7. In 1817, he married Miss Harriet Emerson of Norwich, Vt.; and has a son, John Sydenham, a physician in Roxbury.

The rank and position which Dr. Flint sustains in the community have been the natural result of the many years of honorable and successful pursuit of the profession of his choice to which he devoted himself.

Dr. Jacob Holmes came into town in November, 1834, from Hubbardston; to which town he had removed from Athol. He was born in Worcester, and studied his profession with Dr. Whiton of Winchendon. He practised some years in Westminster before living in Athol. He purchased and occupied a part of the house formerly erected by John Wilder, and afterwards that of Mrs. Washburn; where he died, Dec. 11, 1847, of apoplexy, aged sixty-nine.

Dr. Holmes was a distinguished physician, and was justly esteemed in his profession as well as in private life. He had earned his reputation before he left Athol, where a principal part of the more active period of his life was spent; but he had lived long enough in his newly adopted home, at the time of his death, to win the respect of the people of the town. His daughter, Catherine R., married Rev. Francis V. Pike of Rochester, N.H., in 1839, but died soon after. His daughter Elizabeth died March 29, 1849. His wife alone survives of the family.

Several other physicians have engaged in business here, for longer or shorter periods of time, within a few years; among whom was the now Rev. Isaac R. Worcester of Auburndale. He married Mary S., daughter of the late Col. Henry Sargent; and, after having been in practice here as a physician, studied theology, and gave up his original profession.

Dr. C. W. Whitcomb, after a year or two, removed to Worcester.

Drs. James P. C. Cummings and E. A. Daggett have also

been practising physicians here, but have removed from town. Dr. Cummings went to Fitchburg, where he died in 1858; and Dr. Daggett returned to Maine.

JUSTICES OF THE PEACE.

Those who have held this office previous to 1850, in town, so far as I have been able to ascertain, were —

Name	Year	
William Ward	in 1728.	
Thomas Steele	previous to 1748.	
Daniel Henshaw	1773.	
Edmund Rawson	1775.	
Hezekiah Ward	1782.	
Seth Washburn	1784.	
William Henshaw	1790.	Quorum, 1799.
David Henshaw	1792.	
Joseph Dorr	1798.	
Ebenezer Adams	1802.	
Thomas Denny	1802.	
Nathaniel P. Denny	1804.	Quorum, 1815.
Austin Flint	1811.	
Bradford Sumner	1817.	
Emory Washburn		
Waldo Flint		
Horatio G. Henshaw		
David Brigham		
Daniel Knight		
Joseph A. Denny		
Henry A. Denny		
Cheney Hatch		
Hiram Knight		

Besides the above, I have reason to believe that Judge Minzies, John Lynde, jun., Thomas Denny, sen., Joseph Henshaw, Col. Samuel Denny, and some others, were commissioned as magistrates.

GRADUATES AT COLLEGES.

I give below the names of all who have become citizens of Leicester, and have graduated at any college, so far as they have been ascertained: * —

Rev. David Parsons	H.	1705.
Hon. Thomas Steele	H.	1730.
Rev. David Goddard	H.	1731.
Rev. Joseph Roberts	H.	1741.
Col. Joseph Henshaw	H.	1748.
Rev. Benjamin Conklin	N.J.	1755.
Rev. Benjamin Foster, D.D.	Y.	1771.
Hon. Phinehas Bruce	Y.	1786.
Ebenezer Adams, Esq.	D.	1791.
Rev. Zephaniah S. Moore, D.D.	D.	1793.
Rev. Luther Wilson	W.	1807.
Rev. John Nelson, D.D.	W.	1807.
Bradford Sumner, Esq.	B.	1808.
Rev. Josiah Clark	W.	1809.
David Brigham, Esq.	H.	1810.
John Richardson, Esq.	H.	1813.
Daniel Knight, Esq.	B.	1813.
Rev. Joseph Muenscher, D.D.	B.	1821.
Luther Wright, Esq. †	Y.	
Rev. Amos D. Wheeler. ‡	W.	1828.
Joseph L. Partridge, Esq. §	W.	1828.
Rev. Samuel May	H.	1829.
George F. Bigelow, M.D. ‖	W.	1843.
Rev. Andrew C. Denison	Y.	1847.
Rev. Amos H. Cooledge	A.	

* Several graduates of college have been employed here temporarily as teachers, whose names are omitted, because not coming within the purview of the work.

† Mr. Wright was preceptor of the Academy from 1833 to 1839.

‡ Mr. Wheeler is minister of a society in Topsham, Me.

§ Mr. Partridge was preceptor of the Academy from 1839 to 1845.

‖ Now a physician in Boston; son of Jacob Bigelow, Esq.

The following is, I believe, a complete list of the persons, natives of Leicester, who have graduated at any college; and, of these, Reuben Washburn and John F. Adams left town in early life, and were residing, one in Putney, and the other in Hanover, when they graduated. The same is true of Josiah Clark, whose home was Rutland when he graduated. St. John Honeywood, who is noticed in this work, Yale, 1782. Nathaniel P. Denny, Harvard, 1797. Samuel Swan, H., 1799. Daniel Henshaw, H., 1806. Reuben Washburn, Dartmouth, 1808. Waldo Flint, H., 1814. John F. Adams, D., 1817. Emory Washburn, Williams, 1817. Josiah Clark, son of Rev. Josiah Clark, at one time principal of the Academy (now principal of an academy in East Hampton), Y. Thomas Denny, son of Col. Thomas Denny (now of the city of New York), H., 1823. Winthrop Earle, son of Winthrop, Y., 1826. Andrew Denny, M.D., son of Nathaniel P. (now a physician in Alabama), Amherst, 1831. Joseph Sargent, son of Col. Henry (now in successful practice as a physician in Worcester, M.D. and M.M.S.), H., 1834. Henry Sargent, brother of the above, M.D. and M.M.S. (late a physician in Worcester, deceased), H., 1842. William A. Smith, son of Mr. John A. (now assistant clerk of the courts of Worcester), H., 1843. John S. Flint, M.D., son of Dr. Edward (a physician, now in practice in Roxbury), H., 1843. John N. Murdoch, M.D., son of Deacon Joshua (now a physician in Paxton), W., 1846. Arthur S., a son of Mr. Henry A. Denny, Brown, 1854. John N. Meriam, son of Reuben Meriam, Amherst.

It will be perceived, that, while other professions and callings in life have been represented by these graduates, not one has been a clergyman.

Of the foregoing graduates, a few deserve something more than the notice of their names.

Joseph Henshaw was the son of Daniel Henshaw, the first of the name who settled here. He was born in Boston, 1727;

was graduated at Harvard, 1748; and was engaged in sea-faring life, having the command of a packet-ship plying between Boston and London.

In 1755, he had a singular experience in his nautical life. It being a time of war between England and France, his vessel was taken by a French frigate, and ordered home to France as a prize. He was himself transferred to the frigate which had captured his vessel. The next day she encountered an English frigate, and, after a severe engagement of four hours, was herself taken. The English frigate, with its prize, sailed for London; and, the next day after her arrival, Mr. Henshaw's vessel, which had, like himself, been retaken, arrived at the same port.

In 1772, he erected the house upon Mount Pleasant, afterwards the seat of Major Swan; and removed into it, from Boston, in the spring of 1773. At the commencement of hostilities, he held the office of lieutenant-colonel of the regiment commanded by Col. Artemas Ward, and marched with it at the Lexington alarm to Cambridge. He remained there on duty about a month and a half, and applied for a similar rank in the new regiment of eight-months' men, under the same colonel. The Provincial Congress, however, preferred the claims of Jonathan Ward of Southborough; who was commissioned accordingly, and Col. Henshaw returned home. Col. Joseph, it will be recollected, was an older brother of Col. William Henshaw, who commanded a regiment of minute-men who marched to Cambridge on the same occasion, and became adjutant-general of the troops. About the close of the war, Col. Joseph Henshaw removed to Shrewsbury; where he resided until his death in 1794. His wife was the daughter of Joshua Henshaw, Esq., who is noticed in this work.

The subject of this notice was one of the little band of leading and influential men who infused into the counsels and measures of this town so much spirit and harmony. His family and personal connections with the leading men in Boston made him early apprised of the measures which originated there; and some of the most spirited resolutions and instructions which were adopted by the town, were, as is believed, from his pen.

His brothers, and his uncle Joshua Henshaw, are noticed in other parts of this work. He was a delegate from Leicester to the first and second Provincial Congresses, in October, 1774, and February, 1775; and a leading member of those bodies.

EBENEZER ADAMS, Esq. was born in New Ipswich, N.H., in 1765; was graduated at Dartmouth in 1791; never studied any profession, but engaged in teaching. He was preceptor of the Academy from May, 1791, to July, 1806; when he removed to Portland. In 1809, he became a professor in Dartmouth College, and resigned in 1833. After that, he lived in retirement until his death in August, 1841.

While in Leicester, he exerted a leading influence in the town, and enjoyed the confidence and esteem of the people to a marked degree. He was appointed a justice of the peace, and was the first postmaster of the place.

Through life, Professor Adams sustained a high reputation as a teacher, as a professor, and as a gentleman of stanch principle, of fearless regard for duty, of great dignity and courtesy of manner; one remembered with pleasure and respect by all who knew him.

Mr. Adams married Alice, daughter of Dr. John Frink of Rutland; who died in June, 1805, aged thirty-seven. She left five children; only one of whom, John F., survives; the others having all fallen victims to consumption before the period of middle life. Mr. Adams owned and lived upon the place now belonging to the Rev. Mr. May.

Rev. JOSIAH CLARK was born in Northampton in 1785; was graduated at Williams College in 1809; succeeded Mr. Wilson as principal preceptor of the Academy in 1812, having been English preceptor the three previous years. In 1818, he was settled as minister of the Congregational Church and Society in Rutland; and remained their pastor till his death in 1845.

He was faithful in all his trusts; an excellent citizen, a devoted minister, and a most estimable man. His principal connection with the town was as a teacher; and in that capacity he displayed eminent qualities, winning the love and respect of his pupils, and exerting a salutary influence in training their intellects and cultivating and improving their moral powers.

Rev. Luther Wilson was born in New Braintree; graduated at Williams College in 1807; the same year, was English preceptor of the Academy; and, from 1809 to 1812, was its principal preceptor. He was settled as a minister in Brooklyn, Conn.; resigned his place after a few years; and now resides upon his farm in dignified retirement in Petersham.

He married Sally, daughter of Abijah Bigelow, Esq., of Barre, — a sister of Mrs. Dr. Nelson of Leicester. He owned and lived upon the place now owned by the Rev. Mr. May.

John Richardson was a native of Woburn; was graduated at Harvard in 1813; was principal of the Academy from February, 1819, to August, 1833; when he resigned, and removed to North Andover, where he resided till his death in 1841.

During most of his residence in town, he owned and occupied the place where Mr. Edward Knowles lives, formerly owned by Dr. Moore.

St. John Honeywood, the son of Dr. John Honeywood, was born in Leicester, Feb. 7, 1763. By the death of his father and mother at an early period of his life, he was left, not only an orphan, but penniless, and dependent on the kindness of his friends. By their aid he was enabled to fit himself for college; and entered Yale, where he soon won the warm friendship of its president, Dr. Stiles, who received him into his own family.

He graduated with high honor and reputation for scholarship, and went to Schenectady to engage as a teacher of an academy. He remained there two years, and then went to Albany, where he commenced the study of the law with Peter W. Yates, Esq., and remained with him two years. After his admission to the bar, he established himself in Salem, in Washington County; and continued in the practice, with an honorable reputation, for ten years.

Like most young men of promise in New York, he was seduced into the arena of politics, which interfered somewhat with his success at the bar. He belonged to the old Federal party, and was one of the electors for President when John Adams was elected to that office.

He died at the early age of thirty-four, Sept. 1, 1798. He married a daughter of Col. Mosely of Westfield, Mass.; but left no children.

This brief outline gives but little idea of the characteristic traits of Mr. Honeywood's mind or genius. I say, genius; for he gave early evidence of having been endowed by nature with the eye of a painter and the sensibility of a poet: and although he did not cultivate these in maturer life, except as matters of pleasant relaxation, his friends were aware that he might have attained to eminence in either department of art.

Among the anecdotes that used to be told of his early days, he was taken to church one Sunday, and, while there, was greatly attracted by the appearance of an old man with a very peculiar physiognomy, who sat in the next pew. Instead of listening to the sermon, his aunt was scandalized to detect him in trying to twist his own face into the expression of the old man near him. On reaching home, she accordingly began to read him a lecture on decorum of conduct, which he had little comprehension of having violated; and, as soon as it was over, he went into another room, and in a few minutes returned with a pen-and-ink sketch, which was so exact a likeness of the face which had attracted him, that his fault was forgotten in the delight which the picture gave his foster-mother. His taste led him to caricature as a painter; and, though without any instruction in his art, he produced some historical pieces of merit.

As a poet, he was the author of many happy and sprightly effusions; and gave such evidence of talent as to win a place among the poets of America. A volume of his poems was collected and published, in 1801, from manuscripts left by him; and contains several pieces which are still read with pleasure.

He had from his childhood many of the eccentricities which are supposed to mark the possession of genius; but he had a warm heart, a delicate and refined sensibility, ready wit and humor, and was much regarded as a companion and friend.

Reuben Washburn, though born in this town, Dec. 30, 1781, early removed with his father, Asa Washburn, to Putney in Vermont. He has for many years lived in Ludlow in Vermont, where he has held a good rank as a lawyer; and, at one time, was a Judge of the County Court in that State. Age has done little to impair the vigor of his mind, or the accuracy of his judgment or memory.

Phinehas Bruce was the son of George Bruce, and born in 1762. He was graduated at Yale in 1786. He studied law, and married a sister of Hon. James Savage of Boston. He established himself in Machias, then a new region; and soon rose to a good degree of eminence in his profession. He was a member both of the House of Representatives and the Senate of Massachusetts, and took a leading position and rank there.

He was a man of fine address and most agreeable qualities, and commanded the public confidence, as well as the personal esteem of his friends. In 1803, he was elected to Congress, but declined the election; and, upon a second election, was again chosen to the same Congress, but never took his seat in that body. He was stricken down by insanity, brought on by ill-health and over-exertion in his profession; from which he never sufficiently recovered to resume his profession. He died Oct. 4, 1809, at the age of forty-seven.

DANIEL HENSHAW was a son of William Henshaw, and was born May 9, 1782; was graduated at Harvard, 1806; and read law in part with Nathaniel P. Denny, and in part with Judge Paine. He was in business twenty-one years in Winchendon. In 1830, he resided in Worcester; and afterwards, for several years, in Lynn, where he had the management of a public newspaper, — the "Lynn Record." On becoming an editor, he gave up his professional business, and continued for fourteen years in the arduous and responsible place of leading editor of a paper; and, after that period, often contributed valuable and interesting articles, chiefly of a biographical or historical character, to sundry newspapers, which were read with interest.*

A distaste for public life deterred him from suffering himself to become a candidate for office; but, with the command of the pen of an easy and vigorous writer, he made his influence felt to an extent to which few mere office-holders could ever attain. After his connection with the paper in Lynn had terminated, he removed to Boston, where he now lives. Delicacy, therefore, forbids me to speak of him beyond the few public acts of his life. He married Miss Deborah Starkweather of Worthington, who died in 1851, leaving one son and two daughters.

SAMUEL SWAN, son of Reuben Swan, was born May 6, 1778; was graduated at Harvard in 1799; studied law with Nathaniel P. Denny, Esq., and Judge Paine; and settled in Hubbardston, where he still resides. He married Miss Clara Hale in November, 1812; and a son of his is now a practising lawyer in Worcester, another a merchant in Boston.

JOHN F. ADAMS was a son of Professor Adams, before

---

* I am happy to acknowledge my indebtedness to him for materials for the present work.

named. He was born in 1800; was graduated at Dartmouth in 1817; was employed for a year as assistant preceptor; studied law, and practised the profession several years in Mobile. Resides in Washington, D.C.

WINTHROP EARLE was the son of Winthrop Earle; was born in 1807. He was graduated at Yale in 1826; but died of consumption, Nov. 9, 1828, aged twenty-one. He was a young man of good promise and fine moral qualities; and his loss was much lamented.

AUSTIN HERSEY, son of Calvin, entered Dartmouth College in 1813, and remained till near the close of the four years, but did not graduate. He died in Philadelphia, Aug. 30, 1825, aged twenty-eight.

SAMUEL D. GREEN, Esq., son of Samuel Green, entered, and was a member of, Brown University till his senior year; when he left college, and entered upon active life. He now resides in Cambridge, Mass.

Among the persons born in Leicester, who have become sufficiently distinguished to be proper subjects of notice in a work like this, was —

HON. WILLIAM UPHAM. — He was the son of Samuel Upham, who lived where the late Deacon Rockwood died, in the south part of the town. At a considerably later period, he removed with his family to Vermont; and died in 1848, aged eighty-seven. His son William had the misfortune to have his right hand crushed in a cider-mill while a child; and was subjected, from the necessity of the case, to the rather original surgical process of having the shattered parts of the bones trimmed off with a hatchet in the hands of the operator. It disabled him from pursuing a life of labor, for which he had been intended; and he turned his attention to obtaining such an education as was within his means. He was a student at the Academy in town during the years 1799 and 1800. After his removal to Vermont, he studied law with the late Judge Prentiss, and became his partner in business. He resided in

Montpelier. He attained to a high rank in his profession, and was a very successful jury advocate. He possessed a great share of wit and humor, and occasionally indulged in sarcasm with telling effect. He was a social, pleasant, and agreeable companion; and had acquired such a degree of popular favor and confidence, that, upon his former partner being appointed District Judge of the United-States Court, Mr. Upham became his successor in the United-States Senate.

After serving out the balance of the term for which he was chosen, he was re-elected; and died, while a member of the Senate, at Washington, July, 1853.

Mr. Upham did not speak often in the Senate; but, whenever he did, it was with much force, directness, and effect. He was stanch and reliable in his political opinions, and commanded attention as an independent thinker, and an outspoken representative of New-England sentiment. He never lost his interest in the place of his nativity, and visited it often enough to keep alive his early memories and associations connected with its localities.

Hon. DAVID HENSHAW was a son of David Henshaw, Esq.; and was born April 2, 1791. His early education was confined to the common school and the academy. At a suitable age, he went to Boston as a clerk or apprentice with Messrs. Dix and Brinley, druggists; and afterwards commenced and carried on business on his own account in that city, for many years, with great energy, enterprise, and success. He was, at the same time, diligently engaged in cultivating his mind by study, and by application to books.

He was a vigorous writer, and wrote much for the public papers, and several more extended articles which he published in pamphlet form, and which gained him much credit at the time.

In 1826, he was elected a member of the Senate from Suffolk; which was the higher mark of confidence, inasmuch as he was always a most decided advocate of political sentiments and opinions adverse to what had been the prevailing sentiments of the people of that county.

In 1829, he was appointed collector of the port of Boston by President Jackson, and held the office nine years to the acceptance of all who had occasion to do business with that department. He had great practical experience, with high executive qualities, and brought these successfully to bear upon the orderly and systematic management of the affairs of the office.

President Tyler appointed him to the department of the Navy, in his cabinet; and he had the charge of it long enough to evince eminent talents and qualifications for the place. From the relation, however, in which President Tyler stood to the political parties in the Senate, that body failed to confirm Mr. Henshaw's appointment; and he retired to private life.

Here, however, he was by no means inactive. He took a leading part in promoting in Massachusetts the railroad interest, then in its infancy. He turned his attention to agriculture, and the improvement of his farm, which had been his father's before him. Though unmarried, he surrounded himself with a large circle of family friends; to whom, as well as to all who visited him, he was kind, liberal, and hospitable.

He represented the town in the General Court in the year 1840; made the Annual Address before the Worcester Agricultural Society in 1847; and, though much of the time struggling with hereditary disease of a painful and prostrating character, he continued to exert an active influence in the community till his death, in 1852, at the age of sixty-one. He was a self-made man, and achieved for himself wealth, political influence and power, and an unquestioned reputation for mental vigor, and energy of purpose, of no ordinary character.

Robert Southgate was a son of Steward, and a grandson

of Richard who came into town from England in March, 1718. He was born Oct. 26, 1741; and studied medicine. In 1771, he went to Scarborough, Me., travelling on horseback; and settled there in the practice of his profession, which he pursued, for several years, with high reputation and much success. He became an extensive landowner, and acquired a handsome estate; and gradually withdrew from the practice of his profession.

He married, in 1773, Mary King (then in her sixteenth year), the daughter of Richard King of Scarborough, sister of Rufus King (so distinguished afterwards in public life), and half-sister of William and Cyrus King, — the one a governor, and senator in Congress; and the other a representative in Congress from Maine.

About the close of the last century, he was appointed a Judge of the Court of Common Pleas; and filled the office, for several years, with great acceptance to the bar as well as the public. He died Nov. 2, 1833, aged ninety-two. He had been the father of twelve children; one of whom (Horatio) was the father of Bishop Southgate, recently of Boston.

Ralph Earle deserves to be remembered as a man of fine genius as a painter; and, among other marks of the estimate in which he was held, was his election as a member of the Royal Academy of London. He was the son of Ralph, and a grandson of the first Ralf Earle who settled in Leicester, the ancestor of most of the families which have borne that name in the town.

He was born May 11, 1751. I have been unable to trace the progress of Mr. Earle in the art which he cultivated. In Dunlap's work upon the "History of the Arts of Design in the United States" is a notice of Mr. Earle as an artist, in which he is spoken of as having painted portraits in Connecticut in 1775; and among his works were "two full-lengths" of Dr. Dwight, painted in 1777. The writer represents Mr. Earle as having marched to Cambridge, in 1775, as one of the

"Governor's guard" of militia: and, soon after, to Lexington. The military part of his history is obviously apocryphal in many respects, if not in all; as the men who marched to Cambridge were any thing but the *Governor's guards*, and the marching to Lexington is generally supposed to have preceded that of the troops to Cambridge.

But, in respect to his history as a painter, the writer is much more accurate, and furnishes some curious facts of much interest. Mr. Earle executed, from sketches taken upon the spot, four historical paintings; believed to be the first historical paintings ever executed by an American artist: one, the battle of Lexington; one, a view of Concord, with the royal troops destroying the stores; one, the battle of the North Bridge in Concord; and one, the south part of Lexington, where the first detachment was joined by Lord Percy. These paintings were engraved, and published by Amos Doolittle of New Haven, Conn., who was with Earle at Cambridge, and is said to have been a soldier there with Earle, under Col. Arnold.

It is certainly no slight distinction to have been the first American historical painter, even if his works at the present day should be found to be of inferior intrinsic merit as works of art. How this is, I am unable to state: but, soon after the peace, we find him in England, pursuing his art under the instruction of his countryman, Sir Benjamin West; and such was his success, that he was elected, as has been stated, a member of the Royal Academy in London.

He returned to this country in 1786, and continued to pursue the business of a painter in different parts of Massachusetts, New York, and Connecticut. He left several works that gained him much credit; and among them was a large one, the "Falls of Niagara," which was much admired. He painted for the late Col. Thomas Denny a landscape of much merit, and great fidelity of representation, embracing the beautiful and picturesque view that spreads out towards the east from the mansion-house on the old Denny Farm, so called; which is still preserved, and in good condition. His productions were chiefly in the line of portraits, many of which might have formerly been found in Northampton and Springfield. Among his last works of this kind were portraits of Governor Strong and family.

He died in Bolton in Conn., in October, 1801. His habits, unfortunately, stood between him and that eminence in his profession which genius had originally placed within his reach. I quote, from the writer mentioned, his professional estimate of his qualities as a painter: "He had considerable merit; a breadth of light and shadow; facility of handling, and truth in likeness. But he prevented improvement, and destroyed himself by habitual intemperance."

JAMES EARLE, brother of Ralph, possessed much of the genius and talent of the latter; and is alluded to by the same author (Dunlap), who is utterly confused and mistaken in respect to him. At one time, he represents him as an English gentleman who painted portraits in Charleston, S.C., about 1792; that Sully saw him when a boy, and, when he went to London, saw his widow, and gave her an account of his death by yellow fever. In a subsequent statement he confounds him with Ralph, and concludes there was but one of the name. The only respect in which he was correct was in his having been engaged as a portrait-painter; and having died in Charleston, S.C., of yellow fever. This took place in September, 1796; and, in a notice of his death, he is spoken of as "an eminent painter."

They both left families; but it was Ralph who married in London, while pursuing his studies there. Mr. Dunlap's work contains an extended notice of his son Augustus, — an eccentric artist of great promise, who was a friend and associate with Leslie and Morse, who were fellow-students with him. Ralph left his wife and children in London when he returned to this country.

CHAPTER VII.

NUMBERS AND NAMES OF SOLDIERS IN THE FRENCH AND REVOLUTIONARY WARS. — COMMITTEES OF CORRESPONDENCE. — NAMES OF EARLY SETTLERS, &c. — PERSONAL NOTICES OF OFFICERS, SOLDIERS, PROMINENT CITIZENS, AND OTHERS.

I HAVE made considerable effort to learn the names of those who have been citizens of Leicester, and were at any time in the service of the Crown, the Province, the Provincial or the Continental Congress; but my researches have been far from satisfactory. I give below the names of such as I have been able to ascertain, with such an account of them as the muster-rolls and other sources of information afforded me.

In 1722, a part of a company were stationed in this town to guard its inhabitants from the Indians; and among them were Thomas Newhall, one of the earliest settlers in the town; and William Ward, who then belonged to Marlborough, but afterwards removed to Leicester. They were sergeants in the company. Ward was much employed afterwards as a surveyor, and is noticed elsewhere in this work.

In 1724, a part of Capt. Chandler's company were stationed in Leicester to guard the inhabitants; twenty-nine men, with out commissioned officers.

The French and Indian war of 1744–8 called into requisition great numbers of Provincial troops, especially the expedition against Louisburg in 1745. From the general interest which that expedition excited, I have reason to believe that a considerable number of men were engaged in it belonging to Leicester. I have ascertained the names only of a few.

Capt. John Brown commanded a company, and was at the surrender of Louisburg.

James Smith* was also a soldier there, and died in the service.

Samuel Call† was, I believe, a soldier in the same; but I have been unable to find the rolls of that expedition. They may have been sent to England as vouchers for the claims for compensation made by the colonists for expenses incurred in its prosecution.

In September, 1746, an order from Col. John Chandler, addressed to Capt. Nathaniel Green, "in his Majesty's service in Leicester,"‡ required a draught from his company of twenty-five men without delay, with ammunition and fourteen days' provision, to march to Boston to repel an anticipated French invasion. The order was executed; but I am not in possession of the names of the persons draughted.

In December, 1747, a detachment of troops was stationed at Colraine to guard against the Indians — among whom was Nathan Whittemore of Leicester — from December to the following April.

In the year 1747–8, there was a detachment of troops stationed at Fort Massachusetts, near what is now Williamstown, to guard that pass against the incursions of the western Indians upon the frontier settlements. Among them was James Smith,§ Moses Peter Attair,‖ and James Richardson.¶

Besides these, several from this town had enlisted, the same year, into what was called "the Canada expedition," whose names I have not ascertained.

Another French war broke out in 1754, and an expedition

---

* He lived upon the farm recently owned by Robert Watson.

† Removed from Malden, and lived in the south part of the town. He married a daughter of Capt. Nathaniel Green.

‡ *Vide* copy of the order in *the genealogy* of Nathaniel Green.

§ Son of James who died at Louisburg.

‖ Called servant of John White.

¶ Son of Thomas Richardson.

under Col. Winslow was sent to the eastern frontier to overawe the Indians. In this, Nicholas M'Daniel, Benjamin Merritt, and Benjamin Edmunds, were soldiers from Leicester.

Silas Bowker was in the expedition against Crown Point, in 1755, under Lord Amherst.

In the spring of 1756, measures were taken to organize a powerful expedition to march to Crown Point. Eleven men were enlisted from Leicester. There was found to be a deficiency in the requisite number, and four more were enlisted from the town. Their names were Daniel Watson, Perley Brown, Elias Bowker,* Francis Stone, John Presson,† Ebenezer Washburn,‡ Nathaniel Sargent, John Cole,§ Samuel Wicker, Josiah Robinson, James Bacon, Luke Converse, Stephen Bell, James Graton, and John Bowker.

Knight Sprague, then of Hingham, afterwards of Leicester, was in the same expedition, as is stated in another part of this work.

In July, 1756, the following were soldiers in Col. Ruggles's regiment at Fort Edward: Thomas Handy,‖ sergeant; Francis Stone, who seems to have re-enlisted; John Ryan,¶ John Cole, re-enlisted; Samuel Pike, Joseph Merritt,** Thomas Bridge.

In August, 1756, at Fort William Henry, in Col. Ruggles's regiment, the following belonged to the army:—

Samuel Call, Alexander Calhoon, Joshua Smith, Elijah Wilson, Daniel Jones; Samuel Wicker, sergeant; Perley Brown, corporal; James Lamb,†† then of Charlton; Caleb Barton, then of Oxford, afterwards of Leicester. Nathaniel Harrod

---

* Married a sister of Col. Washburn's wife.

† Was eighteen; born in Framingham; re-enlisted; was returned "killed or taken."

‡ Brother of Col. Seth Washburn.

§ Born in Concord; called laborer.

‖ Born in Ireland; called trader.

¶ Born in Ireland; laborer.

** Born in Scituate; cordwainer; twenty-seven years old.

†† Twenty-three years old; born in Leicester.

joined the army in September. The term of enlistment of these men continued till Dec. 21, 1756. David Smith, Silas Waite, and Thomas Gleason, were impressed with Harrod, and joined the army with him.

Nathan Parsons, son of Rev. David, then of Cold Spring, was a sergeant at the surrender of Fort William Henry, Aug. 9, 1757.

In the same year, Samuel Call, sergeant; John Brown, do.; William Green, ensign; Jabez Swan, corporal; Elijah Dewing, Israel Green, Michael Nagels, Nathaniel Parmenter, Darby Ryan, James Trumbull, Ephraim Taylor, James Calhoon, privates, — were in the service from Leicester, in Capt. Joseph Cheny's company.

The number of officers and soldiers from the town, in the last great struggle with the French which resulted in the capture of Quebec in 1759 and the conquest of Canada the following year, considerably exceeded any former levies for the army. Among them were Samuel Call, James Brindley, Silas Bellows, John Call, John Dean, Benjamin Ellis, Samuel Garfield, Nathaniel Harwood, James Hill, Jason Livermore, John Poore, Joseph Ryan, Edward Saunderson, James Stebbins, Joseph Shaw, Thomas Sargeant, Nehemiah Scott, Jonathan Stoddard, Oliver Segur, Nathaniel Thompson, John White, and John Watson. Thomas Steele was surgeon's mate in Brig.-Gen. Ruggles's regiment in 1759. In 1760, James Taylor (then of Greenwich, born in Leicester), Peter Harwood, Eliphalet Harwood, John Earle, Ezekiel Earle, Oliver Newton, and Timothy Howe.

Joel Cutler, William Dunton (servant of Solomon Parsons, who was probably surgeon of the regiment to which they belonged), and Ebenezer Saunderson, were in the service; the last from April, the two first from July to December, 1761.

In 1762, from July 5 to Nov. 14, Timothy How, and, from March to November, Ebenezer Smith and Benjamin Ellis, were soldiers in an expedition which was sent into the country west of North River.

William Henshaw was a lieutenant in Capt. Jeduthan Baldwin's company of the Provincial troops, from March to November of 1759, at Ticonderoga and Crown Point, as is more fully stated in another part of this work.

Jacob Washburn, who came from Bridgewater, and lived in the north part of the town of Leicester, was a lieutenant in the French War. He was son of Gideon, and cousin of Seth.

SOLDIERS ENGAGED IN SERVICE IN THE WAR OF THE REVOLUTION.

It is not supposed that the list which I here present is by any means complete. Such as are here recorded have been chiefly ascertained by a recurrence to the Revolutionary rolls.

I find there were twenty-seven draughts for soldiers, towards which Leicester supplied two hundred and forty-seven men, between May, 1775, and June 28, 1780. Subsequent draughts were made, which I suppose were principally answered by the classes into which the town was divided; one of which, July 19, 1781, I have found for six men.

This does not embrace the company of minute-men under Capt. Washburn; nor the standing company, under Capt. Thomas Newhall, who marched to Cambridge on the 19th of April, 1775; nor the draughts made by resolves of Jan. 26, 1777, for six months; June 5, 1780, for three years; Dec. 2, 1780, for three and five months; June, 1781, for three years; or March, 1782,—the numbers of which I have not ascertained.

The minute-men belonged to a regiment of which William Henshaw was colonel; Samuel Denny, lieutenant-colonel; and John Southgate, adjutant; all of whom marched to Cambridge on the 19th of April. Col. Henshaw's pay was made up for thirty-four and a half days; Lieut.-Col. Denny's, ten and a half days; and Southgate's, nineteen and a half days.

Col. Artemas Ward commanded a regiment of men; and Joseph Henshaw, then of Leicester, was his lieutenant-colonel, and marched to Cambridge on the 19th of April, and remained one month and ten days in the service there.

For some reason not explained, but much to his dissatisfaction, in organizing the "eight months' men" into regiments, Jonathan Ward of Marlborough was appointed, in Col. Artemas Ward's regiment, lieutenant-colonel in place of Lieut.-Col. Henshaw. The Provincial Congress decided the question on the 25th of May against Col. Henshaw; but Col. Artemas Ward had been commissioned on the 19th May. This probably terminated the period of Col. Joseph Henshaw's service.

The members of the Leicester Company of Minute-men, who marched on the 19th April, 1775, were —

Seth Washburn, captain.
William Watson, 1st lieutenant.
Nathaniel Harrod, 2d lieutenant.
Samuel Watson, sergeant.
Henry King, „
Ebenezer Kent, corporal.
Jonathan Newhall, „
Benjamin Converse.
Abner Dunbar.
Thomas Parker.
Ambrose Searle.
Jesse Green.
Jonas Southgate.
Samuel Richardson.
Jesse Smith.
Peleg Hersey.
John Brown.
William Crossman.
Hezekiah Saunderson.
Daniel Hubbard.
Abijah Stowers.
Adam Gilmore.
David Newhall.
Daniel Denny.
Ebenezer Saunderson.
Elijah Comins.
Elias Green.
John Weaver.
Isaac Livermore.
Jonathan Sargent.
Job Stetson.
James Greaton.
Morris Higgins.
Nathan Craige.
Phinehas Green.
Perley Brown.
Stephen Taylor.
Samuel Sargent.
William Brown.
David Sargent.
Jason Livermore.
James Tucker.
Jonathan Jackson.

Seth Washburn, then of Wilbraham, a son of Capt. Seth, was among those who marched to Cambridge on this alarm.

The members of the Standing Company, who marched the same day, were —

Thomas Newhall, captain.
Benj. Richardson, 1st lieutenant.
Ebenezer Upham, 2d lieutenant.
Loring Lincoln, sergeant.
Isaac Choate, „
James Whittemore, „
Phinehas Newhall, corporal.
Phinehas Sargent, „
Peter Silvester, jun.
Jonathan Johnson.
Nathaniel Richardson.
Moses Hovey.
Micah Livermore.
Elijah Howe.
Jonathan Sargent, jun.
Elisha Ward.
Benjamin Leviston.
Thomas Snow.
Thomas Green.
Reuben Lamb.
Phinehas Barton.
Caleb Nichols.
David Carpenter.
Reuben Earle.
Wait Upham.
Richard Bond.
Reuben Swan.
Solon Green.
Isaac Livermore, jun.
Daniel Sargeant.
Elijah Cumings.
Israel Saunderson.
John Weaver.
Daniel Newhall.

On the 23d April, 1775, the Congress resolved to raise thirteen thousand six hundred men immediately, from Massachussetts, for its defence. Enlisting papers were prepared on the 24th, and printed; and the enlistments began the same day. Capt. Washburn signed, on the 24th April, the one for raising the company which he was to command. The term of service was to be eight months; the number of men in each company to be fifty-nine, including three officers. The names of the Leicester men who enlisted into this company were as follow: —

Seth Washburn, captain.
Joseph Livermore of Spencer, 1st lieutenant.
Loring Lincoln, 2d lieutenant.
Peleg Hersey, sergeant.
John Brown, „
Anthony Sprague, „
William Crossman, sergeant.
Hezekiah Saunderson, corporal.
Daniel Hubbard, „
Elijah Southgate, then of Spencer, corporal.*
Elijah Torrey, fifer.
Joseph Washburn.

* Southgate was of the Leicester Family, and lived just over the Leicester line in Spencer.

Abijah Stowers.	James Richardson.
Adam Gilmore.	William Brown.
Daniel Newhall.	James Tucker.
Daniel Denny.	Phinehas Green.
Ebenezer Saunderson.	Phinehas Green, jun.
Elijah Converse.	Perley Brown.
Elias Green.	Stephen Taylor.
Israel Saunderson.	Samuel Sargent.
John Weaver.	Abner Livermore.
Isaac Livermore, jun.	Thomas Green.
Jonathan Sargent.	John Green.
John Stetson.	Daniel Sargent.
James Greaton.	Jason Livermore.
Morris Higgins.	Jonathan Jackson.
Nathan Craige.	Matthew Jackson.

The balance of the company were enlisted from other towns, — seven from Spencer, three from Paxton, four from Oakham, two from Holden, two from Weston, one from Worcester, one from Brookfield, and one from Gloucester.

The promptness with which the Leicester men enlisted, and the proportion of the two companies then at Cambridge, if it had been followed by the troops from the other towns, would have rendered the new general order of the 27th April unnecessary. This called upon all who were not enlisted, and intended to remain, to enlist at once; with an assurance that they should be officered by those appointed by the Committee of Safety until the particular regiments and companies were completed.

The field-officers were charged to see that *one-fifth* part of the training soldiers of each town from which the companies came, should be immediately enlisted out of the troops assembled in camp; and, if a sufficient number could not be enlisted agreeable to an equal quota, the deficiency of such quota should be immediately forwarded by a recruiting officer to each town; and, in the mean time, a sufficient number of troops present should be retained until the *quota* of the troops for this Province should be raised.

By the 8th May, there had been thirteen regiments officered. One of them was called "Gen. Ward's;" and, to that, Capt. Washburn's company was attached.

The proportion of one-fifth of the troops in the trainband of the town would not have been over twenty; whereas twenty had enlisted before the date of the second order: ten enlisted on its date, and seven before the middle of May, besides six who enlisted in other companies; making forty-seven in all.

The above order explains why numbers of the Minute Company and that of Capt. Newhall were retained in service, as many of them were, after the companies were actually disorganized by the enlistments for the eight months' service.

Of the men who were thus enlisted from Leicester, all except Thomas and John Green, who did not enlist until July, and William Brown, James Tucker, and Daniel Sargent, who had left the company, were present at and took part in the battle of Bunker Hill, on the 17th June, under Capt. Washburn.

William Brown enlisted into Capt. Burbank's company of artillery, in Col. Gridley's regiment, as corporal, on the 15th June, and was in the battle. Perley Brown enlisted in the artillery at the same time, but was with this company in the battle. Nine of the above were supplied by the Province; all the others by themselves.

On the 5th September, orders were issued for organizing a detachment of officers and men to march to Canada, under Gen. Arnold, by the way of the Kennebec River. Among the volunteers from Leicester in that enterprise were Morris Higgins from Capt. Washburn's company, and Thomas Whittemore from Capt. Williams's company, in Gen. Heath's regiment.

Besides the above, I find the following names of Leicester men in the "eight-months'" service: Elijah Green, who died in the service, at Roxbury, December, 1775, aged sixteen; Andrew Brown, in Col. Larned's regiment; Reuben Earle, in the same company; Richard Lamb, in Capt. Larned's company; Nicholas M'Daniel and Waite Upham, — the two last in the artillery, Foster's company.

Dr. Absalom Russell was in the same service as a surgeon's mate, in Col. Doolittle's regiment. He joined the regiment on the 21st July. Steward Southgate was a second sergeant in the same service. The term of this service expired in December, when a new enlistment of men took place for two months; and sixteen men from Leicester joined a company, under the command of Capt. Seth Washburn, which was stationed at Dorchester. The major being absent, Capt. Washburn performed the duty of that officer by reason of his seniority in office.

I am unable to give the names of these sixteen, as I am of many of the twenty-six subsequent draughts. A second enlistment for two months, after the expiration of the first, was made; and Capt. Washburn still continued in command of a company.

In January, 1777, a company was raised, of which Adam Martin was captain;* William Crossman, lieutenant;† and Joseph Washburn, ensign, — the two latter officers from Leicester. The company was attached to Col. Bigelow's fifteenth regiment, in the Massachusetts line of Continental troops; and were enlisted for three years, or during the war.

Among the members of the company from Leicester were —

Asa Harrington, February, 1777. During the war.

James Tucker, April, 1777. During the war. Was sergeant; served forty-four months. He was under Col. Rufus Putnam at West Point in 1781, together with Harrington.

John Hubbard, March, 1777. During the war. Was a black man.

---

* Martin belonged to Sturbridge.

† Crossman was soon cashiered, and Washburn promoted to lieutenant. Crossman had been a sergeant in Capt. Washburn's company, and was wounded at Bunker Hill. He lived a little south of where Mrs. Hobart lives.

Jethro Jones, April, 1777. During the war. Was a black man, thirty-three years old.

Solomon Parsons. March, 1777. During the war. Was wounded at Monmouth, and is noticed hereafter.

Zephaniah Tucker, April, 1777.

Among the names of those to whom bounties were paid by the town, on their enlistment into the Continental service for three years, I find, besides the above, —

William Tolly. Enlisted January, 1777.

Elijah Cummings. Enlisted January, 1777. Was in Capt. Smith's company, thirteenth Massachusetts regiment.

Waite Upham. Enlisted January, 1777.

Asa Waite. Enlisted January, 1777. Was in the service four years; a part of the time, in Capt. Brown's company, whose name was Benjamin. He was sergeant in the sixth light infantry.

Otho Silvester. Enlisted February, 1777. Was in Brown's company for during the war. Died May 20, 1778.

Israel Saunderson. Enlisted February, 1777. Was in Capt. Brown's company, corporal. Served four years.

Asa Souther. Enlisted February, 1777. Was in Brown's company. Served forty-seven months; corporal, six months.

Benjamin Chamberlin. Enlisted March, 1777. Was in Capt. Brown's company, a sergeant, eighth regiment, Col. Michael Jackson.

Elisha Gill. Enlisted March, 1777.

Abijah Stowers. Enlisted April, 1777. Enlisted in Brown's company during war. Served twelve and a half months. Died in the army.

Jesse Harwood. Enlisted April, 1777. Was in Capt. Brown's company.

Timothy Earle. Enlisted April, 1777. Was in Brown's company. Died in the army, Nov. 3, 1777.

Elisha Wood. Enlisted April, 1777. In Brown's company. Served three years.

Patrick M'Mann. Enlisted January, 1777.
Gershom Comings. „ „ „
John Davis. „ November, 1777.
Stephen Witt. „ December, „
Samuel Wood. „ November, „
John Eares. „ January, 1778.
Samuel Low. „ „ „

Abraham Huet. Enlisted January. 1778.
Richard Hill. Enlisted January, 1778. Was in Capt. Brown's company.
Robert Green. Enlisted January, 1778.

In September, 1777, a detachment of troops was ordered to join the Northern Army, and rendezvous at Claverack, in the Provincial service. Col. Samuel Denny was detailed to command the regiment. Dr. Isaac Green of Leicester was surgeon. The term of service was for a single month; but in June, 1778, a detachment from Col. Denny's regiment was made for nine months, and marched to Fishkill. The following Leicester men were in it (they were between the ages of twenty and twenty-six): Zachariah Smith, Joseph Vinton, John Edmunds, William Sargent, James Graton.

In 1779, June 23, the following Leicester men joined Capt. Marshall's company in the "Continental service" (they were between the ages of nineteen and twenty-three): Levi Chilson, Pardon Dolbee, Hosea Sprague, James Snow, and William Webber.

In the return for January, 1781, of the troops enlisted for three years, or during the war, is the name of Daniel Coburn of Leicester, in the light dragoons.

James Tucker was returned as sergeant in Capt. Houdin's company.*
Thomas Saunderson, drummer, in the same company.
Israel Saunderson, corporal, in the sixth light infantry.
Asa Souther, corporal, in fourth company.
Asa Waite, sergeant in sixth light infantry.

Several of the men who enlisted in Capt. Martin's company had by that time been transferred to Capt. Houdin's company, in the fifth regiment. Thomas Seaver of Leicester was at that time, with James Tucker and Asa Harrington, in Col. Rufus Putnam's Massachusetts regiment at West Point.

---

* Houdin was a Frenchman, who came over and joined our army, and received a commission as captain.

In July, 1781, seven men from Leicester enlisted into the Continental service for the term of three months; viz., Jotham Smith, Isaac Denny, Ebenezer Upham, Asa Matthews, Asa Green, Marshall Newton, John Hapgood Howe. Some of these were not quite sixteen years of age.

The same summer, Dr. Austin Flint, then of Shrewsbury, was surgeon of Col. Drury's regiment at West Point, from July 26 to Dec. 20, 1781. He had been a soldier in the army at the surrender of Burgoyne, in October, 1777.

Col. William Henshaw, the adjutant-general of the troops at Cambridge until the arrival of Gen. Washington, has been mentioned at length in another part of this work.

Daniel Davis of Leicester was in Col. Brooks's regiment in 1777.

James Richardson, James Redfield, and David Bryant, were in Col. Wade's regiment of Massachusetts State troops, stationed at Rhode Island, one year from January, 1778.

The roll of Capt. Woodbridge's company, in the thirteenth Massachusetts regiment, has the name of Ebenezer Lane, as enlisted during the war from Leicester.

Isaac Robinson enlisted in Capt. Brown's company, eighth regiment, for three years. He died in the army, after ten and a half months' service, Feb. 14, 1778.

Benjamin Brown * was captain of a company of Continental troops in the eighth (Col. Michael Jackson's) regiment. He was in command of the company from January, 1777, to July 23, 1779; when he resigned.

Joseph Washburn was in the service from Jan. 1, 1777, to Dec. 31, 1779,—three years; of which time he was twenty-six months ensign, and ten lieutenant. He was at the taking of Burgoyne at Saratoga, and afterwards in the army under Gen. Washington in New Jersey. Among the persons to whom Leicester paid bounties in April, 1779, was Amos

* He was a son of Capt. John Brown of Leicester.

Gleason. Abel Green was in the three years' service in 1779.

The company which Capt. Martin had commanded* was called, in the returns of 1782, "the Major's company." There was one company in the regiment called "the Colonels;" and one, the "Lieutenant-Colonels."

John Holden was an officer in the Continental service from January, 1777. He was in the storming party under Gen. Wayne, which took the works on Stony Point; one of the most gallant, daring feats of the whole war.

Peter Salem, who is noticed in another part of this work, and who, while a soldier, belonged to Framingham, was in Capt. Holden's company in 1779; and Cain Bowman, who had been a slave in Leicester, was mustered as a soldier in 1778.

Among those who received pensions for services in the Revolutionary Army were Elijah Southgate and Jonas Stone, then living in Shrewsbury, though belonging to Leicester before their removal to that town.

Besides those already mentioned as members of Capt. Martin's company in September, 1777, at Albany, then under command of Ensign Washburn, were the following belonging to Leicester:—

Elias Green, enlisted for eight months.
Phinehas Green, " " " "
John Green, " " " "
Pliny Green, " " " "

I have before mentioned Seth Washburn, son of Col. Seth, as having marched to Cambridge in April, 1775, from Wilbraham. He afterwards lived in Hardwick; and in July, 1777, was a soldier in an expedition to Providence and Rhode Island. In August, the same year, he marched to Bennington in Col. James Converse's regiment. He was afterwards in the service, and died in the army, in New York, on Governor's Island.

---

* He resigned June 28, 1779.

In the regiment of Col. Brown, in the eight months' service in 1775, Ebenezer Washburn, brother of Capt. Seth, who had removed from Leicester to Hardwick, was quartermaster.

In July, 1780, a draught of seventeen men was made from Leicester to join the Continental Army for six months in Capt. Frothingham's company of artillery, in the fourth division. The following young men were drawn, then being between the ages of seventeen and twenty-one, — only four as old as twenty-one: —

John Sargeant.	Gershom Cummings.
Thomas Harmon.	Benjamin Hubbard.
Pardon Dolbee.	Hosea Sprague.
Ebenezer B. Upham.	John Green.
James Trumbull.	Joseph Washburn, jun.*
Daniel Brown.	James Smith.
Luther Ward.	John Hasey.
Isaac Morse, jun.	Abijah Craige.
Abiel Johnson.	

I find the memorandum of an order of July 10, 1781, in these words: "Lieut. Josiah Brown ordered to go with the men to Yarmouth for three months."

The same date, "Lieut. Nathan Craige ordered to go with the men to Rhode Island for five months." But the names of those who constituted the companies or detachments in either of the above requisitions, I cannot ascertain.

After the expiration of his time in the eight months' service, Mr. Craige joined the company of Capt. Prouty, Col. Cushing's regiment, in 1777, and marched to Bennington; from there to Half Moon, on North River; and returned to Bennington the day of the battle, but after its close.

He was at the surrender of Burgoyne. After that, he was a sergeant in Capt. Harrington's company at Roxbury; and was detailed upon the guard over Burgoyne's men, then prisoners of war.

He was five months at Newport, in 1781, in Capt. Elliot's

* Was a nephew of Col. Seth.

company, in Col. Turner's regiment. The captain belonged to Sutton.

Samuel Sargent, who married Capt. Washburn's daughter, was in the same company, and messed with Mr. Craige at the taking of Burgoyne.

William Todd of Leicester was commissioned as captain of a company of artillery in October, 1776. John Southgate was his "captain-lieutenant." The company was the eighth in the regiment, and was raised partly in Leicester. It was attached to Col. Craft's regiment, and was in service two or more years. They were stationed, some of the time, at Boston, some at Dorchester; twice were ordered to Rhode Island; and, in the autumn of 1777, took part in an engagement with the enemy at Tiverton.

David Henshaw, brother of Col. William, commanded a company in the same regiment as Capt. Todd.

Col. William Henshaw, after retiring from the army in 1775, was appointed lieutenant-colonel in Col. Little's regiment of Continental troops in April, 1776; and accepted office at the personal solicitation of Gen. Washington. He joined Gen. Green's brigade at New York; had an engagement with the enemy at Flatbush; was with Gen. Washington's army at Trenton, Princeton Battle, &c. He was also in the battle of White Plains: but of this more has been said in the notice of Col. Henshaw in this work; my object being chiefly to enumerate the men, and their rank in the army, who belonged to or were immediately connected with Leicester.

Among those to be mentioned indiscriminately, because it is not known to what companies they were attached, was Peter Silvester, jun., who was at Saratoga at the taking of Burgoyne.

Joseph Bass was in the "water-service," under Com. Tupper in 1776, and was engaged in an attempt to destroy the British frigates in North River, of which an account is given in this work. Elijah Hersey and Nathaniel Sargent were soldiers in the service. Capt. Livingston was paid by the town for the expense of a horse "to go to the taking of Burgoyne;" and the presumption is that he was accompanied by a part or all of the company under his command.

The company of artillery commanded by David Henshaw, already mentioned, was organized in September, 1776, and attached as the tenth company to the regiment of Col. Thomas Crafts. It belonged to the Continental establishment in the three years, or during-the-war service. Upon the roll of that company I find the following Leicester men: viz., Peleg Hersey, sergeant; Nathan Green, corporal; Jabez Paine, Bailey Bond, Ebenezer Upham.

In Capt. Todd's company, Samuel Sargent, son of Jonathan (to distinguish him from one of the same name already mentioned), was enlisted; but in the muster-roll of December, 1776, of that company, the only Leicester names it contains are William Laughton, (Lawton); Nathaniel Richardson; Thomas Dunbar, sergeant; Benjamin Leviston, corporal; William Gilkey, Hosea Sprague, Andrew Scott, John Works, Abner Snow.

Dr. John Honeywood joined the army as a surgeon in Col. Brown's regiment, and died at Ticonderoga, while in the service, November, 1776.

Dr. Isaac Green was a second time surgeon in the service at Saratoga, at the taking of Burgoyne, in October, 1777.

Incomplete as the foregoing list may be, it speaks highly in favor of the patriotism and public spirit of the town, when it is recollected, that, in 1781, the whole number of names borne upon the "train" and "alarm-list" of soldiers in town, and capable of bearing arms, was but one hundred and fifty-one, of whom forty-nine were upon the alarm-list.

COMMITTEES OF CORRESPONDENCE, ETC.

I am unable to ascertain when the first committee of this kind was chosen, or the names of its members. The suggestion of such committees seems to have come from the House of Burgesses of Virginia. There was such a committee existing here in December, 1773; and, in 1774, William Henshaw was its chairman. The other members were Thomas Denny, Joseph Henshaw, Benjamin Conklin, Hezekiah Ward, and Thomas Newhall. In 1775, Col. Samuel Denny was added, in May. The same year, in July, William Green, Samuel Green, and Joseph Sargeant, were added.

In March, 1776, the committee consisted of Joseph Henshaw, James Baldwin, jun., Robert Craige, Benjamin Richardson, and Loring Lincoln.

In September, Hezekiah Ward and Robert Henry were added.

In 1777, Joseph Henshaw, John Fletcher, Benjamin Richardson,* James Baldwin, jun., Isaac Green, Phinehas Newhall, and William Henshaw.

1778, Samuel Denny, William Henshaw, Joseph Sprague, Thomas Green, John Fletcher, Joseph Sargent, and Dr. Isaac Green.

1779, Samuel Upham, Henry King, Benjamin Watson, Matthew Scott, Jonathan Sargent.

As the Constitution was adopted early in 1780, and a regular government soon after organized, the committee last named were probably the last elected.†

Their powers were undefined by any statute; nor was there any precedent to guide them in the administration of their office. They derived their existence and authority from the condition of the country, and were discontinued the moment the necessity for such a body of officers ceased.

---

* Mr. Richardson moved out of town in 1777.

† I find an election in 1782 of the following persons as a "Committee of Safety;" viz., William Earle, John Southgate, Thomas Newhall, Ebenezer Kent, and William Green. But the nature of their duty is not stated. It probably answered to the old Committee of Correspondence; and was intended to aid in furnishing men and stores for the army, as requisitions might be made.

The early tax-lists furnish considerable information as to the general and individual condition of the people of the town at that day. Thus, in 1729, John Lynde was assessed for 1,520 acres of land; Samuel Green, 929; Richard Southgate, 600; Thomas Steele, 736; William Ward, 500; William Green, 425; Thomas Richardson, 313; James Southgate, 300; Thomas Newhall, 282; and Joshua Nichols, 270.

In 1731, Richard Southgate, Thomas Newhall, Thomas Green, and Thomas Gill, were each taxed one shilling for "negers;" which were set down in the list as "personal estate."

In 1735, I find one tax assessed "to pay the schoolmaster," £21. 6s. 6d.; another, "to pay the town's debts," £300; another, "the ministry rate for 1734," £75; another, "the county tax," £7; another, "the Province rate," £48. 16s. 8d. In March, 1736, a tax was assessed of £30 "to pay Jonathan Sargent to entertain the Council."

One thing to be remarked, in examining these tax-lists, is the singular equality of taxable property in the north and south parts of the town, as divided by the Great Post Road. Of the Province tax, in 1735, of £48. 16s. 8d., £24. 15s. 4d. were assessed upon those living upon the north side, and £24. 1s. 4d. upon those on the south side, of this line.

Another thing to be observed is the general equality of wealth among the citizens of the town. Of the tax of £300 in January, 1735, while no one was assessed more than £8. 8s. 11d., and only one as high as £8, one alone is assessed below £1; and only sixteen, out of a total of ninety-seven, were assessed below £2. Probably the reason of the difference there was in the valuation between the north and south parts of the town was, that in the former there were fifty-four persons, and in the latter forty-three, to be taxed.

In 1735, Onesephorus Pike paid the highest tax in town; John Lynde, the next; Richard Southgate, the next; John M'Master, the next; and Thomas Green, the next.

There were thirteen taxes assessed between 1722 and 1729, including those years, amounting to more than £1,000; illustrating what I have elsewhere stated, — the heavy burdens to which the town was at first subjected.*

The following families were residing here in 1721, and many of them at an earlier period: William Brown, John Burton, Aaron Bell, Joshua Barton, Bartholomew Curtis, Peter Carlisle, Arthur Carey, who came from Billerica, settled on Carey Hill, and removed to Brookfield; Daniel Denny, Ralf and William Earle, Samuel Green, John Peters, who came from Lexington; David Parsons, the minister; Thomas Richardson and Nathaniel Richardson, from Malden; Hezekiah Russ, from Lexington; James and Richard Southgate, John Smith, from Weston; Samuel, John, and Joseph Stebbins, from England; Thomas Smith, Moses Stockbridge, from Billerica; William Green, William Keen, John Lynde, from Malden; Daniel Livermore, from Weston; John Menzies, Joshua Nichols, from Malden; Thomas Newhall, from Malden; James Smith, John Smith, jun., Samuel Thomas, Rowland Taylor, Adam Taber, James Wilson, from Lexington; William Ward, from Marlborough; and Thomas Westcott and Oliver Watson.

The following are mentioned in the records in 1722, though they were probably here prior to that date: John Boynes, John Potter, John Saunderson, Benjamin Johnson, and John Watson.

In March, 1771, the selectmen made a report of the names of the persons who had come into town since April, 1767, with the places from which they came; which, with two or three additional names, are as follow: —

Zaccheus Ballard, from Framingham, May, 1770. He had a family, and lived on Ballard Hill, where there is now a cellar.

Jonathan Barton, from Spencer, April, 1774.

---

* Among the sums paid during this period was "a bill allowed to Mr. Richard Southgate for making ye stocks, and stuff to mend ye pound," 16s.

Joseph Allen, from Boston, November, 1771; afterwards of Worcester.

Mary Allen, from Boston, November, 1771. Married Rev. Mr. Avery, Holden.

Samuel Allen, from Boston, November, 1771; afterwards of Worcester. County treasurer.

William Crossman, from Hopkinton. Lived on the South Road, a short distance beyond Mrs. Hobart's.

Adam Collins, from Pelham, N.H., 1769.

Michael Carey, from Boston, spring, 1770.

Jonathan Collier, from Weymouth, 1770.

Isaac Choate, from Ipswich, 1773. Lived at the Elliot Place, on the North County Road.

Caleb Earle, from Chester, N.Y., 1770.

Thomas Faxon, from Braintree, 1770.

Watt Fannel, stranger, 1769.

Ezekiel Fosgate, from Bolton, winter, 1769. Trader; built and traded in store on what is now the Common.

Joseph Gleason, from Oxford, 1770.

Semple Gilkey, from Plainfield, Conn., April, 1773.

William Gilkey, Hannah his wife, and Rebecca his daughter, from Plainfield, May 19, 1773.

Daniel Hayden, from Gloucester, R.I., 1770.

Sarah Hunt and Richard Hunt, children of Hayden's wife, from Gloucester, R.I., 1770.

Cornelius Holton, from Union, Conn., 1769.

Elijah Howe, from Paxton, spring, 1769. On Mount Pleasant, opposite the Moore Place.

John Boulster Hubbard, from Brinfield, 1769.

Thomas Hammond, from Newton, 1770. Afterwards removed to Vermont.

Lucy Hammond and Anna Hammond, from Newton, February, 1771.

Jonathan Johnson, and Rachel his wife, from Petersham, January, 1774.

Silas Kendal, from Winchendon, 1770.

Isaac Lynde, from Spencer, 1769.

Hannah Niles, from Braintree, October, 1769.

John Newhall, Dorothy Newhall, Mercy Newhall, and Phebe Newhall, from Spencer, 1774.

Alexander Parkman, from Westborough, 1770. Clothier, in Cherry Valley.

Jonathan Phillips, from Oxford, 1770.
John Phillips, from Smithfield, R.I., 1771.
Ebenezer Prescott, Jerusha his wife, Patience, Ebenezer, and Fortune, children, from Paxton, December, 1773.
James Richardson, from Spencer, 1768.
Benjamin Sherman, from Swanzey, 1771.
Thomas Sibley, from Boston, 1770.
Luther Torrey, from Abington, fall, 1770.
Peter Valentine, from Plainfield, Conn., 1773.
Hezekiah Ward, from Grafton, 1768. Lived at what is now the Town's Farm.

In 1776, the town was divided into nine school districts; and the names of the several families constituting these, except the ninth, were recorded. I have copied them, first, to show who were the active citizens of the town during the Revolution; and, second, the places of their residence, which has already become, and will hereafter be more, a matter of interesting inquiry.

FIRST DISTRICT.

Thomas Steele lived at the Rawson House.
Seth Washburn, where J. Loring lives.
Elijah Lathrop, tavern; where Hiram Knight's house is.
Nathan Waite, tavern; opposite Meeting-house.
Benjamin Richardson, where Mrs. S. Newhall lives.
Joseph Allen, where the old Academy stood.
Benjamin Conklin, where Mr. May lives.
Peter Silvester, where cellar is on east side of Meeting-house Hill.
Reuben Earle, at tan-yard at foot of the hill.
Phinehas Sargent's farm, at Nathan Waite's tavern.
Joshua Crossman and William Crossman, cellar beyond Mrs. Hobart's, on east side of the road.
Richard Bond, house north of Eber Bond's.
Benjamin Bond, south of the house where Eber Bond lives.
Jonathan Bond, house where S. Gleason lived.
William Watson, where Mr. Lyon lives.
James Graton, cellar in pasture west of Eber Bond's.

James Harwood, cellar west of J. Graton's.

Thomas Hutchinson, farm.

SECOND DISTRICT.

Joshua Henshaw and Col. Joseph Henshaw, Mount-Pleasant House.

Perley Brown, on M'Intire Farm; house next east of schoolhouse, on the Great Road.

Ephraim Mower and Thomas Mower, farm formerly of Col. H. Sargent.

Elijah Howe, cellar opposite Mowers'.

Jonathan Sargent, jun., where Artemas Lamb lives.

Nathan Hersey, next east of Capt. Trask's.

Elijah Hersey, Capt. Trask Place. Elijah Hersey built the Capt. Trask House.

John Watson's farm, next west of Capt. Trask's.

Ebenezer Warren, where Elijah died; was father of Elijah Warren.

Jonathan Warren, where Jos. Warren lives.

Thomas Newhall, where R. Watson lived and died.

Richard Southgate, cellar west of Burntcoat Brook. Baptist Elder.

Richard Southgate, jun., where David Lumb lived.

Anthony Sprague, old house near O. C. Silvester's.

Ephraim Mower, jun., cellar north-west of Peter Silvester Place.

John Brown, where Peter Silvester died.

Nathaniel Harrod, opposite where William Silvester lives.

THIRD DISTRICT.

William Todd, the Henshaw Farm.

John Southgate, where he died.

Richard Gleason, and Richard Gleason, jun., cellar in Samuel Waite's Pasture.

Alexander Parkman, where Rufus Upham lived.

Thomas Earle, where Heman Burr lives.

Matthew Watson, saddler; where N. Holman lives.

Peleg Hersey, house near the Cutting House.

Ebenezer Upham, shoemaker; house where Shepherd lived.

Joseph Sargent, house east of where Asa Sargent died.

Nathan Sargent, where Sewall lives.

Daniel Henshaw, opposite Edwin Waite's.

David Henshaw built Edwin Waite's house in 1770.

William Henshaw, Lynde Place.

Nathaniel Waite, Samuel Waite Place.
Mrs. Denny, widow of Thomas; the old Denny Farm.
Robert Henry, Robert Young Place.
Matthew Scott, farm south of Robert Young's.
Judge Chandler's farm.

FOURTH DISTRICT.

Jabez Green, where Abel died.
Antipas Earle, in the hollow west of Abel Green's.
Gardner Earle, Gardner Wilson's.
Ebenezer Kent, and Ebenezer Kent, jun., where Capt. Daniel Kent died.
Robert Earle, the Pliny Earle Place.
Robert Earle, jun., house between Pliny and Timothy Earle Places.
Joshua Silvester, where Erastus Wheaton lived.
John Dunbar, where John Silvester lived.
William Earle, Nathaniel Earle House.
Loring Lincoln, house east of A. Marshall's.
John Wheaton, A. Marshall's; formerly Silas Earle's.
Phinehas Newhall, tavern; where Eddy lives. House removed, and new one built.
Reuben Swan, where L. G. Sturtevant lives.

FIFTH DISTRICT.

Hezekiah Ward, the Poor Farm. Moved to Paxton, and Timothy Sprague bought the farm.
John Potter and Nathaniel Potter, Jonah Earle Place, west of Quaker Meeting-house.
Joseph Sprague, Capt. William Sprague Place.
Daniel Hubbard, where Jacob Bond died.
Jabez Pain, next east of Jos. Whittemore's.
James Whittemore, Jos. Whittemore Place.
Timothy Sprague, Holden Place, north of Hubbard's.
Daniel Snow, old house south of B. Upham's Place.
Nathan Snow, George Upham's; formerly Barnard's.
Sarah Denny, next north of Barnard Upham. Afterwards married Seth Washburn.
Isaac Choate, the Elliot Place.
Jonathan Knight, next to Horace Knight's house.
Jacob Wicker, west of Mr. Knight's, on the Eddy Road.

SIXTH DISTRICT.

Samuel Denny, south side of Moose Hill.
Thomas Snow, where Abner Snow died.
John Watson and Samuel Watson, Asa B. Watson Place.
Joshua Converse, cellar east of the Watsons.
Benjamin Liviston, house gone; where Joel Marsh lived.
Dr. Solo Parsons, at the Gage Place.
John Williams, next to James Whittemore's. He was a shoemaker.
Widow Sawin, west of Benjamin Livingston's.
Jacob Briant, Jos. Bryant Place.
William Thompson, farm north-east of Braddyl Livermore's.
Widow Goodenow, farm near Braddyl Livermore's.
Jabez Green, jun., where Zolvah lives.
Christopher Wheaton, the David Wicker Place.
Benjamin Saunderson, the George Bond Place.
Benjamin Converse, the Eddy House.

SEVENTH DISTRICT.

William Green, Amos Whittemore Place.
Thomas Green's farm, occupied by John Greaton; Elijah Thayer Place.
John Wilson, Mrs. Kingsbury's Place.
Deacon Fletcher, Jonathan Warren's old place.
Gideon Smith, Elkanah Haven Place.
Jonathan Newhall, opposite N. Craig's house, Sadler Place.
John Brown, jun., Daniel Muzzy Place.
Nathan Lumb, where Isaac Livermore died.
Rev. M. Foster, where Caleb Barton lived.
Dr. Isaac Green, Charles Barton's.
Abijah Stower, Baptist Parsonage.
Phinehas Barton and Cornelius Houghton, various places.
Samuel Green, old Tavern House.
Samuel Richardson, Copeland Place.
Ebenezer Upham, house next south of Deacon Rockwood's.
Samuel Upham, Deacon Rockwood Place.
Caleb Nichols, on cross-road, north-west of Eben Dunbar's.
Henry King, John King Place.
Isaac Livermore, at foot of Livermore Hill, west side of road.
Jockton Green, Richard Bond, jun., Place.

Jonathan Newhall, jun., opposite Baptist Meeting-house.
Micah Livermore, Daniel Livermore Place.

EIGHTH DISTRICT.

William Gilkey, the Trask Place.
Matthew Scott, Eben Dunbar Place.
Jonas Livermore, Salem's Place.
Benjamin Watson, where he died.
Nathaniel Richardson, Bridge's Place.
Dr. Clark's farm.
Eight families living in what is now Auburn.

NINTH DISTRICT.

Names not given. Among them were—

Solomon Green, in the Wilby Cottage.
Thomas Parker, the John Parker Place.
Benjamin Baldwin.
James Baldwin.
Ebenezer Baldwin.
Stephen Baldwin.
David Baldwin.
Jos. Trumbull.
Peter Trumbull.
Robert Craig.

PERSONAL NOTICES.

Several of the persons contained in the foregoing list of families deserve a fuller notice than has thus far been given of them.

Col. William Henshaw stands prominently among these. He was born in Boston, 1735; and removed to Leicester, with his father (Daniel Henshaw, Esq.), in 1748. While he resided in Boston, he attended school, studied Latin among other things, and was partly fitted for college.

He remained with his father till he was of age; about which time he was commissioned as a lieutenant in the Provincial troops; and, in 1759, was under the command of Gen. Amherst at Ticonderoga. After a service of two campaigns, he returned home to his farm.

The approach of the Revolution found Mr. Henshaw ready to go with the country, and prompt to engage in all the popular measures which engaged attention preparatory to the vindication of the rights of the Colonies by resort to arms. He was one of the jurors who, at the April Term of the Superior Court at Worcester, refused to be sworn if Chief-Justice Oliver was to be present and act. The remonstrance was drawn by him, and is a spirited and able paper.

There were several county conventions held in Worcester between the 9th August, 1774, and 21st April, 1775, in which he took a prominent and active part; and it is said, that, at one of these, he was the first to propose the measure which was so readily adopted among the militia of the Province,—to form companies of "minute-men," so called, because they were to hold themselves ready to march upon a moment's warning if any demonstration should be made towards coercing the Colony by military force. He was made colonel of a regiment of minute-men raised in the county of Worcester.

Upon hearing of the march of the British troops to Lexington, he issued his orders to his field and subaltern officers and their companies to meet him at Worcester at ten o'clock that night. Before twelve, he, with his regimental officers, was on his way to Cambridge, which they reached the next forenoon.

Upon the organization of the troops at Cambridge by an enlistment of men for eight months, Col. Henshaw was appointed adjutant-general, though he was not commissioned as such till the 27th June; and held office until the arrival of Gen. Washington at Cambridge with Adjutant-Gen. Gates, under a commission from the Continental Congress.

In May of that year, he was a member of the Council of War; and, as chairman of a subcommittee of that body, made a reconnoissance, and reported upon the subject of occupying and fortifying Bunker Hill.

This report was dated on the 12th May; and it was by the advice of the Board of officers, of which he was a member, that works were laid out which were to be occupied by the American troops; the attempt to do which led to the battle of the 17th June.

After the arrival of Gen. Gates, Col. Henshaw, at his personal solicitation, continued to act as his assistant for the term of five or six months, when he returned to Leicester.*

In 1776, he was appointed a lieutenant-colonel, under Col. Little, of the twelfth Massachusetts regiment, in the Continental service; and accepted the office at the personal desire of Gen. Washington. He joined the army at New York, in Gen. Green's brigade; and was actively engaged in the operations against the enemy, upon Long Island. In the severe and bloody encounter with the British troops at Flatbush, he was, with his regiment, surrounded by the enemy's forces; and, after the surrender of Gen. Sullivan, cut his way through their ranks in a most gallant manner, and reached Brooklyn. The battle was a disastrous one; but gained, for those who took part in it, great credit for bravery and resolution.

After retreating from Long Island, the army took up its position at last at White Plains; where another battle was fought, in which Col. Henshaw took an active part.

In November of 1776, he was offered the post of colonel of a regiment, but declined it, though he continued in the service. He was attached to that part of the army which was under Gen. Lee, and marched into New Jersey. After the capture of that general, he was under the command of Gen. Sullivan; and, in the absence of Col. Little, had command of the twelfth regiment. He was with Gen. Washington in the passage of the Delaware, and at the attack on Princeton,— two of the important and memorable events of the Revolution.

He continued with the army till February, 1777; when he

* He was, by special vote of the House, allowed compensation as adjutant-general from 27th June to 1st August, 1775.

resigned, and returned home. His zeal and activity in the cause of the Revolution did not cease with his retirement to civil life. He was an active patriot, and an enlightened, high-minded citizen; and did much to keep alive the spirit which carried the country through that struggle and its subsequent difficulties.

He was repeatedly chosen to represent the town in the General Court, and was for many years an active magistrate. He was of that class which, unfortunately, is becoming a matter of history, — a gentleman of the old school. There was a courtesy of manner, a dignity of bearing, and a self-possessed deportment, in their intercourse, which characterized the officers of the higher grades in the army, which they acquired in their association with each other and by their habits of command, which they retained through life.

Col. Henshaw had these to a remarkable degree. He retained the costume of his earlier *régime*, — his cocked hat, boots, and spurs. He rode a horse with much grace; and moved, when he walked, with a firm step and an erect person. He was social in his feelings and habits, an agreeable talker, and a pleasant and interesting companion. He was a liberal supporter of the religious and educational institutions of the town. He died February, 1820, at the age of eighty-five. He lived, for many years before his death, where Mr. Edwin Waite now lives, upon the farm which had belonged to his father.

He married Ruth Sargent, daughter of Jonathan Sargent, in 1762, for his first wife; and Phebe Swan, a sister of Reuben Swan, in 1771, for his second. The names of their children will be found in another part of this work.

DAVID HENSHAW was the youngest son of Daniel, and brother of Joseph and William. He was born in Boston, 1774; and removed with his father to Leicester at the age of four years. His school education was principally acquired in Boston.

In September, 1776, he was commissioned as captain in Col. Crafts's regiment of artillery in the Continental service. The regiment was principally employed in the vicinity of Boston; but, more than once, parts of it were ordered to Rhode Island, and took part on one occasion, under Gen. Spencer, in an encounter with the enemy at Tiverton. He remained in the service three years, when he resigned, and retired to his farm. He was, many years, an active magistrate in the county. He had a strong and vigorous mind, a resolute will, and an independent judgment.

He married Mary, daughter of Nathan Sargent, in 1773. Their children are mentioned in another part of this work. He died May 22, 1808, in the sixty-fourth year of his age. For several years before he died, he owned the farm known as the "Henshaw Farm," near the Pond; which is still owned by descendants of the family.

JOSHUA HENSHAW was brother of Daniel, above named; and was born in Boston in 1703. He was one of the leading spirits in the early movements of the Revolution; and many of the measures of the day were discussed and planned at his house in Boston, where Warren and Hancock, Adams and Otis, used often to meet. He was elected to the Council in 1769; and his rejection by Gov. Bernard only added to the popular influence, and strengthened the confidence which he enjoyed.* About the year 1773, he removed to Leicester; where his son-in-law, Col. Joseph Henshaw, who had married his daughter Sarah, was then residing.

He boarded for a while in the family of the Rev. Mr. Conklin, in whom he found a congenial spirit. After that, he was occupying the Mount-Pleasant House with his son-in-law in 1776. The following year (1777) he was residing in Ded-

* The persons elected to the Council with him, who were rejected by Gov. Bernard, were William Brattle, James Bowdoin, Joseph Gerrish, Thomas Saunders, John Hancock, Artemas Ward, James Otis, Benjamin Greenleaf, Jonathan Bowers, and Nathaniel Spooner.

ham, in the family of the Hon. Samuel Dexter; where he died Aug. 5, 1777.

I have had occasion to remark more than once upon the constant and intimate connection which was kept up between the people of Leicester and the leaders of the Revolutionary movements in Boston, by which the sentiment of the latter found a ready and immediate response from the former.

Mr. Joshua Henshaw was one of the mediums through which this was effected. He was, as I have stated, a confidential friend and adviser of the Adamses, Otis, Warren, and the other leaders in the popular cause. He was, for instance, a member of the committee, with Samuel Adams and James Otis, who demanded of the governor the removal of the troops from Boston after the Boston Massacre, as it was called.

He had two nephews and a son-in-law in Leicester, all public and active men; and his letters, had they been preserved, would doubtless have given us in detail the steps by which the Revolution was commenced, and carried on up to his removal from the scene of action. His health, for a few years before his death, was feeble; and he had withdrawn from an active participation in public affairs.

John Southgate, though he occupied a much more limited sphere than some of those I have mentioned, deserves to be noticed among the prominent citizens of the town. He was the oldest son of Steward Southgate, who was born in England, and came to Leicester with his father Richard in 1717. He was born Jan. 15, 1738, and was the brother of Dr. Robert Southgate, of Scarborough in Maine. He was well educated for the time in which he lived, and was much employed as a surveyor of lands, in which he seems to have had great skill and accuracy. He married Eleanor Sargent, daughter of Jonathan Sargent, 2d. Their children are mentioned hereafter. He was the adjutant of the regiment of minute-men commanded by Col. William Henshaw, and marched to Cambridge on the alarm of the 19th of April,

1775. Upon the organization of the troops in the "eight months'" service, he returned to Leicester.

In September, 1776, a regiment of artillery was raised under the command of Col. Thomas Crafts, of which James Swan, afterwards a resident in Leicester, was major. One of the companies (the tenth) was commanded by Capt. William Todd of Leicester, who then lived at the Henshaw Place; and another, by David Henshaw, already mentioned.

John Southgate was commissioned as second officer in the company of Capt. Todd, under the title and style of "captain-lieutenant." They were immediate neighbors, and strong personal friends.

This regiment was regarded as an important arm of the service, and is often alluded to in the proceedings of the General Court of Massachusetts, by whom its officers were commissioned, although in the Continental establishment. The company to which Capt. Todd and Southgate were attached was stationed a part of the time at Boston; a part at Dorchester Point and Governor's Island; and, in the autumn of 1777, was ordered to Rhode Island; as it was again in September, 1778: both of which expeditions took place during the temporary absence of Capt. Southgate on visits to his family.

From several letters * left among the papers of Capt. Southgate I select a few extracts, as they serve to give an insight into the condition of the army at the times when they were written. In one from Capt. Todd, dated Nov. 22, 1776, written at Boston, he tells Capt. Southgate that he had seen the regiment; that they looked well; and desires Mr. Southgate to inform the men he should bring with him, that they would be noticed, and, if not in uniform, probably rejected. "All the old companies are clothed, and most of Capt. Cushing's and

---

* For these I am indebted to the kindness of his grandson, Dr. George F. Bigelow of Boston.

Henshaw's.* I should be sorry to see my men appear any worse than the best of them."

Soon after this, he writes again: "I would request you'd do all in your power to promote the design of regimental clothing; would hint to you, the officers look well; *would not have you* get a *home-spun coat, if you can help it.* No man will have an opportunity of being *gunner* or *bombadier* in the company, without a uniform; as regimental orders are, they shall appear in regimental dress. Let all the men bring down with them whatever arms or accoutrements they can procure, — quite scarce here. Desire them to do what they can in getting them. . . . The 2d of December we have a regimental muster, — a grand appearance."

On the 25th of the same November, 1776, he writes from "Camp Boston:" "Sir, you must inform Mr. Richardson, he must either get a tye wig, or else let his hair grow." — "Am well now. My men all arrived; all well. Have received good provisions, and will pass muster to-morrow."

Perhaps some allowance should be made for this fastidiousness about dress and outside appearance to the fact that Capt. Todd had been an English gentleman before coming to this country, and, of course, familiar with the dress and appearance of neatness in the uniform of the English Army at home. He had removed from Boston to Leicester, and purchased and lived upon the farm formerly belonging to Judge Steele, and subsequently to David Henshaw, Esq. His sister Rachel married William Sargent, brother of Capt. Southgate's wife; which formed an additional bond of intimacy between the families.

After the war, Capt. Todd removed to Keene, N.H.; and was living there in 1793.

But to resume the notice of Capt. Southgate. I give an extract from a letter of his to his wife, dated in April, 1777,

* Capt. David Henshaw of Leicester.

which he sent "by Rev. Mr. Conklin," who, I suppose, was then a chaplain in the army. I give it in order to show to what straits people, in even comfortable circumstances, were reduced for the common articles of necessity in their families. "I sent you *a paper of pins* by Capt. Newhall."—"I can't get any *calamanco* for shoes, nor any shoes I think will fit you, yet."

All these letters were by private hands; for, as it will be recollected, it was long anterior to the establishment of a regular postal arrangement for general use.

Capt. Southgate left the army in the summer or autumn of 1778, but still continued active in promoting the success of the Revolution.

In 1781, he was first assessor of the town, and had the duty of dividing the people of the town into classes; each of which was required to furnish one or more men for the army, according as the requisition might be upon the town. In the class to which he himself belonged, there were thirty-one whose names were borne upon the tax-lists of the town.

The prostration of business and credit, and the exhaustion of the pecuniary resources of the country, consequent upon the war, ripened at last into that unhappy feeling of hostility to the government in Massachusetts, which led to open resistance in what was called Shay's Rebellion, in 1786–7.

The sober and reflecting portion of the people stood by the government; but many, who had been good and devoted soldiers during the Revolution, were found enlisted under the banner of revolt.*

The aim of the insurgents was to put a stop to the courts, in order to prevent the collection of debts by legal process and the punishment of those who should resist the law.

I hardly need say that Capt. Southgate was found in sup-

* Shays and Wheeler, who were among the leaders in the insurrection, had been captains in the army of the Revolution.

port of the government; and one or two extracts from letters addressed to him at that time will give some idea of the feeling that then existed. One is dated Sept. 5, 1786, and is from a kinsman living in Palmer. "Your aunt and I were summoned as evidences to Northampton court last week. On Tuesday morning, there were a company of horse of about fifty or sixty; and followed them a company of foot, armed with guns and bayonets in regular order, drums, fifes, &c.; besides smaller bodies continually marching through the street and crossing the river. It being a very rainy forenoon, did not think best to go over; being very unwell, and expecting a tumult, and perhaps much confusion. All the afternoon, for six or eight hours, could not see man, woman, or child, in Hadley Street. Next day, I went over to Northampton; but the mob had stopped the court, so that they never attempted to go into the Court House, but adjourned without day. The mob were all retired to their homes; and such people as I had opportunity to see said but very little, but seemed concerned at the consequences."

The other, of a different character, is from Col. William Henshaw, and is characteristic of the times and the man. It bears date Sept. 19, 1786. "I shall go by the way of Major Newhall's* to Worcester, and see what number we can raise that may protect the court from insults, if any should be offered. I was at Worcester yesterday; and it was the opinion of some that a party would try to stop the court. Others were of opinion they would not. It is best to guard against the worst. If you are with me in opinion, it will be best to invite such persons as you think are friendly to government to appear at Worcester with their arms as early as may be in the day, to rendezvous at Patch Tavern. Capt. Henshaw,† Mr. Stone,‡ Capt. Lyon and sons, Col. Washburn

---

* He kept a tavern on the North County Road, where Mr. Eddy lives.

† David. ‡ Jonas.

and sons, Mr. Denny,* and Swan,† I believe, will go. Worcester will stand ready to join us. Perhaps you will find others ready to go in so good a cause." — Col. Henshaw was not mistaken in his supposition; but the history of that affair belongs to another part of this work.

Capt. Southgate engaged extensively in purchasing wild lands in Maine. He owned a pretty large tract a few miles above Bangor, on the Penobscot River. After the death of his oldest son, which is mentioned in another part of this work, he had occasion to visit these lands from time to time, to dispose of them, and protect them from trespassers.

On the 7th of August, 1806, having occasion to be at Stillwater for this purpose, and wishing to pass a short distance down the river, he got upon a couple of logs in the stream, in company with a man by the name of Reed, and was soon after thrown into the water in some way; and was drowned, though an excellent swimmer, within a few rods of the shore. Strong suspicions of foul play were entertained at the time; but no measures, I believe, were ever taken to investigate their truth. His body was soon recovered, and buried at Kenduskeag Point, on the banks of the Penobscot.

Capt. Southgate lived in the easterly part of the town, near the junction of the County Road from Charlton with the old Great Road, where it passed along the side hill, instead of its present course through the valley. One only of the family remains.

THOMAS DENNY was the son of Daniel, the first of the name who settled in Leicester. He was born in 1724. He married Tabitha Cutler of Grafton in 1752, and had four children. He must have been a man of more than ordinary ability, and of an education superior to most of his contemporaries, who were brought up, as he was, in a country town.

He held many places of responsibility and trust in the town

---

* Thomas. † Reuben.

and county, and early engaged in the controversy with the mother-country. Some of the spirited and statesman-like resolutions and instructions adopted by the town, to which I have alluded, were from his pen. He was, too, in correspondence with the leading public men in Boston and its vicinity, and was regarded by them as a wise and patriotic counsellor.

For five years in succession, next previous to his death, he represented the town in the General Court; and was a mem- of the first Provincial Congress in 1774. This covered a most eventful and trying period of our history. During the early part of 1774, there were several meetings of delegations from the towns in the county of Worcester, in convention, in which Col. Denny took a leading part, and was one of a committee of three selected by the convention to present to Gov. Gage a remonstrance against the course of measures which the government were pursuing. The delegates from this town to this convention were Col. Thomas Denny, Capt. William Henshaw, Capt. Joseph Henshaw, and Rev. Benjamin Conklin. Spencer and Paxton united in their election. Of these, William Henshaw was chosen clerk of the convention.

The congress met in October, 1774. Soon after its convening, Col. Denny was obliged to return home on account of sickness; which terminated his life, Oct. 23, at the age of forty-nine.

He seems to have been a ready and popular debater as well as writer; and his death was a public loss, and lamented as such. He had held the office of colonel of a regiment of militia, which was then regarded as a mark of distinguished honor. From his qualifications for public life, and his experience and familiar acquaintance with the affairs of the Province, there is every reason to believe, that, had he lived, he would have filled an important part in that drama of which he saw only the opening scene. Col. Denny lived upon what was long known as the "Old Denny Farm," where his father had first settled.

L. Grozelier's Lith.

Thos. Denny

Col. Thomas Denny, a son of the above, was born in May, 1757. He married Lucretia Sargent, daughter of Phinehas Sargent. He early engaged in active business, and accumulated a large estate. He often represented the town in the General Court; was many years postmaster of the town, having succeeded Mr. Adams in that office; was a member of the Board of Trustees of the Academy; an active magistrate; colonel of a regiment of cavalry,* — the first raised in the county; besides being called to fill many places of trust in the town and elsewhere.

He was extensively engaged in the manufacture of cards and in merchandise, and did much towards sustaining and fostering a branch of manufacture upon which the wealth and business of the town have greatly depended.

Col. Denny, with some of his contemporaries, did much by their enterprise, and the encouragement and employment they afforded to active and industrious young men, in laying a foundation for the prosperity of the town; for which the town owes a debt of gratitude to their memory.

He died suddenly, in the midst of his usefulness, Dec. 5, 1814, aged fifty-seven. His wife survived him until her ninetieth birthday; retaining her faculties and her cheerfulness unimpaired to the last, and enjoying the respect and esteem of a wide circle of friends and acquaintance. Her death was very sudden, and with her passed away almost the last link between the present generation and the ante-revolutionary age.

Many valuable memories, that might have lent an interest to these pages had they been preserved, have died with her; and her rich store of personal recollections of individuals and events is now lost beyond recovery.

Col. Denny lived, after his marriage, on the Denny Farm; but, though he continued to own the estate, he lived, many

---

* He succeeded Col. Crafts of Sturbridge, and was chosen March, 1791.

years before his death, in the house opposite the Academy, recently altered and repaired by Dr. Daggett.*

Col. Samuel Denny was a brother of the first Col. Thomas; and, though not so distinguished as a public man, held a prominent and leading place among the men of his day. He was born in 1731. He married Elizabeth, daughter of Daniel Henshaw, Esq.; and had a large family of children, who are mentioned elsewhere. He was engaged with the Henshaws and others in the early movements of the Revolution, and was lieutenant-colonel of the regiment of minute-men which marched upon the Lexington alarm.

In February, 1776, he was elected colonel of the first regiment in the county of Worcester; and, in November of that year, was stationed with the army at Tarry Town. In September, 1777, he was detailed to command a regiment of militia that was ordered to join the Northern Army. The term of his service at the last time was but a single month. He represented the town in the General Court in 1778; and was a member of the Convention which was called to act upon the ratification of the Constitution of the United States, in January, 1788. Col. Denny lived upon his estate upon Moose Hill, in the north-west part of the town. He died in 1817, at the age of eighty-six.

Col. Seth Washburn. — No one, who has followed the course of the narrative of this work, will doubt the propriety of noticing this gentleman among the leading men of the town in his day; and yet the relation in which I stand to his memory is such as to hazard the character of any judgment I may have formed of his public measures or personal merits. I can at best give but a meagre detail of even the few incidents which go to make up his history.

He was born in Bridgewater in 1723. His grandfather

* His manufactory and store stood where the brick store stands, in which the Bank is now established.

came to Duxbury in 1635; and was, as is believed, the son of the first secretary of the Massachusetts Company, before its charter was removed to New England. He afterwards removed to Bridgewater; where his son Joseph,* father of Seth, was born. He removed to Middletown, Conn., in 1739 or 1740; and lived there till about 1745, when he removed to Leicester with his family. Seth was then twenty-seven years old. The father was a blacksmith, and lived where there is now a cellar, on the west side of the road leading to William Silvester's, some fifty rods from the Great Road. His shop was at the junction of the Silvester Road with the Great Road. Seth also was a blacksmith, and served his apprenticeship in Middletown. In April, 1750, he married Mary, the daughter of Capt. Nathaniel Harrod, who had removed with her father from Lunenburg, where she was born. He is spoken of, in a deed dated 1756, as innkeeper; and is supposed to have kept the public-house where Capt. Knight now lives, which was afterwards burned in 1767. He afterwards lived in the house which belonged to him, standing where Mr. John Loring lives, and forming a part of it, but enlarged by him in 1780. After his second marriage, to Mrs. Sarah Sargent, a sister of Col. Samuel Denny, in April, 1788, he lived four years upon what is now called the Slade Place, — the farm afterwards owned by John Howard, two miles north of the Meeting-house. He then returned to his former residence, where he died.

Col. Washburn is chiefly interesting, as a study, from his being a fair representative man of his time. His qualities had never been developed by early education, and lay dor-

* Joseph's mother was grand-daughter of Mary Chilton; the first white person, it is said, who stepped upon the Plymouth Rock. She married John, brother of Gov. Winslow.

The mother of Seth was Hannah Johnson of Hingham. One who knew her described her as a woman of superior endowments; and added, that, "if any of her children had any smartness, they owed it chiefly to her."

mant until drawn out by the emergency of the occasion. His education must have been very limited. He wrote an indifferent hand, and often violated the rules of spelling and grammar. He had, however, a ready command of language; was a fluent and forcible speaker; and exhibited a coolness and self-possession, which made him an effective debater. But probably he would have gone through life, as thousands are constantly doing, without knowing that he had courage, firmness, sagacity, or executive talent, beyond what was necessary to manage his shop and command the respect of his neighbors, if it had not been for the call upon his best energies which he found in the Revolution.

He had been a soldier in one expedition against the Indians in New Hampshire in 1749. He held various subordinate town-offices, from time to time, after 1758; but had not attained to the dignity of a selectman before 1769; and it was 1773 before he was placed at the head of the Board. He was first chosen representative in 1777, and a senator in 1780. The first of his military offices, in which he afterwards acquired much credit and importance, was in 1770, when he was chosen lieutenant of a company of volunteers, of which William Henshaw was captain. In April, 1774, he was commissioned as lieutenant of the second company of foot in Leicester, of which Samuel Denny was captain. When the company of minute-men was raised in January, 1775, he was made their captain: and in the eighth months' service, after the war began, he was the captain of a company; as he was in the two successive terms, of two months' service, at Roxbury and Dorchester, which succeeded. In one of these, as senior captain in the regiment commanded by Col. Whitney, he did the duty of major. From that time till the close of the war, he was constantly in the public service, though not attached to the army. Of the part he took in the battle of the 17th June, 1775, I have elsewhere spoken.

The military commissions he afterwards received were in

the militia. In February, 1778, he was chosen by the General Court and commissioned as major of the first regiment in Worcester; and in July, 1781, became its colonel. It then embraced Spencer, Paxton, Ward (Auburn), Worcester, Holden, and Leicester; and contained nine companies, of six hundred and eighteen men in the whole. How long he held the office, I am not able to state; but he had the command at its first regimental muster, which took place in September, 1785. Though his rise into public notice and confidence must have been sudden and rapid, I find no evidence of his having afterwards lost or forfeited that confidence. The duties he was called upon to perform, after leaving the army, were, most of them, such as indicated a reliance upon his judgment and sagacity as well as his fidelity.

I have mentioned, in a subsequent part of this work, his having been muster-master for the county, and superintendent for military purposes of the county, by repeated elections, as well as storekeeper of portions of the supplies for the army.

In June, 1776, an order of the General Court was adopted for raising five thousand men to co-operate with the Continental troops; and a committee of one for each county was chosen to go into the several counties to promote the enlistments. Mr. Washburn was chosen for the county of Worcester. The same service was done in July, the same year, to enlist every twenty-fifth man to re-enforce the Northern Army.

In May, 1777, he was appointed by the General Court to proceed to Ticonderoga to learn on the spot the exact condition of the garrison, and to see that the supplies destined for it were forwarded with despatch; but he was unable to comply with the order, and another was appointed in his place. Massachusetts was to raise fifteen battalions of troops for the Continental service, but was to have the commissioning of their officers.

In June, 1777, a committee, consisting of Azor Orne,

George Partridge, Jonathan Webster, Seth Washburn, and Joseph Hosmer, was raised by the General Court "for commissionating the officers now raising men," &c., in this State.*

Certainly this was a delegation of great power and discretion. But that which was conferred the same month upon another committee, of which Mr. Washburn was a member, was hardly less. It was to examine accounts against the government for services done or articles supplied, and pass upon the accounts of commissaries for men raised for defence of the seacoast. And in August, 1779, he was on a similar committee; and whatever accounts were approved by the committee were to be allowed and paid, without any further order or action upon them.

In these and similar duties his time was occupied until peace was established. In 1776, '7, '8, and '9, he represented the town in the General Court, and was elected in 1780, '82, and '84; but, having been elected to the Senate in 1780 and '84, his seat in the House was vacated for those years.

In 1777, he was one of a committee of seventeen chosen by the Legislature to draught a Constitution for the people; and, in 1779, was chosen a delegate to the Convention that framed the Constitution which was adopted by the people. In that Convention he was the senior monitor of the body, served upon some of its most important committees, and took an active part in the discussions which arose during its sessions.

He was elected a member of the first Senate under the Constitution, and was re-elected in the years 1783, '84, '85, '86, and '87. In 1788, he was again a member of the House.

In March, 1781, he was commissioned as a justice of the peace; an office which everybody did not hold at that day, as will appear from the very few who were commissioned in

* In the Revolutionary records at Boston is an account of the number of commissions delivered to each of this committee, of "the men to go to Canada." Eight were confided to "Capt. Seth Washburn."

the town as such before 1800. They did not exceed half a dozen in seventy-five years.

He has always been described to me by his contemporaries as having a light complexion, high forehead, and blue eyes; about five feet ten inches in height; thin, active, and muscular. This was shown by his bringing off Sergeant Brown in his arms from Bunker Hill, and his seizing and disarming the sentinel at the door of Mr. Allen during the Shays insurrection. He was represented as being a man of agreeable, winning manners and address; a fluent and effective speaker; of fearless courage and great firmness; as exerting a marked influence in his own town, and commanding the confidence and respect of the public bodies of men with whom he was at various times connected.

His wife * was, I apprehend, what would now be called a strong-minded woman, shrinking from no duty or sacrifice to which the emergencies of the times called upon the women of that day to submit. They reared a large family of children, whose descendants may be found in various parts of the Union; but not one remains in the town or county where he had lived. He had around him at Cambridge, and engaged with him in the battle of the 17th June, a brother, two sons, and one soon to be a son-in-law.

He died of dropsy, Feb. 12, 1794, at the age of seventy-one, in the full possession of his intellectual powers, and in the consciousness of a life filled up with honest industry and honorable usefulness. In the notice of his death, in the papers of the day, we read, "Of whom it may be truly said, that he was an honest man, a true patriot, a kind husband, an indulgent parent, an obliging neighbor, and a friend to mankind."

Though for many years employed in places of trust, involving, at times, the disbursement of considerable sums of money,

* She died in September, 1787.

he left but little for his heirs beyond the inheritance of a good name. Among the so-called property he gave up, was that of a slave by the name of Titus, who had become his by some means other than a direct purchase. When his attention was called to the question of holding slaves, by the discussions as to the rights of the Colonies, he at once emancipated Titus; who, on the other hand, declined to leave the employment of his former master, and continued in the family till his death. Col. Washburn married Mrs. Sarah Sargent, widow of Thomas Sargent, and daughter of Daniel Denny, the first of the name, in 1788. She survived him.

I have mentioned his sons. One of them (Joseph) was born May 18, 1755. At the age of seventeen, his father bound him as an apprentice to a housewright; where he remained till the war commenced, when, just before he was twenty years of age, he enlisted into the company commanded by his father.

After leaving the service in April, 1776, I do not find that he engaged in it again till the 1st of January, 1777; when he was commissioned as ensign of a company commanded by Capt. Adam Martin, in Col. Bigelow's fifteenth Massachusetts regiment, in the Continental service. On the 2d March, 1779, he was promoted to a lieutenancy in the same company; which office he resigned, and was honorably discharged 13th April, 1780.

This regiment was chiefly composed of men from Worcester County; and we have the testimony of a careful historian,* that "a braver band never took the field or mustered to battle." It saw a great deal of service which required much physical endurance, as well as a good share of heroic courage. Its first destination was to join the Northern Army under Gen. Gates. After the capture of Burgoyne, in which the regiment took a part, it marched into New Jersey.

Without attempting to trace its movements together or in

* Mr. Lincoln, in his History of Worcester.

detail, I may refer to one or two incidents in which it took a part. It went into winter quarters with the American Army at Valley Forge, the winter of 1777–8, and shared in the frightful want and destitution which made that so memorable a scene ever after, when the sufferings and endurance of the army in the war of the Revolution were spoken of. Worn down with hard service, without proper food or shelter, without blankets or clothing, during a winter of unusual severity, when the men might be tracked in the snow by the blood from their naked feet, the condition of an officer was hardly less tolerable than the humblest soldier in the camp. A letter from the subject of this notice, addressed to his father (then a member of the Legislature), giving a detailed account of the condition and destitution of the army, was read by the latter before the House, and is said to have aroused the attention of that body to provide, in some measure, for the immediate relief of the suffering troops.

The following season, the company to which Mr. Washburn belonged was in New Jersey, under Gen. Washington, and took an early and active part in the battle of Monmouth, memorable alike for the desperate courage with which the Americans fought after the disasters of the early part of the engagement, and for the dreadful suffering of the troops from heat, fatigue, and exhaustion; where, it is said, as many met their death by imprudently quenching their intolerable thirst at the wells and streams, to which they rushed when the action was over, as from the shot of the enemy.

The only attempt I shall make to describe the battle will be while speaking of the experience of one of his company (Solomon Parsons), who was dreadfully wounded on the occasion. Being a neighbor and personal acquaintance of Mr. Washburn, he discovered and removed him, from where he had been lying many hours under a burning sun, to a place where his wounds could be dressed; and did every thing in his power to alleviate his sufferings.

I am unable to give in detail the points and places in which the company was engaged while Mr. Washburn remained in the service. After his return from the army, he worked a while at his trade, and built the house where Mr. Knowles lives, at the corner of the Great Road and the road to Charlton, which he afterwards sold to the Rev. Mr. Moore. In 1787, he married Ruth, daughter of Ebenezer Davis, Esq., of Charlton; and occupied the farm on the west side of the Charlton Road, at the foot of the Livermore Hill. He sold that farm, and purchased the one on which he lived, till his death, March, 1807. A part of it now belongs to Mrs. Newhall, half a mile from the Meeting-house, upon the west side of the Rutland Road.

As early as the summer of 1789, he was appointed a deputy-sheriff of the county; and held the place, through all the changes in the office of sheriff, until his death.* He shared liberally in the favor and confidence of his townsmen, so far as that might be evinced by the various offices, and places of trust, which he held. He died in the vigor of life, and in the midst of active usefulness. He left seven children. His widow died March 22, 1827, at the age of sixty-one. It would be, indeed, a poor privilege to have been permitted to write these pages, if delicacy thereby forbade my bearing a humble tribute of respect to parents, one of whom I have spoken of chiefly from information derived from others; and of the other, — her life of humble piety, her wise counsels, her untiring devotion as a mother, and her beautiful exhibition of womanly virtues, which I so long witnessed, will, I trust, justify me in inscribing this simple record of affection and respect to her memory.

The other son of Col. Washburn (Asa Washburn) early removed to Putney, Vt.; where he sustained, through a long

* There had been two incumbents of the office in Leicester before Mr. Washburn. Capt. Ephraim Mower was the first: he removed to Worcester. Timothy Sprague succeeded him. The office was vacant during 1788 and a part of 1789.

life, a high rank and reputation as a magistrate, and a man of worth and intelligence.

I have had occasion to speak of Mr. SOLOMON PARSONS in his connection with the period of his service in the Revolutionary Army.

He was born in 1757, a son of Dr. Solomon Parsons, and grandson of the Rev. David Parsons. I find, by memoranda which he left, that he entered the army in 1775, and went through two campaigns before 1777, the particulars of which I am unable to ascertain. In March, 1777, then twenty years of age, he enlisted in the Continental service during the war, in Capt. Martin's company, in Col. Bigelow's fifteenth Massachusetts regiment; and was in the various battles, marchings, and hard service, to which that distinguished regiment was subjected. It was chiefly, however, to speak of the sufferings he endured in the battle of Monmouth, that I began this notice.

That battle was fought on Sunday, the 28th June, 1778, between the main English Army, on their march through New Jersey, after having evacuated Philadelphia, under Gen. Clinton, and the main American Army, under the immediate command of Gen. Washington, having with him Generals Lee, Lafayette, Green, and Wayne, and other distinguished officers.

It is not my purpose to attempt to describe the battle, any farther than it may be necessary to understand the extract I give below, from Mr. Parsons's written account of his own participation in it. His account, by the way, is another of the many illustrations we have of how little one who is engaged as a soldier or subordinate officer knows of the actual movements of an army, as a whole, in a battle.

The enemy were moving across New Jersey towards the Raritan Bay. Washington's army was a few miles to their left and in their rear. He was inclined to bring them to an engagement, but was not sustained in this by a majority of his officers in council. He, however, pressed upon their line of march; and, for that purpose, sent forward Gen. Maxwell's brigade with the New-Jersey militia, and Col. Morgan with a select corps, to interrupt and impede their progress. On the 24th June, he ordered forward another detachment, under Brig.-Gen. Scott, to aid in annoying the enemy, while he moved on with the main army to Kingstown, — a point near to the enemy, who were moving very slowly through the country at that time, in the direction of Monmouth Court House. The line of march of Clinton's army, as appears on the map, was nearly east; that of the American, more south-easterly, and, of course, approaching the left flank of the enemy.

On the 26th, he sent forward a select corps of one thousand men under Brig.-Gen. Wayne, with Gen. Lafayette to command the whole advanced corps, with orders to take the first opportunity to attack the enemy's rear. Martin's company were a part of these troops. These advanced corps, that night, took position on the Monmouth Road, about five miles from the enemy's rear; but, as that brought our troops too far to the right of the main army, it was ordered to file to the left, to a point between the enemy and the American main army. This was on the 27th. The main body then marched up to within three miles of Gen. Lafayette's advanced corps. Morgan's troops were on the right flank of the enemy; and Gen. Dickenson, with the Jersey militia, on their left. The enemy were about a mile and a half beyond the Court House, where they halted till the morning of the 28th. On the evening of the 27th, the command of the whole advanced corps having been given to Gen. Lee, he encamped at English-town, about five miles to the left, and in rear of the English Army. The main body of the American Army was about three miles in his rear.

Gen. Washington resolved to commence an attack upon their rear the next morning, as soon as the enemy should move from their ground; and gave his orders to Lee accordingly. These orders were repeated in the morning, and the main army moved forward to support him.

Lee advanced with Wayne's and Maxwell's brigades; and, as he came up with the enemy, he sent forward Wayne to engage their rear, while he proposed to attack their leading columns. The enemy had, at this time, a wood upon either flank; and were otherwise favorably situated for making a stand.

The battle was begun, and Washington was pressing forward with the main body of the army to sustain the attacking forces; when, to his amazement, he met Lee in full retreat. With great effort, he succeeded in arresting this retreat of the Americans, and in bringing them to a stand, until the main army could come up to their support. Wayne was in advance of the American forces, and was opposed to the centre of the English Army, where he maintained himself for some time. Col. Stewart's, and the other corps of American artillery, were also very effective in keeping the enemy in check till the main army could be brought into the action.

After a severely contested battle, the enemy, towards night, retreated back on to the ground where Lee first encountered them in the morning; and, in this position, the Americans lay on their arms during the night, intending to renew the fight in the morning. During the night, the enemy silently withdrew, and abandoned the field.

This was the battle of Monmouth, rendered memorable in the annals of the war by the gallantry of our troops, after the disastrous retreat of Lee in the morning, the dreadful sufferings which they endured from long and heavy marches, heat, thirst, and the desperate resistance of the enemy, and by the confidence with which it inspired the country. Every point, from the first advance of the enemy in the morning till their retreat in the afternoon, was sharply contested, notwithstanding the disgraceful retreat of that part of the advance which was with Gen. Lee.

Capt. Martin's company, to which Mr. Parsons belonged, as I gather from his narrative, formed a part of Gen. Wayne's command; having been of the detachment sent forward on the 26th, as above stated, under his and Gen. Lafayette's command.

It was, I infer, after Lee's retreat, when Wayne was obliged to give way, and after an order from Gen. Washington for the brigade to maintain its position, and when, for a second time, the front ranks of Wayne's command fell back upon Stewart's artillery and the other American troops as they came up, that Mr. Parsons was wounded. He must have fallen near the British lines as they were advancing; and the army passed over him, both in its advance and retreat, as well as the American Army in its advance upon the retreating forces of the enemy.

In his narrative, which I purposely somewhat abridge, though I retain his language in whatever I have copied, he mentions the movements of the detachment of the thousand men to which he belonged, on the 26th and 27th, and the part they took in the skirmishing in the morning of the 28th, and the retreat of his regiment with that of Col. Stewart's artillery, and their meeting an officer ordering them to halt. He then describes their return into the action, encountering the head of the enemy's column, and their being fired upon by their artillery.

"The regiment were ordered to incline to the left, to let our artillery in. They commenced to fire most vehemently. We had orders to march forward to a growth of wood a little to our left, where we soon met the enemy. The smoke gave way. I beheld the red-coats within eight rods. I was loaded with a ball and six buck-shot. I took aim about waistband-high. I loaded the second time, and made attempt to fire; but my gun did not go. I jumped into the rear, where I saw Major Porter. I told him my gun would not go off. He said, 'Take care of yourself: the enemy are just upon us!' I stepped into the front rank, and discharged my piece, the enemy within six rods. I loaded the third time. As I returned my ramrod, I found our men four rods distant, and the enemy the same. I wheeled to the left, and observed that the enemy had flanked our men which were out of the woods. I then ran out of the woods. I got ten rods, and the enemy came out of them, and fired a platoon upon me. One ball struck my heel, which much disabled me. The next platoon on the left fired on me, and broke my thigh. I then raised myself upon my right arm, and looked toward the enemy, and saw a man coming towards me. He came upon the run within a rod of me. I begged for quarter. He came within four feet of me. I begged for quarter. He says, 'You damned rebel, I have none for you!" He drew back, and stabbed me through the arm. I *twitched* back my arm and seized the bayonet, one hand by the hilt and one hand by the point, and *twitched* it to the ground. Then he went to twitching it, and twitched it five or six times. He twitched me off the ground, and tried to stab me with the bayonet a number of times. I defended my body. He then drawed me about fifteen feet. I then began to faint. I looked over my shoulder, and saw the flourish of a cutlas, which was by a British officer, who said, 'Why ain't you in your rank?' I let go of the bayonet, and they went off.

"I then was beset by two men. One took my piece, and said, 'I will blow your brains out with your own gun!' He snapped it at me; but, not being loaded, he run upon me like a mad bear. A man standing by says, 'Let him alone: he has got enough.' One cut away my canteen of rum and my time-piece. I had three days' provision and thirty rounds of cartridges, which I had in my blanket. The cry of all was, 'Damn the rebel! why don't you kill him?'

"Here there came a man, and demanded my money. I told him I would not; but, if he would help me to a shade, I would give it to him. He took towards eight dollars. He took hold of my arms, and took me up on my feet; and my *bones grated*, and I fainted; and he laid me down in the same place. I was alarmed by a British sergeant with twelve men. They wore green coats, which we call tories. The sergeant, a Britoner, I had some talk with. I heard some one cry, 'Have you got there a rebel? Why don't you kill him?' Two light-horse-men appeared. One came towards me, and I gave myself up; but the horse, having more mercy than the man, jumped over me. The horseman struck at me, which came very near me.

"I lay in imminent danger from our artillery. The balls came every side of me: one of them came right over me. The sun was so hot, that I could not bear my hand on the ground. I covered myself with my blanket to keep off the sun. The enemy were continually passing. I asked them to help me to a shade. I happened to look out, and saw Gen. Clinton with his life-guard, with several parade-officers. The aide-de-camp rode up towards me, and says, 'My lad, are you wounded?' I told him I was: 'I received my wounds, by balls and three bayonet-thrusts, since I fell into your hands. You give no quarter to-day.' He says, 'There is no such order.' He says, 'The men are rash.' I told him, 'Rash or not, this is what we get for using your men like brothers. I was at the taking of Burgoyne, where we took their whole army. I never saw one of them abused.' They did not want to hear of that. They asked me the state of our army, and where they were. I told them that I had news from them every minute; that our whole park of artillery were playing upon them now, which were six and thirty pieces of artillery. They asked me how many men we had. I told them we had a numerous army. They asked what detachment I belonged to. 'To Marquis Lafayette's.' They asked me what division I belonged to. I told them, 'Gen. Green's division, and Gen. Glover's brigade; Col. Bigelow's regiment, and Capt. Martin's company.' They asked me what town I belonged to. I told them, 'Leicester.' They asked me where. I told them, 'Leicester in the county of Worcester, in the Massachusetts Bay;' and I was not ashamed of it.

"I lay in a deplorable situation. The sun being about an hour high, I perceived their men on the retreat. I then laid myself in the very posture of a dead man, as near as possible. Their main body marched over me; and I heard their officers say they would halt in that growth of woods, and refresh themselves. I heard another party, which was the covering party of the artillery; which marched over me. The artillery came on, which I expected would go over me. They just cleared my head. They trotted. I perceived somebody at my breast. I suppose I stirred. They asked one another whether that man was dead. He said he did not know. I heard the piece move, and I knew no more till our men passed by. I beckoned to the officer: he came with six men, and carried me to the village meeting-house."

That officer, as already stated, was Lieut. Washburn. From Gen. Washington's letters giving an account of this battle, the general action must have begun about noon; and I infer, from the whole of Mr. Parsons's account, that he, a young man never very rugged, scarce twenty-one years of age, must have lain in that burning sun, without shelter or any means of quenching his raging thirst, — with his hip dreadfully shattered, and his arms thrust through, — from about twelve o'clock till the sun was nearly down. As one reads this minute account of a single experience upon a battle-field, he is almost ready to believe that there must be some exaggeration, — that human nature could not have endured so much. But, in the first place, every circumstance which he details in writing co-incides with the official accounts of the battle. Besides, his own character needed no corroboration to confirm his statement. The crippled condition in which he was, from the wounds he then received, for life, was of itself a confirmation; and I have heard him, more than once, converse with the officer who discovered and rescued him, of the experiences of that day, as a thing familiarly known to them both.

From the Monmouth Meeting-house, into which, with the other wounded, he was carried, he was removed to Princeton College; and from thence to Trenton, until he was able to be removed home by his father, Dr. Parsons; where he suffered intensely for seven years, before he sufficiently recovered to engage in any business.

Another Revolutionary incident may here be related, from the part which was taken in it by one long a citizen of Leicester, — Mr. Joseph Bass. He removed here soon after the war, having married the mother of Mr. John Hobart.* A considerable part of the time, he occupied the house opposite Mrs. Newhall's, upon the Rutland Road. He was, while a young man, engaged in a seafaring life. The following narrative I took from his own dictation; though, so far as I could compare it, I found it fully confirmed by the published history of the war: —

In July, 1776, two English frigates, the "Phœnix" and the "Rose," succeeded in sailing up the Hudson, and stationed

* She died in 1816, aged sixty-eight.

themselves near Tarrytown; cutting off the communication, by the river, between the different portions of the American Army. In the latter part of that month, a gallant attack was made upon them by six row-galleys, under the command of Com. Tupper, from Tarrytown.

This attempt being unsuccessful (I borrow Irving's language in his "Life of Washington"), "a gallant little exploit, at this juncture, gave a fillip to the spirits of the community. Two of the fire-ships recently constructed went up the Hudson to attempt the destruction of the ships which had so long been domineering over its waters. One succeeded in grappling the 'Phœnix,' and would soon have set her in flames; but, in the darkness, got to leeward, and was cast loose without effecting any damage. The other, in making for the 'Rose,' fell foul of one of the tenders, grappled and burnt her. The enterprise was conducted with spirit, and, though it failed of its main object, had an important effect." They soon escaped down the river.

Bass, who had been in the "water-service" under Com. Tupper, was, according to his narrative, put in charge of one of these fire-ships: the other was under the command of Capt. Thomas, of New London. Bass's vessel, called the "Polly," was a sloop of about a hundred tons, nearly new: Thomas's was of a smaller size.

These little vessels were anchored in the mouth of the "Spuit-in-Devil Creek." They had been prepared with fagots of very combustible wood, dipped in melted pitch; and bundles of straw, cut about a foot in length, and prepared in the same way. These fagots filled the deck, and communicated with a trough of fine gunpowder, which extended along under the deck, from the hold into the cabin; and into this was inserted a fuse, that might be fired by a person in the cabin, who might escape, by means of a door cut in the side of the vessel, into a whale-boat which was lashed to the "quarter" of the sloop.

Besides these combustibles, there were ten or twelve barrels of pitch in each vessel; and a great number of yards of canvas, cut in strips about a foot wide, covering the yards and rigging, and extending to the deck, all of which had been dipped in spirits of turpentine.

Bass had nine men to his vessel; three of whom he stationed in the whale-boat; one acted as pilot; while he stationed himself in the cabin with a lighted match to fire the materials.

Besides the two frigates, there were a bomb-ketch and two tenders in company, and moored near them.

The night was dark and cloudy, with occasionally a little rain. The vessels lay moored in a line, about north and south, — first the "Phœnix," next the "Rose," then the ketch, and above them the tenders. The fire-ships, on starting from the creek, took a course near the middle of the river; and the darkness of the night, as well as the high bank in their rear, prevented their seeing either the hulls or masts of the vessels; and the first thing that apprised them of their approach, was hearing, immediately on their left, the twelve-o'clock bells of the vessels, and the cry of the sentinels, of "All's well!" from their decks. For the same reason, they could not distinguish the situation of the vessels sufficiently to ascertain their size, or which of them were the frigates.

Bass was considerably in advance of Thomas; and, upon hearing the cry of the sentinels, bore down at once upon the line of the British fleet. He was already near the bomb-ketch before he was perceived by the enemy; who immediately began a severe cannonade upon his vessel, which damaged her rigging and mast, and some of the shot entered her hull. But he was under too much headway, and was already too near to retreat if he had been inclined. As soon as he saw himself near enough to the vessel towards which he was steering, to be sure she would not escape, he gave orders to his men to take to the boat, and, touching the fuse, leaped into the whale-boat, and cast off from his ship. Her course had been surely directed; and, the next moment, the grappling-irons upon her bowsprit and yards became interlocked with the rigging of what proved to be the ketch, and they were both immediately in a blaze. The fire of the burning ship lighted up the surrounding scenery with a horrid glare of splendor. The ketch, with most on board her, were burned or drowned; a few only escaping.

Capt. Thomas, by the light of Bass's ship, bore down upon the "Phœnix," and became grappled with her. He then applied the match; but, becoming entangled with his own fire, was obliged to leap into the river. He lost five of his men, while Bass escaped without the loss of one. The "Phœnix" succeeded in cutting loose from her dangerous assailant by cutting her rigging and slipping her cable.

It was an exceedingly bold and hazardous enterprise; and, if it did not accomplish all it proposed, it infused so much terror into the minds of the commanders of the British vessels, that they immediately withdrew from so dangerous a vicinity.

This account, substantially as above given, was prepared and published in a periodical more than thirty years ago,* as taken directly from the principal actor himself, — an unlettered man; and the co-incidence of his statement, even in minute particulars, with the authentic narrative of history, leaves no reasonable doubt of its correctness even in its details.

I have spoken in another place of the black man, by the name of PETER SALEM, who shot down Major Pitcairn at the battle of Bunker Hill. After the war, he came to Leicester, and continued to reside there till a short time before his death. The history of the town would be incomplete without

---

* Mr. Bass died in 1829, aged seventy-five.

giving him a place; and I am happy that I can borrow from so authentic and interesting a history as Mr. Barry's, of Framingham, for the early life of this "hero of '76."

He was born in Framingham, and was held as a slave, probably until he joined the army; whereby, if not before, he became free. This was the case with many of the slaves in Massachusetts; as no slave could be mustered into the army. If a master suffered this to be done, it worked a practical emancipation. Peter served faithfully as a soldier, during the war, in Col. Nixon's regiment. A part of the time he was the servant of Col. Nixon, and always spoke of him in terms of admiration.

He lived in various places in the town; but his last abode was a cabin which he built for himself, on the south side of the road leading to Auburn, about a quarter of a mile from the house formerly of William Watson. In front of his cabin he planted and reared two or three poplar-trees; and, around it, dug and cultivated a little garden, in which, besides the few vegetables that he planted, a few clumps of flowering shrubs and a stinted rose or two, with a few sweet-smelling herbs, gave evidence of his unequal struggle with a hard and rocky soil.

Horticulture, however, was not his forte. He earned a precarious livelihood by making and mending baskets, bottoming chairs, and the like; which gave him admittance into everybody's house, where his good nature rendered him a universal favorite, especially with the children. His military training in the army had given him a sort of instinctive soldierly bearing; and his habits of obedience there to his superiors, infused, into all his intercourse with the considerable people of the town, a marked courtesy of manner, which he never omitted or forgot.

It was always a pleasant sight to observe the promptness and precision with which the heel of Peter's right foot found its way into the hollow of his left one, his body grow erect, and the right hand spring up to a level with his eye, to salute Massa Moore or Mistress D. on passing, in return for the salutation or nod of recognition with which everybody greeted him.

It was a treat, too, for the younger members of the family to gather around Peter, while engaged in mending the household chairs; or, sitting in the chimney corner, with the youngest on his knee, while the flickering blaze lighted up his black face, to listen to his stories of the war, and what he had seen "when he was out with Massa Nixon."

He was especially at home at the firesides of those who had been in "the service," and generally found a welcome chair at the hospitable board. They were, to him, companions in arms; and he never seemed to think he could grow old while any of them remained to answer his roll-call.

But though Peter had gone through seven years' hard service unharmed, and had not lost a jot of his freshness of feeling, age crept upon him unawares at last. His erect form began to stoop; his military step grew unsteady; the thinned and whitened covering which had concealed an ugly *wen* or two, that had perched themselves upon the top of his head, no longer served to screen this defect in his personal symmetry. His resources grew smaller and smaller; till, at last, the hand of charity had to supply the few wants which the old man required.

In this respect, there is a frightful equality in the law. Overseers of the poor never heed whether the man that is hungry is a saint or a sinner. If he needs fire to warm or clothes to cover him, though scarred all over in the service of his country, it is their "duty" to hunt up his "settlement," and give notice, as the law requires.

Peter's settlement was in Framingham, and the good people of that town took early measures for his removal thither.

It was a sad day to Peter; but, before taking his final departure, he went around and made a farewell visit to each of his favorite haunts, and to such of his old friends as time had spared. With a heavy heart, he paid them his last salute, and disappeared from the spot which had been his home for so many years. His cabin soon went to decay. A rough stone chimney served for many years to mark where it had stood; and the lilac and the rose he planted, bloomed for a few years, and were then broken down, and died. The last object that marked the spot was a poplar-tree; and even that has grown old, and will ere long disappear.

But will any one say that this humble black man, whose hand did such service in the very redoubt on Bunker Hill; who perilled his life, through some of the most trying and arduous scenes of the war, for that freedom for others which he had never been permitted to share till he won it personally by personal valor, — will any one say that his name does not deserve a place among those whom it is the purpose of these simple annals to commemorate?

He died at Framingham, Aug. 16, 1816.

Of Capt. John Holden, I have been able to learn very little. From one of his descendants, I find that he was born at Concord in 1753; entered the army, and was at the battle of Bunker Hill; served through the war; and left the army, at the peace, with the rank of captain. I have mentioned elsewhere his having been of the party which so gallantly stormed Stony Point under Gen. Wayne, — one of the most signal acts of bravery which took place during the war. I have often heard him allude to it, though never in detail.

After leaving the army, he went to reside in Holden; where he married Zipporah Hall in 1789. He removed from there to Paxton, and thence to Leicester, previous to 1804. He had a numerous family of children, and lived in a house (now removed) which stood on the east side of the Rutland Road, a little north of the Hubbard House, where Jacob Bond lived. His wife died in January, 1827: he died March 13, 1828. He had lived long enough in the town to be familiarly known to its citizens, and sufficiently identified with its history to be mentioned in connection with it.

CHAPTER VIII.

CONNECTION OF THE TOWN WITH THE GENERAL HISTORY OF THE COMMONWEALTH. — FRENCH AND REVOLUTIONARY WARS. — CONSTITUTION OF THE UNITED STATES AND OF THE STATE. — WARS WITH FRANCE AND ENGLAND. — CONCLUSION.

In attempting to trace the part which the people of this town took, from time to time, in the general affairs of the country, it will be obvious that the topics must be few in number.

They bore their share in the wars which preceded the final expulsion of the armies of France from Canada, upon its conquest in 1759 and '60. In the controversies with the mother country, they took an early and active part; and, in the struggle of the Revolution, evinced a prompt and cordial co-operation in all the public measures it involved. After the peace, the town was, in the maintenance of government and order, true to its early history; and in none of the agitating questions which engaged the attention of the people at large was it an indifferent or an inactive spectator.

Somewhat may be said of the history of the town in these particulars; and, though it may involve much that might seem to be altogether local in its interest, it has seemed to me to be the most fit connection in which to present what I have been able to glean upon the subject from the limited materials within my reach.

I found it impossible to ascertain the names or numbers of all its citizens who were called into actual service during the wars which preceded the Revolution. I have discovered a few of these by researches in the muster-rolls which are to be found in the State House in Boston; but I am apprehensive that it is far from embracing the entire number.

In a chapter of this work upon the "Army, &c.," I have preserved the names of those from Leicester who took part in the wars before the Revolution as well as during that struggle, so far as they have been ascertained; and, consequently, shall have no occasion to repeat them again in this.

Troops were stationed here in the Indian War of 1722; it being then a frontier settlement.

The war which was declared against France in 1744 aroused a general enthusiasm and zeal in the Colony; and the expedition which was organized the following year to make a descent upon Cape Breton, with a view of conquering the military works at Louisburg, called out such a proportion of the entire military of Massachusetts, that I am justified in assuming that Leicester contributed liberally of men towards the enterprise.

Massachusetts furnished three thousand two hundred and fifty of the four thousand troops, by whom, chiefly, that stronghold was taken, — an exploit that shed lustre upon the fame of the Provincial troops, and told upon their courage and self-reliance in after-days when their children met the descendants of their former companions and associates of '45 at Lexington and Bunker Hill. John Brown of Leicester commanded a company in that expedition. Two only of the number have I been able to trace; and, whether the balance of his company was from this town, I have no means of saying.

The following year, the country was greatly alarmed by an invasion, threatened by a formidable French fleet; which was planned, and so far carried out as to have arrived off Nova Scotia, under the command of Duke D'Anville. A draught of twenty-five men was made from Leicester, to march, without a moment's delay, to Boston. The order for this draught, and the pressing nature of the call for troops, will be found in another part of this work, when speaking of Capt. Nathaniel Green, to whom it was addressed.

The draught was answered, and the men marched; but, fortunately, there was no occasion for their services. The French fleet was scattered by a storm, the commander committed suicide, and the expedition was abandoned.

To guard the frontier settlements, during this war, from the Indians, troops were stationed at Coleraine and at Fort Massachusetts, between what is now Adams and Williamstown. I find one man from Leicester among the troops at Coleraine during the winter of 1747–8, and three at Fort Massachusetts. Besides these, an expedition was planned in 1747 against Canada; in which Massachusetts, as usual, took a leading part, and furnished a large proportion of the troops. Leicester bore her share in the enterprise; and I find the following entry upon her records, though I am unable to ascertain the names of the persons alluded to. In the warrant for March meeting, 1748, it is recited, "Whereas there has been several persons that have enlisted into the Canada expedition, these are to see if the town will abate them of their rates the year past."

The treaty of Aix-la-Chapelle, in October, 1748, put an end to this war; nor were hostilities commenced until 1754, and then without any formal declaration of war. This war, though not formally declared till two years after the commencement of hostilities in America, became memorable as the last of those French and Indian wars which had kept the Colonies in a state of danger and alarm, and cost them so much blood and treasure. It was the opening scene in the military career of Gen. Washington, and was signalized by the disastrous defeat of Gen. Braddock, the massacre of Fort William Henry, the taking of Quebec, and the final subjugation of Canada; and the part which the colonists took in the various expeditions and battles to which this war gave rise became such a school for the practical training of their troops, that the opening scenes of the Revolution found officers already educated and men already disciplined for the camp and the field.

In 1754, an expedition of eight hundred men, under Gen. Winslow, was sent into Maine to hold the French and Indians in check. I find the names of three men from Leicester upon the rolls of that expedition, in the service from April to November of that year.

In 1756, an expedition was planned against Crown Point, to consist of ten thousand men; and an order was issued for enlisting a thousand men within the counties of Worcester and Hampshire. Under this order, eleven were enlisted from Leicester, and belonged to the company of Capt. John Stebbins, who had formerly belonged to Leicester, but then lived in Spencer, and died, while in the service in this expedition, in 1756. The company belonged to the regiment of Col. Ruggles, afterwards the famous Brig.-Gen. Ruggles, of Hardwick. There being a deficiency in the requisite number of men, four more were enlisted from Leicester.

In July, three more joined the army at Fort Edward, in addition to one who had previously joined it; and, in September, four more were called for, and two of them impressed for the same service. They joined the army at Fort William Henry. Two others, who had been, or soon after became, inhabitants of the town, were in the same expedition.

It will be perceived that there were draughted more than twenty men in a single year from a town containing scarcely six hundred souls, struggling with all the difficulties of a new settlement, and little able to spare the services of its active young men who were called to join the army. It serves to show the nature of the struggle in which the Colonies were engaged, and the extent to which a people thus situated were willing to make sacrifices for a common cause.

Of all this number, two only did not voluntarily enlist; nor were those who joined the army mere adventurers, or such as were willing to throw off the restraints of home for the greater license of the camp. They were of various ages, from nineteen to thirty. Several had wives, and most of them had connections of family and homes, which they must have given up with reluctance and regret. For instance, Parley Brown, a son of one of the most considerable men in the town, was nineteen years old; while the father-in-law, brother-in-law, and brother, of Seth Washburn, who had served in one expedition himself against the Indians in 1749, were of the number who enlisted in that of 1756.

The operations of the year 1756 were, however, mostly unsuccessful; and the French, at the opening of the campaign of 1757, continued to advance upon the English posts in the northern parts of New York. Under Gen. Montcalm, they invested Fort William Henry, on Lake George, in August, and compelled the garrison to surrender. This was followed by what has been ever since known as the "Massacre of Fort William Henry."

Among those who were present in the fort at the time of its surrender was Mr. Knight Sprague, then of Hingham, but, for most of a long life, a citizen of Leicester; from whose narrative I have transcribed the incidents of which he was a spectator, and in which he participated. He belonged to Col., afterward Gen. Benjamin Lincoln's regiment; and was, at that time, only sixteen years of age.

According to his account, the fort was surrendered about ten o'clock on Wednesday morning. The English were detained till the next morning, and, during that time, were guarded by the French troops, and protected from the savages: but as soon as the army had left the fort to take up their march towards Fort Edward, according to the terms of the capitulation, the Indians rushed upon them, and began to kill and strip them; and every effort on the part of the French to restrain them was unavailing. Sprague escaped, after having been partially stripped, and made his way to Fort Edward. On his way, he passed his captain, who had been entirely stripped, and many women who were in no better condition. The yells of the savages, the groans of the wounded and dying, the shrieks of the affrighted women and frantic soldiers, and the dead who lay scattered around them, made it a scene of unsurpassed horror. Fifteen out of his own company of fifty were killed soon after leaving the fort. Nor is it surprising that the massacre of Fort William Henry became one of the memorable events in that last, protracted death-struggle for ascendency on the part of France, in a country over which, at one time, she seemed destined to become the acknowledged mistress.

Mr. Sprague often saw Munroe, the English commander of the fort; as well as Montcalm, the general of the French trooops. The former he represented as a dignified gentleman of about fifty years of age; the latter, a finely formed, active, and graceful man, of small stature. The following year, Sprague had the satisfaction of taking part in the attack upon Fort Frontinac, on Lake Ontario, under Col. Bradstreet, and to witness the surrender of that fortress.

The scenes in which these and the other Provincial troops of that day were engaged have become all but classic ground. History and fiction have combined to keep alive the interest which no one can fail to feel on visiting these fields, on which the fathers of New England fought with a courage and devotion worthy of the best days of Greece or Rome. Every rock and glen teems with the associations of events which are so intimately connected with a most important historic period of our country. Here Baron Dieskeau and Col. Williams fell in 1755; and here the same flag was struck down on the ramparts of William Henry by Baron Montcalm, in 1757, which in 1759 waved in triumph over his grave on the heights of Abraham, and floated above the citadel of conquered Quebec.

No sound of war now breaks the silence which reigns over the spot where the crumbling bastions of that once memorable fortress stood; and forest-trees were a few years since growing within its intrenchments, to shelter it, as it were, from the decay which was fast obliterating its embrasures and breastworks.*

If these simple annals may serve to preserve the names of a few of the humble actors in those scenes, its purposes will not have entirely failed.

The war terminated practically in America by the surrender of Quebec; but levies continued to be made until the peace of 1763. In 1761 and '62, I find six, at least, drawn from Leicester for military service, though the length of the service is not specified. One of the expeditions in which three of these were engaged was beyond the North River; but the place of its destination does not appear upon the roll from which the names are copied.

No circumstance of a public nature appears to have occurred, after the close of the last French War, to call upon the town for action, until those measures of the British ministry which began to awaken the attention of the Colonies, and led on, step by step, to their final severance from the mother-country.

The part which this town took in carrying forward the measures of the Revolution is one of which her sons had a right to be proud. To appreciate these, and to understand the circumstances under which the town acted, it is necessary that we should consider for a moment the situation and resources of its inhabitants.

I suppose, that, at no time during the war, the population of the town exceeded nine hundred persons; and a statement, professing to be authentic, places it below that number. As for its actual wealth, I have no valuation taken during or immediately preceding the war to guide me. It was, however,

---

* I speak of this fortress as it appeared upon a visit to it thirty years ago. From advertisements in the newspapers, a magnificent hotel, it would seem, had sprung up upon a spot so long memorable in the annals of our Colonial history.

a mere agricultural community, without trade or manufactures; and its soil a hardy and unproductive one. The whole number borne upon the list of the trainbands of the town in 1781 was but a hundred and fifty-one, of whom forty-nine were upon what was called the "alarm-list;" leaving only a hundred and two supposed to be competent for active military duty.

But, with no other than ordinary means of education, the town seems to have possessed an unusual proportion of not only strong-minded, but well-educated men. The record they have left of the public papers which were produced between 1765 and 1776 bears honorable testimony to the patriotic zeal, the scholarly attainments, and the sound statesmanship, of those who took a lead in the utterance of the public sentiment of the town. One circumstance had an important influence in producing a harmony of feeling and a promptness of action on the part of the town; and that was the intimate family connection which existed between several of the people of Leicester and the leading men of Boston, where most of the early Revolutionary movements originated.

The mother of the Hon. Joseph Allen, who had himself removed from Boston in November, 1771, was a sister of Samuel Adams. The Henshaws, Joseph and William, had also come from Boston, and were connected with many of the patriot families there; and Joshua Henshaw, who came into town just before the Revolution broke out, and whose daughter had married Joseph Henshaw, was on terms of intimate association and correspondence with the Adamses, James Otis, Warren, and the other leaders of public opinion in Boston. If, then, it might seem that the town took a prominent and leading part in these measures, disproportioned to its relative magnitude and resources, it may not have been that they were actuated by any warmer or more devoted zeal for the cause; but because, by being earlier advised than some of the towns in respect to the measures to be adopted, they may have taken earlier action, and held a more prominent position, than other communities equally deserving of commendation.

In its early history, the town must have been eminent for its loyalty to the crown. In the notice of Judge Menzies, given in another part of this work, it will have been seen, that, while a representative from the town, he was expelled from the House for his excess of loyalty to the king. Judge Steele, long a leading and influential citizen of the town, remained true to his loyalty to the last; but, when the war broke out, there was, besides him, not a single man of influence who was not a thorough and decided "liberty man." Prominent among these were Joseph Allen, John Brown, the Dennys, the Greens, the Henshaws, Seth Washburn, Hezekiah Ward, John Southgate, and others, whose names will appear in the following pages. They could not fail to shape the opinions and give direction to the judgment of such a community.

But in maintaining the assumption, that this town furnished its full share of wise counsellors, brave soldiers, and patriotic citizens, towards achieving our national independence, it will be necessary to do little more than give in their order the facts which the records of the town furnish of the sacrifices made, the services rendered, and the moneys expended, by them in the prosecution of the war. If, in these respects, she was surpassed by any of her sister-towns, it is believed that the history of those towns is yet to be written.

In the matter of scholarship, Joseph Henshaw had received a collegiate education; Joseph Allen and William Henshaw had had the advantages of the classical schools of Boston; and Thomas Denny must have cultivated a taste for reading, and skill in composition. But of some, if not most, of the others, they had few if any advantages beyond the most limited teachings of schools for a few weeks each year. The grammar and spelling of many of the public papers which some of these men were called upon to prepare, indicate but little familiarity with these graceful and convenient, if not necessary, accomplishments in a writer.

In the matter of military skill and experience, the people of the town must have possessed a good share of that element. John Brown had been a captain at Louisburg; William Henshaw had served as a subaltern officer under Gen. Abercrombie in 1756; and Seth Washburn had served in one campaign against the Indians. Besides these, four or five of Capt. Washburn's company of minute-men had served in the campaigns against Ticonderoga and Crown Point; and others were living in the town at the time, who had learned war under officers of the crown.

Not to anticipate, it will be my purpose to present, in a chronological order of events, the part which the town took in the affairs of the Revolution; but being, as it was, the great historical event of the State, as well as of all the older towns of the Commonwealth, the reader ought not to expect any thing new or original in the narrative.

Not to go farther back into that chain of causes which led to the scenes of 1775, Parliament had, in 1763, passed the "Acts of Trade," which bore hardly upon the business and commerce of New England. The plan of taxing the Colonies was thus early broached and discussed, but not then adopted. This led to a correspondence between Massachusetts and others of the Colonies. In 1764, the "Sugar Act," as it was called, was passed, and was intended as an incipient measure of taxation. A Stamp Act was proposed, but did not then pass; but a measure quite as offensive was adopted, by which all breaches of the revenue laws were required to be tried in Courts of Admiralty, without the intervention of a jury. The alarm thus created was general: for the people had regarded trial by jury as one of the great safeguards of their liberties; and, as such, it had come down to them with the common law which their fathers had brought with them from England.

This was followed by the famous Stamp Act of 1765. The Colonies were aroused by a sense of impending danger; and Massachusetts proposed a General Congress of the Colonies, to be held in October of that year. In the mean time, riots occurred in various places; and one of the most memorable and disgraceful of these outbreaks was that by which, on the 26th August, 1765, the costly mansion-house of Lieut.-Gov. Hutchinson, with its furniture, plate, and, above all, his invaluable collection of books and manuscripts, were destroyed; a loss which no one, interested in the early history of the Colony, can ever cease to deplore. In this agitated state of the public mind, the people of Leicester, Spencer, and Paxton, then forming one district for representative purposes, were called together, on the 17th October, 1765, "to see if the town will give instructions to their representative in this critical conjuncture."

John Brown was their representative, and had been since 1761. Daniel Henshaw, Thomas Denny, Jonathan Newhall, of Leicester; Benjamin Johnson, who had removed from Leicester to Spencer; Joshua Lamb of Spencer; and Jonathan Knight, whose son and grandson afterwards lived in Leicester, of Paxton,—were appointed a committee to prepare these instructions. Their report was adopted after some additions, and entered of record as a part of the proceedings of the town. It was probably from the pen of Thomas Denny. These resolutions will be found at large in the Appendix. to this work, and will amply repay by their perusal any one who wishes to understand the tone of public sentiment at that time, and the intelligent basis upon which it rested.

The next recorded action of the town was the adoption of resolutions, Sept. 19, 1768; setting forth in plain and forcible language the political duties and rights of the Colonies, as they were apprehended by the people of this town. These, too, will be found in the Appendix; and are an unmistakable index of the thoughts and sentiments which had been occupying the minds of the people between their former meeting in 1765 and the time of their adoption. They had studied their rights as Englishmen; and, while they never thought of compromising their loyalty to the king, they insisted upon the privileges and protection guaranteed to them by Magna Charta and the Bill of Rights. The paper is worthy of the men, the time, and the cause to which it owed its origin.

It was during this year (1768) that Massachusetts addressed a circular to the other Provinces upon the subject of the grievances which they were suffering in the duties and taxes imposed upon them by the mother-country. This called down upon them the severe animadversions of the Earl of Hillsborough, in a communication which was laid by Gov. Bernard before the Legislature. This led to a reply on the part of the House, and a message to the Governor, which so exasperated him that he dissolved the Legislature. It was followed by a spirited convention of representatives of the several towns, held in Boston; which fills quite a space in Hutchinson's third volume of his History. Leicester was represented in that convention by Capt. Brown; and that fact, as well as the occasion for calling it, are alluded to in the resolutions above referred to. This convention was called by the people of Boston assembled in town-meeting. It met, Sept. 22, 1768, in Faneuil Hall, and continued in session till the 29th. Its purpose professed to be that such measures might be concerted and advised as his majesty's service, and the peace and safety of his subjects in the Province, might require. As the occasion for calling it was the refusal of the Governor to convene the Legislature after proroguing it on the 30th of June, and then dissolving it by proclamation on the 1st of July, it was decidedly a revolutionary measure; and so it was esteemed by the government here and at home, and gave great cause of uneasiness. Circulars had been addressed to the various towns of the Province, ninety of whom had responded by sending delegates, authorized and ready to adopt any measures which the exigencies of the times demanded. "That it was a high offence," says Hutchinson, "it was generally agreed. Some would make the act of the selectmen of Boston to be treason; and pains were taken to procure and preserve some of the original letters signed by them."

A compact was entered into by most of the merchants and principal people of Boston, in August, 1768, not to import English goods; especially tea, paper, glass, and the other things upon which duties had been imposed.

The next measure of the ministry which served to excite new fears and create new causes of alienation on the part of the Colonies, was the threatening to visit upon them the consequences of treason and rebellion, and to transport them for trial to Great Britain. This was followed, on the part of Virginia, by resolutions not to import British goods; in which they were joined by like resolutions on the part of South Carolina, Maryland, Delaware, North Carolina, and New York.

In January, 1770, the people of this town assembled, and voted not to purchase any thing of those merchants in Boston who imported goods from Great Britain; and adopted a resolution of thanks to those merchants, who, by refusing to import such goods, sacrificed their own interest to the good of their country. This meeting was called upon the petition of twenty-eight persons, which was drawn by William Henshaw, dated Dec. 25, 1769, in the following words:—

"Whereas there are several persons in this Province who have sordidly detached themselves from the public interest, and have taken advantage of the agreement entered into by the merchants for non-importation, thereby endeavoring to defeat their noble design of saving their country from slavery; we, the subscribers, will endeavor by all lawful means to prevent their base designs: and, for that end, we pray that you will grant a warrant for the calling a town-meeting to act on the following articles; viz., to vote that any person, being an inhabitant of Leicester, who shall, directly or indirectly, purchase any goods or merchandise of John Barnard, James and Patrick M'Masters, John

Mien, Ann and Elizabeth Cummings, all of Boston; Henry Barnet of Marlborough; Dunkin and Campbell of Worcester; or any other person who imports goods from Great Britain, or shopkeeper who purchases of any imported contrary to the agreement entered into by the merchants of Boston, — such persons so offending shall be deemed enemies to America, and, as such, shall be recorded in the town's book of records."

The loss of trade arising from these compacts not to purchase English goods had such a disastrous effect upon the business of that country, that, in March following (1770), it was voted to repeal all these obnoxious duties, except that upon tea. Nothing could have been more misjudged than retaining this. It showed, by the repeal of the other duties, how much the country had been troubled by the retaliatory acts of the Colonies; and it did little more than keep alive the source of irritation which drove them at last to exasperation.

We see, as we trace the events that took place at this period, how the people grew more and more bold and resolute in their resolutions till the final rupture. Resolutions were followed by acts. They first studied and settled in their own minds what were their rights, and next took measures to maintain them.

In May, 1770, a company of forty-six men belonging to this town formed an association to familiarize themselves with the drill and manual of the soldier; and devoted afternoons every week to the purpose, although the season of the year rendered such a loss of time from the business of their farms especially inconvenient. They elected William Henshaw, captain; Seth Washburn, lieutenant; and Samuel Denny, ensign.

In 1771, the town took the decided step of voting to purchase one hundred pounds of powder, with bullets and flints in proportion.

Until this time (1771), the Governor had been dependent upon the Legislature for the payment of his salary; but, in order to relieve him from the constant annoyance to which he had been subjected during the growing controversy between the prerogative and the people by their refusing to provide him a proper support, it was resolved by the government at home to pay him a fixed salary of an adequate amount out of the American revenue. This gave great umbrage to the people. The General Court, in 1772, adopted strong and decided resolutions against it, as being an infraction of their charter; but it was from Boston, as usual, that the most systematic efforts emanated for enlightening and arousing the public mind.

One of the memorable town-meetings of Boston was called on the 2d November, 1772; when a large committee, at the head of which was James Otis, was raised, "to state the rights of the colonists, and of this Province in particular, as men, as Christians, and as subjects; to communicate and publish the same to the several towns in the Province, and to the world, as the sense of this town, with the infringements and violations thereof that have been, or from time to time may be, made. Also requesting of each town a free communication of their sentiments on the subject."

When it is remembered, that, in addition to its chairman being James Otis, that committee embraced among its numbers Samuel Adams, Joseph Warren, and Josiah Quincy, it is unnecessary to say that their report presented the rights and the wrongs of the Colony with a power and an effect that were felt throughout Massachusetts and beyond its borders.

Leicester received one of these reports, and immediately convened its inhabitants "to hear a letter from the town of Boston, with a pamphlet accompanying it, wherein the rights of the colonists are stated, with the infringement thereof; and to consider and advise thereon, and come into such measures as the town may think proper, in co-operation with the other towns in the Province, either by instructing our representative, or any other means that may appear to them best to contribute to the restoring those privileges we are deprived of, or establishing those we enjoy."

This meeting was held on the 4th January, 1773. At this meeting, the town voted,—

"1st, That the rights, as therein stated, do belong to the inhabitants of this Province.

"2d, That they would choose a committee of nine persons to take the matter into consideration, and report, as soon as may be, what they think proper for this town to do."

The committee consisted of Capt. Brown, William Henshaw, and Hezekiah Ward, of Leicester; Moses Livermore and Joshua Lamb, of Spencer; Capt. Witt, Capt. Brown, and Willard Moore, of Paxton.*

The committee prepared a series of resolves; which, with the instruction at the same time adopted, to be communicated to their representative, will be found in the Appendix. These papers were undoubtedly from the pen of William Henshaw. Additional instructions were adopted, in May following, at the election of their representative. Seth Washburn was moderator of the meeting; but the record does not indicate who prepared these. Several of the papers of that day were the productions of the ready and vigorous pen of Joseph Allen, Esq. The instructions are copied into the Appendix, and speak, in their language, the spirit that dictated the measures of the men who had then assembled.

Every thing, in the mean time, had been growing more and more threatening. The tea had been thrown into the dock at Boston. The letters of Gov. Hutchinson to the ministry had been discovered by some mysterious agency, and published in the Colony; and the governor had become suspected, and detested by the people generally.

Great injustice was undoubtedly done to Gov. Hutchinson in regard to the measures of the ministry. He was a

* This was Major Moore, who was killed at the battle of Bunker Hill.

loyalist, ambitious of royal favor, and shared largely in the royal patronage; but Massachusetts was his birthplace and his home; and the printed works that he left show with what sentiments of affection he ever regarded her.

In December, 1773, another meeting of the people of Leicester, Spencer, and Paxton, was held; and resolutions were adopted, which will be found in the Appendix. A committee of fourteen was appointed "to inspect any teas that may be sold or consumed in the town and district aforesaid, and report, at the annual meeting in May, the names of the persons so offending; and it was ordered, that the proceedings of the meeting should be recorded, and forwarded by the Committee of Correspondence to the committee in Boston.

Parliament, exasperated by the destruction of the tea, now maddened the people still more by undertaking to punish Boston by passing the famous "Boston Port Bill" early in 1774. The Boston Committee of Correspondence thereupon addressed letters to the several towns in the Colony. Many of the replies to them have recently been published by the Massachusetts Historical Society.

It is difficult for us, at this time, to understand how slow and infrequent was the communication between one part of the country and another. It was almost impossible to reach the great body of the people. Instead of a press sending out its newspapers daily into every hamlet, and almost every house, in the land, so that what is said or thought in Boston in the morning is read by or before the next morning all over the State, the only way of communicating with the masses was by pamphlets and circulars sent to the several towns by special messengers, and then calling the people formally together, and reading these in their hearing.

I happen to have before me a memorandum in a private diary, which illustrates the slow transmission of news at that day. The tea, it will be recollected, was destroyed in Boston on the evening of the 16th December. The entry in the diary I am speaking of — and it was that of a man much engaged in public business at the time, and living upon the Great Post Road — was "Monday, 21st December, spent at home. *Heard of the destruction of the East-India Company's tea in Boston* by a body of three hundred men; taken out of the vessels, and thrown overboard."

The efficiency of these Committees of Correspondence was manifested in various ways during the whole struggle with the Royal Government. It is hardly too much to say, that, at times, they were the government. Whatever emanated from the central body was sure, in a few days, to reach every part of the Colony.

In May, 1774, in addition to instructions to their representative, the town voted to answer a letter just received by them from the Committee of Correspondence in Boston. A committee, for the purpose of preparing resolutions, was raised, consisting of James Baldwin, jun., Joseph Henshaw, Oliver Witt, Joseph Allen, Oliver Watson, Lieut. Lamb, and Willard Moore; while the letter was referred to the Committee of Correspondence of the town. The resolutions and letter which were reported and adopted are copied into the Appendix. The letter was transmitted by the clerk of the town to the town-clerk of Boston.

The ministry went on madly in their measures of alienation and exasperation by the appointment of "Mandamus Councillors" in the place of their being elected, as provided in the Province Charter; and by prohibiting the assembling of the people in their town-meetings, except for specific purposes.

The people grew justly alarmed at these strides towards despotic power; and a town-meeting was held in Boston, from which an appeal emanated in May to their own fellow-citizens and the people of the other Colonies. The proposition was made for the suspension of all commerce with Great Britain.

In June, there was a warrant issued for a meeting of this town, on the 6th July, to consider the state of the public affairs. They uttered their sentiments, as usual, in the form of resolves. The committee who were to prepare these seem to have been carefully selected, and consisted of Thomas Denny, Joseph Henshaw, and Joseph Allen, of Leicester; James Draper and Joseph Wilson, of Spencer; and Oliver Witt and Ralph Earle, of Paxton. They are quite extended; but their perusal is the best means I have for exhibiting what the people thought and how they felt at that time. They may be found in the Appendix.

The same meeting raised a committee to present the "covenant," not to purchase or import any goods from England, Ireland, or the West Indies, for signature, to all who had not signed it, in order that they might have the opportunity to do so. In such a state of feeling, few could have dared, even if they had wished, to decline such an invitation. The ban of public opinion was too formidable to be encountered by men of ordinary courage. I have no reason, however, to suppose that the measure did not meet the cordial assent of all the people of the town, with the exception of Judge Steele.

On the 6th September, 1774, in pursuance of an invitation from a Convention of the Committees of Correspondence of the county of Worcester, a body of six thousand men assembled at Worcester, and so effectually blocked up the access to the Court House, that the Inferior Court, then about to assemble, were unable to open the term, and never afterwards resumed their functions.

The journal of the meetings of this Convention, which was published more than twenty years ago, enriched as it was by notes of its accomplished editor, the late William Lincoln, Esq., added much to the fund of information before possessed as to the movements in the county preliminary to the Revolution. It first met Aug. 9, 1774. At that time, the Committee of Correspondence of Leicester, who attended, were Thomas Denny, William Henshaw, Joseph Henshaw, and Rev. Benjamin Conklin. William Henshaw was elected the clerk of the convention. It was opened by prayer by the Rev. Mr. Conklin, who was second to no one in zeal and earnestness in the cause for which it had assembled. At its meeting on the 30th August, the resolution which called for this mass meeting of the people as a body was reported by Joseph Henshaw, which was in these words: "In order to prevent the execution of the late Act of Parliament respecting the courts, it be recommended to the inhabitants of this county to attend in person the next Inferior Court of Common Pleas and General Sessions, to be holden at Worcester, in and for said county, on the 6th of September next." As it was anticipated that the royal troops would be sent to sustain the court, the people were recommended to come properly armed, if they should have intelligence of such troops being on the march.

The convention itself met on that day. The people were under the command of officers of their own election, each town being under a separate command, and marched in military array. They were formed into two lines; and through these the justices and officers of the court were compelled to march, stopping at brief intervals, and repeating a written declaration of their submission to the public will. They were followed by forty-three royalists belonging to Worcester, who had made themselves obnoxious by protesting against the revolutionary movements of the patriots, but who now read a recantation of their errors.

The Court of Sessions then consisted of all the justices of the peace in the county. A paper was accordingly prepared for these to sign, addressed to the people of the county, assuring them that the court would stay all judicial proceedings. This paper bears the signature of Judge Steele; and, among other justices, that of Daniel Henshaw; while a separate assurance was signed by Gardner Chandler, the sheriff, and Rufus Chandler, John Sprague, and Nathaniel Chandler, as attorneys of the court.

A portion of these justices, among whom was Judge Steele, had addressed a congratulatory letter to Gov. Gage on his arrival. These were required, in addition to the general confession and promise, to make an acknowledgment of their fault in writing. The name of Judge Steele stands at the head of the paper.

It is not my purpose to follow the journal of this convention, any further than may be necessary to illustrate the action of this town. At its various meetings, Leicester was uniformly represented; and the records of its proceedings show that the representatives of that town held a prominent place among their associates. The committees of Worcester and Leicester were made a standing committee for the county, to correspond with other Committees of Correspondence; and call a County Congressional Convention, whenever they thought proper; and to them were added Thomas Denny and Joseph Henshaw of Leicester, and Joshua Bigelow of Worcester. Hezekiah Ward and Thomas Newhall had been elected members of the committee of Leicester, in the places of Col. Denny and Col. Henshaw, since the first meeting of the convention. The convention, among other things, adopted a spirited remonstrance, addressed to Gov. Gage; and appointed Joseph Henshaw, Thomas Denny, and Willard Moore, to present the same. The paper bore the names of Joseph Henshaw, chairman; and William Henshaw, clerk. The date of these proceedings was the 21st September, 1774.

It will be recollected, that, though no open rupture had taken place, there had, practically, grown up a separation between the Royal Government and the people of the Colony. In June, the Governor had dissolved the General Court. Early in September, writs for the election of a new House of Representatives were issued, to meet, on the 5th of October, at Salem; but, before that day arrived, the order for the election was revoked by proclamation.

Those who had been chosen representatives, however, were instructed by their respective towns to meet at the appointed time and place, and to resolve themselves into a Provincial Congress, and repair to Concord to hold their meeting. This was in accordance with the advice of the Worcester Convention. In anticipation of the result, the Convention divided the county into seven regiments; recommended that the towns choose their company-officers, and those the field-officers; and that the company-officers of the minute-men should meet at Worcester on the 17th October, and proportion their regiments and choose their field-officers.

The Convention, in fact, felt themselves called upon to exercise many of the functions of government, although it could only be done by the way of advice and recommendation; and never was public sentiment better united or more potent in its action than at this moment in the Colony.

As an instance of the manner in which it made itself felt, I would refer to a convention of blacksmiths, which was held at Worcester on the 8th September, 1774; at which Ross Wyman of Shrewsbury presided, and Timothy Bigelow, afterwards the distinguished colonel of the fifteenth regiment of the Massachusetts line in the Continental service, was clerk. Seth Washburn of Leicester was among its members. They resolved, among other things, that they would not work for any whom they esteemed enemies to the country, — viz., Tories, councillors by mandamus who had not resigned, and those who addressed Gov. Hutchinson on his departure; and specified by name Timothy Ruggles of Hardwick, John Murray of Rutland, and James Putnam of Worcester. They put under the ban all who had not signed the "non-consumption covenant," and appealed to all classes of artificers to form similar associations.

In the military organization adopted by the County Convention, one-third of all the men able to do duty, between eighteen and sixty, were to be enrolled as "minute-men." The first regiment was made up of the towns of Worcester, Leicester, Spencer, Holden, and Paxton.

It would occupy too much space to refer any more, in detail, to the proceedings of this County Convention; though, for a considerable time, this and similar conventions in other counties practically constituted the governing power of the Province. The House of Representatives which the Governor had dissolved in June was the last that was assembled under the Royal Charter. The power of the Charter Government had come to a stop; the courts of justice were closed; the Province was without any body to make or expound the laws; and the staff of the executive was broken in pieces. But such was the force of public sentiment, such the sense of right and wrong which pervaded the community, and so significant was the judgment which was expressed in their public assemblies, that never was there less complaint of justice denied, or injustice done between man and man, than in this interval of courts and legislation. Leicester voted in town-meeting, that, whatever differences might arise in the town, they should be settled by such indifferent men as the parties should agree upon; and this recommendation was, I believe, uniformly observed.

The last meeting of the Superior Court in Worcester had been in April; when, in anticipation of Chief-Justice Oliver being present and presiding, the grand jury drew up, and fifteen of them signed, a protest against serving in that office if the Chief-Justice were to be present. This protest was drawn by William Henshaw, and bore his name and that of Moses Livermore of Spencer. The Chief-Justice did not attend, and the business of the term was suffered to proceed.

The term of the court, which was to have met at Salem on the 1st November, was adjourned by the sheriff, without the judges having come together at all.

Pursuant to the original notice from the Governor, this town proceeded to elect a representative to attend the Legislature at Salem; but in anticipation of the subsequent course pursued by him, and pursuant to the recommendation of the County Convention, they instructed him to unite in forming a Provincial Congress. The representative chosen was Thomas Denny; and the instructions, which will be found in the Appendix, were prepared by a committee, consisting of Joseph Henshaw, John Brown, Joseph Allen, of Leicester; Deacon Muzzy and Dr. Ormes, of Spencer; and Phinehas and Willard Moore, of Paxton. This was on the 29th September. The same committee, on the 10th October, prepared new instructions to Col. Denny, as a member of the Provincial Congress, which were then adopted by the town.*

There had been, however, a meeting of the town on the 3d of October, at which the inhabitants voted that the cannon be mounted on a proper carriage; and appointed Seth Washburn, Benjamin Richardson, and Capt. Newhall, to cause this to be done; and directed the selectmen to act in their prudence respecting persons not furnished with firearms.

The Provincial Congress met at Concord on the 11th October, and Mr. Denny attended: but he was soon attacked with sickness, which compelled him to return home; where he died on the 23d October.

His death was not only a severe loss to the town, but to the whole Province. He had won the confidence and respect of the leading men of the day, and is spoken of by Hutchinson, in his third volume of the "History of Massachusetts," in connection with Joseph Hawley, James Warren, and several others, who, he says, "may be considered as most active and zealous" of those who, in 1770, were "in the opposition to Parliament."

---

* They are also copied in the Appendix.

His place was supplied by the election of Joseph Henshaw on the 20th October; to whom the same instructions were repeated, with an additional one, that he should use his "influence that Dorchester Point should be immediately taken possession of and fortified by this Province."

Another meeting of the town was held on the 7th November, when it was voted to provide ammunition for the cannon belonging to the town, — two and a half barrels of powder and four hundred-weight of shot or balls. A committee was at the same time raised "to supply those persons with provisions who might be called to march from home in defence of our rights and privileges."

In December, the town chose a committee of nine * to carry into execution the resolves and proceedings of the Continental and Provincial Congresses; in short, to take the place of the executive, so far as the town was concerned. Eight men were selected to manage and exercise the town's cannon; and a subscription was recommended for the relief of the poor in Boston "suffering in the common cause," and a committee raised to carry this vote into effect.

This was the last of the *eighteen* meetings which the town had held during the year 1774: but on the 9th January, 1775, another meeting was held; when it was voted to raise a company of minute-men in the town, and that a number should be draughted for that purpose from the trainbands in the town. A committee † was raised to draw up articles for the men to sign.

A company of nearly fifty men was accordingly raised, of which Seth Washburn was elected captain; William Watson and Nathaniel Harrod, first and second lieutenants. The

* These were Joseph Henshaw, Hezekiah Ward, Jonathan Newhall, Joseph Sargent, William Green, Seth Washburn, Samuel Denny, Thomas Newhall, and Samuel Green.

† Jonathan Newhall, William King, Samuel Denny, Seth Washburn, and Joseph Henshaw.

standing company in the town was under the command of Thomas Newhall, with Benjamin Richardson and Ebenezer Upham, first and second lieutenants. This, it should be remembered, was not altogether a new movement in town. They had had, as already stated, a company of volunteer minute-men since 1770; and this new organization was only to comply with the recommendation of the Provincial Congress.

So intent were the members of this volunteer company in the necessary preparation for active service, that they hired a drill-officer, who had been in the regular army, to train them; meeting weekly or oftener for drill, and for several days before the 19th April, 1775, doing so daily: so that, when the alarm reached Leicester of the march of the British troops to Lexington, every man was found ready to move, literally, at a minute's warning.

It was not, as some writer has said, that the battle of Lexington roused a warlike spirit in the community: it found that spirit already roused and organized. The people who, upon the alarm of the 19th April, gathered by fifties and by hundreds, to more than twelve thousand in all, in Cambridge and its vicinity, on the 20th and the few following days in April, 1775, were not a mob, nor a mass of men drawn together by accident or passion. They rushed to the scene of action to do service as soldiers, already organized into companies and regiments; and if without the discipline, they were without the habits and vices, of the camp.

The anxiety of the town for the restoration of an orderly government is elicited by the instructions * which they gave to Joseph Henshaw, their delegate to the Provincial Congress, Jan. 9, 1775; and they show in all their proceedings a disposition to perserve order. Thus we find them voting

* The committee who prepared them were Joseph Allen, Seth Washburn, Samuel Green, of Leicester; Deacon Mussy and Dr. William Frink, of Spencer.

in town-meeting in March, that they would aid and assist the sheriff and constables in apprehending and securing any riotous or disorderly persons. At the same meeting, they voted, that, "as it was probable some interesting events might turn up between that time and May meeting, each minute-man should be allowed the sum of six shillings as a bounty for his service; and, if called upon to march, to be allowed Province pay." They further voted to procure pouches for the use of the company.

They were right in their conjectures. Interesting events did turn up before May meeting; events, compared with which, the history of no nation can present any thing of deeper interest, — the opening scene of the American Revolution. Early in the afternoon of Wednesday, the 19th of April, a horseman rode furiously through the little village of the Leicester of that day; and stopping for a moment in front of the blacksmith-shop of the captain of the minute-company, a little west of the present house of Mr. John Loring, announced, in a hurried voice, that "the war had begun, the regulars were marching to Concord!" and rode on to carry the alarm to the towns lying west of Leicester. He stopped for no explanation; nor was any needed. Who he was, or by what authority he came, no one inquired, nor can I find that it was ever known.

The captain threw down the ploughshare upon which he was at work; seized his musket, which stood by him, ready loaded for the purpose (for there was no bell in town with which to ring an alarm), and, rushing into the street, discharged it. The signal was understood; and, without waiting for further orders, the appointed messengers were at once on their way to arouse the men of the company. These were scattered in the various parts of the town, — many of them three or four miles from the place of their parade, and engaged upon their farms; but, before four o'clock, every man of that company was on the Common, by the Meeting-house, ready to answer to the roll-call. Some of them had literally left their ploughs in the furrow. Not one of them had a uniform. They hastily changed their working-dresses for a more fitting garb; seized their fire-locks, — most of them of that kind known as the "Queen's arms," from having come down to them from the wars of Queen Anne's time, — with their powder-horns and bullet-pouches; and, on foot or on horseback, made their way in the shortest and nearest routes, and across the fields, where, by so doing, they could sooner reach the point of rendezvous; and were mustered, and actually on their march, some time before sunset.

But there were others besides soldiers gathered, that afternoon, on that little muster-ground. There were groups of spectators, who shared in the excitement of the scene, and witnessed this hurried preparation with apprehension and alarm. There were the fathers and mothers, and in many instances the wives, of this little band; bringing with them such few necessaries as they were able to supply for the night-march that was before them, and the battle-field or the camp to which they were hastening.

In that solemn moment, the most thoughtless grew serious; and when the clergyman of the parish (the Rev. Mr. Conklin), while the men rested upon their muskets, lifted up his voice in prayer for their protection and safe return, every head was uncovered and every murmur hushed, and every heart gathered new strength to meet whatever emergency awaited this little band.

I have heard this scene, as well as many of the little incidents connected with it, described in simple terms by more than one eye-witness. The mother of the commander of the company, then an aged woman, had come with others to witness their departure. With deep emotion, which she struggled to suppress, she came near her son as he was giving the word to march, to bid him God's speed; when, turning to her, with a cheerful voice he said, "Mother, you pray for me, and I will fight for you;" and, at the "Forward" which followed, the march was begun.

Among the spectators on that occasion was Dr. Honeywood, who is mentioned in another part of this work. He had been born and educated in England, and had never believed that the colonists would dare to push measures to an actual outbreak with the mother-country; but when he saw the alacrity with which that company had come together, and the readiness and coolness with which they took up their line of march, on that occasion, his convictions were changed. Addressing those around him, he exclaimed, "Such men as these *will* fight; and, what is more, by G—! they won't be beat."

It was about an hour and a half before sundown when the company began their march. The group of spectators stood gazing upon them till the last platoon had disappeared below the hill on which the village is built; and, when the sound of the drum had died away in the distance, they dispersed to their several homes. "But I need not tell you," said an eye-witness to me, "that that night was a solemn one to the people of Leicester. Soon after Capt. Washburn's company had left, they were followed by the standing company of the town, under Capt. Newhall. Soon after dark, we heard the Spencer Company pass; and, before morning, the company from Brookfield followed them. Lights shone from the windows along the highway, and not an eye was closed that night in the village."

In this company of minute-men was a son of Nathan Sargent, who lived near the line of Worcester, where Mr. Sewall Sargent now lives. As the company came up, they halted in front of his house. Mr. Sargent came out to greet them, and inquired of the captain if they were supplied with ammunition. On hearing that there was a deficiency in bullets, he went back into his house, took from his clock the leaden weights that carried it, and, melting them down, cast them into bullets, which he brought out, and distributed to the men.

Soon after sundown, the company reached Worcester; where they were joined by other companies, and continued a rapid march till near morning; when, having heard that the regulars had retreated into Boston, they halted at Marlborough. The next day, they moved forward to Watertown; and, the day following, to Cambridge. Between Worcester and Marlborough they found lights burning in every window by the wayside, and were greeted on their way by groups of people who were gathered to witness so novel and exciting a spectacle.*

Eighty men marched on that occasion from this town; while Col. William Henshaw, Lieut.-Col. Samuel Denny, Lieut.-Col. Joseph Henshaw, and Adjutant John Southgate, from the same town, were early on their way to the scene of action to take charge of their respective regiments.†

The rolls and periods of service of these men, as well as of those who enlisted and held office in what was called the "eight-months' service," may be found in another part of this work.

The company which Capt. Washburn enlisted for the eight-months' service consisted of fifty-nine men, chiefly from Leicester, from his own and Capt. Newhall's companies. The remainder of these men, after a service varying from thirteen to twenty-six days, were discharged, and returned home. This company was attached to the regiment of which Artemas Ward was colonel; Jonathan Ward, lieutenant-colonel; Edward Barnes, major; and Timothy Bigelow, second major.

* Many of the details of this day I have derived, as I have elsewhere stated, from the personal narrative of the late Nathan Craige, Esq., who was a member of Capt. Washburn's company; some from a daughter of Capt. Washburn, who was present when the company was mustered; and some from the late John Sargent, a son of Nathan Sargent, who was present when they halted in front of his father's house.

† Spencer sent fifty-six men, under Capt. Mason; and Paxton, thirty-four, under Capt. Phinehas Moore.

As Artemas Ward was soon made the commander-in-chief of the forces, Lieut.-Col. Ward was promoted to the command of it; though it was still called Gen. Ward's regiment. Jonathan Ward belonged to Southborough; so did Major Barnes: Major Bigelow, to Worcester.

One or two facts should be mentioned in the history of the town, before noting the part which its soldiers took in the events subsequent to the new organization of the troops.

In May, 1775, Col. Joseph Henshaw was appointed by the Provincial Congress to repair to Connecticut, and consult with the Government of that Colony upon what measures should be adopted in order to maintain possession of Fort Ticonderoga, which had just before that capitulated to Ethan Allen, in obedience to his demand, "in the name of Jehovah and the Continental Congress."

Oliver Watson was chosen to represent Leicester and Spencer in the Provincial Congress, in the place of Mr. Henshaw. He belonged to Spencer; having, some years before, removed there from Leicester.

In the same month of May, the Congress had undertaken to relieve the poor of the town of Boston by assigning them to the towns in numbers proportioned to their ability to aid them. Five hundred and thirty-nine were assigned to the county of Worcester: of whom Leicester was required to relieve thirty-six; Spencer, thirty-one; and Paxton, twenty.

At this time, also, an estimate was made, and returned to the Congress, of the quantity of powder, belonging to the several towns, which could be spared by them for the public service; and it was found to amount only to the paltry sum of sixty-seven and three-quarter barrels. Only forty towns in the State could furnish any. Of these, Leicester was to furnish one barrel; Worcester, one; and Lancaster, one. The whole Province stock of powder, in 1774, was but seventeen thousand four hundred and forty-four pounds; that of all the towns, three hundred and fifty-seven barrels.

The idea, at this day, of commencing a war with such an inconsiderable amount of an article as essential as gunpowder, would be thought worse than absurd. Nor was there any means at hand to supply more. There was not a powder-mill in the Province; nor had they saltpetre in quantity to manufacture powder, if there had been. While upon this subject, I may anticipate by saying, that on the 13th February, 1776, the Legislature offered a bounty of £50 to the person who should erect the *first* powder-mill in the Province, capable of manufacturing fifty pounds per day; and should actually manufacture a thousand pounds, if erected within six months from that time.* They had, a few days before, offered a premium of ninepence per pound for manufacturing saltpetre, from mines or ores, in this Colony; and it was amongst the saddest circumstances in the battle of Bunker Hill, that the field was finally lost more from the want of ammunition than from the superiority in numbers, or prowess of arms, in the enemy.

To return to our narrative. On the 15th June, Congress recommended that the several towns should deposit, for the use of the Province, such fire-arms as, it was estimated, they could spare; which amounted in all to a thousand and sixty-five.† Of these, Worcester County was to supply five hundred and fourteen; and the proportion of Leicester was twelve; Spencer, ten; and Paxton, six.

As we approach the events of the 17th June, it seems proper to speak of these by themselves. The reader may find, in the full and accurate "History of the Siege of Boston" by Mr. Frothingham, an interesting account of the condition of the army, and the disposition of the forces, while carrying on the siege which had been commenced almost

* This was to be exclusive of the mill at Stoughton and one at Andover, which were then in process of erection by order of the Province.

† The whole number of fire-arms in the Province in 1774, including Maine, was twenty-one thousand five hundred and forty-nine.

immediately after the affair at Lexington. I shall speak of these only so far as persons from Leicester were connected with those events. There has been a great deal said and written and felt upon the question, "Who commanded at Bunker Hill?" If by it is meant, "Who directed the operations upon the hill on the night of the 16th? and whose orders, from his position during the battle and from being known and recognized as the leader of the enterprise, were obeyed, so far as they could be communicated?" Prescott must undoubtedly be considered as the commander on that occasion. But if the inquiry embraces, "Who planned the enterprise? who detailed and directed particular troops to take particular posts and perform particular duties while upon the field?" it would be a much more difficult question to answer.*

The truth seems to be, that, whatever was the original plan as a whole, in many of its parts there were material departures from that, by design or by accident; and, when it was apparent that the enemy would attack them, most of the principal officers — among whom no one was more active or prominent than Putnam — entered into the fight with little order or system, but with a spirit and zeal which supplied the necessity of special directions from any superior officer. Each corps, as it came into the field, took up its position, and maintained it till the general retreat.

In May, Col. William Henshaw, Col. Gridley, and Mr. Richard Devens, examined the heights of land in Charlestown and Cambridge, with a view to their occupation. This was done at the request of Gen. Ward. On the 12th of May, a report was made to the Committee of Safety, who seem to

* The judgment of the court-martial who tried Major Scarborough Gridley, of the artillery, for defect of duty on the 17th June, found him guilty, and dismissed him from the service; "but on account of his inexperience and youth, *and the great confusion which attended that day's transactions in general*," they did not hold him disqualified to hold office again.

have had, in connection with the Council of War, the general direction as to the operations of the army. It was signed by Dr. Church, Chairman of the Subcommittee from the Committee of Safety, and William Henshaw, Chairman of the Subcommittee from the Council of War; and related to erecting military works upon Prospect, Winter, and Bunker Hills, and intermediate points. But it is not necessary to transcribe it here, as the position occupied by the intrenchments on the 16th June was nearer to the point where the enemy landed than Bunker Hill Proper would have been.

Gen. Ward, as commander-in-chief, was stationed at Cambridge, and gave directions what regiments should march to Charlestown on the occasion of occupying the hill, and, the next day, to help to maintain it. A part, at least, of his own regiment, under Lieut.-Col. Ward, was stationed at what was called Fort No. 2, which is said to have been upon what is now known as Dana Hill. It was here that Capt. Washburn's company were stationed. Though the enemy landed about one o'clock, it was past three o'clock in the afternoon, according to the account given by Mr. Frothingham, before the battle actually commenced. He speaks of a part of Lieut.-Col. Ward's regiment arriving at a critical time of the battle, and of the part taken by Capt. Washburn's company, with other companies mentioned, in maintaining the position of the American troops at the rail-fence, and "gallantly covering the retreat."

The British finally took possession of the hill about five o'clock, so that the heat of the action must have lasted about two hours.

With this preliminary statement, drawn from other sources, I propose to give a detailed account, as near as I have been able to gather it from those who took part in them, of the movements of the Leicester men on that day. I am chiefly indebted for my facts to Mr. Nathan Craige, a member of the company, given many years since, when a clear and unimpaired memory and a character for honesty and integrity which was never impeached, gave to his statement the force of truth. Nor will it be found to conflict with any well-authenticated account of the details of the battle.

It seems that, between one and two o'clock, a re-enforcement had arrived from Boston to join the troops which had previously landed at Moulton's Point. This, according to a statement in Ward's "History of Shrewsbury," — the connection of whose author with Gen. Ward gave him an opportunity to understand something of the motives of his movements, — so far satisfied the general that the enemy would not attempt to land, and attack his position in Cambridge, that he ordered Lieut.-Col. Ward to march his regiment with the utmost despatch by the way of Lechmere Point to Charlestown, keeping a strict look-out towards Boston in its march. The regiment, according to Mr. Craige's recollection, were paraded under arms, ready for marching, soon after noon. On reaching Lechmere Point, they halted for near an hour. The reason for this delay he never understood. While here, they heard the "cracking of the musketry over in Charlestown," as well as the roar of the cannon. They were then ordered to march for Charlestown Neck, in order to reach the scene of the battle, which had already begun. Before they arrived at the Neck, they were met by a man on horseback (said to be Dr. Church), who told the commander to halt his men; that orders had been sent, that no more troops should go into the action.* Major Barnes, who was then in command, gave the order to halt. Whereupon Capt. Washburn, stepping out of the column, addressing his men, exclaimed in a loud voice, "Those are Tory orders: I shan't obey them. Who will follow me?" Every man of his company at once left the column, and passed on towards the hill. Capt. Wood

* The same circumstance, though in a little different language, was repeated by a member of another company in the regiment, as stated by Mr. Ward in his History, p. 55.

of Northborough, with his company, and, as appears by Mr. Frothingham's narrative, Capt. Cushing also, left the regiment, and came into the action about the same time that Capt. Washburn did.

When the company reached the Neck, the shot from the British frigate were sweeping across it; and the captain, halting his men, addressed a few words to them; told them that they saw the danger before them; that if any of them wished to avoid it, or was afraid to go forward, they might then go back. No one left the ranks; and, after a moment's pause, the captain said cheerfully, "Then we'll all go together." The whole company started upon a full run across the Neck, to avoid the balls from the frigate as well as they could. As they ascended the hill, they saw the houses in Charlestown on fire, and met numbers bringing off the wounded from the field. Near the summit of the hill they saw an American officer swinging his sword, and beckoning them to come in that direction; which they obeyed. The men, at this time, had about fifteen rounds of cartridges each. As they came in sight of the British troops, and were moving steadily on towards the breastwork below the redoubt, a ball struck the cartouch-box of the captain, — for he was, like his men, armed with a musket; and he, supposing the shot had come from one of his own men, coolly turned round, and said, he believed one of them had hit him, and cautioned them to be careful, and not shoot our own men. After the battle, however, he found the ball lodged in his cartouch-box; and its direction showed that it was received from the enemy.

The company rushed forward as soon as they had surmounted the hill, and took their station at the rail-fence, and began firing as fast as they could. The enemy, by this time, had mounted the redoubt; and, in about twenty or thirty minutes after the company had entered the action, the order was given to retreat. This they did, at first, slowly and in regular order; keeping together, and doing what they could to cover the retreat: but when they saw that the enemy were gaining upon them, and threatening to cut them off on the flank, the company broke, and hurried down the hill.

But, in this retreat, they showed nothing like panic. Sergeant Brown received a shot in his thigh, and another in his foot, which disabled him from walking. The captain, who was the last to leave the ground, finding him in this condition, and being an athletic though not a large man, took the wounded man under one arm, and his musket (with his own) in the other, and carried him till he was out of immediate danger. He there left him, and hurried on till he overtook Brown's brother Perley and Jonathan Sargent (another of the company), and sent them back for the wounded man; whom they brought off in safety.* Daniel Hubbard wore a cue, braided in two strands, which hung down his back. As he passed by, Mr. Craige saw him *dodge* his head; and it was afterwards found that a musket-ball had cut off one of these strands so close to his head as to graze the skin. Kerley Ward of Oakham, one of the corporals of the company, was wounded in the arm; and Sergeant Crossman, in the leg. Abner Livermore had the cord of his canteen cut off by a musket-ball while retreating; and, as it fell, it rolled a considerable distance towards the enemy, who were firing and pressing upon the left flank of the company. His brother Isaac, seeing the disaster, and knowing what the canteen contained, stopped, with the exclamation, "It will never do to lose that rum!" and, running after the canteen, picked it up, and brought it off the field, in the face of the fire from the British. Samuel Sargent, another of the company, was less fortunate in saving his liquor. While stopping to prime his gun, a musket-ball struck his canteen, and, passing through one end of it, lodged in the other, which rested upon his hip.

* The General Court, in April, 1777, granted Brown a pension of twenty shillings a month on account of his wounds.

He lost the contents, but saved the ball; and it was, for many years, preserved in the family as a trophy. The captain wore a wig, and had on, that day, a camlet frock-coat. He found, after the battle, that, besides the one through his cartouch-box, four balls had passed through his coat, and one through his wig; though he was himself wholly unharmed. The ball that lodged in his cartouch-box he brought home after his tour of duty was over.

It is by personal anecdotes that the true character of a battle may be understood, much more than by the statistics of killed and wounded. The published accounts of the day tell us of the dreadful sufferings of the gallant Major Moore of Paxton (who fell mortally wounded in the early part of the action) from an agony of thirst, without a drop of water to relieve it, as he lay bleeding and dying beneath the hot sun of that bright June afternoon. An incident occurred in the retreat of the Leicester men, illustrative of what occurred in the battle. As Mr. Craige was passing a house near the Neck, which the fire had not reached, the lieutenant called to him that there was a soldier lying in the house, wounded and bloody, and unable to speak; and added, "We must take him with us, or he will be burnt up!" Four of the men, accordingly, placing him in a blanket, carried him nearly half a mile; when, overtaking some Connecticut troops, they found he was the sergeant of their company, and they took charge of him.

Instead of returning with his company to Cambridge after the battle, Capt. Washburn, with three other captains and eighteen men, undertook a voluntary patrol, during the evening and night, between Cambridge and the Neck, in order to protect the property in the houses which had been abandoned, and save it from being burned. Three of these houses were, in fact, set on fire the next morning, and destroyed.

Besides those in Capt. Washburn's company, there were others, who previously had been, or afterwards were, citizens of Leicester, and took part in the battle of the 17th June. Among them was John Holden of Col. Doolittle's regiment, which went into the action under the command of Major Moore. He was afterwards a lieutenant, and, before the close of the war, was promoted to a captaincy, in the Continental service. Ebenezer Washburn, a brother of Capt. Washburn, who had removed to Hardwick, was quartermaster in Col. Brewer's regiment; and Seth, the oldest son of the captain, who had removed to Wilbraham, and Caleb Barton, then of Oxford, were also in the battle.*

There was one other, whom I have noticed elsewhere, who was in that fight, — Peter Salem, a black man, belonging to Col. John Nixon's regiment. All the accounts of the battle speak of the gallant conduct of Major Pitcairn, of the British marines, on that occasion. He was shot down as he mounted the redoubt, crying out exultingly, "The day is ours!" and fell into the arms of his son, who tenderly bore him off the field to a boat, and thence to a house in Prince Street, Boston, where he died. That shot was, undoubtedly, fired by Peter; and the death of Major Pitcairn, with its accompanying circumstances, formed one of the most touching incidents of that eventful day.

It may seem to some that I am devoting too much space to the incidents of a single battle; but my object has been, not merely to do justice to the physical courage and endurance of those of whom I am speaking, as soldiers, but to their higher qualities as men and as citizens. Many of the company were young men, some not seventeen years of age; and quite a number between that age and twenty-one. The commander was at the mature age of fifty-two; a serious, reli-

* I would notice another fact indirectly connected with the history of the town, and illustrating the history of the times. Israel Green, whose sister married Hezekiah Ward, was a native of Leicester. He married, and had three children born in Leicester. Before the war, he removed to Hubbardston. He had three sons in the battle of Bunker Hill. One was killed; and one received a wound, of which he died. The third subsequently fell in the battle of Monmouth.

gious man, known personally to all his men, to whom he stood in a relation more parental than authoritative: and their conduct in camp as well as in action showed that the confidence of the parents of these young men in their commander, in allowing them to enlist at so early an age, was not misplaced.

All the forenoon of the 17th, the troops in and around Cambridge were in a state of intense excitement. The incessant boom of the cannon from Copp's Hill and the British frigates in the stream, the mustering of the various companies and regiments, the occasional roll of drums, the hurried movements of adjutants on horseback, the still more stirring sound of the alarm-bells in Cambridge, and the beat to arms and hurried march of troops towards Charlestown as soon as it was known that the British had landed, presented altogether a scene calculated to agitate and alarm any one, unaccustomed to war, who was momentarily expecting orders to move forward to take part in the action, which it was now known must take place.

It was amidst surrounding circumstances like these, that Capt. Washburn, a few moments before orders came for his regiment to form, called his men together, and spoke to them of the action in which they were about to engage, and what would be expected of them; and closed by offering up a fervent prayer for their safety and protection, and the success of the cause in which they were enlisted. Every thing was done coolly and calmly; and some of them often spoke, in their old age, of the unfaltering confidence with which, after this, they went through the experiences of the day.

Several of these soldiers were personally known to many of the present generation as among the substantial and respectable citizens of the town. Six of them were alive in 1826,* fifty-one years after the battle; and Nathan Craige,

* Daniel Hubbard, Nathan Craige, Thomas Sprague, Isaac Livermore, Matthew Jackson, and Elias Green.

the last survivor, died April 2, 1852, wanting but seventeen days of seventy-seven years from the time he marched at the Lexington alarm.*

In resuming the narrative of what may be more properly considered the general history of the town, I may still be obliged to refer with some minuteness to subsequent events of the Revolution. To do justice to the part which the town took in furnishing men and material for the war would require a much greater accuracy of detail than, unfortunately, can now be obtained. So far as I have been able to ascertain the names of these men, I have given them elsewhere; though I am well aware that the list is far from complete. I must content myself with referring to these.

After his service at Roxbury and Dorchester, which expired in the spring of 1776, Capt. Washburn withdrew from the army, but continued in various posts of duty in public life, through the war. I refer to his name in this connection, to explain one or two things which might not be readily understood otherwise. Leicester seems to have been made a place of deposit of more or less of the public stores; which I cannot readily account for, unless it was that the well-known unanimity of sentiment of the town, as well as the prominent part which some of its citizens had taken, indicated it as a safe and secure place.

Thus, as early as Feb. 21, 1775, the Committee of Safety and Supplies of the Provincial Congress voted unanimously,

---

* One is surprised, now that the consequences of the stand made by the colonists at Bunker Hill have become a matter of familiar history, to see how little its true importance was appreciated at the time. I have before me the orderly-book of Col. Henshaw, containing the orders of Gen. Ward at that time. No order is promulgated on the 17th June, except the usual parol and countersign, and an order to Gen. Thomas to send two cannon to Cambridge. On the 18th, there is no special order; and the 21st is the first time the battle is alluded to, requiring the officers to make returns of numbers fit for duty, "absent on furlough, deserted, sick, killed, and wounded, in the *late engagement*, and missing upon account thereof." On the 24th is an order tendering the thanks of the general to the officers, soldiers, &c., "who behaved so gallantly at the late action in Charlestown."

that the powder which was then at Concord should be removed to Leicester; and, on the 24th, voted that eight field-pieces, with the shot and cartridges, and two brass mortars, with their bombs, be deposited at Leicester with Col. Henshaw.*

On the 14th April, they voted that the cannon-powder at Leicester should be removed to Concord, one load at a time, and made into cartridges. On the 17th, this vote was reconsidered, and all the ammunition was voted to be deposited in nine different towns, of which Leicester was one. "*The* eleven hundred tents" were voted to be deposited in equal quantities in seven different towns, of which Leicester was one.

In May, 1776, the House chose deputy-commissioners for the several brigades into which the militia had been divided; and Joseph Allen, Esq., then of Leicester, was elected for the Worcester Brigade. How early the office of muster-master was created, I am unable to fix; but on the 28th

---

* To show with what caution this was done, I insert a copy of a letter from Joseph to Col. William Henshaw: —

CONCORD, 25th March, 1775.

DEAR BILLY, — The bearer hereof will bring six or seven hogsheads: two of which, would have you put in your barn, in some dry place where no wet or damp will come at the same; two others, would have you order to Major Denny's, to be deposited with the same care in his custody; two others, would have you order to Capt. Samuel Green's, to be with him stored with the same care; and the remaining one be sent to Thomas Newhall's, to be by him taken the same care of.

You will conduct this matter with the greatest secrecy, and in a way the least liable to suspicion. You will take care that no candle goes near the cask, and enjoin the same on those to whom the others are sent. Be careful also to enjoin the strictest secrecy on them respectively.

When I return home, shall take further order concerning the same; and am your affectionate brother,

JOS. HENSHAW.

Would have you, after you have lodged your two hogsheads, proceed with the other team to the westward; and, when you get to Mr. Allen's shop, press him to proceed with one team down the South Road to Capt. Green's. After giving Mr. Allen the necessary directions, than proceed to Major Denny's, by the way of Thomas Newhall's, if that road will do to go with the teams. As soon as the team destined to Newhall's is discharged of the one hogshead, proceed to Denny's, and unload the last team. The teamsters had better agree to meet together at Noah Jones's, after discharging their contents, in order to return together.

December, 1776, Capt. Thomas Newhall of Leicester was appointed, by the General Court, muster-master for the county of Worcester. It seems to have been an important and responsible office. He judged of the fitness of the men who were enlisted or draughted for service; took care that they should be forwarded into service; in case of desertion, took measures to arrest the offender; and when, as at last grew to be not an unfrequent case, any controversy arose between different towns as to which might claim a soldier as having been furnished by such town, the muster-master determined the question. How long Capt. Newhall held the office, I cannot tell: but I find Capt. Washburn commissioned and acting as such in February, 1778; and believe he held the office till the close of the war.*

In February, 1777, the General Court seems to have adopted the course of having stores of boots, shoes, blankets, &c., collected for the use of the army, and deposited in the several counties, under the charge of military storekeepers, to be held subject to the orders of the Board of War. By a resolve of the date of Feb. 7, 1777, the several towns were required to furnish as many pairs of boots and stockings and shirts as were equal to one-seventh of the males in the town of sixteen years of age or upwards. Seth Washburn was chosen such storekeeper for the county of Worcester, and was furnished with £300 for the purpose.

In April, 1778, the General Court elected *superintendents* of counties, to receive and send forward the men whom they at that time resolved to raise in order to fill the fifteen battalions of the Continental troops which Massachusetts was to supply; and in June of the next year, and November of

---

* I copy the form of one of his certificates in that office; viz.: "Leicester, July 24, 1780. This may certify whom it may concern, that on the 23d day of February, 1778, Cain Bowman, a negro man, appeared, and passed muster: presented as a free man, as it was contrary to my orders to muster any slaves. Said Bowman was mustered in Col. Marshall's regiment, Capt. King's company. Received £20 bounty."

1780, similar officers were appointed. In each of these instances, Seth Washburn was chosen for the county of Worcester. These votes are noticed as explanatory of some of the orders which appear upon the minutes of the Board of War. In August, 1777, I find a memorandum of that body, that "there were at Seth Washburn's store, at Leicester, a hundred and ninety-one shirts, a hundred and thirty-nine pairs shoes, six hundred and sixteen pairs hose. "See his return for the 5th inst."

On the 30th September of the same year, an order is made, "that Seth Washburn deliver Deacon Davis, or order, four hundred and seventy-two pairs shoes he has collected for the use of the State;" and again, on Feb. 5, 1778, it was "ordered that Capt. Seth Washburn, of Leicester, deliver Messrs. Otis and Andrews five hundred and ninety-two pairs stockings."

If we attempt to estimate the share which Leicester bore in the sacrifices and expenses occasioned by the war, it must, at best, be but an approximation. To a considerable extent, we can trace the number of specific articles paid into the public store; but this does not include the clothing and provisions furnished by the towns to the soldiers directly, and to their families in their absence. And, when we come to the matter of levies and contributions of money, we lack for a safe and proper measure of value, in consequence of the rapid depreciation of Continental money down to total worthlessness. It will be my object to refer to the several votes upon the subject, and then to endeavor to furnish as near a standard of admeasurement of value as I can command, by which to estimate the surprising amount of taxation which the town, somehow, sustained while the war was in progress.

Among the votes which I have noticed upon the journal of the General Court, bearing upon this subject, are the following: —

Jan. 5, 1776.—To collect four thousand blankets, to be contributed by the towns; the share of Leicester being fourteen.

Jan. 19, 1776.—To raise four thousand three hundred and sixty-eight men for the army, to maintain the fortifications at Cambridge and Roxbury, to serve till April 1: Leicester was assigned thirteen, and actually furnished sixteen, besides the commander of the company.

June 25, 1776.—To raise five thousand troops to co-operate with the Continental army in Canada and New York; two battalions from certain towns in Worcester to go to New York: twenty-five assigned to Leicester.

July 10, 1776.—To raise every twenty-fifth man to re-enforce the Northern Army.

Sept. 10.—To raise one-fifth of the entire militia not in actual service, to march to "Horse Neck" to re-enforce the army in New York.

Jan. 20, 1777.—To procure five thousand blankets, to be furnished by the towns: Leicester, fourteen.

Jan. 6, 1777.—To raise every seventh man above the age of sixteen, to complete the quota of the Continental Army.

Aug. 9.—To draught every sixth man in Suffolk, Essex, Middlesex, York, Worcester, and Berkshire, to join the army, in consequence of the taking of Ticonderoga; to serve till the last of November, unless sooner discharged.

April 20, 1778.—To fill up the fifteen battalions of Continental troops: Leicester to furnish six.

June 8, 1779.—To raise two thousand men on the Continental establishment: Leicester to furnish six.

June 21, 1779.—That the towns furnish shirts, shoes, and stockings for the army, equal in number to one-sixth of the male inhabitants: Leicester to supply thirty pairs of each. Seth Washburn to receive them for the county.

May 4, 1780.—To furnish shoes and stockings and shirts equal to one-tenth of the male inhabitants, and half as many blankets: Leicester, twenty-one shirts, &c., and eleven blankets.

Sept. 25, 1780. — To supply beef for the army: Leicester, four thousand five hundred and sixty pounds.

Dec. 2, 1780. — To raise four thousand two hundred and forty men to supply the defect in the State's quota of the Continental force: Leicester, eleven men.

Dec. 4. — To supply the army with provisions: Leicester, eight thousand seven hundred and sixty-one pounds beef.

Jan. 22, 1781. — To supply the army with provisions: Leicester, three thousand six hundred and twenty-four pounds of beef; sixteen shirts, pairs stockings, and shoes; and eight blankets.

June 30, 1781. — To raise two thousand seven hundred men, for three months, to re-enforce the Continental Army: Leicester, nine men.

March 7, 1782. — To raise fifteen hundred men to re-enforce the army, for three years: Leicester, four.

I have given the foregoing votes partly as independent facts of interest, and partly as a proximate mode of comparison by which to judge of the relative proportions of the public burdens borne by the town. It is, however, by no means a reliable one; for these draughts do not seem to have been regulated by any fixed proportion. In one case, for instance, where Worcester furnished ten men, Leicester did six. In another, Worcester, twenty-nine; Leicester, eleven. In another, Worcester, twenty-three; Leicester, nine. In another, Worcester, nine; and Leicester, four. When we come to examine the votes of the town, we are able to form a more positive judgment in the matter.

In the first place, I have before me the certified returns of twenty-seven draughts of men between May, 1775, and June 28, 1780; amounting to two hundred and twenty-seven men in all, — more than twice as many as were borne on the entire muster-roll of the train-band in the town as fit for active duty; together with the sums paid by the town for bounties upon their enlistment. It does not include the companies which marched at the Lexington alarm, nor the draughts made after the 28th of June, 1780; of which there were several, either paid for by the town, or by the classes into which its inhabitants were divided.* In one of these (July 19, 1781) the town paid seven men twenty pounds each in silver money, with a right to receive their wages for the three months for which they enlisted.

I have copied into the Appendix the interesting document to which I have above alluded, as a matter of curious reference; and would venture to commend it, with the other papers found there, as worthy the attention of the reader.

So numerous and heavy were the draughts for men, that the traditions may easily be credited which have come down to us, that the labor in the fields was in many cases performed by women, because every male member of the family was absent. It is a matter of record on the part of the town, that, in 1776, they had to choose two new selectmen because the others were absent in the army; and in January, 1778, they were obliged to choose a new assessor for the same reason.

In 1780, if not earlier, the custom began of dividing the towns into classes, each of which, when called on, was required to supply a man, by enlistment, from their number, or by hiring a substitute; which partially withheld from the town as immediate action upon the subject as they had before been accustomed to take.

In respect to the direct appropriations by the town for the purposes of the war, I find that, in April, 1776, the town voted to procure ammunition, intrenching tools, &c., agreeably to a requisition from the General Court; and, in May, they allowed Samuel Cole seven shillings for carting pro-

* The town voted to divide the inhabitants into ten classes in 1781.

visions to Watertown the previous year. But the cost of either of these is not stated.

In May, 1777, the town abated the poll-tax of all soldiers in the Continental Army belonging to town. In October of the same year, the selectmen were directed to furnish such of these soldiers as had enlisted for three years, or during the war, with the necessaries of life.

In January, 1778, the town voted to raise twelve hundred pounds, and loan it to the State Treasury, on interest.

In March, they directed the Committee of Correspondence to provide for the families of the soldiers in the Continental Army; and, a few weeks after, it was voted to provide clothing for Continental soldiers, by purchasing it with money to be drawn out of the town-treasury, and to make such provision for the families of the officers from the town in the Continental service as the selectmen should think fit.

In May, 1778, the selectmen were authorized to pay, out of money of the town or to be hired for the town, thirty pounds for each Continental soldier raised within the town, by the 20th of the month.

In March, 1779, they voted three hundred dollars for each company, to be distributed to such of the company as had done more than their proportion in the war; and a thousand pounds for hiring men for the war.

In June of the same year, they granted four thousand pounds to pay the hire of soldiers and contingent charges.

In October, 1779, they raised five hundred pounds for the same purpose.

In March following, the Committee of Safety were allowed £92. 10s. 8d. for taking care of the soldiers' wives; Capt. Leviston was allowed £3. 15s. "for a horse to go to the taking of Burgoyne;"* and £5,000 was raised for employing

---

* Capt. Leviston commanded one of the standing companies of the town. How many of his company went with him, I cannot ascertain.

soldiers. The town had, in the mean time, — between January, 1778, and March, 1780, — furnished Jethro Jones and Asa Harrington supplies, equal, as near as I can calculate the depreciated currency, to at least a hundred and twenty dollars; as well as sundry other supplies, the amounts of which are not ascertained.

In July, 1780, they raised £11,058. 5s. 7½d. for hiring soldiers, and the same amount to pay "the six-months' men who are gone in the Continental Army." It was voted, moreover, to give to each soldier a hundred and ten bushels of corn; they allowing the town to draw their wages.

In October, they raised two hundred pounds to purchase beef for the army. This was "new money;"* and the rate at which it was reckoned shows what was then regarded as the depreciation of the old, — one of new for ninety of old.

The town, at the same time, abated £20. 8s. tax per head, or about 4s. 6d. per man, to all the "three and six months'" men. The next month, they raised six thousand pounds to pay soldiers.

In January, 1781, they again abated the poll-taxes of the three and six months' men; raised a committee to go into other towns to hire men to go into the service; and voted two hundred and twenty pounds, *silver money*, to buy beef for the army. The town was, at the same time, divided into classes to supply the draughts for soldiers.

In July, they raised a hundred and twenty-seven pounds, *silver money*, and thirteen thousand pounds of, I suppose, Continental currency, with which to purchase beef; and the committee were directed to provide not less than a thousand

---

* The "new money" was an emission of bills by Massachusetts, guaranteed by the United States, in May, 1780. They were payable in silver in six years, with five per cent interest, payable annually. It was never equal to par, and never seems to have depreciated like Continental money. In February, 1781, it was to specie as one and seven-eighths to one; in May following, two and a quarter to one. It run down to four to one in June; and in September, 1781, the issue of any more bills was stopped. — *Felt's Currency*, pp. 188 and 196.

pounds of beef, to send to the army the present month. And, in September, they raised four hundred pounds, *in silver money*, to meet the charges of the town for beef, pay of soldiers, &c. This was the last specific vote for raising money on account of the war, which I find recorded; and the reader may have thought that the detail which I have given is too minute for a work like this: but it seemed to me, that it was by such details only that the people of this day could judge of the magnitude and extent of the cost and sacrifice which the actors in the Revolutionary War were willing to sustain for the boon for which they were contending.

It was by no means the men alone who went into the army that sustained hardships and endured privations. The farmer toiled without ceasing for the means of feeding and clothing the soldier and his family. The fruits of the mechanic's days and nights of labor went into the treasury of a common cause. Woman, too, bore her full share in these incessant labors; stinting herself, moreover, of the very necessaries of life, to supply the wants of husbands and fathers and brothers in the camp and the field.

There are, indeed, few records of these unostentatious sacrifices; and one reason was, they were too common, too universal, to be thought worthy of being noticed. They heeded little what posterity might think or say; the present absorbed their chief attention: and now, when we look for a history of the period, we are left to personal recollections of individuals, to be read in the light of what is known of the general condition of the country at the time.

I have spoken of the part which the women took in tilling the soil and gathering the crops. Instances were frequent among the men who remained at home, whose stock upon their farms, though inadequate to their necessities, had to be surrendered or disposed of to pay their war-tax. Such was the case, for instance, with Mr. Nathan Sargent, one of the substantial farmers of the town. I was assured by his son, that, time and again, he sold, from his stall or his pasture, animals that he greatly needed, in order to meet his share of the common burdens of the war.

Besides, the clothing of the husbands and brothers who were in the army for short terms of service was the product of household manufacture, spun and woven and made up by wives and sisters; and, when the requisitions for stockings and shirts and blankets for the army were to be supplied, it was the busy fingers and nervous arms of the women that furnished them. The State had neither commerce to supply, nor money with which to purchase, these homely necessaries for the soldier.

The simple truth was, every nerve and sinew, every article of personal possession, as well as the credit both public or private of the country, were devoted to one absorbing object; and it was not until after that object had been substantially obtained, that men began to look coolly around them, and measure with any thing like accuracy what it had cost them.

What reflects great credit upon the people of the town is, that though there was no law which could be enforced against them if they suspended their schools, as some other towns had done, they rejected the proposition when it was made, and, in fact, new-districted the town in 1776. In 1778, they voted £108 for schooling; and, in the next year, added £500 to the Rev. Mr. Conklin's salary. As an example of the frequency of the public calls upon the town, in addition to the moneys which they raised for other purposes, I have before me three State warrants for taxes in the months of June, September, and November of 1780, which were sent to a constable of the town to enforce against its inhabitants in a single year.

If we should set down the sum of eighteen thousand dollars as approximating the actual amount paid by the town to carry on the war, it would, I am persuaded, fall much below the truth. Nor should it be overlooked, that, of these sums, there were voted and raised over fifteen thousand dollars between January, 1777, and September, 1781, — more than three thousand three hundred dollars a year, — in addition to the other expenses and burdens of the town and its share of the State charges.* When, before or since, has there been a period, when, for so long a time, such burdens as these would have been borne without a murmur?

Of the importance of the Committees of Safety and Correspondence as a means of carrying on the war, I have spoken elsewhere. They were at first voluntary bodies, depending upon moral force for their power; but as early as February, 1776, they were recognized by the Legislature as an existing institution; and in February, 1777, towns were by law authorized to elect them annually. I give in another place the names of as many of this committee in Leicester as I have been able to ascertain. As an effective police, pervading the community and acting as the executive organ of public sentiment, their power and influence in preserving order at home, while they were promoting the operations of the army in the field, were an indispensable agency in carrying on the war. Nor was this the only interposition which served to suppress every manifestation of hostility to the government. The people took up the matter in their primary assemblies.

In June, 1777, Col. William Henshaw was chosen a committee to procure what evidence was to be found of the inimical disposition of any inhabitant of the town towards this and the United States, who might be voted, in the opinion of the town, as coming under this class. But the only person I can find answering this description in the town was Nathaniel Scott: and, in his case, the town, upon further investigation,

* The State-tax of Leicester is set down, for 1781, at £855. If this is reckoned as new-emission money, I suppose it would amount at par to about $1,500. It would vary according to the time of the year to which the computation should relate.

were satisfied that the imputation was groundless; and his name was stricken from the list of suspected persons.

A more signal instance of the jealous scrutiny exercised by the public over the conduct and opinions of individuals in the community was in the case of Mr. Allen, one of the truest, most consistent, and firmest patriots of the day. "Dec. 19, 1775. — Whereas a report has been propagated that Mr. Joseph Allen hath violated the ninth article of the Constitutional Association, in taking undue advantage of the scarcity of goods, the Committee of Inspection for said town, having examined into the grounds and motive of said report, are of opinion that they are cruel, false, and malicious. By order of the committee: Joseph Henshaw, chairman."

In other places, where there was occasion to apply this inquisitorial power, the obnoxious person was sometimes merely denounced as a suspicious person; in others, he was required to confine himself to his own farm; in others, he was actually imprisoned for a longer or shorter time: but, in one form or another, no man could escape the jealous watchfulness of the public eye.

In 1775, the Provincial Congress, in the absence, as we have seen, of any organized government known to the law, applied to the Continental Congress for advice as to what measures ought to be adopted in the emergency. It was recommended that the people should choose a House of Representatives, as had been done under the Charter; that a Council should be chosen, as provided in the Charter; and that the executive power should be lodged in this Council.

This recommendation was followed; and on the 19th July, 1775, the House of Representatives convened at the Meeting-house in Watertown, and the government was organized as advised. Hezekiah Ward was elected a representative from Leicester; and the instructions to him, which were adopted, were doubtless drawn by Joseph Allen, Esq., the chairman of the committee. They may be found in the Appendix; and they give the clearest and readiest view I could offer of the sense of intelligent men upon the wants and condition of the country at that period. From this time till the adoption of the State Constitution, all commissions were signed by a majority of the Council.

In May, 1776, Seth Washburn was chosen a representative; and the instructions given him on the occasion are the last of those remarkable papers which I have copied from the records of the town. Nor do I deem any apology necessary for occupying so much space with them, when they are regarded in the light of historical documents.

Two things were at this time agitating the public mind,— the formation and adoption of a constitution of government for the State, and the problem of declaring the Colonies *independent.* With whom, or precisely when, the idea of national independence originated, I am unable to state; but as early as May, 1776, the plan had been so far matured, that a meeting of the people of Leicester was held on Monday, after the 22d of that month, upon a warrant containing this article: "To see if the town, in case the Honorable the Continental Congress should declare an independence of Great Britain, will support said Congress, *at the risk of their lives and fortunes,* in effectuating such a measure, agreeable to a resolve of the late General Assembly of this Colony."

The House of Representatives had, on the 9th of May, recommended to the several towns to give instructions to their representatives with respect to independence. The vote of the town was, "by the inhabitants then present, unanimously, that, in case the Honorable the Continental Congress should declare these Colonies independent of Great Britain, they would support said Congress in effectuating such a measure, *at the risk of their lives and fortunes.*" That measure having been adopted by the Congress, upon a motion first made on the 7th of June, the people of the State were left to consider the matter of their own form of government. The king's name had been retained in judicial proceedings, until it was expunged by order of the General Court in June, 1776.

When independence was declared, the General Court was in session; and a proposal was made at once to prepare a form of government for the State: but no measures were actually taken at that time. In September, it was proposed to the people to elect their representatives to the General Court, with power to adopt a constitution. This did not find general favor. The people of this town voted, in October, that the House of Representatives ought not, at that time, to present any new form of government or constitution; and a series of resolutions were adopted, to be communicated to the General Court, embodying the views of the town upon the subject.

The Legislature, however, of 1777, resolved themselves into a Constitutional Convention on the 17th of June, and chose a committee of seventeen to consider and report upon the subject. The town was represented that year by Seth Washburn and Samuel Green. Mr. Washburn was one of this committee. Thomas Cushing was its chairman. This measure was taken in consequence of the votes of the towns to whom the Legislature had appealed on the 5th of May previous. The vote of Leicester was in favor of the Council and the House uniting in one body in framing a constitution for the acceptance of the people. This committee of seventeen reported a form of a constitution to the General Court in December; which was submitted to the people in March, 1778. It was rejected by a most decided vote. Among the objections to it, it had no Bill of Rights. There were hardly votes enough for it to be thought worth while to make returns in many of the towns.

The matter remained in this state until February, 1779; when the Legislature referred the question to the people, whether they would have a convention called for framing a new constitution. There were forty-seven votes in this town in favor of, and none against, the proposition. It found so much favor with the people, that a convention of delegates from the several towns was held at Cambridge in September, 1779. The place of meeting was the old Meeting-house in Cambridge. Seth Washburn and William Henshaw were delegates from Leicester. The records of that body would show, that, among the congregated talent and wisdom of the State, these delegates held an honorable position, and took important parts in its proceedings, especially as members of its leading committees.

The constitution was submitted to the towns, for their approval or disapproval, in March, 1780. It was adopted by a vote of more than two-thirds of the people in its favor. In September, an election of State officers was held; and in October, 1780, the government under the constitution was organized. Seth Washburn was the first representative under the constitution; and, of the votes for governor, John Hancock received sixty-nine out of seventy-two that were cast.

After a struggle so long maintained, so exhausting in its effect upon the resources of the country, — with industry crippled, commerce suspended, public credit prostrated, the currency depreciated, and a frightful debt accumulating, — it is not to be wondered at that the people began to manifest symptoms of uneasiness and discontent. Nor was it less surprising that they sought, as had been so often done before, to avert the evil by undertaking to regulate prices and business by conventions and resolutions and pledges. A convention for the purpose was held on the 14th July, 1779, at Concord; which was attended by delegates from all parts of the State. They came together to consult upon the adoption of measures for the relief of the people under their difficulties. Among other things, they proceeded to fix a scale of prices of produce and merchandise. At the same time, they recommended, in strong terms, the encouragement of schools, and the cause of education generally. Leicester, by vote, approved of the proceedings of the convention, and pledged themselves to abide by the same.

A second convention, at the same place and for the same purpose, was held in October following; at which the town was represented by Henry King, and a more detailed system of prices was adopted.* These prices show the scarcity of meats, of butter and cheese; the difficulty in the way of importing coffee, tea, or sugar; and the almost total want of cotton in the country, — one pound of cotton being worth as much as six bushels of rye, or four of wheat. But the people found, by sad experience, that the laws of political economy are far more potent than the resolutions of popular assemblies.

Men may vote that labor shall be be high or low, that provisions in a time of scarcity shall be no higher than in years of plenty, and they may attempt to brand as an enemy to his country the man who disregards the scale of prices which consumers may prescribe as just and fair; but they might about as well vote a wet spring or a warm summer, with an expectation of regulating the weather, as to attempt by resolutions to infuse generous sentiments and a spirit of self-sacrifice into men of cold hearts and selfish natures.

The peace of 1783, though it crowned the work of the Revolution with a recognition of our national independence by the world, was very far from bringing immediate relief for the embarrassments of the people. The army was, indeed, disbanded; and the exhausted granaries and stalls of the people were no longer to be taxed to feed them. But they had come home unpaid, feeling that their services and their sufferings had not been duly appreciated; while those who,

---

* Some of the prices, beyond which no one was at liberty to charge, were as follow: West-India rum, 6s. 6d. per gallon; molasses, 4s. 7d. per gallon. Coffee, 18s.; brown sugar, 14s.; Bohea tea, 16s.; *cotton*, 36s., — all these per pound. Corn, 4s. 10d. per bushel; rye, 6s.; wheat, 9s. Beef, 6s. and 5s. per pound; mutton, 4s.; butter, 12s.; cheese, 6s. per pound.

at home, had strained their last sinew to pay bounties upon their enlistment, and to feed and clothe them, and pay their wages (though in part), felt that it was a common lot of suffering and sacrifice, and should be borne by all as men embarked in one vessel, which, under the favor of Providence, had at last reached its haven. There were, besides, officers residing in the towns, who, after having gone through the period of the greatest peril and sacrifice during the war, had only retired when their services were no longer necessary, but who, by having then resigned, would lose their claim to the extra allowance made to such as remained till its close.

In view of these things, the town, in 1782, instructed their representative to endeavor to have the General Court petition Congress not to pay the officers who should be "deranged out of the army" more than half-pay for a single year. Another reason for this expression was, undoubtedly, the change which had come over the composition of the army itself towards the close of the war. In addition to the many who had joined it from motives of patriotism alone, there were others — and they were growing more numerous every year the war lasted — who were influenced by mercenary motives, and were ready to enlist because of the bounties and pay which they were to receive, and to whom the reckless and exciting life of the camp had more attractions than the hard work of a farm or a workshop in the seclusion of a country town. It is not, therefore, surprising that some grew discontented, and regarded those things as grievances which were the legitimate result of a protracted state of war and exhausted resources.

There was, accordingly, as early as March, 1781, a convention called by the people of Sutton, who seem to have been the first to manifest restlessness, to which Hezekiah Ward and John Lyon were delegates. Little was attempted, and, I believe, nothing done.

In 1786, another convention was held, at the call, again, of the people of Sutton; professedly to consider the subject of an excise duty, but embracing, in fact, the evils generally which they deemed to be grievances. It met at Worcester, and Col. Samuel Denny was a delegate from Leicester: Ebenezer Davis, Esq., of Charlton, was the president. This was but the muttering of the storm that was about to shake the fabric of the body politic of the State to its foundation in the insurrection of 1786.

We should, however, be doing injustice to many, and perhaps most, of those who attended these early popular gatherings, if we suppose they did so to fan a sentiment of discord among the people. So far from it, many of them went for the purpose of allaying the spirit of misrule, and to infuse wiser counsels and cooler judgment into their deliberations. A memorable instance of this occurred in the case of a convention, called, as the others had been, from Sutton, which met at Leicester in May, 1786. Willis Hall, of Sutton, presided on the occasion. David Henshaw and Col. Thomas Denny were delegates from Leicester. They were firm in their adhesion to the government, resolute in their purpose, and shrewd and discreet in their measures. The attendance was thin, and the convention adjourned to the 15th August. At the adjourned meeting, thirty-seven towns were represented; but so effectually clogged were the measures of the convention by the concerted action of these gentlemen with other friends of the government, that it contented itself with raising a committee to report a memorial for its adoption, and adjourned to Paxton on the 25th September. It met and adjourned from time to time till January, 1787; when the outbreak of the insurgents had so far developed itself, that the town deliberately resolved not to be any longer represented in such a body, and dismissed their delegates.

Though there were several here who sympathized with those who opposed the government in that insurrection, the measures of the town were so far under the control of a few leading minds, that they were always upon the side of law and order. In the adoption of many of the important votes passed by the town at that time, its action was unanimous. In 1778, a list was made of every man in town of the age of twenty-one and upwards; and every one was called upon to take the oath of allegiance to the State, upon the peril of being reported to the town. No one, however, hesitated to comply; and the record, to this extent, is without a stain.

The events of the insurrection belong to the history of the State rather than to that of a single town. The friends of the government wore, by way of distinction, a white fillet of paper in their hats; their opponents, a sprig of green. There were a few of the latter in the town, and it is fitting that oblivion should rest over their names. No one, at this day, can appreciate or understand the weight of the pressure under which they acted. It was little less than the impulse of despair. I find the names of seventeen who were required, between the 9th February and 22d March, 1787, to take the oath of allegiance; and nine of these were required to surrender their arms.

Numerous anecdotes were once rife in this community of the parts which individuals took in resisting this attempt to foment civil war. One great object of the insurgents was to stop the courts of justice. For this purpose, great numbers assembled in Worcester in September and November, 1786, and January, 1787. To prevent the Clerk of the Court, — Hon. Joseph Allen, — whom they knew no threats could intimidate, from attending the court, a sentinel was posted at his door with a fixed bayonet, with peremptory orders not to suffer him to come out, or any person to go in to render him aid. Seth Washburn, having business with the court, and occasion to see Mr. Allen, was approaching his door, when his right of passing was fiercely challenged by this sentinel, with a bayonet at his breast. Before, however, the sentinel could collect his thoughts sufficiently to act in so new a duty, Mr. Washburn sprang upon him, and, seizing his musket with one hand and his person with the other, disarmed him; and the clerk was liberated from his confinement.

Luke Day, one of the insurgent captains from the western part of the State, had occasion to pass from Worcester, through Leicester, on his way to Springfield. The winter was a remarkably cold one, and the day of which I am speaking was severe for the winter. He was on horseback, wore a military dress, and carried a sword in his hand. His appearance was imposing, and his bearing imperious and haughty. Upon reaching the house of Mr. Nathan Sargent, the first one in Leicester on his way from Worcester, he stopped, dismounted, fastened his horse, and went into the house to warm him.

Laying his hat and sword upon the table, and taking a chair to sit down by the fire, he asked Mr. Sargent, as a thing which he was going to take at any rate, if he might warm him by his fire. Mr. Sargent, who had been silently observing his free and easy manners and his imperative air, replied, "Not till I know who you are. These are suspicious times, and I must know who it is I am to entertain." Day, dilating himself to his full height, and assuming more than his usual consequence, replied, that "he was Capt. Day." — "Then get out of this house!" said Mr. Sargent; and, seizing Day's hat and sword, threw them out into a snow-drift, and drove Day after them. Gathering them up, he resumed his ride; swearing a vengeance upon Mr. Sargent, which he never found it convenient to inflict.

Excursions of government-men were sent out from time to time, from Leicester, to seize insurgents, and break up their haunts in other towns, — once, certainly, as far as New Braintree. On the other hand, the insurgents in this and the neighboring towns were not passive. Several of the prominent government-men were obliged to secrete themselves to avoid personal insult and violence. This was the case with Mr. Conklin. More than once, he was compelled to find lodgings in other houses than his own, to escape the midnight attacks which were planned for his arrest.

Several from the town — among whom I might mention Dr. Flint, and, as I have been told, Joseph Washburn — were with Gen. Lincoln in his memorable night-march through the trackless drifts of a blinding snow-storm, from Hadley to Petersham, which struck a final blow at the hopes of the insurgents.

Fortunately, the wild storm of passion which had been agitating the community like that of the elements of the night of the 3d and 4th of February, 1787, was followed by a day of sunshine and calm. The people returned to the allegiance to their own laws and institutions. Industry, at last, wrought out that independence for men individually which courage and perseverance had done for the nation; and it has long since faded away into tradition, how troops were quartered, in the time of peace, in this farmer's house and upon that mechanic's premises; and how houses were searched for arms, under an apprehension that their inmates were plotting treason, or collecting the means for resisting the law.

Few events have occurred of a public nature, since the suppression of "Shay's Rebellion," in regard to which Leicester can be said to have a history of her own.

When the United-States Constitution was submitted to the States for their ratification, the people of the town chose for their delegate Col. Samuel Denny, to attend the convention that assembled at Boston on the second Wednesday of January, 1788. When that body met, a majority was undoubtedly against the adoption of the Constitution. The delegate from Leicester voted against it to the last; but, fortunately, enough of its members were convinced that the future stability of the government, and the ultimate success of the attempt to maintain national independence, required them to waive their first impressions, to carry the measure of its adoption, and settle the question as a national one, which had, till then, hung doubtful or preponderating against it.

Nor were they mistaken. Every year has shown that it was under the banner of the Union which was then formed, and under that alone, that this nation of yesterday has gone on in its growth of power and prosperity, till it stands to-day the equal of the proudest and oldest of the family of nations.

When the harmony of our relations with France was disturbed in 1794, and measures were taken to raise an army, the town promptly responded to the call, and voted bounties to such as should enlist, and an addition to the pay offered by the General Government.*

But there were few laurels won by the "Oxford Army." No blood was shed; and, when peace came, it took no time to heal old wounds; and every thing went on again in quiet.

The time has not come to write the history of those measures upon which the public mind was divided before and during the war of 1812. Posterity is doing justice to the memory and the motives of the actors on both sides; and time may, if it has not already done so, settle the measure of wisdom which dictated the policy which the General Government adopted. All that I have to do with the subject is to record the fact, that the town was opposed to the policy of the government. In 1808, they passed a vote condemning the embargo, and adopted an address to Mr. Jefferson for its repeal.

In 1812, they, by vote, disapproved of the war with Great Britain; but when orders for draughts of men, who should

---

* I have before me the original receipt of the following soldiers who volunteered as minute-men in September, 1794, and received a bounty of six shillings each from the town: Sergeant, Elisha Towne; corporal, Nathan Beers; John Fessenden, Joshua Sprague, Jacob Hobart, Asahel Matthews, Reuben B. Swan, Joseph Whittemore, Joseph Elliot, jun., Lanson Morse, David Watson, Joseph Henshaw, Baley Bond, Joel Woodard, Thomas F. Newhall, Abraham Walker, Nathaniel Hammond, 3d, Daniel Wilson, Simeon Phelps, Daniel Baldwin, John Adams.

be ready to march at the earliest notice, came, they were promptly complied with. As there was then no light company in town, the order under which the light troops of the State were called into service in and around Boston did not affect its inhabitants; and none of them, except a few who may have enlisted into the regular army, were required to do active duty during the war.

An incident connected with one of these draughts may not be inappropriate here, however it may reflect upon the courage and patriotism of the soldiers of 1812 compared with those of 1775.

The first order was, I think, for five or seven from the South Company. It was then pretty generally believed, that whoever was drawn would have service to do in repelling the attacks of the enemy upon our coast. No one seemed anxious to win laurels in that quarter. Instead, however, of drawing, as was first proposed, the names of the requisite number by lot, it was thought best to offer an opportunity, to such as were willing, to enlist freely. It was, accordingly, proposed, that, the company standing in open ranks, the drummer should proceed from the right of the company down its rear, and then up in front, beating the proper call; and that such as were willing to enlist should fall in, and follow him up to the right of the company. The captain, after addressing a few patriotic words to his men, gave the proper order. The drummer went beating his drum down the rear, and up the front of the line to his place; but no one moved. Each waited for his courage to come or his neighbor to go; and soldiers and spectators stood waiting to see what was to be the next movement.

The order was repeated: and again the drummer began his round, and had reached about the middle of the front of the company, with no better success than before; when Mr. S——, a soldier of the Revolution, — who had brought from the service a wound which had made it convenient to use a staff, but in whom the spirit of 1776 was by no means dead,—stepped from the group of spectators who were witnessing the scene; shouldered his staff, as he had so often done his musket more than thirty years before; and filed in behind the drummer, with a measured step and soldierly bearing, and followed him up the line. Another and another of his old companions in arms, who were present, filed in behind him; and, before the drummer had reached the head of the company, more than the requisite number of recruits had paraded on the spot, amidst the applause of the spectators, as volunteers again ready to march, if their country needed them.

We have reached a period, however, in reviewing the past, of which history may not presume to speak at present. It remains for some one, less identified with the character of passing events, to do justice to these and their actors. And yet, in closing this outline of what goes to make up the general history of the town, it seems to be a proper occasion to present to the mind some of the more striking circumstances which characterize the present and the past.

In the first place, the most remarkable contrast is in what goes to make up life itself. Men live a great deal faster, and fill up life a vast deal more completely, now, than they did seventy or eighty years ago. Without newspapers or post-offices; with few books, and those exceedingly expensive; with no means of intercourse, for common people, but on foot or on horseback,—life upon their farms (for there were few workshops to serve as places of neighborhood resort) must have stagnated for want of something to rouse the mind to action.

It is difficult for one, standing in the whirl and go-ahead movement of every thing around him in our day,—railroads, which bring him nearer to New York than his grandfather was to the next town that adjoined him; mails everywhere, and from three to half a dozen times a day, between points which it then took a fortnight to connect; newspapers (political, theological, scientific, and literary), embracing all interests and sects and subjects, thrown into every man's door, to tell him, among other things, of what took place two hours ago at St. Louis or Halifax, and placing him, as it were, upon one great central point, where, through the sensitive wires of the telegraph, he can feel every pulsation of the moving millions upon the globe, — I say, it is difficult for such a one to comprehend the dull, monotonous, do-little life of the first generation of those who planted these towns in the interior of Massachusetts. Every thing partakes of the change; and every man seems to be on a chase with his fellow-men, which shall go farthest and fastest.

In the schools, instead of a few rudiments of elementary teaching, the whole encyclopædia of science is to be mastered by boys and girls of a dozen years old: and, in matters of religion, — instead of a minister settled for life, preaching his two sermons of a Sunday, and working his farm and studying his ponderous tomes of polemical divinity of a week-day, — there are not days enough in the week for the lectures and meetings, the sewing-circles, the society-gatherings of all imaginable phases of benevolence; in all which, everybody, especially the minister, must take a part, — to be used up and dismissed the moment he ceases to be able to "keep alive the interest of his people."

We often hear, and always with something like a feeling of reflected merit, of the courage and patriotism, the puritanic virtues and primitive simplicity of habits, of our ancestors; and yet, loose as may be the sentiments of our own day, it seems to me that there has been a decided improvement upon the state of morals which existed immediately and for many years after the war.*

---

* I copy the following memorandum from a private diary as a singular statement; although it ought by no means to be regarded as a specimen of the morals of the town at that day. I omit the names, as I believe every one of them came to precisely such

The war and the camp had had their usual effect upon those who had served through the Revolution. Indisposition for systematic labor, and profanity and intemperance, were the natural fruits of a soldier's life. These were witnessed in high life as well as low. Some of the grosser vices were more openly tolerated then than they are now; because the tastes of the community are more cultivated, and less tolerant of grossness in any form, than they once were. On the other hand, in the intercourse of life — in the respect for age, for eminence in rank or station; in the bearing of children towards their parents, and in the young towards the old — there has been a change which no man can fail to deplore.

There was a courtesy, and dignity of intercourse, in their associations in the army, between our well-bred superior officers and those who had been trained in the schools of Germany and France, which impressed itself upon every little community in which they settled after the war, and which has given place to the precocity of Young America, and the deference which the young, now-a-days, extort from the middle-aged and the old.

The style of dress, of the houses in which men live, of their social entertainments, and, in short, the whole matter of living, has fully kept pace with the progress of other changes. What man, much less what woman, would be content with the furniture that satisfied our grandmothers? — sanded or painted floors, without a carpet; an hour-glass, it may be, but no clock; a pillion, but no chaise or carriage of any kind. Instead of a piano, the daughters learned the use of a spinning-

---

an end as might have been anticipated; and it can be of no use to revive the memory of forgotten wrecks.

"In January, 1772, the 'Club' met at —— Tavern, and drank, and played cards, and quarrelled, all night. They met again in February, and carried on the same game: and in March, on Monday, they met and staid till Tuesday night; and they gave D.'s wife a mug of flip to kiss B. The names of some of these are W. B. R., and others. And, on 23d May, there was fiddling and dancing kept up in said tavern; and, in July 5, the same again: all which is against law."

wheel and loom, in which the garments of the household were wrought. The household arts have indeed, within that time, wholly disappeared, and a "quill-wheel" or a "reel" has become a curiosity suited to a museum of antediluvian fossils. On the other hand, schools have vastly improved; the standard of education of all classes has advanced, especially among the so-called educated men, in an equal ratio; and branches of science, which were not known, even by name, to our ancestors, are now familiar studies. Books have been multiplied, especially such as are suited to the popular taste, and their prices reduced to an extent of which no man could have conceived three-quarters of a century ago; while newspapers and magazines, in the purposes to which they are applied, are all but the discoveries of the last half-century.

As to the condition of woman, if her *equality* of rights and duties be a test of the social condition of an age in the matter of comparative advancement, — saying nothing of the conventionalities of social intercourse and fashion, — many of the things which women are now holding conventions and making harangues and adopting resolutions that they have a right to do, our mothers did, without dreaming that they were heroines or martyrs. I have mentioned more than once what they did in the culture of their farms while their husbands were away in the army. Time and again, the wife of the representative of the town accompanied him on horseback to Boston to make her own little purchases, and lead back the animal which the husband had ridden, as the only mode of travelling at that day; and when the muster-master of the Continental troops was absent on public duty, and men offered themselves for inspection, the wife did not hesitate to perform the duty, and deliver the proper certificate in order to their being mustered into the army.*

* This was repeatedly done in the case of the muster-master in Leicester.

Nobody spoke of these women as "strong-minded," or expected to find them any the less better wives or mothers, because they shared in the rough but common experiences of a community of which they were a part.

I say nothing of any comparison between the standard of political qualification and success during the last quarter of the last century and our own day. Some have thought the scale of morals, of disinterested devotion to country, and of qualification for office; learning, fitness, and honesty, — had not been elevated or improved since the days of Hawley and Adams and Madison and Jay. It may be that posterity will perceive beauties and excellences, in the policy and measures and deportment of the last Congress or two, which have escaped the attention of those who stood too near them to judge of the harmony into which the light and shade of their grouping upon the canvas may blend at a period of observation more remote.

One change in the people of this community, since the close of the Revolution, cannot escape the attention of the most casual observer. That contest found New England, at its commencement, an industrial, a homogeneous race of men, of pure Anglo-Saxon stock. The Revolution introduced a new element, to an inconsiderable extent, by the deserters and those taken prisoners, who chose to remain here, of the British and German troops.

In March, 1780, by a vote of the General Court, "Robert Todd, a British soldier of the troops of the Convention of Saratoga, is permitted to reside in Leicester; having taken the oath of allegiance and paid taxes in Leicester, and produced a certificate of the selectmen that he appears to be a good member of society."

Even within the recollection of many now living, the sight of an "old countryman" was rare in country towns forty miles from the seaboard. But now their numbers have become so great, that the national prejudice thereby awakened was made the basis of a short-lived party organization, impotent indeed of good; and the Constitution of the Commonwealth has been amended, to counteract, as it is assumed, the un-Americanized action of naturalized citizens.

But, in a work like this, it is only in reference to its local and social effect that this change is referred to. Nor is it to be wondered at, that those who remember the old and stable families that have given place, as proprietors of the soil in many of our towns, to names of less familiar patronymic origin, should regret the change, even if they were conscious of no national prejudice or jealousy.

Fortunately, the process of assimilation goes on so rapidly, that no effort to create a caste in social or political rights, based on birth alone, can ever be successful for any great length of time. By the second generation, every one is fused into an American citizen, and the birthplace of the ancestor is forgotten.

As we thus glance over the past, we can hardly fail of the conviction, that, in every thing that goes to make up what is called the progress of the age, Leicester has kept pace with the other towns in the Commonwealth; but, when we turn to the future, it cannot be concealed, that there are causes at work, in this and every town similarly situated, adverse to its retaining its relative importance, although it may be making a positive progress in wealth and numbers.

There has been — especially of late years, and since the opening of so many railroads — a tendency to *centralization*, drawing men of capital and enterprise to the focal points of business. It is seen in the counties in this Commonwealth, and in the great business republic of the country. The smaller towns and cities do not keep pace, in their relative rank and influence, with the larger ones; and, so long as a wide field offers more attractions for the man of enterprise than a limited one, this will continue to go on. One sees it in Worcester, in Boston, and in New York. There is scarcely a town in all New England that is not more or less largely represented in each of the two last-named cities.

At a social gathering in Worcester, a few years since, of natives of Leicester resident in that city, some sixty or more sat down together to indulge in the pleasant memories of their birthplace. These embraced men in almost every business and profession. They were among those whose industry and moral worth had been adding wealth and respectability to the flourishing city of their adoption. It was from no feeling of alienation towards the home of their childhood. It was no sudden exodus from the place where their fathers had lived contentedly and independently. They came one by one, and as the superior advantages of their new homes for business offered attractions sufficiently strong to break the ties that bound them to those they left. That something like this is to operate upon the hopes and reasonable ambition of young men hereafter, is doubtless to be expected.

If, however, mechanics and traders and professional men shall continue to seek elsewhere a wider or more tempting field for their enterprise and skill, the town has little cause to apprehend a decline, if she will but avail herself of the attractions which she will continue to command in the literary institution* which is planted here, and in the associations which she may offer of moral, cultivated, and refined society; and will lend, to the natural beauties of scenery of a locality of unsurpassed healthfulness, the adornments of taste which a wise liberality and a generous public spirit would dictate. It was of the past, however, that I undertook to speak: and I cannot review what I have written, — meagre and unsatisfactory as it may seem, — without congratulating her sons, wherever they may be found scattered through this wide continent, that the past is at least secure; that, among con-

* A history of this institution, in a pamphlet of 158 pages, having been published in 1855, further notice of it has been purposely omitted in this work, to avoid repetition; both being from the same pen.

temporary civil communities, none more faithfully, more zealously, or more consistently, acted up to the line of duty, of honor, and of patriotism, as well in the hours of danger and difficulty as of prosperity and success, than the one in whose councils their ancestors took a part, and within whose soil their ashes are reposing.

CHAPTER IX.

GENEALOGIES, &c.

The reader should be apprised that this chapter is exceedingly defective, from the impossibility, with the means and opportunity I could command, to make it complete. It has been my aim to record the names, and dates of birth, of all persons born in Leicester in the first century after its settlement; and, so far as these have been recorded in the registry of births in the town, I believe it has been done. Beyond that, I have depended upon published family genealogies in part, and in part upon the aid which individuals have been able to afford me.

If, therefore, many names and certain families are omitted, who, from their social position and influence, might be expected to hold a place in such a record, it must be ascribed only to the want of means of obtaining the requisite information. Imperfect as it is, this record will be found to contain about three hundred families; in procuring the account of which, I have to acknowledge the aid derived from the "Genealogical Sketch of the Descendants of Thomas Green," by Samuel S. Green, Esq., of Providence; the "Genealogy of the Vinton Family," by J. A. Vinton; the "Genealogy of the Sargent Family," by Aaron Sargent, Esq., of Somerville, Mass.; the "Genealogy of the Parsons Family," by S. G. Drake, Esq., published in the "Genealogical Register;" and personal communications from Dr. Pliny Earle, Lyman Waite, Esq., and Joseph A. Denny, Esq., of Leicester; Hon. Judge Hayward of McConnellsville, O., in relation to the Brown Family; Henry H. Silvester, Esq., of Charleston, N.H.; and the valuable "History of Spencer," by Hon. James Draper, to which reference has more than once been made. To Mr. William S. Denny — whose transcript of the records of the births, marriages, and deaths, was kindly furnished for my use — I am also much indebted for the means of testing the accuracy of the information derived from other quarters.

ADAMS, EBENEZER, m. Alice Frink of Rutland, and had *Amelia*, b. June 2, 1796; m. Rev. Mr. Murdock, and d. in Portland, Me. *Adeline A.*, b. Jan. 17, 1798; d. unmarried. *John F.*, b. Nov. 3, 1799; m. Elizabeth, dau. of Hon. Lovell Walker; now lives in Washington, D.C., and is noticed in this work. *Charles A.*, b. Oct. 2, 1801; d. in early life in Portland. *Harriet R.*, b. Sept. 14, 1804; m. Hon. John Aiken, now of Andover; d. in Columbia, S.C., where she had gone for health, leaving two children, one a professor in Dartmouth College. Mrs. Adams d. June 20, 1805, aged thirty-six.

ALLEN, JOSEPH, Hon., removed here from Boston, Nov. 17, 1771; m. Anne, dau. of Judge Steele, and had *Thomas*, b. Nov. 16, 1774; d. March 30, 1775. Mrs. Allen d. May 10, 1775, aged twenty-four. In 1776, Mr. Allen was appointed Clerk of the Courts of the County, and removed to Worcester. He is noticed in this work. He held many offices of honor and trust, — Councillor, Member of Congress, Presidential Elector, &c.; and d. Sept. 2, 1827, aged seventy-eight.

ALLEN, AARON, m. Catherine Cummings, July 10, 1739; and had *Elizabeth*, b. Oct. 4, 1739.

ALLEN, LEWIS, m. Mary Adams of Worcester, but had no children. He was from Shrewsbury. He lived on the Mount-Pleasant Place, then in fine repair; and d. Nov. 7, 1782, aged thirty-four. He was buried in the garden of the place on which he lived. He was spoken of at his death as "a great loss to his friends and the public."

Bass, Joseph, was early a seafaring man and a ship-master in the West-India trade. He came from Plymouth County to Leicester with his family. His wife was mother of John Hobart, Esq. Their children were *Manly; Matilda*, m. a Reed; *Saba*, m. William Lynde; *Warren*, removed to Lisbon, N.H.; *Betsey*, d. unmarried. Mr. Bass is noticed in another part of this work. His wife d. 1816; he in 1829, aged seventy-five. He lived in the house opposite Mrs. Newhall's.

Beers, Nathan, m. Betsey, dau. of Isaac Southgate, Mar. 4, 1790; and had *Sally*, b. June 17, 1790; m. Amos Warren, Esq., of Woodstock, Vt., 1854. *Melissa*, b. Feb. 10, 1798; m. R. Bancroft, 1821. *Horatio*, b. May 10, 1802. *Alphonso*, b. Dec. 26, 1805; d. April 22, 1843. *Almira*, a twin; m. William Woodcock of Leicester, 1838. *Albert*, b. July 13, 1800; and *Adeline*, b. Nov. 4, 1813. Mr. Beers was a manufacturer of shoes; and, the latter part of his life, lived in Cherry Valley, in the house afterwards occupied by Moses Shepherd.

Bruce, George, m. Hannah Lovett, March 30, 1758. He was born in Mendon; was a commissary in the army of the Revolution; and removed to Rutland. From thence he came to Leicester about 1783. He lived in various places in the town; and, at one time, kept a tavern in the Mount-Pleasant House. He died May 3, 1788. He had ten children, all of whom were born before his removal to Leicester; but most if not all of them lived at some time in Leicester. Among them were *Phinehas*, b. Jan. 7, 1762; mentioned among the college graduates. *Hannah*, b. Dec. 27, 1767; m. Daniel P. Upton, Esq., of Eastport, Me., and was the mother of Hon. George B. Upton of Boston. *George*, b. Nov. 21, 1769; d. in Billerica in 1826; had been a merchant in Boston. *Patty*, b. May 10, 1771; m. Nathan Waite, jun., afterwards of Sterling; d. July, 1794, leaving one daughter. *Abigail*, b. July 14, 1773; died unmarried at Billerica, 1843. *Stephen*, b. Aug. 21, 1775; d. in Worcester, unmarried. *William*, b. Feb. 14, 1778;

d. in Bangor, 1841; a merchant. *Charles*, b. Sept. 29, 1781; d., unmarried, 1817; had been a merchant in Charleston, S.C. None of the family remain in Leicester.

BARTON, JOSHUA, came from Oxford in 1720. He had *Timothy*, b. April 13, 1732; *Nathan*, b. July 23, 1734; *Reuben*, b. March 28, 1738. He removed to Spencer in 1737. His wife's name was Anna.

BARTON, PHINEHAS, m. Elizabeth, dau. of John Hasey, 1772. They had *Betsey*, b. Sept. 3, 1776; m. Alexander Westley. *Elijah*, b. Oct. 25, 1778; m. Hannah, dau. of Luther Ward, 1810; was an ingenious mechanic; removed from Leicester, before 1817, to Connecticut, where he now lives. *Samuel*, b. Dec. 24, 1782. *Phinehas*, b. May 12, 1785. *Phinehas*, 2d, b. Oct. 27, 1795; lives in the city of New York. *Horace*, b. Dec. 17, 1799. Mr. Barton was a laboring man, and lived in various places in Leicester. Edward, a son of Betsey, is a well-known gentleman of business in New York; and is one of the proprietors of the "New-York Times," which he helped to establish.

BARTON, CALEB, brother of the above, came originally from Oxford. He lived in the south-west part of the town, and is mentioned among the soldiers of the Revolution. He had *Caleb, jun.* *David.* *Charles*, b. in 1795; now living in Leicester. *Otis*, who lives in Oakham. And *Brigham N.*, now in business in Philadelphia. His daughters were *Rebecca*, who m. Knight Sprague, jun. *Sally*, m. J. Gilbert. *Patty*, m. Philip Earle. *Roxa*, m. Charles King; and d. 1843, aged fifty-three. *Mehitabel*, m. a Hixon of Medway. *Huldah*, m. a Clark of Medway. *Harriet*, m. a Prentiss of Auburn. *Adeline*, m. a Blake of Hopkinton. Mr. Barton had two wives: first, Polly, dau. of Samuel Upham; and, second, Betsey Lamb.

BROWN, WILLIAM, was born in England; came to this country before 1686, and to Leicester before 1721. He was a soldier in the Indian and French wars. He died in Leicester in 1752. His wife's name was Martha. They had *William*, 2d;

John, b. about 1703; *Zachariah;* and *Samuel.* He lived on the farm now belonging to William Silvester.

Brown, William, 2d, son of the above. His wife's name was Martha. They had *Martha*, b. April 30, 1724; *William*, 3d, b. Dec. 12, 1727. He lived where William Silvester now lives.

Brown, Zachariah, son of William, 1st; m. Patience Converse, 1730; and had *Joshua*, b. June 3, 1732. *Zachariah*, 2d; b. Oct. 6, 1739. His house was south-west of William Silvester's, and upon the south side of the road.

Brown, Samuel, son of William, 1st. His wife's name was Mary. They had *Eunice*, who married Elder Richard Southgate, grandfather of Capt. Isaac Southgate; and *Abram*, b. Feb. 8, 1740.

Brown, John, 1st, son of William, 1st, was a soldier in the French wars, and commanded a company in the Louisburg expedition in 1745. He was a leading man in the town, and its representative in the General Court for twenty years. He d. 1791, at the age of eighty-eight. His first wife was Lydia Newhall. He lived where Peter Silvester lived and died, in the south-west part of the town. Their children were *John*, b. 1733. *Perley*, b. May 27, 1737. He was a soldier in the French War. He built and lived in the old house lately owned by Mr. Thomas Sprague. *Dorothy*, b. Aug. 23, 1728; m. Simeon Wilson, 1746. *Lydia*, b. Nov. 14, 1730; m. Edward Hale of Uxbridge, 1748.

Capt. Brown m., for his second wife, Mary Jones, aunt of Hon. John Coffin Jones, and had *Mary*, b. April 24, 1743; m. Daniel Reed, Uxbridge, 1765. *Rebekah*, b. Sept. 9, 1744; m. Isaac Southgate (1769), father of Capt. Isaac. *Benjamin*, b. Oct. 6, 1745; m. Jean, dau. of Archibald Thomas, 1792. He commanded a company of Continental troops, in the Revolution, three years; removed to Ohio in 1797, and died in 1821. *Lucy*, b. Oct. 8, 1747. *Sarah*, b. Nov. 23, 1750; m. John White, 1785. *Hannah*, b. Nov. 24, 1752; m. Frederick

Baylies, 1773. *Elizabeth,* b. Dec. 16, 1754; m. Jeremiah Chase, 1780. *William,* b. June 15, 1758. *Caleb,* b. Feb. 16, 1760. *Daniel,* b. Dec. 17, 1761. *Opphia,* b. April 13, 1765. *Aziel,* and three other children; making nineteen in all. Of these, John, Perley, and William were in the battle of Bunker Hill; making, with Benjamin, four in the Revolutionary service.

Brown, John, 2d, son of John, 1st, m. Rebekah Baldwin, 1757; and had *Samuel,* b. June 1, 1758; *Lydia,* b. May 12, 1760. He is mentioned among the members of the company that took part in the battle of Bunker Hill, and was severely wounded in that engagement. He lived in the south-west part of the town, where Daniel Mussy lived. He removed to Washington County, O., after the war; and d. September, 1821, aged eighty-eight.

Of the numerous families of Brown above mentioned, no descendant of the name, it is believed, remains in Leicester.

Bond, Baley, m. Elizabeth Hopkins, 1740; and had *Baley,* b. Oct. 26, 1740.

The families of this name came to Leicester from Beverly.

Bond, Edward, formerly kept the tavern which stood where H. Knight, Esq., lives, and was burned in 1767. His wife's name was Experience. Their children were *Edward,* b. Dec. 28, 1737. *Experience,* b. Dec. 16, 1739. *Emma,* b. 1741; m. Richard Bond, 1768. *Benjamin,* b. June 28, 1743. *Abigail,* b. May 16, 1745. *Jonathan.* He lived in a house which stood where Capt. Gleason recently lived.

Bond, Benjamin, 1st, son of above, m. Elizabeth, dau. of Nathaniel Harrod, 1765; and had *Jacob,* b. Dec. 2, 1766. *Elizabeth,* b. 1763; d. unmarried. *Hannah;* m. John Sargent, formerly of Hubbardston. *David. George. Polly;* m. John Boice. *Benjamin,* jun., b. 1776. Mr. Bond lived in the north-west part of the town, in a house that stood near where his son George afterwards lived and died. He d. 1812, aged sixty-seven: his wife d. the same year, aged seventy.

BOND, JACOB, son of the above, lived, for some years before his death, in a house one mile north of the Meeting-house. His wife's name was Hannah. They had *Jacob*, b. Nov. 18, 1795. *Nathan D.*, b. Jan. 20, 1798. *Nathaniel*, b. Jan. 3, 1800. *Joseph*, b. April 6, 1807; and a dau., who married a Clark. Jacob lives in Oxford. The father d. May 20, 1838, aged seventy-one.

BOND, BENJAMIN, jun., brother of above, m. Betsey, of Killingly, Conn.; and had *Oliver B.*, b. April 10, 1806. He studied medicine; but d., just as he was commencing practice, Sept. 11, 1832. *William*, b. Feb. 13, 1810. *Sewall B.*, b. Aug. 12, 1812; a merchant in Boston. Mr. Bond lived in the house with his father. He d. July 4, 1813, aged thirty-seven.

BOND, JOHN, m. Lydia Graves, January, 1740; and had *John*, 2d, b. Jan. 8, 1741. *Jacob*, b. Jan. 18, 1743. *Ephraim*, b. Dec. 3, 1740. Mr. Bond d. Feb. 4, 1802, aged ninety-two.

BOND, JONATHAN, son of Edward, m. Sally Crossman, and lived where Silas Gleason, Esq., lately lived. Their children were *Nancy*. *Edward*. *Cynthia*. *Jonathan*, jun., — a well-known musician, — m. Betsey, dau. of Elijah Warren; removed to the State of New York. *Hannah*. Mr. Bond died of an injury, which rendered the amputation of his foot necessary, July, 1810.

BOND, BENJAMIN, 2d, lived on the Oxford Road, one mile south of the village, in a house next to the one recently occupied by Capt. Silas Gleason. His wife's name was Mary. Their children were *Benjamin*. *Richard*, b. Dec. 11, 1747. *Mary*, b. Dec. 25, 1755; m. Daniel Tenny; d. 1806. *Elizabeth*, b. 1758; d. unmarried, 1813: known to all as "Aunt Betty;" and in the notice of her death, in the "Massachusetts Spy," it is said, "She was justly endeared to each of her acquaintance for her many virtues and amiable qualities." *Thomas* and *Baley*. He built the house in which he lived.

BOND, RICHARD, son of above, lived in a house, a little north of where Mr. Eber Bond lives (on the Oxford Road), which he built in 1768. He m. Emma, dau. of Edward Bond, 1768; and had *Experience*, b. May 2, 1769, who d. unmarried, 1825. *Polly*, b. March 6, 1770; m. Amos Whittemore. *William*, b. March 1, 1773; removed to Jamaica, Vt. *Richard*, jun., b. Nov. 1, 1774. *Eber*, b. 1784; m. Minerva Stetson, and has a family of children now living. *Lydia*, b. 1778; and *Sally*, b. 1781, d. 1759. Mr. Bond was a shoe-manufacturer. He d. Sept. 17, 1819, aged seventy-two.

BOND, RICHARD, jun., son of above, m. Elizabeth, dau. of Carey Howard, who lived where Mr. Amos Whittemore died, on the Charlton Road. They had *Jeremiah*, b. Oct. 6, 1800; lives in Worcester. *Louisa*, b. Jan. 15, 1799; m. Rev. Otis Converse. *Narcissa*, b. April 21, 1803; m. a Collyer of Troy, N.Y. *Zephaniah*, b. Feb. 23, 1805; now lives in Pennsylvania. *Mary*, b. April 9, 1807; m. Hastings Bridges. *Carey*, b. Dec. 6, 1809; d. at the age of twenty-two. *Lydia*, m. Dexter Trask; b. March 28, 1814. Mr. Bond lived a little east of the house of the late John King, Esq. His wife d. 1832: he d. 1838.

BOND, THOMAS, son of Benjamin, 2d; m. Sarah, dau. of James Harrod, 1779; and had *Samuel*, b. April 2, 1784. *Benjamin*, b. June 29, 1787. *Eli*, b. July 28, 1790. *Patty*, b. March 28, 1794. *Maria*, b. Feb. 23, 1799.

Mr. Bond lived at the north foot of the Livermore Hill, where Joshua Lamb, Esq., has recently lived. He removed to Lanesborough.

BOND, BALEY, son of Benjamin, 2d; m. Elizabeth Charles of Brimfield, 1780; and had *Charles*, b. Feb. 18, 1781. *John*, b. April 18, 1783. *Linus*, b. Aug. 28, 1785.

Mr. Bond, with his family, removed to Brimfield.

BLAIR, WILLIAM. His wife's name was Jane; and his children were *Sarah*, b. March 18, 1745. *Hannah*, b. Oct. 21, 1746.

BABBIT, SAMUEL. His first wife's name was Abigail. They had *Abigail*, b. Sept. 8, 1762. His second, Bathsheba; and they had *Silas*, b. Oct. 1, 1764. *Sanford*, b. Dec. 17, 1765.

BALDWIN, STEPHEN, m. Elizabeth Baldwin, 1759; and had *Elizabeth*, b. Oct. 8, 1760. *Stephen*, b. Oct. 26, 1761. *Samuel*, b. April 4, 1765, and m. Rebekah Green. *James*, b. June 20, 1767. *John*, b. June 25, 1769.

BALDWIN, EBENEZER, m. Phebe Baldwin, 1772; and had *Phebe*, b. Dec. 7, 1774. *Winnifred*, b. Aug. 18, 1776. *Mary*, b. Aug. 26, 1778. *Rebekah*, b. Jan. 22, 1781. *Ebenezer*, b. May 31, 1783. *James*, b. March 3, 1787. *Aaron*, b. June 25, 1789.

BALDWIN, JAMES. His wife's name was Lucinda. They had *Lucy*, b. April 16, 1807. *John S.*, b. Sept. 26, 1808.

BALDWIN, BENJAMIN. His wife's name was Betsey; and had *Roxana*, b. Dec. 15, 1811. *Horace*, b. Nov. 24, 1813. *Nancy*, b. April 17, 1816. *Dexter*, b. Sept. 2, 1818.

BELL, AARON. The name of his wife was Isabel. They had *Mary*, b. March 19, 1721. *Martha*, b. April 1, 1724. *Elizur*, b. July 8, 1726. *Sarah*, b. July 4, 1728. He lived where there is now a cellar, south of Mr. Robert Young's.

CAPEN, SAMUEL, came from Dorchester and settled in Leicester about 1733, and remained there about five years, when he removed to Spencer. His wife's name was Deborah. His children, born in Leicester, were *Samuel*, b. March 14, 1734. *Elizabeth*, b. Jan. 14, 1735; d. March, 1735. *John*, b. May 1, 1737. *Hannah*, b. May 22, 1739. *Edmond*, b. July 16, 1740.

CALL, SAMUEL, m. Mehitabel Green, dau. of Capt. Nathaniel Green, in 1746. He came from Malden. His children, born in Leicester, were *Samuel*, b. Oct. 12, 1754. *Mary*, b. Nov. 4. 1756. *Elizabeth*, b. March 25, 1758. *Amos*, b. Dec. 9, 1759. *Winnifred*, b. June 4, 1761.

Mr. Call came from Louisburg, Cape Breton, to Leicester, at the time of his marriage.

CHOATE, ISAAC, came from Ipswich in 1773. He was a tanner, and lived upon the Elliot Farm, so called, in the north part of the town. His wife's name was Sarah. They had *Mary*, b. Feb. 10, 1772. *Jacob*, b. Dec. 20, 1773. His second wife's name was Patty Craige, dau. of Dr. Robert Craige. They had *Hannah*, b. Jan. 26, 1785. *Polly*, born Nov. 15, 1787. *George*, b. July 1, 1789.

Mr. Choate was a deacon of the Congregational Church. He, with his brother Francis, emigrated to the West. An account of their being made prisoners by the Indians will be found in another part of this work.

CHOATE, FRANCIS, brother of the above, was a cordwainer, and lived on the same place with his brother. His wife's name was Betsey Lyon, m. 1780; and they had *Sally*, b. April 20, 1782. *Susannah*, b. March 20, 1784. *John*, b. March 6, 1786. *Betsey*, b. May 18, 1788. *Polly*, b. Nov. 26, 1790. *Francis*, b. Dec. 9, 1792.

CHOATE, JONATHAN. His wife's name was Lois; and had *Lois*, b. Oct. 6, 1792.

CERLEY, JOSEPH, m. Sarah, sister of Col. Seth Washburn, Feb. 7, 1750; and had *Joseph*, b. Dec. 7, 1751. *Hannah*, b. May 26, 1753. *Sarah*, b. April 3, 1754.

Mr. Cerley removed to Whitingham, Vt.; and d. 1817.

CONKLIN, BENJAMIN, Rev., m. Lucretia Lawton, 1769; and had *Joseph*, b. April 25, 1770. *Benjamin, jun.*, b. May 28, 1772. *Elizabeth*, b. March 20, 1774; m. William Harris.

CONKLIN, BENJAMIN, Jun., m. Rebekah Browning of Rutland; and had *Lucretia*, b. Aug. 8, 1795; *Benjamin; Austin F.; George B.;* and *Henry*, now of Worcester. Lucretia m. William Hatch; Benjamin m. Hannah Woodcock.

CUTTING, DARIUS, came from Rutland; was the son of Abraham. He m. Sally Waite, September, 1789; and had *Lewis*, b. Jan. 2, 1790; who m. Rebekah, dau. of John Sargent, and removed to Worcester. He now lives in West Boylston. *Absalom*, b. Jan. 29, 1792. *Alice*, m. Daniel Hastings, 1817, and removed to Petersham. *Eliza*, m. Elijah H. Trowbridge, 1818, and removed to the western part of New York. *Charles*, b. July 6, 1801; d. 1859, unmarried. *William D.*, b. Jan. 2, 1804. *George*, b. May 11, 1806. *Sarah Ann*, b. Nov. 14, 1810. *Otis*, b. Jan. 23, 1813.

Capt. Cutting once commanded one of the military companies of the town. He was by trade a hatter, and carried on his business in a shop next west of the tavern, and near the house which he built, and is now standing. After that (about 1807) he removed to Cherry Valley, where he lived the remainder of his days. He died Sept. 18, 1830, aged sixty-six. He was a man of much pleasantry and good-humor, and was esteemed by his neighbors and friends.

Craige, Robert, Dr., m. Martha, dau. of Dr. Thomas Green, in 1753; and had *Nathan*, b. June 11, 1754. He m. Sarah, dau. of Francis Choate; is noticed among the soldiers of the Revolution; lived a considerable part of his life in Spencer, near the line of Leicester, in the south-east part of the town; and died April 2, 1852, aged almost ninety-eight, — a man of great worth and respectability: his son lives upon what was once the farm of Jonathan Newhall; his daughter was the wife of Mr. Samuel Watson. *Olive*, born Dec. 24, 1755. *David*, b. Oct. 16, 1757. *Jemima*, born Sept. 19, 1759; m. Joseph Bemis. *Abijah*, b. July 3, 1761; removed to Auburn. *Martha*, b. April 4, 1763; m. Isaac Choate. *Amos*, b. March 23, 1765. *Hannah*, b. Dec. 26, 1766; m. Samuel Stone of Oxford. *Esther*, b. Dec. 27, 1768.

Dr. Craige is noticed among the physicians of the town. He lived in the south part of the town, where his son Amos afterwards lived, and where, after giving up the practice of medicine, he manufactured spinning-wheels. He d. 1805, at the age of seventy-five. Some persons may recall him as a seemingly old man, who used to attend meeting, and, on account of his defect in hearing, sat in the pulpit on Sundays.

Craige, Amos, son of the above, lived in the south part of the town; and d. in 1843, at the age of seventy-one. He was a farmer. His wife's name was Phebe. Their children were *John*, b. May 6, 1800. *Eliza*, b. Sept. 18, 1803.

Converse, Josiah. His first wife's name was Hannah. They had *Sarah*, b. November, 1729. His second wife was Eleanor Richardson, m. 1732. They had *Mary*, b. July 17, 1733. *Eleanor*, b. March 21, 1734.

The original Converse families, it is understood, came from Woburn to Leicester. The next in order (John) is known to have come from there. He removed to Brookfield.

Converse, John. His wife's name was Abigail. They had *Benjamin*, b. May 20, 1732. *Luke*, b. Oct. 6, 1734. *Robert*, b. April 20, 1737. *Abigail*, b. March 5, 1739. He m. Mary Damon, 1751; and had *Phebe*, b. March 22, 1752. *Daniel*, b. March 2, 1754. *Deliverance*, b. Oct. 3, 1756; d. 1759. *Elijah*, b. Sept. 27, 1759.

Mr. Converse was a blacksmith, and came from Woburn, as above stated.

Converse, Benjamin, son of John, m. Prudence Harrington of Spencer (1754); and had *Phinehas*, b. Dec. 15, 1754. *Abiel*, b. March 26, 1756. *Abraham*, b. Dec. 31, 1757.

Mr. Converse lived in the north-west part of the town, where he built the house afterwards occupied by Azariah Eddy, but now taken down.

Converse, Luke, son of John, m. Ruth Lamb of Spencer (1759); and had *Lydia*, b. Feb. 10, 1760. *Jude*, b. May 17, 1762. *Ruth*, b. Oct. 31, 1764. *Patience*, b. March, 1767. *Reuben*, b. April 25, 1769. *Esther*, b. Nov. 20, 1771. *Asaph*, b. April 22, 1774. *Tamar*, b. Aug. 29, 1776. *Uriah*, b. March 13, 1779.

Mr. Converse at one time lived in Charlton, afterwards in Spencer; and, for several years before his death, lived in the house west of the mills at the Burncoat Pond, which he managed. He d. June 10, 1810, aged seventy-six.

Converse, Robert, son of John, m. Sarah Newton, May 24, 1762; had *Dinah*, b. Sept. 29, 1762. *Jonas*, b. Oct. 6, 1764.

Converse, Joshua, m. Mehitabel Wicker, 1772; and had *Francis; Chloe; Henry.*

Mr. Converse lived near the house where George Bond lived, in the north-west part of the town, where there is now a cellar; the house having long since disappeared.

Converse, Reuben, had *Silas*, b. July 17, 1801. *Pamela*, b. July 12, 1803. *Thomas W.*, b. Feb. 10, 1805.

Clark, Uriah, came to Leicester from Watertown. He married Ruth Hastings; and had *Mary*, b. Aug. 25, 1744. *Uriah*, b. Aug. 10, 1746. *Ruth*, b. April 23, 1748. *Thomas* and *Richard*, b. July 7, 1750. *Uriah*, b. Aug. 29, 1752. *Rebekah*, b. Oct. 12, 1754. *Daniel*, b. Dec. 31, 1756.

Mr. Converse's sister, Joanna, m. James Lawton of Leicester.

Damon, Daniel. His wife's name was Deliverance. They had *Daniel*, b. June 9, 1734. *Mary*, b. April 26, 1736. *Elijah*, b. July 31, 1738.

Mr. Damon lived in the north part of the town, on the estate owned by Amasa Southwick. He owned land bounding upon "Tea Lane" (so called). Deliverance Damon — who, I suppose, was his widow — m. Robert Woodward in 1743.

Denny, Daniel, was the common ancestor of all of the name in Leicester. His removal to Leicester is mentioned in another part of this work. The Rev. Thomas Prince — the annalist of New England, and minister of the Old South Church in Boston — m. Deborah, sister of Mr. Denny, in Leicester. They came from Coombs, England. Mr. Denny's wife's name was Rebekah. They had *Thomas*, b. March 19, 1724; who is spoken of in this work. *Mary*, b. April 22, 1727; m. Nathan Sargent, 1750. *Rebekah*, b. April 10, 1729; m. John Lynde, 1755. *Samuel*, b. May 20, 1731. *Sarah*, b. May 5, 1733.

Mr. Denny's brother — "Major Denny" — settled in

Maine; became a prominent citizen there: at his death, was the Chief-Justice of the Court of Common Pleas for the County of Lincoln.

Denny, Thomas, son of the above, m. Tabitha Cutler of Grafton (1752); and had *Daniel*, b. July 22, 1753; d. 1754. Mr. Denny m., for his second wife, Mary Storrs of Pomfret; and had *Thomas*, b. May 15, 1757. *Mary*, b. April 17, 1758; m. Joseph Sargent, father of Col. Henry. *Tamison*, b. Sept. 15, 1760; m. Peter Webb, Esq., of Windham, Conn., 1783; mother of Mrs. Isaac Southgate, and Thomas Webb, Esq. (a lawyer in Warren, O.).

Mr. Denny was a prominent patriot in the Province, in the early part of the Revolution, and is noticed in this work. He lived upon the Denny Farm, which had been his father's.

Denny, Thomas, son of the above, m. Lucretia, dau. of Phinehas Sargent (1791); and had *Maria*, b. May 16, 1793; m. James Smith, Esq., who is mentioned in another part of this work, and now lives in Philadelphia, — a wealthy, public-spirited, and influential gentleman. *Lucretia*, b. January, 1795; m. Mr. Charles Bertody, an accomplished ship-master in the India trade: he retired from this several years before his death, and was living in New York; where, having business in one of the West-India Islands, he sailed thence; but was lost, on his return voyage, at sea, — the vessel never having been heard from; his life was one of singular incident and peril in the prosecution of his profession; he had the confidence and esteem of all who knew him; he left four children. *Thomas*, b. June 29, 1797; was a cadet, educated at West Point; and died in Virginia, while engaged upon a public work. *Adaline*, b. Nov. 26, 1799; m. Rev. Elizur G. Smith of Ogdensburg (1830), where she d. *Sarah*, b. May 26, 1802; m. Col. James W. Ripley, of the United-States Army (1824). *Phinehas S.*, b. Nov. 15, 1804. After the death of his brother, he took the name of *Thomas;* graduated at Harvard in 1823, and resides in New-York City.

Col. Denny is among those who are spoken of more at length in the body of this work.

Denny, Samuel, son of Daniel; m. Elizabeth, dau. of Daniel Henshaw and sister of Col. William, 1757. He lived in the north-west part of the town, near Moose Hill. He was an officer in the Revolutionary service, and is noticed in the body of this work. Their children were *Daniel*, b. Aug. 6, 1758; m. Nancy, dau. of Matthew Watson, 1783; and lived in Cherry Valley till after the birth of *Elizabeth* and *Daniel*, when he removed to Worcester. *Elizabeth*, b. March 1, 1760; m. Thomas W. Ward, Esq., of Shrewsbury. *Samuel*, b. April 21, 1762; early went to Ohio; afterwards lived and died in Oakham. *David*, b. Jan. 7, 1764; removed to Vermont. *Isaac*, b. Nov. 27, 1765; removed to Vermont: his widow m. John Sargent, and d. 1859. *William*, b. Sept. 17, 1767. *Sally*, b. May 23, 1769; m. Stephen Harris, who afterwards moved to Norfolk, Va., where he left a family: his son Charles is an enterprising and public-spirited gentleman of that city. *Thomas*, b. July 21, 1771; afterwards took the name of *Nathaniel P.*, and is noticed in this work. *Polly*, b. Aug. 21, 1773; m. Rev. Mr. Miles of Grafton. *Joseph*, b. April 2, 1777.

Mr. Denny m. a second wife, Phœbe Rich, in 1794; and a third, in 1809, — Sarah Meriam.

Denny, William, son of the above, m. Patty Smith of Paxton, 1788; and had *Elizabeth*, b. Sept. 10, 1789; m. Col. Henry Sargent. *John A.*, b. April 30, 1791; lives in the west part of the town. *Mary*, b. Mar. 4, 1795; m. Aaron Morse, who formerly kept the hotel opposite the Meeting-house; removed to New Haven. *Charles*, b. April 6, 1793; m. Miss Sibley of Spencer; was engaged in trade in Leicester, and died there.

Mr. Denny m., for his second wife, Ruth, dau. of Reuben Swan; and had *Martha*, b. Aug. 11, 1798; d. unmarried. *Horace*, b. April 2, 1800; d. under age of twenty-one. *Caroline*, b. Dec. 10, 1801; d., unmarried, 1859. *William*, b. Dec. 23, 1803; d. in infancy. *Julia Ann*, b. Oct. 22, 1805; m. Thomas Gilbert of North Brookfield. *William*, b. Aug. 8, 1807; died young. *Catherine*, m. Charles E. Miles, and lives in Worcester. *Rachel S.*, b. Aug. 21, 1809; m. Mr. Ayers of North Brookfield.

Mr. Denny m., for his third wife, Mrs. Upham, widow of Barnard Upham, in 1827. He kept a tavern for many years in a house standing where Capt. H. Knights lives. After selling that, he removed to Spencer. He d. in North Brookfield.

DENNY, NATHANIEL P., son of Samuel, m. Sally, dau. of Reuben Swan, Nov. 18, 1798; and had *Sarah*, b. July 21, 1799. *Marcia*, b. July 13, 1802; m. Alfred Willard, Esq.; removed to and lives in Indianapolis, Ind. *Edward*, b. May 19, 1806; is a manufacturer in Barre; has been a member of the Executive Council. *Lucia*, b. June 10, 1808; m. Joshua Clapp, a merchant and extensive manufacturer, from whom the village of Clappville took its name: he d. in Boston, leaving a family of children; she lives in Cambridge. *Andrew*, b. April 30, 1812; is a physician in Alabama. *Reuben S.*, b. June 22, 1814; has been an extensive woollen manufacturer in Clappville: he now lives there. *Thomas*, b. Jan. 26, 1819; was a merchant in Boston, and d. unmarried.

Mr. Denny m., for his second wife, Mary Denny of Worcester. He soon after removed to Norwich, Conn.; and d. in Barre.

DENNY, JOSEPH, son of Samuel, m. Phebe, dau. of Col. William Henshaw; and had *Theodore V.*, b. Feb. 21, 1800; went to Indiana, m. and had a family, and d. there. *Catharine H.*, b. July 25, 1801; m. Otis Sprague; removed to the West; lives in Milwaukie. *Henry A.*, b. Oct. 10, 1802; m. Eliza E. Sprague, dau. of Capt. William, 1825: now lives in Worcester. *Joseph A.*, b. May 13, 1804; m. Mary Davis of Rutland; lives in Leicester; an acting magistrate; has represented his district in the Legislature, and is one of the most active and public-spirited citizens of the town. *Lucinda H.*, b. April 3,

1806. *Christopher C.*, b. Jan. 10, 1813. *Phebe H.*, b. June 4, 1815.

Mr. Denny m., for his second wife, Lucinda, dau. of Col. William Henshaw; and had *Sarah H.*, b. Feb. 10, 1817. *Harriet F.*, b. Dec. 13, 1818. *Elizabeth H.*, b. April 12, 1821.

After Mr. Denny's death, his widow, in 1825, m. Samuel Daugherty, and removed to Belchertown. Mr. Denny was a card manufacturer, and lived in the western part of the village, where Mr. John Loring lives. He was an active citizen; for several years deputy-sheriff; and died in the midst of his usefulness.

DUNBAR, JOHN. His wife's name was Abigail. Their children: *Lucy*, b. April 26, 1741; m. Thomas Parker, jun., of Charlton. *Sarah*, b. Aug. 30, 1744; m. Samuel Parker of Charlton. *Nabby*, b. April 10, 1746; m. Phinehas Sargent, 1772. *David*, b. Feb. 22, 1747; m. Hannah Hammond, 1773; *Thomas*, b. Aug. 1, 1750; d. May, 1796. *Abner*, b. April 9, 1753.

Mr. Dunbar d. March, 1802, aged ninety-two. He lived in the north-east part of the town, where John Silvester lived.

DUNBAR, THOMAS, son of the above, m. Lucretia Smith; and had *Thomas*, b. Feb. 11, 1774. *Nancy*, b. Dec. 25, 1775. *James*, b. Sept. 19, 1779. *Betsey*, b. Jan. 29, 1782. *Chloe*, b. Jan. 29, 1784. *Lucretia*, b. Jan. 13, 1786. *Lucy*, b. Oct. 28, 1789.

Mr. Dunbar d. May 4, 1796, aged forty-five. His widow m. Jonas Lamb of Spencer, Aug. 25, 1803. Mr. Dunbar kept a tavern in the house opposite the Mower House, on Mount Pleasant.

DUNBAR, ABNER, m. Lydia, dau. of Ebenezer Warren, Mar. 31, 1774; and had *Sarah*, b. Nov. 3, 1774; d. unmarried. *Ebenezer*, b. March 29, 1777; now lives in the south part of the town, east of Clappville. *Lydia*, b. May 6, 1779; m. David Legg, 1804. *Abigail*, b. April 9, 1782. *Simeon*, b. Oct. 27,

1785. *Polly*, b. Oct. 5, 1791; m. Artemas Haven, 1814. *Daniel*, b. June 13, 1794; went to New York.

Mr. Dunbar was a mason by trade.

DIX, BENJAMIN. His wife's name was Mehitabel. Their children: *Elijah*, b. March 5, 1744. *Eunice*, b. July 4, 1747. *Sarah*, b. April 7, 1750. *Lois*, b. Sept. 24, 1751. *Joseph*, b. July 7, 1753. *Jonathan*, b. Dec. 20, 1754. *Hannah*, b. Sept. 21, 1759. He lived in the north-west part of the town, on what is called Dix Hill; and came originally from Watertown.

EARLE, RALPH, was the ancestor of the families of the name in Leicester. He came from Rhode Island in 1717, and d. in 1757. He m. Mary Hicks, and had *William*. *Elizabeth*, m. Job Lawton of Newport. *John*, b. Feb. 24, 1694; lived in Swansea. *Robert*, b. 1706. *Mary*, m. Sheffield. *Benjamin*. *Patience*, m. Benjamin Richardson.

Mr. Earle settled in the north part of the town, and lived where Gardner Wilson now lives.

EARLE, WILLIAM, son of above, m. Annah Howard; and had *William*, b. April 27, 1714. *Elizabeth*, b. May 12, 1716; m. John Potter. *Mary*, b. Feb. 28, 1719; m. James Lawton, jun. *David*, b. Aug. 16, 1721. *Judith*, b. Aug. 11, 1723; m. George Cutting. *Ralph*, b. Nov. 13, 1726. *John*, b. March 1, 1729.

Mr. Earle came to Leicester with his father, and lived at one time on the Amasa Southwick Place; then on the Abel Green Place; afterwards removed to Shrewsbury.

EARLE, ROBERT, son of Ralph, m., for his first wife, Mary Newhall; and had *Martha*, b. Nov. 3, 1726; m. David Earle, and afterwards Hezekiah Ward, 1768. *Nathan*, b. May 12, 1728; m. Elizabeth, dau. of Benjamin Richardson. *Mary*, b. Aug. 10, 1730; m. Jonathan Sargent. *Elizabeth*, b. Oct. 18, 1732; m. John Whittemore. *George*, b. March 3, 1735. *Thomas*, b. Aug. 27, 1737. *Esek*, b. Feb. 10, 1741. *Robert*, b. Oct. 10, 1743. *Lydia*, b. Aug. 15, 1746; m. John Wilson.

Marmaduke, b. March 8, 1749. For his second wife, he m. Hepsibah Johnson; and had *Phebe*, b. Dec. 22, 1756. *Timothy*, b. March 13, 1739.

Mr. Earle came to Leicester with his father; owned and lived upon the Mulberry-Grove Place. George was a captain in the Revolutionary service. He, with Nathan and Esek, removed to Vermont. Timothy died in the service in the Revolutionary War. Marmaduke lived in Paxton.

EARLE, BENJAMIN, son of Ralph, m. Abigail Newhall; and had *Newhall*, b. March 15, 1735; *Antipas*, b. June 1, 1737. *John*, b. Nov. 18, 1740. *Gardiner*, b. Feb. 21, 1744. Mr. Earle lived on his father's homestead. Newhall removed to Vermont, 1774.

EARLE, WILLIAM, 2d, son of William, 1st, m. Mary Cutting; and had *John*, b. Dec. 3, 1740. *Lois*, b. Jan. 25, 1743; m. Nathan Whittemore. *Oliver*, b. March 21, 1745. *Reuben*, b. May 8, 1747. *Jabez*, b. Jan. 7, 1754. *James*, b. April 10, 1757. *Joel*, b. July 6, 1759.

Mr. Earle built and lived where his son Capt. James lived, a short distance north of where Pliny Earle lived. He d. 1805, aged ninety-one. John removed to New York; Oliver, to Vermont; Reuben went to New York; and Joel, to Hubbardston. Mr. Earle was a remarkably active man, and rode on horseback the day before he died.

EARLE, RALPH, son of William, 1st, m. Phebe Whittemore; and had *Ralph*, b. May 11, 1751; distinguished as a painter, and noticed in the body of this work. *Clark*, b. April 17, 1753; lived in Paxton; was in Capt. Phinehas Moore's company of minute-men in 1775. *James*, also an artist; noticed in this work.

Capt. Earle commanded a company in the Revolutionary service. He lived in what is known as the Joseph Penniman Place, in Paxton.

EARLE, THOMAS, son of Robert, 1st, m. Hannah, dau. of Nathaniel Waite, 1760; and had *Asahel*, b. Dec. 21, 1761.

Hannah, m. Joseph Newhall. *William*, went to Baltimore; d., unmarried, 1799. *Sylvanus*, b. March 28, 1773; m. Eunice Southgate, and removed to Ohio. *Winthrop*, b. May 5, 1775. *Electa*, b. April 27, 1778; m. Luther Nye of New Braintree. *Betsey*, m. Zenas Studley. *Polly*, d. 1804.

Mr. Earle resided in Cherry Valley, in the house where Mr. Heman Burr lives. He planted the fine rows of sycamores that stood in front of it, on the day of the battle of Lexington. He was distinguished for his mechanical skill and ingenuity. He manufactured a gun of exquisite workmanship for Col. William Henshaw, in 1773; and when Col. Henshaw marched to Cambridge, in 1775, he took it into the service. Here it fell under the observation of Gen. Washington, who admired it so much, that he ordered one of the same pattern. Mr. Earle, having completed it, loaded and primed it, and placed it under water, all but the muzzle, during a night; and, taking it out in the morning, discharged it as if it had just been loaded. He carried it to New York, where the army then lay, and delivered it personally to Gen. Washington; having travelled the distance on foot, and carried it upon his shoulder. It received great commendation for its perfection of workmanship.

Earle, Robert, son of Robert, 1st, m. Sarah Hunt; and had *Pliny*, b. Dec. 17, 1762. *Jonah*, b. Aug. 10, 1765. *Silas*, b. May 26, 1767. *Elizabeth*, b. July 5, 1769; m. David Hoag. *Persis*, b. Sept. 19, 1771; m. Edward Halloch. *Henry*, b. March 13, 1774. *Lydia*, b. Jan. 16, 1776; m. John Fry of Bolton. *Timothy*, b. March 2, 1778. *Sarah*, b. Jan. 1, 1781; m. Jonathan Fry of Bolton.

Mr. Earle lived a little south of Pliny Earle's house, in the north part of the town. He was a man of great integrity, and much respected; and the regard in which he was held was indicated by the friendly title by which he was generally known, — "Uncle Robert."

Earle, Antipas, son of Benjamin, 1st, m. Mercy Slade;

and had *Benjamin*, b. Sept. 27, 1761. *Slade*, b. Nov. 22, 1764. *Jonathan*, b. Dec. 22, 1767; was an extensive card manufacturer; owned the place, on Mount Pleasant, where N. P. Denny, Esq., afterwards lived; and d., unmarried, July 1, 1813,—a man of active enterprise, and success in business. *Abigail*, b. April 7, 1774; m. George Read. *John*, b. Oct. 13, 1777; removed to Vermont.

Mr. Earle lived in the north-east part of the town, about half a mile east of the Gardner Wilson Place.

EARLE, JAMES, son of William, 2d, m. Deborah Sargent, dau. of Nathaniel; had *Aaron*, b. April 22, 1781. *Nathaniel*, b. July 23, 1783; d. 1859, in Leicester. *Charlotte*, b. May 3, 1786; m. Asa Sargent. *Arnold*, b. Nov. 7, 1788. He m. Lydia Kelly; was by trade a hatter; built the house now occupied by Denny and Bisco for a factory; and removed to the West. *Charles*, b. June 8, 1790; lives in Worcester. *Daniel*, b. Jan. 11, 1793; went to Ohio. *Reuben*, b. Sept. 8, 1795. *Homer*, b. May 30, 1798; studied medicine, and settled in Ohio,—as did Reuben.

Mr. Earle commanded one of the military companies in town in 1794, and was always called "Captain." He was a farmer; upright, and respected by his townsmen. Aaron d. 1846. He lived in the house next south of Amasa Southwick's.

EARLE, ASAHEL, son of Thomas, m. Persis Newhall. Had *Clarissa*, b. Sept. 29, 1786; m. John Thornton. *Melinda*, b. Feb. 28, 1788; d. 1815. *Austin*, b. May 16, 1792. *Ormacinda*, b. Oct. 31, 1795; d. 1839. *Adeline*, b. April 8, 1798; m. Gardner Wilson. *Elvira*, b. Sept. 5, 1800; m. George Earle. *Louisa*, b. Nov. 13, 1802; d. 1819. *Lydia*, b. Dec. 9, 1805; d. 1828. Austin removed to Kentucky. Mr. Earle had a good deal of his father's ingenuity and skill in mechanism. He lived on the North-County Road, where Mr. Knowlton now lives. He d. April 9, 1837.

EARLE, WINTHROP, son of Thomas, m. Persis Bartlett, and

had *Almira*, b. Mar. 1, 1800; m. William Newhall. *Theodore*, b. Nov. 13, 1801; d., unmarried, 1822. *Otis D.*, b. July 23, 1805; went to New Haven; d. unmarried, Dec. 15, 1830. *Winthrop*, b. July 2, 1807; d. Nov. 10, 1828.

Mr. Earle was an active business-man, extensively engaged as a card-manufacturer; much respected; and his early death, in 1807, was greatly lamented. His widow m. Alpheus Smith. He lived in the west part of the Col. Denny House, lately altered by Dr. Daggett.

EARLE, PLINY, son of Robert, jun., m. Patience Buffum, 1793; and had *John Milton*, b. April 13, 1794; has been a senator; now lives in Worcester. *Thomas*, b. April 21, 1796; removed to Philadelphia; was a lawyer; and d. there, 1849. *Lydia*, b. March 24, 1798; m. Anthony Chase, Esq., of Worcester. *Sarah*, b. April 8, 1800; m. Charles Hadwin of Worcester. *William B.*, b. Dec. 20, 1802; now lives in Boston. *Lucy*, b. May 7, 1805. *Eliza*, b. June 8, 1807; m. William E. Hacker of Philadelphia. *Pliny*, b. Dec. 31, 1809; a physician; resides in Leicester.

Mr. Earle is noticed in other parts of this work. He was at one time extensively engaged, in connection with his brother Jonah, as a card-manufacturer. He was a man of much intelligence. He lived where Mr. Billings Mann now lives. His wife was a woman of strong and cultivated intellect, and their house was the seat of a generous hospitality. The daughter (Lucy) and the son (Dr. Pliny) alone remain of the family in town. Mr. Earle d. 1832; Mrs. Earle, in 1849.

EARLE, JONAH, son of Robert, jun., m. Elizabeth Southgate; and had *John Potter*, b. Nov. 11, 1795. *Nathaniel P.*, b. April 17, 1798; d. May 17, 1853. *Amos S.*, b. April 22, 1800; d. January, 1853, leaving a family. *Rebekah P.*, b. May 20, 1802; m. Joseph Anthony.

Mr. Earle lived in the house near Mann and Marshall's factory. He was a man of great integrity and benevolence. He d. Jan. 21, 1846.

EARLE, SILAS, son of Robert, jun., m. Rachel Thornton; and had *Hannah*, b. March 16, 1796; m. William Keese of Ausable, N.Y.; d. 1859. *Anna*, b. Dec. 26, 1797; m. Harvey Chase of Rhode Island. *George*, b. Jan. 17, 1800; d. 1827. *Mary*, b. Feb. 9, 1802; d., unmarried, 1835. *Elisha*, b. April 18, 1804; d. 1827. *Robert*, b. May 18, 1806; m. Anna M. Brown of Salem, and now resides near Philadelphia. *Rachel*, b. May 11, 1808; d. 1836. *Silas*, b. March 29, 1806; d. 1833. *Stephen*, b. April, 1813; d. 1836. *Timothy*, b. Aug. 14, 1820; lives in Valley Falls, R.I. Mr. Earle d. in 1842. He built the large house where Mr. Marshall lives, on the North-County Road; had a large farm, and carried on card-manufacturing extensively and successfully, by which he accumulated a handsome estate. He once represented the town in the Legislature, and was highly esteemed and respected in the town. None of the family remain in Leicester.

EARLE, HENRY, son of Robert, jun., m. Martha Aldrich for his first wife, and had one child. His second wife was Miriam Fry. They had *Narcissa*, b. May 3, 1800; m. George Earle, and afterwards John Mann. *Melisssa*, b. April 1, 1803; m. Nathan Babcock, and afterwards Blaney Palmer. *Sarah*, b. April 8, 1805; m. Reuben Randall. *Henry W.*, b. 1810. Mr. Earle m. the widow of Timothy Earle for his third wife; and had *Timothy K.* and *Thomas*, b. Jan. 11, 1823. *Oliver K.*, b. Sept. 8, 1824. All of whom live in Worcester.

Mr. Earle built a large house upon the North-County Road, west of the Asahel Earle Place, but gave it up several years before his death. He d. in 1837.

EARLE, TIMOTHY, son of Robert, jun., m. Ruth Keese; and had *Anna K.*, b. Oct. 12, 1806; m. Samuel H. Colton, of Worcester. *Edward*, b. Feb. 10, 1811; lives in Worcester. *Mary B.*, b. Feb. 5, 1819; m. Jonathan Slocum.

Timothy Earle was a card-manufacturer; a man of active enterprise and energy. He lived in a large house, which he built, about a quarter of a mile south of Pliny Earle's. He

d. in 1819, in the midst of a prosperous and successful business, at the age of forty-one.

EARLE, BENJAMIN, son of Antipas, had *Slade*, b. Aug. 9, 1802; d. 1849. *Benjamin*, b. Aug. 6, 1804; lives in Leicester. *Elizabeth*, b. Dec. 25, 1829; m. Cutler Snow. Mr. Earle lived several years upon the farm now belonging to the town. He d. in 1834.

EARLE, SLADE, m. Elizabeth Earle. Had *Antipas*, jun.; b. Nov. 13, 1787; d. April 30, 1828; m. Amy Chase. *Joseph*, b. Dec. 28, 1788; m. Lydia Fowler. *Mary*, b. June 29, 1791; m. Smith Arnold. *Waldo*, b. Oct. 11, 1796; m. Sarah Aldrich. All except Antipas removed early from Leicester: he lived at the Ralph Earle Place.

If it were not for the known migratory habits of the people of New England, it might seem remarkable, that of the above nineteen families, comprising more than a hundred individuals who have lived or been born in Leicester, not more than half a dozen of the name remain in town.

FLINT, AUSTIN, Dr., m. Elizabeth Henshaw, 1785; and had *Joseph H.*, b. April 20, 1786; he was an eminent physician; lived in Petersham, afterwards in Northampton, and, for several years before his death, in Springfield; d. at Leicester, Dec. 11, 1846. *Sally*, b. June 5, 1787; m. Calvin Spear of Boston. *Edward*, b. Nov. 7, 1789. *Elizabeth C.*, b. May 3, 1792; m. John Clapp. *Waldo*, b. Sept. 4, 1794; is noticed in this work; President of the Eagle Bank, Boston. *Laura*, b. Nov. 1, 1796.

Dr. Flint is noticed in the body of this work.

FLINT, EDWARD, m. Harriet Emerson of Norwich, Vt., November, 1817; and had *Charlotte E.*, b. June 10, 1821. *Sally*, b. Oct. 12, 1822. Both d. unmarried. *John S.*, b. March 6, 1824; a successful physician in Roxbury.

Dr. Flint is noticed in this work.

FAY, EBENEZER. His wife's name was Sarah. They had *Sarah*, b. Jan. 3, 1743.

FAY, DAVID. His wife's name was Jemima. They had *Hannah*, b. June 26, 1748. *David*, b. Dec. 23, 1749. *Ebenezer*, b. Dec. 5, 1751. *Jemima*, b. March 31, 1754; m. Peter Buck of Worcester, 1779.

Jedidiah Newton m. Jemima Fay in 1758, who was probably widow of David. The family seem to have disappeared from the records after that time.

GREEN, SAMUEL, was the first of the family of this name who settled in Leicester, and may be considered the Nestor of this little community. The part of the town where he settled is now called Greenville. He was born in Malden, 1670; and came to Leicester, a few months, it is believed, before Mr. Denny and the Southgates. He married Elizabeth Upham, dau. of the ancestor of the early families of that name in Leicester; and had *Elizabeth*, b. 1693; m. Thomas Richardson, an early settler in Leicester. *Rebekah*, b. 1695; m. Samuel Baldwin of Leicester. *Ruth*, m. Joshua Nichols of Leicester. *Thomas*, b. 1699. *Lydia*, m. Abiathar Vinton; and afterwards Samuel Stower, who came from Malden to Leicester. *Barsheba*, m. Elisha Newers. *Abigail*, m. Henry King of Leicester. *Anna*, m. Ebenezer Lamb. That he was regarded as a man of intelligence and worth, is shown by the early action of the town. At the first recorded meeting of the inhabitants, he was chosen first selectman, moderator, first assessor, and grand juror; and he continued to hold offices of trust and responsibility in the town as long as he lived. He early became a proprietor of the township; and was one of the committee of the proprietors, in 1722–3, to select the half which should be conveyed to the settlers, and to convey the same. This he did in 1724. In that deed he is named as proprietor of lots No. 28–31, two mill-lots, and one other mill-lot in connection with his son-in-law, Thomas Richardson. He afterwards purchased the whole of this lot, and erected a gristmill and the first sawmill in the town upon them, upon the site on which the mills in Greenville now stand. In 1727, he was the owner of nine hundred and twenty-nine acres of land in the town.

He was the first captain of the first military company raised in the town; an honorable mark of distinction, which is carefully recognized in all documents and records afterwards in which he is named. He built and occupied the house opposite the Baptist Meeting-house in Greenville; and continued to be a leading man in the town until his death, Jan. 2, 1736, at the age of sixty-five. The influence of the character and example of the first settlers of such a town, upon the little community growing up around them, is often felt through successive generations; and, among those to whom the town of Leicester owed its progress and character, the memory of Capt. Green ought ever to be held in grateful respect.

GREEN, THOMAS, son of the above, was a more prominent and leading man than his father. He is noticed at length among the clergymen of the town. He m. Martha, dau. of Capt. John Lynde of Malden, and sister of one of the early settlers of the town, January, 1726; and had *Samuel*, b. 1726. *Martha*, b. 1727; m. Dr. Robert Craige. *Isaac*. *Thomas*, b. 1733. *John*, b. 1736; a physician; removed to Worcester; became eminent in his profession; and had a son and grandson, of the same name and profession, in Worcester. *Solomon*. *Elizabeth*, m. Rev. Dr. Foster. Mrs. Green d. June 20, 1780: Dr. Green d. Aug. 19, 1773. Among the descendants of Dr. Green is Mrs. Mary H. Pike, authoress of "Ida May," a work of fiction of considerable reputation. She is the wife of F. A. Pike, Esq., of Calais, Me.

GREEN SAMUEL, 2d, son of Dr. Thomas (sometimes called "Captain," as he was at one time in command of the military company of the town, but more generally known as "Deacon"), m. Zerviah Dana of Ashford, Conn., for his first wife, and a Mrs. Fisk of Sturbridge for his second. His children were *Samuel*, 3d, b. November, 1757. *Elijah*, b. May 3, 1760; entered the service in the Revolutionary War; joined the army at Roxbury; and died in camp, December, 1775, at the age of fifteen.

Capt. Green was the one appointed to notify the company of minute-men in case of alarm; and did so on the 19th April, 1775, as stated in this work. He accompanied his son when he joined the army at Roxbury, and remained in that vicinity till his death. In 1777, he represented the town with Col. Washburn in the General Court. He was deacon of the Baptist Church for more than fifty years, and one of the main pillars of the society. After the removal of Dr. Foster, he had charge of and supplied the pulpit until a successor was appointed. He lived in the house built by his grandfather, opposite the Meeting-house in Greenville. He died Feb. 20, 1811, at the age of eighty-four; and his wife, June 28, 1797, aged sixty-five.

Green, Isaac, son of Dr. Thomas, was a physician, and is noticed in another part of this work. He m. Sarah Howe, and had *Sarah* and *Mary*.

Green, Thomas, 2d, son of Dr. Thomas, m. Hannah Fox, and afterwards Anna Hovey of Sutton; and had *Elias*, b. Jan. 25, 1756; he m. Mary —— in 1782, and removed to Cambridge, Vt. *Thomas*, b. 1757: he became a physician, and lived in Auburn, then Ward; d. 1812, aged fifty-five. *Isaac*, b. 1759; was also a physician; was in the Revolutionary service; and removed to Windsor, Vt., in 1788. He m. Ann Barrett, and became a wealthy and influential citizen of that town. *Abiathar*, b. 1760: he, too, was in the service in the Revolution; he removed to Farmington, Me.; d. 1831, aged seventy-one. *Asa*. *Hannah*, m. Howard Putnam. *John* and *Rebekah*, twins. *Daniel*, b. 1778; is a physician in Auburn.

The father was a farmer, though not a very thrifty one. He once owned the farm, in the south part of the town, where Elijah Thayer formerly lived. After that, he lived in various places, and, at one time, in the house that stood on Flip Lane. He died in Auburn, October, 1813, aged eighty.

GREEN, WILLIAM, 1st, was b. in Malden in 1683. His father was cousin of Capt. Samuel. He m. Sarah Sprague, a branch of the same family which settled in Leicester; and had *Mary*, b. 1710. *Sarah*, b. Sept. 13, 1711; m. Hezekiah Ward, Esq., of Leicester, 1737. *Hepzibah*, b. June 13, 1714. *William*, b. July 6, 1716. *Israel*, b. 1721. *Charles*, b. 1724. *Nahum*, b. 1729. *Mary*, b. 1731.

Mr. Green removed to Leicester about 1719 or '20. He purchased Lot No. 36, and must have built the house thereon, recently occupied by the late John King, Esq. At the first recorded town-meeting, he was elected a tithing-man; then an office of consequence, especially in the matter of Sunday police. He held sundry other offices of trust in the town. He d. subsequently to 1755. The mother of Mr. Green m. Capt. John Lynde of Leicester for her second husband.

GREEN, NATHANIEL, brother of the above, was b. in Malden, 1689; and m. Elizabeth Sprague, sister of the wife of his brother. He lived in Stoneham previous to his removal to Leicester in 1723. Their children were *Elizabeth*, b. 1714; m. Benjamin Saunderson of Leicester, 1737. *Winnifred*, b. 1716; m. Benjamin Baldwin of Leicester, 1749. *Nathaniel*, b. 1721. *Mehitabel*, b. 1724; m. Samuel Call of Leicester, 1746. *Phinehas*, b. 1728. *Benjamin*, b. 1731.

Mr. Green was captain "of the first foot company in Leicester" in 1743. I copy from the work of Mr. Green, of which I have made liberal use in these genealogies, an order addressed to Capt. Green; which shows that it was no holiday matter to command a military company at that time. The conquest of Louisburg took place in 1745. The next year, the whole of New England was alarmed by the intelligence, that an immense armament had reached Nova Scotia from France, on its way to attack the Colonies, and destroy Boston. This led to the following order from Col. Chandler:—

"SIR, — This moment I received the Governor's express; and, pursuant thereto, you are required, in his majesty's name, on your utmost peril, to draw out of your military ward twenty-five men, completely armed, and furnished with ammunition and fourteen days' provision, and march them, without the least delay, to Worcester, and from thence to Boston; a French invasion being every moment expected. I say, Fail at your peril!

"JOHN CHANDLER, *Col.*

"WORCESTER, SEPT. 22, 1746.

"Either you or Capt. Whittemore, with two more commissioned officers, must go; and don't fail.

"In his Majesty's service,
Capt. NATHANIEL GREEN, in Leicester."

Capt. Green d. Sept. 27, 1774.

GREEN, NATHANIEL, son of the above, was b. in Stoneham; came to Leicester, with his father, in 1723; m. Tabitha Prentice; and had *Lemuel,* b. 1749; lived in Spencer. *Susannah,* b. 1751. *Tabitha,* b. 1753. *Nathaniel,* b. 1755. *Lydia,* b. 1758. *John,* b. 1760; was a minister in Coleraine, and d. 1800. *Rufus,* b. 1762; went to Calais, Vt.; d. 1844. *Mary,* b. 1764. *Chloe,* b. 1766; m. Adams Wheelock. *Ebenezer,* b. 1769; removed to Belchertown; d. 1848.

This Mr. Green was known as "the Rev.;" having been ordained as a Baptist minister after he was forty-three years old. In the latter part of his life, he removed to Charlton; where he d., 1791, at the age of seventy.

GREEN, PHINEHAS, brother of the above. His wife's name was Judith. They had *John,* b. 1759; removed to Ohio. *Pliny,* b. 1761. *Silas,* 1762. *Judith,* 1765; d. unmarried. *Phebe,* b. 1766. *Daniel,* 1768. *Mary,* 1770.

He d. in 1776, at the age of forty-seven. He is spoken of as a "teacher of penmanship." There was a Phinehas Green, jun., in the same company with the above, at the battle of Bunker Hill; but I am unable to ascertain his parentage.

GREEN, BENJAMIN, brother of the above; m. Lucy Marston of Spencer in 1754; and had *Benjamin,* 1775, who removed to

Spencer. *Lucy,* 1757. *Asa,* 1761; removed to Deer Isle, Me., 1797. *Elizabeth,* 1763. *Olive,* 1766. *Hannah,* 1768. *Lydia,* 1770.

After the births of his children, Mr. Green removed to Spencer.

GREEN, SAMUEL, son of Deacon Samuel; m. Hannah Kinney of Sutton. Had *Elijah,* 1780; d. 1796. *Lucretia,* July, 1783; m. D. Fairbanks, and d. 1820. *Sophia,* May, 1785; m. John King, Esq.; d. 1854. *Samuel D.,* 1788; entered Brown University; left college in his senior year; now lives in Cambridgeport. *William K.,* 1790; lived in Woodstock, Conn. *Hadassah E.,* 1792; m. Asa Mann; removed to Canada West, and d. there.

Mr. Green lived in the house next west of the mills in Greenville, and once kept a tavern there. He removed late in life to Pembroke, N.Y.; and d. there, 1832, at the age of seventy-four.

GREEN, WILLIAM, son of William, 1st, m. Rebecca Tucker of Milton, 1737. Had *Joel,* 1738; who, I suppose, was the Joel Green that commanded a company in Col. Larned's regiment, in the Continental service. *William,* 1742. *Jeduthan,* 1744. *Ira,* 1746. *Rebecca,* 1749. *Asenath,* 1750; m. Isaac Center, 1772. *Jesse,* 1752. *Oliver,* 1754. *Jeruiah,* 1756. *Jehiel,* 1758. There was a *Jockton* Green, who is believed to have been the son of the above-named William, and probably was born in 1740.

Mr. Green was a farmer, and lived where Amos Whittemore died, formerly the house of Andrew Scott, on the Charlton Road.

GREEN, NAHUM, brother of the above, m. Dorcas Sanger of Woodstock; and had *Mary,* 1751; *Uzziah,* 1753; *Irijah,* 1756; *Mercy,* 1758; *Jeruiah,* 1760; *Amasa,* 1762; *Pamela,* 1764; *Jared,* 1765; *Zerviah,* 1767; *Nahum,* 1770.

Mr. Green was a farmer, and lived upon a part of his father's farm; where, as I suppose, Richard Bond, jun., lived and died.

GREEN, ISRAEL, brother of the above, was married, and had three children in Leicester; removed to Petersham, and then to Hubbardston; d. about 1790. Had four sons in the battle of Bunker Hill, — one of them killed, and the other mortally wounded, in that battle. The third, then a lieutenant, was killed at the battle of Monmouth. The fourth was in the battles of White Plains, Bennington, and Saratoga, and in the campaign in New Jersey, — the only one of the four who survived the service.

GREEN, JOCKTON, son of William, 2d, as is believed, m. Esther Newhall, dau. of Jonathan, 1762. Had *Esther*, 1763; m. Elkanah Haven, 1785. *Jonathan*, 1765; *Persis*, 1768; *Francis*, 1770; *Josiah*, 1772; *Salmon*, 1775; *Eli*, 1778.

Mr. Green lived in the house east of the late John King, Esq., where Richard Bond, jun., lived and died.

GREEN, JABEZ, came from Malden about 1750. His grandfather was brother of the first Samuel who came to Leicester. His wife's name was Mary; and they had *Jabez*, June 13, 1743. *Mary*, Jan. 7, 1749. *Nathan*, went to Gardner, Dec. 27, 1752. *Joseph*, Dec. 30, 1754; went to Vermont. *Stephen*, Aug. 7, 1757; known as "Deacon." *Elizabeth*, March 8, 1762. *Hannah*, Dec. 28, 1764. *Abel*, September, 1767.

Mr. Green lived in the north-east part of Leicester, where his son Abel lived for many years. He was a farmer; and d. Oct. 1, 1806, aged eighty-eight.

GREEN, JABEZ, son of the above, m. Lucy Kent of Leicester, 1764; and had *Hannah*; m. John White of Leicester. *Zolvah;* who lives on the same farm where his father lived, in the north-west part of the town. *Josiah* and *Jabez;* who removed to Spencer, and are now living there.

GREEN, ABEL, brother of the above, m. Eunice Wicker, whose mother was sister of Seth Washburn. Had *Harriet*, 1790; *Eunice*, 1795; *Julia*, 1797; *Laura*, 1800.

Mr. Green lived in the north-east part of the town; a farmer; d. 1743, aged seventy-six.

GREEN, JOEL, son of William, 2d. His wife's name was Chloe. They had *Joel*, 1762; *Chloe*, 1764; *Seth*, 1767.

GREEN, JESSE, brother of the above, m. Grace Hall, August, 1777. Had *Martin*, 1779; *Jacob*, 1780; *Sarah*, 1783; *Iddo*, 1785.

There were several other families of Green; some of whom, after marrying and settling in Leicester, removed from the town. Among them, *Elias*, son of Thomas, 2d, above mentioned. He m. *Mary Scott* of Leicester, 1782; and had *Tamisin*, Oct. 27, 1784; d. 1808. *Sylvanus*, April 6, 1787. In 1796, he removed to Cambridge, Vt.

There was a Thomas Green, a hatter, who came here about 1807 or '8, and raised up a pretty large family.

GREEN, SOLOMON, son of Dr. Thomas, m. Elizabeth Page, and lived in what used to be called the Wilby Cottage, in the south part of the town. His children were *Timothy; Solomon; John; Archelaus; Lynde; Isaac; Mary.*

The Greens have been the most numerous of the Leicester families; and the number of those whose names are found on the rolls of Revolutionary service furnish the strongest proof of the energy which characterized them as men, as well as the patriotic influences under which they were educated: and yet, like so many of the early families of the town, they have almost all disappeared; while their descendants may be found scattered all over the Union.

GODDARD, Rev. DAVID, m. Mercy Stone of Watertown. Had *Daniel*, Sept. 19, 1738. *William*, April 27, 1740. *Mercy*, Nov. 10, 1741. *Edward*, Dec. 12, 1742. *Mary*, Oct. 16, 1744. *Susannah*, Feb. 17, 1747. *Mercy*, Feb. 3, 1750.

The family disappear after the death of the Rev. Mr. Goddard.

GRATON, JOHN, m. Abigail Baldwin, 1772. Had *Rowena*, May 3, 1773. *Tryphena*, Sept. 23, 1774. *John*, Feb. 17, 1777. *Cyrus*, April 29, 1779. *Alvin*, April 20, 1781. *Abigail*, May 7, 1783. *Hannah P.*, Aug. 27, 1785.

Mr. Graton came from Spencer. The family were originally from Medford. He lived a little west of John Parker's house, in the south-west part of the town. Mr. Graton d. 1827, aged seventy-eight.

GAGE, JONATHAN. His wife's name was Mary. They had *Levi*, b. Aug. 9, 1786; *Silas*, 1788; *Polly*, 1790; *Brigham*, 1793.

Mr. Gage lived in the north-west part of the town, where Dr. Parsons once lived, on the road leading by Joseph Whittemore's, opposite the road leading to Zolva Green's. The house is removed.

GILMORE, ADAM, m. Martha, dau. of James Harwood, 1788. Had *James*, March 9, 1799; d. young. *David*, Jan. 22, 1783.

Mr. Green lived in various places in town; a part of the time, on Mount Pleasant, in the small house opposite the place once Major Swan's. He d. 1808; his wife, 1834.

HAVEN, ELKANAH, was the son of Elkanah; b. in Framingham. He m. Esther, dau. of Jockton Green, Nov. 24, 1785. The father d. in 1794 in Leicester. The children of Elkanah, jun., were *Persis*, b. 1788; m. Daniel Muzzy. *Jockton G.*, b. 1789. *Artemas*, b. 1793. *Harriet*, b. 1796; m. Asahel Barber of Framingham. *Lucetta*, 1802; m. George W. Hartwell, Oxford. *John.*

Mr. Haven lived on the County Road, in the south-west part of the town.

HARWOOD, NATHANIEL, removed from Lunenburg to Leicester. His wife's name was Hannah. He lived in a house opposite where William Silvester lives. He was a soldier in the French wars; afterwards commanded the military company of the town; was a respectable farmer, and seems to have been a man of considerable influence in the town. His children were *James; Nathaniel; Jesse*, 1750; *Mary; Elizabeth; Lucy; Hannah*, — though not born in the above order; there being no record of their births. A part or all of them were born in Lunenburg.

Nathaniel went to North Brookfield; Jesse moved to the West; Mary m. Col. Seth Washburn, 1750; Elizabeth m. Benjamin Bond, 1765; Hannah m. Micah Whitney of "Narraghanset, No. 6" (Templeton), 1759; Lucy m. Jonas Gleason, 1773. The name in the records is sometime *Harwood*, and sometimes *Harrod*. It has been used in both forms in this work.

HARWOOD, JAMES, son of the above, m. Martha Barnes, 1755. Had *Martha*, March 4, 1756; m. Adam Gilmore. *Sarah*, March 5, 1758; m. Thomas Bond. *Hannah*, July 31, 1759; d., unmarried, 1818. *Rebekah*, May 16, 1761; d., unmarried, 1840. *Mary*, Feb. 8, 1763; m. Isaac Very. *Eliphalet*, b. 1764. *Susannah*, m. a Hill. *James*. *Nathaniel*.

Mr. Harwood lived in a house, now removed, that stood in the pasture west of Eber Bond's. He d. 1803; his widow, 1817, aged eighty-eight.

HARWOOD, NATHANIEL, son of Capt. Nathaniel, m. Sarah Grimes of New Salem, 1770; and had *Betsey*, 1773; m. Asa Scott of Ward. *Nathaniel*, 1775.

HAMMOND, EBENEZER. His wife was Hester. Had *Ebenezer*, Aug. 17, 1744; *Samuel*, 1746; *Nathaniel*, 1748. Both d. 1754.

HAMMOND, JONAS. His wife's name was Elizabeth. Had *Margaret*, July 29, 1740; *James*, Dec. 20, 1742; *Elizabeth*, April 13, 1745; *Mary*, Feb. 19, 1747; *Hannah*, May 30, 1751; *Lydia*, Nov. 25, 1753. Hannah m. David Dunbar, 1773.

HASEY, SAMUEL. His wife's name was Sarah. They had *Sarah*, March 28, 1746; *Samuel*, Aug. 19, 1747; *Zaccheus*, 1751; *Mary*, 1755; *Jerusha*, 1757.

HASEY, JOHN, m. Tabitha Thomas of Leicester, Nov. 22, 1748. Had *Tabitha*, 1749; m. Abijah Stowers. *Elizabeth*, m. Phinehas Barton, 1753.

HOPKINS, THOMAS. Had *Judy*, b. Aug. 4, 1716; *Elizabeth*, Jan. 13, 1718; *Sarah*, April 15, 1721. Elizabeth m. Baley Bond.

Mr. Hopkins's wife's name was Sarah. He lived on the Oxford Road, where Silas Gleason recently lived.

HENRY, ROBERT. His wife's name was Susannah. They had *Hannah*, 1766; *Robert*, 1772; *Mary*, 1774; *Martha*, 1777; *William Y.*, 1779; *Elizabeth*, 1782; *Foster*, 1784. He lived upon the farm, owned by Robert Young, which Robert Henry (probably his father) purchased in 1728. He removed with his family from Leicester to Charleston, N.H. (No. 4), in 1794. His dau. Hannah m. Ezra Silvester, 1787.

HERSEY, PELEG. His wife was Lucy. Had *Peleg*, May 6, 1764; *Samuel*, June, 1766. Lived in what is now called Cherry Valley. His house stood where Capt. Cutting lived and died.

HERSEY, NATHAN. His wife was Mary. They had *Thomas*, b. March 24, 1771: is noticed elsewhere as a physician in town. Mr. Hersey lived where Calvin Hersey afterwards lived, in the west part of the town. The house was afterwards burnt.

HERSEY, ELIJAH. His wife's name was Beulah. They had *Achsa*, 1782; *Harvey*, 1784; *Elijah*, 1786; *Nathaniel S.*, 1788; *Sarah*, 1791. Mr. Hersey lived where Capt. Trask afterwards did, in the west part of the town. He built the house.

HERSEY, MARTIN, m. Mercy Brown, Sept. 24, 1789. Had *Betsey*, Aug. 10, 1790; *Huldah*, 1792; *Isaac B.*, 1794. He lived where J. A. Denny lives.

HERSEY, CALVIN. His wife's name was Sally. They had *Thankful*, 1792; m. Uriel Johnson. *Charles*, 1794; went to Canada West. *Austin*, 1797. *Martha P.*, 1799; m. a Goddard. *Clarissa Alvira*, 1801. *Zephaniah S. M.*, 1805; went to Canada West. He lived in the house next east of the Capt. Trask Place.

HUBBARD, DANIEL, came to Leicester from Spencer in 1750; was a native of Worcester. He m. Elizabeth Linde, 1747; and had *Jonathan*, 1750; m. Elizabeth Parsons, dau. of Dr. Parsons, and lived in Paxton. *Daniel*, 1753. *Elizabeth*, 1757;

m. Samuel Cheever. *John*, 1761. *Benjamin*, 1763. *Molly*, 1766; m. Joseph Thurston. *Esther*, 1768; m. Aaron Moore.

Mr. Hubbard d. 1805, aged seventy-nine. He lived where his son Daniel once lived.

HUBBARD, DANIEL, son of the above, m. Mary Sargent, dau. of Nathaniel, Feb. 22, 1776; and had *Jonathan;* m. Betsey Kent; removed to Vermont. *Betsey*, m. Barnard Upham, 1802. *Sally*, m. John Sprague, 1801. *Mary*, m. a Brigham. *Persis*, m. Lot Hancock, 1816. *Nancy*, b. 1784; m. Silas Bullard; d. 1839. *Catherine*, b. 1795; went, with her father, to Vermont.

Capt. Hubbard lived one mile north of the Meeting-house. He was a farmer, and, for several years, steward of the Academy; a man much respected. He once commanded one of the military companies of the town. In the latter part of his life, he removed to Wallingford, Vt.; where he died.

HONEYWOOD, Dr. JOHN, is noticed among the physicians of the town. He m. Elizabeth, dau. of Judge Steele (1761); and had *St. John*, 1763; noticed among the college graduates. *Mary*, 1766; m. Nathaniel Lyon. *Elizabeth*, 1769; m. Samuel Allen, Esq., many years Treasurer of the County of Worcester. *Henry*, 1771.

HOBART, JOHN, b. 1768, in Abington; m. Charlotte Spear, 1788. He was, by trade, a blacksmith. He came to Leicester in 1793; purchased, and for many years carried on, the public-house opposite the Meeting-house, with general favor and success. After that, about 1816 or '17, he built the house where Mr. Hobart lives, and lived in it till his death. He represented the town several times; was often in town-office, and held a commanding influence in town. His children were *Relief*, b. 1789. *Mehitabel*, 1790; m. Roswell Sprague, Esq., now of New York. *John*, 1792; *Polly*, 1795; b. in Leicester. *Billings*, 1797. *Otis*, 1800. *Louisa*, 1802; m. Emory Drury. *Harriet B.*, 1804; d., unmarried, 1831. *George*, 1806; lives in Philadelphia. *Sally*, 1809. *Edward*, 1812; lives in Philadelphia. *Maria*, 1814. John went to Indiana; Billings, to Virginia. Otis went to the West, and d. there, 1849. Mrs. Hobart is still living.

HENSHAW, WILLIAM, is noticed in another part of this work. He m. Ruth, dau. of Jonathan Sargent, 1762; and had *Sarah*, 1762; m. Andrew Scott, 1780. *Elizabeth*, 1764; m. Dr. Austin Flint, 1785. Col. Henshaw's second wife was Phebe Swan, dau. of Dudley W. Swan; and had *Ruth*, 1772; m. Dr. Asa Miles, and afterwards Rev. Lysander Bascom. *Joseph*, 1774; d. in Belchertown. *Phebe*, 1777; m. Joseph Denny; d. August, 1815. *William*, 1780; lives in Leicester. *Daniel*, 1782; noticed elsewhere. *Catherine*, 1784. *Lucinda*, 1786; m. Joseph Denny for his second wife. *Horatio Gates*, 1788. *Benjamin*, 1793. *Almira*, 1796; d. unmarried.

Col. Henshaw's first wife d. 1769, aged twenty-five; his second, 1808, aged fifty-six. He lived upon the farm where Mr. Edwin Waite lives, in the east part of the town.

HENSHAW, DANIEL, ancestor of all of the name in Leicester; came from Boston, and lived where Mr. Edwin Waite lives. His wife was Elizabeth, dau. of Joseph Bass, Esq., of Boston. They were m. in 1724; and had *Joseph*, 1727; mentioned in this work as Col. Joseph. *William*, 1735. *David*, 1744. *Hannah*, m. John Jopp of Oxford, 1763. *Mary Belcher*, m. Amos Wheeler of Worcester, 1762.

Mr. Henshaw d. Nov. 18, 1781, aged eighty.

HENSHAW, DAVID, son of Daniel, m. Mary, dau. of Nathan Sargent, 1773. Had *Mary*, 1774; d. 1790. *Elizabeth*, 1776; m. Nathaniel Dodge, 1823. *Anna*, 1778; d. unmarried. *Joshua*, 1779; lived many years in Ohio; d. in Leicester. *Andrew*, 1783; removed to Alabama; d. there. *Fanny*, 1785; d. 1801. *Sarah*, 1787; m. Andrew H. Ward, Esq. *Charles*, 1789; lives in Boston. *David*, 1789; is noticed in this work. *Laura*, 1795; m. Oliver Fletcher, Esq., 1822. *John*, 1798; many years a merchant in Boston; d. in Cambridge, 1859.

Mr. Henshaw is noticed in this work. He d. 1808, aged sixty-four: his wife d. 1831, aged seventy-six.

HODGKIN, JOHN, came from Fitchburg; m. Sarah, dau. of Col. Seth Washburn, 1789. Had *Eber*, 1790; *Lucy*, 1793. Soon after that, he removed to Putney, Vt.; where he lived the remainder of his life.

JACKSON, JAMES, lived where Mr. Eber Bond lives, on the Oxford Road. His wife's name was Martha. They had *James*, 1731; *Thomas*, 1733; *John*, 1734; *Mary*, 1739; *Martha*, 1741.

JACKSON, MATTHEW, m. Elizabeth Works, 1781. He came to Leicester, just before the close of the Revolution, from Brookfield. He had been a soldier in Capt. Washburn's company in the eight-months' service, and at the battle of Bunker Hill, and then belonged to Rutland. He first bought the Tanyard Place, at the foot of the Meeting-house Hill. In 1789, he bought the house-lot, where he built his house and shoemaker's shop, of Seth Washburn.

Here he afterwards lived and died. He was a shoemaker. His children were *Joseph*, 1784; d. unmarried. *Elsey*, 1788; married a Cushman; lived in New-York State. *Elizabeth*, 1790; d., unmarried, Oct. 25, 1850. With her, the family became extinct. Elizabeth was a lady of a cultivated mind and poetical taste, and often contributed fugitive pieces for the press. She left the following touching allusion to the extinction of her family, which a friend caused to be inscribed as an epitaph upon the headstone at her grave:—

"Ah! who shall shed a tear for me
When 'neath the silent turf I lie?
Will there be friends — who may they be?—
To stand around with weeping eye?
The clouds of heaven alone will weep,
The winds of heaven sigh, where I sleep;
And here and there a wild-flower shed
Its fragrance round my lowly bed,—
The last of her family."

JOHNSON, BENJAMIN, lived in a house, now gone, standing

north of Eber Bond's, on the Charlton Road. His wife's name was Rebekah. Their children: *Rebekah,* 1719; m. Daniel Lynde. *Esther,* 1721; m. William White. *Mary,* 1724; m. Samuel Bemis. *Abigail,* 1726; m. John Prouty, 1745.

Capt. Johnson removed to Spencer in 1747. While he lived in Leicester, he was a man of influence in the town.

KENT, EBENEZER. His wife was Sarah. They had *Ebenezer,* 1745. *Reuben,* 1747. *Jacob,* 1750; m. Desire Prouty. *Elizabeth,* 1752; m. Benjamin Flagg, 1776. *Lydia,* 1755; m. John Campbell, 1783.

Mr. Kent d. Feb. 3, 1786, aged sixty-nine. He lived in a house near the Kent Place.

KENT, EBENEZER, Jun., son of above; m. Esther Stone, 1772; and had *William,* 1773; m. Katy Wheaton. *Sarah,* 1774. *Daniel,* 1777; m. Ruth Watson, 1805, for his first wife; and Miranda Cunningham, 1829, for his second; he lived where his father had lived, about two miles north-easterly from the Meeting-house; he once commanded one of the military companies in the town; d. 1849, leaving a family of children. *Elias,* 1780. *Polly,* 1787. *Betsey,* m. Jonathan Hubbard.

Mr. Kent and wife both d. in 1806.

KING, HENRY, came from Sutton to Leicester. His wife's name was Prudence. They had *Tamar,* 1774; *John,* 1776; *Henry,* 1779; *Charles* and *Charlotte,* 1783.

Capt. King was a well-known citizen of the town, and commanded one of the military companies; lived where his son John afterwards lived and died, on the Charlton Road. He is mentioned several times in the body of this work. He d. 1822, aged seventy-four.

LIVINGSTON, BENJAMIN, usally written Leviston in the town-records. He came from Billerica. He m. Margaret, dau. of Alexander Scott, February, 1769; and had *Martha,* December, 1769; m. John Phillips, and went to New York. *Matthew,* 1774. *James,* 1777. *Benjamin,* 1780. *Nabby,* 1782. *Amasa,* 1784.

Capt. Livingston lived about half a mile north-westerly of Joseph Whittemore's, in a house, now removed, which stood twenty or thirty rods from the road. He once commanded a company in Leicester during the Revolution, and was in the service at Saratoga at the taking of Burgoyne. After the war, he removed to Townsend, Vt. James, after removing to Vermont, m. Nabby Wheaton of Leicester; and, in 1833, was living in Peacham, Vt.

LIVERMORE, JONAS, came from Weston; b. 1710. Daniel — who, I suppose, was his father — was a proprietor and settler of the town before 1720. He settled upon Lot No. 29, lying at the foot of Livermore Hill, in the south part of the town, on both sides of the road. Jonas lived upon the east side of the road. His wife's name was Elizabeth Rice of Sudbury. They had *Jonas*, 1736. *Micah*, 1738. *Mary*, 1743; m. a Scott. *David* and *Elizabeth*, 1745; m. Samuel Tucker. *Elisha*, 1751. *Beulah*, 1753; m. Levi Dunton. *Lydia*, 1755; m. Asa Prouty. Mr. Livermore's will is dated 1773. His wife d. 1799.

LIVERMORE, JONAS, son of the above, lived in the south part of the town, where Salem lived and died. He was a carpenter as well as farmer. His wife's name was Sarah. They had *Hannah*, 1762; d. 1767. *Jonas*, 1764; d. 1790. *Sally*, 1766; d. 1833. *Patty*, 1768; m. Samuel Upham, jun., 1791, father of William Upham, senator in Congress from Vermont. *Salem*, 1770; lived in the south part of the town; d. 1858. *Bathsheba*, 1772. *Lovisa*, 1774; m. Gall; d. 1800. *Daniel*, 1776. *Rebecca*, 1778.

Mr. Livermore d. 1825; his widow, in 1832, aged ninety-four.

LIVERMORE, ISAAC, lived in the house opposite where Jonas, sen., lived, at the foot of Livermore Hill. His wife's name was Dorothy. They had *Isaac*, 1746; who was in Capt. Washburn's company at Bunker Hill. *Abner*, 1749; also in the same company. *Dorothy*, 1751; m. George Rogers. *Abraham*, 1753. *Elijah*, 1755. *Lucy*, 1758.

Livermore, Jason. His wife's name was Abigail. They had *Jason*, 1750; *William*, 1752; *Abigail*, 1758; *Josiah*, 1761.

Livermore, Jason, Jun., son of the above, m. Mary ——; and had *Daniel*, 1773; *Mary*, 1775; *Jason*, 1778.

Lynde, John, the ancestor of the families of the name in Leicester, came from Malden, and was here before 1721. He was one of the persons named as grantee in the deed to the proprietors of the eastern half of the township, and was the proprietor of Lot No. 18. He was married, and had five children, before he left Malden: viz., *Hannah*, 1710; *John*, 1712; *Samuel*, 1714; *Daniel*, 1717; and *Mary*. His first wife died in Malden. His second wife's name was Hannah. They had *Abigail*, 1721; who m. Benjamin Wheaton. *Elizabeth*, 1724; m. Daniel Hubbard, then of Worcester, 1748. *David*, 1726. *Benjamin*, 1731; d. 1737.

The will of Mr. Lynde, dated April 7, 1749, gives his son John, among other things, half of his tan-yard on his home place in Leicester, together with "my negro slave named Pompey." To Samuel he gives the farm "where —— Houghton now lives, late the estate of Benjamin Johnson," which lies next north of Eber Bond's. He gives his son Daniel his lands on the east side of Rutland Road, by Oliver Wilt's.

Mr. Lynde seems to have been a leading man in the town, a large landholder, and a man of wealth and influence. He d. 1756. He lived at what is called the Elliot Place.

Lynde, John, Jun., son of the above, seems to have been of superior education to those of his day. He was the schoolmaster of the town in 1733, when hardly twenty-one years old; and afterwards is described in a deed as "John Lynde, Esquire." If he was a justice of the peace, he was one of the earliest in town. In 1750, he owned the Elliot Farm, as it was afterwards called, in the north part of the town, then containing three hundred acres, which had been his father's homestead. His children were *John*, 1736. *Isaac*, 1741.

James, 1743. *John*, 1745. *Benjamin*, 1747. *Ruth*, 1749; m. Daniel Upham, 1765.

The wife of Mr. Lynde d. 1751.

LYNDE, SAMUEL, brother of the above, m. Dorcas, widow of James Smith; and seems to have moved on to the farm which had been her husband's, in the west part of the town. His house was destroyed by a hurricane, as mentioned in this work. His children were *Samuel*, *Lucy*, and *Mary*.

LYNDE, DAVID, brother of above, m. Jerusha Paine of Holden, 1754; and had *Jerusha*, 1755; *David*, 1756; *Charles*, 1758; *Hannah*, 1760.

LYNDE, DANIEL, brother of the above, m. Rebekah Johnson, 1740. Had *Johnson*, 1741; who went to Spencer, and lived on the Sibley Farm.

LOCKE, JOSIAH, was born in Marlborough; came to Leicester from Westborough. He had five children at that time. From Leicester he went to Hardwick. While residing there, he commanded a company at Roxbury in 1775. He died in Litchfield, N.Y., 1819; and his wife, in 1839, at the age of a hundred and three years and five months. His wife was Persis Matthews of New Braintree. While in Leicester, they had *John*, 1762. *Persis*, 1765; m. George Jenkins. *Josiah*, 1766.

LARKIN, WILLIAM, came from Boston; owned and lived on the place now owned by Mr. May. He is sometimes called "trader," and sometimes "yeoman," in contemporary papers. They had *Sarah*, 1730; *Elizabeth*, 1735; *Thomas S.*, 1737.

LOVE, JOHN, was a poor man. The town gave him a piece of land on the top of Carey Hill, where he lived in a small house which long since disappeared; the traces of which, with a pear-tree near it, which he planted, were lately visible. His wife's name was Susannah. They had *Sarah*, 1736; *Rachel*, 1741; *Moses*, 1745; *Rhoda*, 1754; *Eunice*, 1759.

LINCOLN, LUKE, is said by the Hon. Mr. Wilder in his "History of Leominster," to have been of the family of Gen. Lincoln of Revolutionary memory. He came from Scituate. His wife's name was Lydia. Their children: *William*, 1738. *Rachel*, 1741; m. Timothy Boutelle of Leominster, 1768: she was the mother of Hon. Timothy Boutelle, late of Waterville, Me. *Loring*, 1746. *Lydia*, 1748. *Mary*, 1751; m. Asa Meriam of Oxford, 1778. *Dorothy* and *Elizabeth* Lincoln were m. in Leicester (one in 1742, the other 1748), and were probably sisters of the above.

LINCOLN, LORING, son of the above, m. Dolly Mower, 1770. Had *Dorothy*, 1773.

Mr. Lincoln was the ensign of the company in the eight-months' service, under Capt. Washburn, which took part in the battle of Bunker Hill. He lived on the North-County Road, in the house next east of where Silas Earle used to live.

MOWER, EPHRAIM, was born in Malden; came first to Worcester, and then to Leicester; d. 1790, aged sixty. His first wife was Mary B. Wheeler of Worcester. They had *Timothy*, b. 1745. His second wife was —— Garfield of Waltham. They had *Ephraim*, b. 1748; *Thomas*, b. 1750; all b. in Worcester, and two children who died in childhood; one b. in Leicester.

MOWER, THOMAS, son of Ephraim, lived upon Mount Pleasant, on the farm once owned by Col. Henry Sargent. He came from Worcester at the age of ten years. His wife's name was Anna Brown of Worcester. Their children: *James B.*, 1773; d. 1832. *Ephraim*, 1778. *Sarah*, 1780; d. 1855. *Huldah*, 1784.; d. 1826. *Thomas Gardner*, b. 1790; d. 1853.

Mr. Mower removed to Worcester in 1792; where his son Ephraim, a wealthy and highly respectable gentleman, is still living. James B. died in the city of New York. Sarah m. John Thayer. Thomas Gardner was graduated at Harvard in 1810, and should have been mentioned among the native-born graduates of the town. He was educated as a surgeon, and commissioned as such in the United-States Army in 1812; saw much service on the northern frontier and elsewhere;

and continued connected with the army till his death, during the last years of his life, in the city of New York. He was a member of the American Philosophical Society of Philadelphia.

There was a SAMUEL MOWER, a cousin of Thomas, who took his farm on his removal to Worcester, and had *Lyman* and *Levi*, who removed to Woodstock, Vt.; and *Nahum*, who removed to Montreal, and became proprietor and editor of a leading newspaper in that city.

MOREY, EPHRAIM. His wife's name was Abigail. They had *Reuben*, 1738; *Simeon*, 1739; *Zenas*, 1740; *Eleanor*, 1744; *Abigail*, 1751; *James*, 1752; *Moses*, 1754; *Elizabeth*, 1756.

MERRITT, BENJAMIN, came from Scituate; was a shoemaker, and lived a little west of the late Joseph Whittemore's. His wife's name was Sarah. They had *Freelove*, 1758; m. Phinehas Converse. *Sarah*, 1760. *Abigail*, 1775. He was a soldier in the French War in 1754.

MORSE, ABNER. His wife was Keziah. They had *Elijah*, 1758; *Stephen*, 1759; *Keziah*, 1762.

NEWHALL, DANIEL, came, as I suppose, from Malden; as Thomas, the first of the name in town, came from there. He was here before 1731. His wife's name was Tabitha. They had *Daniel*, 1734; *Elizabeth*, 1736; *Phinehas*, 1742; *Samuel*, 1744. He lived in the north-east part of the town.

NEWHALL, DANIEL, Jun., m. Elizabeth Stebbins, 1754. Had *James*, 1756; *Sarah*, 1757; *Daniel*, 1760; *John*, 1762; *Elizabeth*, 1765.

NEWHALL, PHINEHAS, son of Daniel, 1st. His wife was Lydia. They had *Joseph*, 1765. *Artemas*, 1768. *Persis*, 1769; m. Asahel Earle. Joseph removed to Phillipston. Col. Newhall kept a tavern, many years, on the North-County Road, where Mr. Eddy lives.

NEWHALL, JONATHAN. His wife's name was Hannah. They had *Thomas*, 1732; a leading, public-spirited man, and a liberal benefactor to the town; he lived where the late Robert Watson d., in the west part of the town; and d., without children,

Oct. 26, 1814, aged eighty-two: he commanded the standing military company of the town, and marched with his company to Cambridge, on the alarm of the 19th April, 1775; and was always known as "Capt. Newhall." *Hannah*, 1734; m. Elijah Harding of Southbridge. *Phebe*, 1736; m. Jonathan Winslow. *Hiram*, 1738. *Dorothy*, 1740; m. Ebenezer Washburn, 1757, brother of Col. Seth. *Esther*, 1742; m. Jockton Green, 1762. *Jonathan*, jun., 1744. *Betty*, 1747; d. 1751.

Mr. Newhall, and his son Jonathan after him, lived at what used to be called the Sadler Place. The house was burned while Mr. Sadler lived there. The farm is now Nathan Craige's, in the south-west part of the town.

NEWHALL, HIRAM, son of the above. His wife was Mary. They had *Hiram*, 1764; *Mary*, 1768; *Joshua*, 1770. He removed to Athol.

NEWHALL, JONATHAN, Jun., brother of the above. His wife was Mary. They had *Mary*; m. Solomon Keyes, Cambridge, Vt. *Anna*. *Thomas*, 1776. *Lucy*, 1778. *Hetty*, 1791. *William*, 1793. The family removed to Warren, R.I. William m. Almira, dau. of Winthrop Earle, 1818; and lived in Leicester many years; then removed to Fall River.

NEWHALL, JOHN. His wife's name was Dorothy. They had *Allen*, 1743; *John*, 1745; *Betty*, 1748. Mr. Newhall came from Spencer to Leicester in 1774.

NICHOLS, JOSHUA, came from Malden; was a tailor by trade; was employed as a schoolmaster at one time; was chosen one of the assessors at the first town-meeting. He m. Ruth, a dau. of Capt. Samuel Green; and had *Catherine*, 1721. *Caleb*, 1722. *Ruth*, 1724; m. Thomas Moore of Worcester, 1746. *James*, 1725. *Abijah*, 1728. *Jeremiah*, 1730. Mr. Nichols lived on the Deacon Rockwood Place, on the Charlton Road.

NICHOLS, CALEB, son of above, m. Lucy Smith; and had *John*, 1752. *Lucy*, 1756; m. Daniel Carpenter. *Catherine*, 1757. *Abigail*, 1759. *Caleb*, 1761. He lived on the cross-road from the Deacon Rockwood Place to the turnpike.

NEVERS, ELISHA, by his wife Bathsheba, had *Phinehas*, 1726; *Nathan*, 1728; *Martha*, 1731; *Samuel*, 1736; *Jabez*, 1738. He lived at the Amos Craige Place, in the south part of the town.

PARSONS, Rev. DAVID. He has been too fully noticed in this work to require any further remark. He was b. in Northampton, 1680; was graduated at Harvard, 1705. His wife's name was Sarah. They had *David*, 1712; graduated at Harvard, 1729; settled as a minister in Amherst, 1739; d. 1781. *Nathan*, 1721; removed to Belchertown, 1746; d. 1806. *Israel*. A daughter, 1724, — name not known. *Solomon*, 1726.

Mr. Parsons d. 1743, aged sixty-three; his wife, 1759, aged seventy-three. Meekness does not seem to have been a distinguishing trait in his character.

PARSONS, ISRAEL, son of the above, m. Hannah Waite of Malden, 1750, for his first wife; and Lois Wiley of Lynn, for his second, in 1761. His children were *Hannah*, 1751; *Sarah*, 1754; *Deborah*, 1755; *Israel*, 1757; *Ebenezer*, 1762; *James*, 1763; *Ruth*, 1765.

Mr. Parsons lived, a part of his life, in the house opposite Mrs. Newhall's, on the Rutland Road; and, a part of it, in the house where his father had lived, north-east of the Meeting-house He d. 1767. But, though all his children were then living, I have been unable to trace them. None of them or their descendants appear in the town for more than fifty years past.

PARSONS, SOLOMON, son of David, was a physician, and also deacon of the Congregational Church. He m. Elizabeth Taylor, 1752; and had *Elizabeth*, 1753; m. Jonathan Hubbard of Paxton, 1771. *Phebe*, 1755; m. Abijah Brown, 1775. *Solomon*, 1757. Dr. Parsons is noticed among the physicians of the town.

PARSONS, SOLOMON, Jun., son of the above, m. Rebecca C. Wesson of Shrewsbury, 1789. He lived on the North-County

Road, till he removed to Worcester, about 1812. He had *Samuel*, 1791; went to Louisiana, and d. 1817. *Elizabeth*, 1793; m. Ira Bryant of Worcester. *Sally*, 1794; m. E. N. Child of Worcester. *Bloomfield*, 1796; d. in New Orleans, 1815. *Maria*, 1794; d. 1804. *Solomon*, 1800; lives in Worcester. Mr. Parsons is noticed in other places in this work. He d. 1831: his wife d. 1836.

PIKE, ONESEPHIRUS. His wife was Mary Saunderson. They had *James*, 1729. *Onesephirus*, 1731; who removed to Sturbridge. And *Mary*, a twin; m. Stephen Tucker, 1750. And, I suppose, *Sarah;* who m. Ephraim Amsden, 1749. He lived north of the Bond Place, in the north-west part of the town. He came from Weston to Leicester.

POTTER, JOHN, Jun. His wife's name was Lydia. They had *Ezra*, 1730; *Lydia*, 1733; *Robert*, 1735; *Hannah*, 1736. His second wife was Elizabeth, dau. of William Earle. They had *William*, 1738; *Lois*, 1741; *Mary*, 1745. Mr. Potter d. 1797, aged seventy-three.

Mr. Potter came from Lynn; was a housewright. His father bought of Benjamin Potter, in 1726, half the lot where he lived, about one mile north of the Meeting-house, previously belonging to Samuel Stimpson, and conveyed it to this John, 1728. The house in which he lived was built by his father John in 1728, and was lately owned by Thomas Smith, and, before that, by Jacob Bond.

POTTER, NATHANIEL, m. Rebekah ——; and had *Nathaniel*, 1732; *Ruth*, 1735; and *Elizabeth*, older than these, who m. Steward Southgate, 1750.

He lived in the northerly part of the town, next east of John Potter, — the Jonah Earle Farm. Mrs. Potter d. 1799, aged seventy.

PIERCE, THOMAS, m. Hannah Locke; and had *Hannah*, b. 1723; m. William Bullard, jun., 1741. *Benjamin*, 1725. *Thomas*, 1726 or '27.

Mr. Pierce came from Woburn about 1722. In 1723, he

was pound-keeper, and had charge of the Meeting-house. He lived on the Oxford Road, on the east side of it, south of Eber Bond's, in a house long since removed. He left Leicester, and went to Hopkinton, in 1728.

PARKMAN, ALEXANDER. He came from Westborough; was a clothier; owned the shop where Samuel Watson afterwards carried on business in Cherry Valley; and lived in the house lately occupied by Rufus Upham, which he bought of the Southgates, 1771. His wife's name was Keziah. They had *Robert Breck*, 1771; *Alexander*, 1773.

PAINE, JABEZ, m. Elizabeth Hubbard of Worcester, 1753; and had *Ruth*, 1754. *Jabez*, 1756; removed to Westminster, Vt. *Ann*, 1758. *Elizabeth G.*, 1761; m. Hezekiah Saunderson, 1780. *Anna*, 1763. *Chloe*, 1765; m. Joshua Wood, Townshend, Vt., 1786. *Rebekah*, 1768; m. Benjamin Hubbard, 1787. *William*, 1769.

Mr. Paine lived in the first house on the road leading by the late Joseph Whittemore's, which was burned, and stood where the present one does. His son William also lived there till his removal with his family to Mercer in Maine. He m. Relief Ward of Worcester, 1797.

PARKER, THOMAS. He lived on the Charlton Road, the last house next to Charlton. His wife's name was Lucy. They had *Thomas J.*, 1764; d. 1769. *Mary*, 1769. *Sarah*, 1771. *John*, 1774; lived where his father lived; d. 1849. *Elizabeth*, 1777. *Thomas, jun.*, 1779; who lived in Charlton; m. Lucy Dunbar of Leicester.

Mr. Parker d. 1815, aged eighty.

RAWSON, EDWARD, Esq., came from Mendon, where he was born 1721, and where his children were born. He came to Leicester soon after the war. He was a descendant in the fourth degree from Secretary Rawson of Colonial memory; a grandson of the eminent divine, Grindal Rawson of Mendon. He represented Mendon in the Provincial Congress and in the General Court; and was a member of the Constitutional Convention, 1779. He was an active magistrate while in Leicester, and highly respected. He lived at one time at the corner of Flip Road; afterwards just east of Town-Meadow Brook, or, as it used to be called, "Rawson Brook," half a mile west of the Meeting-house; where he d. Feb. 11, 1807, aged eighty-six.

Only two of his eight children came to Leicester, — *Edward* and *Nancy*; who d. unmarried, 1848, aged ninety-one.

RAWSON, EDWARD, son of the above, was b. 1754; was a physician; m. Margaret Steele, dau. of Judge Steele; and had *Mary*, b. 1779. *Benjamin Pemberton*, 1781. *Margaret S.*, 1784; d. 1785.

Dr. Rawson is noticed elsewhere. He lived where his father died. His wife died Sept. 6, 1784. His son, Benjamin P., went to Hudson, N.Y.; and, on the death of his sister Nancy, the family became extinct in Leicester.

RUSS, HEZEKIAH, came from Lexington. His wife's name was Deborah. Their children were *Deborah*, 1710; *Margaret*, 1714; *Abigail*, 1718; *John*, 1720.

Mr. Russ was in Leicester before 1721. He was chosen constable at the first town-meeting, and was one of the grantees of the settlers' half of the town; being proprietor of Lot No. 8, about a half-mile from the Main Street, on the Charlton Road.

RICHARDSON, THOMAS, came from Malden. His wife's name was Elizabeth. They had *Elizabeth*, 1718. *Samuel*, 1722. *James*, 1723. *Philip*, 1725. *Mary*, 1729. *Rebekah*, 1731; m. James Smith of Leicester, 1751.

His second wife was Jane. They had *Lucy*, 1740. *Elizabeth*, 1741; m. Nathan Lamb of Spencer.

Mr. Richardson lived in what was the Baptist Parsonage House.

His son Philip commanded a company of men in Col. Ruggles's regiment, at Fort William Henry, in August, 1756.

RICHARDSON, BENJAMIN. His wife was Patience. They had

Abigail, 1725. *Benjamin*, 1731. *Elizabeth*, 1734; m. Nathan Earle. *Nathaniel*, 1737.

Mr. Richardson was a housewright by trade.

RICHARDSON, BENJAMIN, Jun., son of the above; m. Eunice Swan, dau. of Dudley Wade, 1758; and had *Abigail*, 1760; *Benjamin*, 1764; *Phinehas*, 1767; *Artemas*, 1768; *Asa*, 1771; *Katy*, 1773.

Mr. Richardson owned and lived on the farm where Mrs. Newhall lives, half a mile north of the Meeting-house, which he bought of Israel Parsons, 1760. He sold this to John Lyon in 1777, and removed to Sterling. When he was married, he was called of Worcester.

RICHARDSON, NATHANIEL, son of Benjamin, 1st, m. Ruth Gilkey of Plainfield. He owned and lived on the Bridge's Farm, in south-east part of the town. They had *William*, 1764; *Semple*, 1767.

RYAN, ANTHONY, was probably from Ireland; as there was a John Ryan from Leicester, a soldier in the French War, who was from there. His wife's name was Margaret. They had *John*, 1743. *Mary*, 1745; m. Walter Fanning, "a Foregnor," 1769. *Katherine*, 1746; m. John Mansfield of Boston. *Sarah*, 1748. *Samuel*, 1750. *Susannah*, 1752. *Daniel*, 1755. *Margaret*, 1760. *Susannah*, 1762. *Hannah*, 1765.

Mr. Ryan owned a part of the Mount-Pleasant Farm.

SARGENT, JONATHAN, belonged to Malden, and came to Leicester before 1728. He built, and kept as a tavern, the house which stood opposite the present Catholic Church, till his death. He was b. 1701; and m. Deborah Richardson, 1726. His children were *Jonathan*, 1728. *Nathaniel*, 1730. *Lucretia*, 1734; m., first, Dr. Pliny Lawton; second, Rev. Benjamin Conklin. *Deborah*, 1739; m. Thomas Newhall. *Ruth*, 1744; m. Col. William Henshaw. *Phinehas*, 1746.

SARGENT, JONATHAN, Jun., son of the above, m. Mary, dau. of Robert Earle, 1750; and had *Jonathan*, 3d, 1752. He lived on Mount Pleasant, where Benjamin Earle has lived; died in the army, in the Revolutionary War. *Mary*, 1753; m. Timothy Sprague. *Eleanor*, 1754; m. John Southgate. *William*, 1756; m. Rachel, sister of Capt. Todd, in 1755; he went to Canada. *Catherine*, m. Amos Livermore, 1790. *Samuel*, 1761. *Elihu*, 1764; d., unmarried, about 1835.

Mr. Sargent lived in the south-east part of the town, on the Auburn Road, a short distance from the turnpike. The house is now standing.

SARGENT, NATHANIEL, son of Jonathan, 1st, m. Anne Garfield, 1753; and had *Nathaniel*, 2d, 1754; d. 1757. *Mary*, 1756; m. Daniel Hubbard. *Deborah*, 1759; m. Capt. James Earle, 1786. *Hadadrimmon*, 1762. *Betsey*. *Ruth*; d., unmarried, about 1809. He lived a little west of the Pond, on the north side of the road.

SARGENT, PHINEHAS, son of Jonathan, 1st, m. Mary Edson of Simsbury, Conn., 1766; and Abigail Dunbar, for second wife, 1772; and had *Lucretia*, April 10, 1768; m. Col. Thomas Denny; d. April 12, 1858: a lady of great worth and respectability; bright, cheerful, and intelligent to the last; forming, while she lived, a connecting link between the ante-Revolutionary period and our own, which no one is left to supply. *Phinehas*, 1770. *Artemas*, 1773; d., 1822, unmarried. *Mary*, 1775; m. William Moffit. His first wife d. September, 1770.

SARGENT, SAMUEL, son of Jonathan, 2d, m. Patty Johnson, 1784. He lived in various places in town, though for many years where his father had lived. He removed to the State of New York pretty late in life; and d. October, 1830. His children were *Samuel*, 1785; lives in Ohio. *Charlotte*, 1787; m. John Pike. *Eleanor*, 1789; m. Elisha Pike. *Lucretia*, 1791; m. Abner Wallen. *William F.*, 1793; lives in Ohio. *Loring L.*, 1794; removed to Ohio. *Arnold G.*, 1796; in Ohio. *Palmer G.*, 1798. *Evelina*, 1800; m. Simon Phillips. Palmer G., 1802; went to New York. *Almira*, 1804; m. Silas Boynton. *Louisa*, 1805; m. George Gierson. *Winthrop E.*, 1808; lives in Brookfield. *Sarah*, 1811; m. David Aldrich.

Sargent, Nathan, brother of Jonathan, 1st, came from Malden; settled on Chestnut Hill, so called, adjoining the town of Worcester, where his grandson Sewall Sargent lives. His first wife was Mary, dau. of Joseph, and grand-niece of Jonathan, 1st, 1742. Their children were *Lydia*, 1743; m., 1st, J. Watson; 2d, N. Kellog. *Nathan*, 2d, 1746; removed to New Braintree. *Mary*, 1749; d. same year. His second wife was Mary, dau. of Daniel Denny, 1751. They had *Mercy*, 1751; m. Micah Reed of Westmoreland, N.H., 1796. *Samuel*, 1754. *Mary*, 1755; m. David Henshaw, Esq. *Rebekah*, 1758; d. 1785. *John*, 1759. *Sarah*, 1763; m. William Sprague of Leicester. *Anna*, 1767; m. John Hayward, 1795.

Mr. Sargent was a stanch patriot. He is mentioned, in connection with the march of the Leicester troops, as having melted his clock-weights to provide bullets for the soldiers. He d. 1799, aged eighty-one. His wife, a very intelligent lady, survived till 1822, ninety-five years of age.

Sargent, Samuel, son of the above, m. Mary, dau. of Seth Washburn, 1781; and had *Ruth*, 1782; m. Benjamin Dunklee; d. 1840. *Mary*, 1784; m. Joel Estabrook; d. 1830. *Margaret*, 1786; m. W. Arnold; d. 1834. *Clarissa*, 1788; m. Ira Gale. *Sarah D.*, 1790; m. Daniel Joy; d. 1836. Mr. Sargent removed to Putney, Vt., about 1790; and his children born after that were born in that town. Among them is the *Hon. Nathan* (b. 1794) of Washington City, once a Judge of Court of Common Pleas in Alabama; once Serjeant-at-Arms of Congress, Registrar-General of the United-States Land Office, and Registrar of the Treasury. *Samuel*, b. 1796; was a physician in New York; d. 1846. Mr. Sargent d. 1825, aged seventy-one: Mrs. Sargent d. 1848, aged eighty-nine. He lived, while in Leicester, in the house which Deacon Murdoch enlarged and occupied, about a half-mile west of the Meeting-house.

Sargent, John, brother of the last, m. Sarah Gates, 1783;

and, for his second wife, Mrs. Isaac Denny, 1818. His children: *Asa*, 1784; m. Charlotte Earle; d. 1854. *Betsey*, 1786; m. David Andrews of Hingham, and is mother of Major-Gen. Andrews of Boston. *Julia*, 1788; d., unmarried, 1818. *Rebekah*, 1792; m. Lewis Cutting; d. 1843. *Anna*, 1795; m. Ebenezer A. Howard; d. 1820. *John*, 1797; lived in Leicester; a trader and postmaster; m. Mary A., dau. of Billings Swan; and, for his second wife, Abigail Ward; had children; d. 1850. *Sally*, 1797; twin with John; m. J. A. Smith, Esq., of Leicester; d. 1849. *Sewall*, 1799; lives in Leicester; m. Laura Woodworth, and has a family of children.

Mr. Sargent lived where his son Sewall now does, and owned a gristmill, which stood where the brick factory now does. He was in the service during the Revolution; a valuable citizen, much respected in the town.

SARGENT, JOSEPH, brother of Nathan's first wife; son of Joseph of Malden, where he was born, 1716. He m. Hannah Whittemore for his first, and Martha Grout for his second wife. His children were *Daniel*, 1750; removed to Holden. *Hannah*, 1754; m. William Waite. *Joseph*, 1757. *Patty*, 1759; d., unmarried, 1831. *Rachel*, 1761; d., unmarried, 1831. *Stephen*, 1762; went to Canada, and died there.

Mr. Sargent lived in a house that stood on the north side of the Great Post Road, west of Mr. John Sargent's, near where Asa Sargent built a new house.

SARGENT, JOSEPH, 2d, son of the above, m. Mary, dau. of Thomas Denny. He lived a part of the time in a house that stood next west of the house in which Dr. Austin Flint lived, now removed, upon what is now a part of the Common; and d. there in 1787. His children were *Henry*, 1783. *Sophia*, 1788; m. Daniel M'Farland in 1813; and, after his death in 1818, m. Horace M'Farland in 1822. *Joseph D.*, 1787. Col. Henry Sargent m. Elizabeth, dau. of William Denny, 1812. He was a very successful business-man; held many offices, civil and military; and was a distinguished citizen in the county as well as the town. He was a member of the Constitutional Convention in 1821; d. 1829. The house in which he lived stood where Mr. Rice's store is, at the corner of Main Street and the Charlton Road. He left a family of children; two of whom were graduates of Harvard University, and both physicians in Worcester. Henry, the youngest, d. 1857. The other (Joseph) holds an eminent rank in his profession. He is mentioned among the graduates of the town. Col. Joseph was also a leading and influential man, and represented the town in the General Court in 1846. He m. Mindwell Jones of Spencer; d. 1849, leaving a family of children. One son (Edward) is now in business in Leicester. Mrs. Sargent d. after her husband.

Sargent, Thomas, came from Malden; was the son of Samuel, and cousin of Jonathan 1st, and Nathan. He was born 1720; m. Tabitha Tuttle. He lived in Leicester some years, and then removed to Hubbardston. His children were *Abigail,* 1750; m. Zaccheus Hasey. *Thomas,* 1752; lived in the north part of the town, next north of where Barnard Upham formerly lived; m. Sarah, dau. of Daniel Denny: he died without children, and his widow became second wife of Col. Seth Washburn. *John,* 1755; m. Hannah Bond, dau. of Benjamin, for his fourth wife: lived sometimes in Hubbardston, and sometimes in Leicester; d. 1837. *Ebenezer,* 1762; lived in Hubbardston. *Samuel,* m. Deborah, dau. of Peter Silvester, 1772; and lived in Marlborough, N.H.

Southgate, Richard, came with Daniel Denny from Coombs, Suffolk, Eng., in 1715. The next year he went back for his family; and brought them over in July, 1717, and with them his brother James. The next March, 1718, the Southgates and Denny removed to Leicester, and settled there. I do not know what circumstance led them to select that spot. Mr. Southgate became an extensive land-owner in the town, and is one of the grantees in the settlers' deed; Lots No. 35,

41, and 42, being conveyed to him by that deed. In 1737, he owned seven hundred and seventy acres in the town.

He was the first treasurer of the town, and was much employed as a surveyor of lands; being a skilful and trustworthy person. The name of his father was John. Richard was born 1671, and m. Elizabeth Steward, October, 1700. They had six children, all born in England; five of whom came to Leicester: *Steward,* b. 1703. *Elizabeth,* 1705; d., 1791, unmarried. *Hannah,* 1709; m. Nathaniel Waite of Leicester, 1737; d. 1754. *Mary,* 1712; m. Daniel Livermore of Weston, 1732. *Richard,* 1714.

He died 1758, aged eighty-eight: his wife died 1751, in the eighty-eighth year of her age. They are said to be the ancestors of all of the name in New England.

SOUTHGATE, STEWARD, son of the above, m. Elizabeth Scott of Palmer, then called the "Elbow," in 1735, while he was living there. About 1740, he returned to Leicester, and spent the rest of his days there. Their children were *John,* 1738. *Robert,* 1741; who was a physician; removed to Scarborough, Me., and is noticed in this work. *Margaret,* 1743. *Sarah,* 1744; m. Azariah Dickinson of Hadley. *Steward,* 1748. He married, and removed to Hardwick, and was a soldier in the Revolution. After the war, he went to Barnard, Vt.; where, in 1795, he lost five children by the canker-rash, within a few days of each other.

Mr. Southgate married Elizabeth, dau. of Nathaniel Potter, for his second wife; and had *Amos,* 1751; who was married, and had a daughter born after his death, who became the wife of Jonah Earle: Amos d. in Boston, 1775. *Rebekah,* 1754; d. 1756. *Ruth,* 1758; d. at Boston, 1777. *Moses,* 1761; d. at Boston, 1777.

His second wife d. 1748: he died 1765. Mr. Southgate was at first a member of the Congregational Church, but became a zealous and leading member of the Society of Friends; to which society his second wife's father belonged prior to 1732. He must have been well educated for his day; and seems to have possessed a clear head, strong purpose, and, withal, great sensibility and Christian resignation. He had a commanding influence among his religious brethren; and the memoranda that he left allude in terms of deep emotion to the afflictions through which he was called to pass.

SOUTHGATE, JOHN, son of Steward, m. Eleanor Sargent, dau. of Jonathan, 1776; and had *Sally*, who d. unmarried. *John*, 1778; d. 1804, unmarried, as related in this work. *William*, 1782; d., unmarried, 1811; he was rather a skilful and talented painter; he had cultivated his taste under several masters; among others, Ralph Earle, to whom he was remotely related; and by instruction of Gilbert Stuart: the department of art to which he devoted his attention was that of portraits, in which he would probably have attained a distinguished reputation, had he diligently devoted himself to it as a profession. *Harriot*, 1792; d., unmarried, 1841. *Eliza*, 1796; m. Jacob Bigelow, then of Montreal; where she died, leaving one son, Dr. George F. Bigelow of Boston. *George W.*, 1800; now living. Mrs. Southgate d. 1825.

SOUTHGATE, JAMES, came with his brother Richard from England, as above stated. He became a proprietor of the settlers' half of the town, as owner of Lot No. 30. At the first town-meeting, he was chosen one of the selectmen, and surveyor of highways. He, with his brother and several other inhabitants of Leicester, addressed a letter to the Governor in 1725, asking for soldiers to guard the town from the Indians.

He was deacon of the church, and took an active part in settling Mr. Parsons in 1720. His wife's name was Mary; and they had one son (*James*), 1718, who m. Dorothy Lincoln in 1741, and had a daughter (*Dorothy*), 1746. But I find no traces of the family after that period. His house was a little north of Mr. Morton's, in the east part of the town.

SOUTHGATE, RICHARD, son of Richard, 1st, came with his father from England; m. Eunice Brown, dau. of Samuel, 1741; and had *Richard*, 1742; removed to Bridgewater, Vt. *Isaac*, 1744. *Samuel*, 1747; lived in various places; d. in Scarborough, 1773. *Elijah*, 1751; m. Patty Hastings; d. in Shrewsbury, 1837, aged eighty-seven, without children. *Jonas*, 1753; m. Mary Whitney, Grafton, 1782; d. 1784. *Eunice*, 1757; d. unmarried. *Judah*, 1761; d. 1799; m. Susannah Taylor of Spencer in 1798. *Mercy*, d. unmarried.

Mr. Southgate was known as "Elder," and was a Baptist preacher. He held meetings in the schoolhouse, when it stood where the brick factory now stands, opposite to where Esquire Rawson lived. He lived in the south-west part of the town, near the line of Spencer; and was a farmer.

SOUTHGATE, ISAAC, son of the above, m. Rebekah Brown, dau. of John Brown, 1769; and had *Rebekah*, 1770; m. a Hodges of the State of New York. Mr. Southgate m., for his second wife, Eunice White, 1771; and had *Asa*, 1772. *Betsey*, 1774; m. Nathan Beers, 1790. *Samuel*, 1776. *Eunice*, 1779; m. Sylvanus Earle; removed to Ohio; d. 1835. *Isaac*, 1782.

Mr. Southgate d. 1800, aged fifty-six. Samuel m. Hannah Waite, 1801; and had a family of children in Leicester. One son (John P.) lives in Worcester; one (Samuel) is in business in Leicester. Isaac m. Maria, dau. of Peter Webb, Esq., and grand-dau. of Thomas Denny, sen. He has been one of the active business-men and public-spirited citizens of the town for many years; a manufacturer of cards. He has represented the town in the Legislature; and has taken an active part, as Trustee of the Worcester-County Agricultural Society, in promoting the interests of that important association.

STONE, JONAS, came from Brookfield. He at first lived at the tan-yard house, at the foot of the Meeting-house Hill. He afterwards lived in the Academy Building, until his removal to Boston about 1806. He m. Lucretia Baldwin of

Shrewsbury, 1784; and had *Lucy C.*, 1785; m. Paul Whitney of Boston. *Henry B.*, 1786; he learned the trade of a saddler, and lived in Leicester till his father removed to Boston; after going to Boston, he became engaged in business of finance, and, by his integrity, skill, and sagacity in that department, won the confidence of all; he was the principal instrument of originating and carrying out the "Suffolk-Bank" system of exchange, as it was called; he was the President of that institution for many years: he m. Elizabeth Clapp, and left several children; but his history belongs rather to the home of his adoption than that of his earlier days. *Lucretia B.*, 1787; d. unmarried. *Artemas*, 1789. *Jonas E.*, 1792; now a merchant in Philadelphia. *Louisa M.*, 1797; d. in Leicester in 1811. *William W.*, 1798; a merchant in New-York City.

Mr. Stone came from Boston to Shrewsbury in 1821. He d. 1851, aged ninety-three: his wife d. in 1847, aged eighty-four. He was a man much respected and esteemed, and had a wide circle of acquaintance and friends.

SMITH, JAMES, m. Dorcas Richardson, 1727; and had *James*, 1728. *Dorcas*. *Abigail*, 1733; m. John Lamb. *Israel*, 1735. *Nathaniel*, 1738. *Deborah*, 1741; m. Elijah Howe, 1759. *Beulah*, 1743; m. Ebenezer Collin, 1770.

Mr. Smith lived on the Robert Watson Farm, adjoining Spencer. He was a soldier in the Louisburg expedition in 1745. His estate was settled in 1750; when Israel is not named in the proceedings. His widow m. Samuel Lynde, and lived on the same estate. James, the son, removed to Spencer. He was a soldier in the French War, and d. in the service. The father is called a housewright, in a deed of 1733.

STOWER, ASA, came from Malden. His first wife was Elizabeth Upham. After her death, he came to Leicester, and m. Rebekah Lynde, 1761; and had *Daniel*, 1762; *Elizabeth*, 1764; *Amos*, 1765; *Thomas*, 1767; *Asa*, 1769; *Samuel*, 1771.

STOWER, ABIJAH, m. Tabitha Hasey, 1761; and had *Samuel*,

1762; *Nathan; Abijah*, 1768. Mr. Stower was a soldier in Capt. Washburn's company, at the battle of Bunker Hill. In 1776, he lived at the Baptist Parsonage-house, in the south part of the town. It is believed he went to Putney, Vt.

SAUNDERSON, JOHN, was a housewright; came from Watertown between 1720 and 1730. He bought a farm in the north-west part of the town, west of the Cedar Swamp and adjoining Peter's Hill, in 1728. His will was dated in 1750; in which he mentions his children, most of whom were born before his removal to Leicester: viz., *Benjamin*, 1707. *Ebenezer*, 1716. *Hannah*, 1704; m. a Kingsbury. *Abiah*, 1706; m. a Coolidge. *Mehitabel*, 1714; m. a Dix. *Prudence*, 1710; m. Joshua Smith. *Tabitha*, 1721; m. Nahum Newton. *Mary*, 1701; m. Onesiphorus Pike. *Lydia*, 1723. He had represented Watertown in the General Court, 1711 and 1712. His wife's name was Hannah Stratton; m. 1700.

SAUNDERSON, BENJAMIN, son of the above, m. Elizabeth, dau. of Nathaniel Green, 1736; and had *Elizabeth*, 1737; m. Ebenezer Call, 1762. *Benjamin*, 1740. *Mary*, 1742; m. Joseph Call, 1762. *John*, 1744. *James*, 1746. *Phinehas*, 1751. *Azubah*, 1754. *Rufus*, 1759.

Mr. Saunderson lived upon the George Bond Place, in the north-west part of the town.

SAUNDERSON, EBENEZER, brother of the above, m. Hannah Whitney; and had *Hannah*, 1747; m. John Saunderson of Hartford, N.Y., 1769. *Ebenezer*, 1748. *Hezekiah*, 1750. *Phebe*, 1754. *Israel*, 1755. *Phebe*, 1757. Hezekiah was corporal in Capt. Washburn's company at Bunker Hill. Ebenezer was in the same company, and also Israel.

SAUNDERSON, BENJAMIN, Jun., son of Benjamin, 1st, m. Rachel Merritt, 1761; and had a dau., 1763; *Beriah*, 1767; *Rachel*, 1768.

SCOTT, MATTHEW, m. Martha Lockard, 1746. Their first child on record was *Andrew*, b. 1759. Mr. Scott lived where Mr. Ebenezer Dunbar lives, on the Turnpike.

Scott, Andrew, son of the above; m. Sarah Henshaw, 1780; and had *Andrew*, 1782; m. Mary Curtis, 1805. *William H.*, 1785; m. Persis Earle, 1811, and had a family of children. *James*, 1788; removed to the West.

Mr. Scott built the house in 1800, and lived, where Amos Whittemore died, in the south part of the town. William H. once commanded the south military company in the town.

Scott, John, by his will, dated 1750, disposed of his property to his widow Martha, and children: *Matthew*. *Nathaniel*, lived on Flip Road; d. 1827, aged fifty-eight. *Thomas*, lived in Auburn. *Jane*, m. a Thompson. *Elizabeth*, m. a Cunningham. *Rebecca*.

Steele, Thomas, is noticed in the body of this work. His wife's name was Mary; d. 1768. Their children were *Thomas*, 1738; d. 1767. *Elizabeth*, 1740; m. Dr. Honeywood. *Mary*, 1741; d., unmarried, 1828. *Jane*, 1744. *Margaret*, 1745; m. Dr. Rawson. *Sarah*, 1746; m. —— Hitchcock. *Samuel*, 1749. *Anne*, 1751; m. Joseph Allen.

Shaw, Joseph, was a blacksmith, and lived in the west part of the town, near North, or Shaw Pond, as it was sometimes called. His wife's name was Dorothy. They had *Joseph*, 1735; d. 1736. *Jeremiah*, 1737. *Mercy*, 1739. *Dorothy*, 1745.

Snow, Daniel. His wife's name was Mary. They had *Jonathan*, 1735; who lived in the north part of the town, next south of where Mr. Barnard Upham lived. *James*, 1748; d. 1811; lived where Barnard Upham lived. *Mary*, 1749.

Snow, Thomas, m. Thankful Bellows, 1756; and had *James*, 1757. *Abner*, 1759. *Sarah*, 1761; m. Amos Muzzy, 1784. *Elizabeth*, 1763. *Seth*, 1765. *Mary*, 1767.

Mr. Snow d. 1804, aged seventy-four.

Swan, Dudley Wade, came from Milton; purchased of John Potter, jun., the Asahel Earle Place, on the North-County Road, in 1736. The name of his wife was Beulah. They had *Ruth*, 1739. *Jabez*, 1736. *Eunice*, 1741; m. Benjamin Richardson, jun. *Seth*, 1742. *Abigail*, 1746. *Reuben*,

1748. *Nathan*, 1750. *Phebe*, 1753; m. Col. William Henshaw. *Dudley*, 1756. Jabez was killed during the Revolutionary War.

SWAN, REUBEN, son of the above, m. Rachel Putnam of Sutton, 1767; had *Ruth*, 1769; m. William Denny. *Sally*, 1771; m. Nathaniel P. Denny. *Reuben Billings*, 1772. *Catherine*, 1774; m. James Watson of Thompson, Conn. *Samuel*, 1778; graduated at Harvard; studied law, and lives in Hubbardston.

Mr. Swan was a farmer, and lived on the North-County Road for several years after he was married. He then purchased the Tavern Estate, where Capt. Knights now lives; and kept a public-house for some time. He then built the house where Mr. J. A. Smith lately lived, and resided there till his death, 1825.

SILVESTER, PETER, came from Scituate, and was born there in 1687. He married Sarah ——, and came to Leicester in 1720. Their children were *Peter*, 1713. *Hannah*, 1716; m. Samuel Tucker. *Joshua*, 1717. *Mary*, 1721. *Levi*, 1723. *Deborah*. Mr. Silvester died 1746.

SILVESTER, PETER, 2d, son of the above, m. Deborah Torrey, 1750; and had *Deborah*, 1751. *Ruth*, 1753. *Peter*, 1755. *Otho*, 1758; he was a soldier in the Revolution, and was killed at Fort Stanwix, 1777. *Amos*, 1760; m. Sally Osland. *Ezra*, 1762. *Elisha*, 1765. *Olive*, 1777.

Mr. Silvester lived for many years in a house on the eastern slope of the Meeting-house Hill, where there is now a cellar, on the north side of the road. He died 1801, aged eighty-eight.

SILVESTER, PETER, 3d, son of the above, was a soldier in the army at Saratoga, when Burgoyne was taken. He m. Mary Sprague, sister of Capt. William Sprague; and lived in the south-west part of the town. His children were *Phebe*, 1782; *Joseph*, 1784; *William*, 1786; *Mary*, 1788; *Oleton C. (Oliver)*, 1792.

SILVESTER, JOSHUA, son of Peter, 1st, m. Ruth Merrit of Mendon, 1758; and had *Joshua*, 1759; *Joseph*, 1761; *John*, 1763; *Elizabeth*, 1764; *Ichabod*, 1767; *Isaac*, 1770.

Mr. Silvester lived in the north-east part of the town, where Erastus Wheaton lately lived.

SILVESTER, ICHABOD, son of the above. His wife's name was Patience. They had *Joseph*, 1795; *Levi*, 1796; *Silas*, 1798; *John*, 1799.

SILVESTER, EZRA, son of Peter, 2d, m. Hannah Henry, 1789, dau. of Robert Henry; and had *Susannah*, 1789; *Henry*, 1791; *Otho*, 1793.

Mr. Silvester and family, with Mr. Henry, removed to Charleston No. 4, N.H., in 1794.

SPRAGUE, JOSEPH, the first of the name in Leicester, was born in 1722, and came from Malden. He married Phebe Hutchinson. He owned the farm, and lived where his son (Capt. William Sprague) lived, about a mile north of the Meeting-house. Their children were *Sarah*, 1748; *Timothy*, 1752; *Mary*, 1755; *John*, 1760; *William*, 1763.

He died 1792; his wife, 1811. Sarah m. Daniel Upham of Templeton, father of Barnard and Daniel Upham of Leicester. Mary m. Peter Silvester.

SPRAGUE, WILLIAM, son of the above, m. Sarah, dau. of Nathan Sargent; and had *Joseph*, 1783. *Rebekah*, 1785. *Roxa*, 1787. *Lana*, 1789. *Otis*, 1791; m. Katherine H., dau. of Joseph Denny; removed to Wisconsin, and died there. *Alice*, 1795; *Laura*, 1800; *Eliza* E., 1806.

Capt. Sprague died 1831, aged sixty-eight; Mrs. Sprague, 1837. He was a well-known citizen of the town; lived where his father had lived; was captain of one of the militia companies of the town; was a deputy-sheriff of the county; and filled many responsible places. Joseph went to Brooklyn, N.Y., where he was at one time mayor of that city; d. 1854. Rebekah was many years a useful and popular school teacher; d., unmarried, 1844. Roxa m. Thomas Edmunds, of the well-known publishing firm, Lincoln and Edmunds; and is the mother of Gen. B. F. Edmunds, and the Hon. J. Wiley Edmunds, late of the United-States Congress. Lana m. Benjamin Edmands; Alice m. Stephen Wiley; Eliza m. Henry A. Denny, now of Worcester.

SPRAGUE, TIMOTHY, brother of the above, m. Mary, dau. of Jonathan Sargent, jun., 1774. Had *Joshua*, 1774. *Polly*, 1776; m. Jonathan Knight. *John*, 1778; m. Sally, dau. of Capt. Daniel Hubbard; removed to the State of New York, 1807. *Phebe*, 1781. *Betsey*, 1786; m. Stephen Trask, 1818. *Katherine*, 1788.

Mr. Sprague lived upon the farm, now belonging to the town, which he purchased of Hezekiah Ward, Esq. He died 1815, aged sixty-two.

STICKNEY, THOMAS, came to Leicester from Boston. He was a native of Newburyport, and had lived in Haverhill and Boston. He purchased the Mt. Pleasant Place (of which there is a view given in this work), where he carried on his mercantile business, and lived in generous hospitality. He d. July 28, 1791. The next year, his widow m. John Lyon, jun.

His children were *John*, b. at Haverhill, 1775. *Thomas*, 1777. *Polly*, 1779. *Joseph*, 1780. *Harry*, 1782; b. in Boston. *Betsey*, 1784. *Harriet*, 1788; b. in Leicester. Thomas, jun., m. a dau. of Rev. Ephraim Ward of West Brookfield, who d. 1859: he was the father of J. Henry Stickney, Esq., of Baltimore, mentioned elsewhere in this work. There were also John and Joseph Stickney (brothers of Thomas), who were bachelors, and came from Newburyport, and were traders upon Mt. Pleasant, in the house which John built, upon the north side of the road, in 1789; the same in which Jonathan Earle and Nathaniel P. Denny afterwards lived. They both d. in 1803,—Joseph in October, and John in December. They were all men of property and influence, and were much respected in town as useful, intelligent, and public-spirited citizens.

Taylor, Edward. His wife was Elizabeth. They had *Samuel*, 1718; *Edmund*, 1721; *Bartholomew*, 1723; *Adonijah*, 1728; *James*, 1731.

Taylor, John, m. Susannah Parsons, 1752; and had *John*, 1753; *Susannah*, 1755; *Sarah*, 1757. His father (John) owned and occupied the Tavern-house Estate, where Capt. Knight lives, in 1749. He is called, in a deed of 1748, a "trader." That deed conveyed to him all the land between the present Charlton Road and the Sturbridge County Road, upon the south side of the Great Road.

Trumbull, Joseph. His wife was Abiah. They had *James*, 1727; *Abiah*, 1729; *Joseph*, 1731; *Mary*, 1734. Mr. Trumbull lived near the Kent Place, in the north-east part of the town.

Trumbull, Joseph, Jun., son of the above, m. Lydia Hammond, 1758; and had *Phinehas*, 1759; *Isaac*, 1763.

Trask, David, came from Millbury (then a part of Sutton), 1764; m. Mehitabel Dwight for his first wife, 1788; d. 1801: and, second, Polly Cooley; d. 1807: third, Abigail Harrington, 1808. He lived in the west part of the town, on the north side of the Great Road. His children were *Anna B.*, 1790; m. John Wood. *Mehitabel D.*, 1794; m. Samuel Hurd. *Mary W.*, 1803; m. Baylies Upham. *James P.*, 1809; d. 1848. *Abby G.*, 1812. *Adeline*, 1815; m. Delphos Washburn. *Jane S.*, 1819. *Frances M.*, 1823. Capt. Trask d. 1831.

Tucker, Samuel, was of Roxbury, and a son of Benjamin, one of the original proprietors of the township. He early came to Leicester; where he m. Hannah, dau. of Peter Silvester, 1st, 1740. He removed to Spencer, 1762. His children were all born in Leicester; and were *Sarah*, 1741. *Samuel*, 1742. *Hannah*, 1745; m. David Baldwin. *Isaac*, 1746. *Ruth*, 1748. *Elijah*, 1751; d. 1777. *Huldah*, 1755; d. 1777. *Ezekiel*, 1757. Mr. Tucker lived in the north-west part of the town, on the road leading to Spencer, by the Bond Place.

Tucker, Benjamin. His wife's name was Mary. They had

Elizabeth, 1730; m. Abel Woodward, 1753. *Mary*, 1732. *Benjamin*, 1734. *Joshua*, 1738. *Abijah*, 1740. *Caleb*, 1743. Mr. Tucker bought his farm, in Cherry Valley, of Nathaniel Richardson, in 1727.

TUCKER, STEPHEN. His wife was Hannah. Their children: *Hannah*, 1739; *Stephen*, 1741; *John*, 1742; *Lucy*, 1744; *Rebekah*, 1746. His second wife, Mary Pike, 1750. They had *James*, 1751; *Nathan*, 1752; *Zephaniah*, 1756; *Mary*, 1759; *Elizabeth*, 1760; *Solomon*, 1761; *Daniel*, 1764; *Sarah*, 1770.

TUCKER, BENJAMIN, Jun. His wife was Martha. They had *Benjamin*, 1762; *Jacob D.*, 1763; *Ichabod*, 1765.

THOMAS, JOHN. The name of his wife was Susannah. They had *Mary*, 1758; *John*, 1760. I suppose him to be son of Samuel Thomas, who was here before 1721, and lived in the north-east part of the town, near the Samuel Waite Place.

TORREY, ABEL. His wife was Mary. They had *Samuel*, 1753; *David*, 1755; *Molly*, 1757; *Abel*, 1761; *Abner*, 1753.

VINTON, ABIATHAR, was born in Woburn in 1700; m. Lydia, dau. of Capt. Samuel Green, 1723; and had *Lydia*, 1724; m. James Wilson of Spencer. *Hannah*, 1726. *Tamar*, 1728; m. James Baldwin, jun. *Elizabeth*, 1730; m., first, Seth Babbitt, 1753; and, second, James Howard. *Abiathar*, jun., 1732. *John*, 1735. *Samuel*, 1737; a physician in South Hadley, 1801.

Mr. Vinton lived a while in Braintree before coming to Leicester. He was a blacksmith, and lived on the Copeland Place, in the south part of the town. He d. in 1740. His son of the same name went to Charlton, and removed to Granby about 1772. He had a son Abiathar, b. 1764, who lived in South Hadley; where his son (Hon. Samuel F. Vinton, now of Washington) was born 1792. He graduated at Williams College; went to Ohio; became an eminent lawyer; and was a member of Congress twenty-two years.

UPHAM, EBENEZER, was the son of Samuel; b. in Malden, 1726. He m. Lois Waite of Malden, 1748. They had *Lois*,

1751. *Waite*, 1753; was in the three-years' service in the Revolution. *Eunice*. *Elizabeth*, 1755. *Tabitha*, 1757. *Ebenezer B.*, 1759. *Mehitabel*, 1761. *Priscilla*, 1765. *William*, 1766. *Joshua*, 1767. *Phinehas*, 1770.

Mr. Upham was a farmer, and lived in the house between the Deacon Rockwood Place and the Copeland Place. He was the lieutenant of the Leicester Company, in 1775, which marched to Cambridge; and his son Waite belonged to the same.

UPHAM, SAMUEL, brother of the above, lived where Deacon Rockwood did, in the south part of the town. His wife's name was Martha. They had *Martha*, 1758. *Samuel*, 1762. *Mercy*, 1765; m. Pliny Green, 1783.

UPHAM, SAMUEL, 2d, son of the above, m. Patty Livermore, dau. of Jonas, 1791. He lived where his father had lived, until his removal to Vermont. His children were *William* (Aug. 5, 1791), who is noticed in another part of the work; d. at Washington, a senator in Congress. *Samuel*, 1793. *Patty*, 1797. *Horace*, 1799.

Mr. Upham removed to Vermont soon after 1800. He d. 1848, at Randolph in that State, aged eighty-seven.

UPHAM, EBENEZER, m. Mary Crowl; and lived in Cherry Valley, where Nathan Beers, and after him Mr. Shepherd, lived. They had *Mary*, 1762. *Ebenezer*, 1764. *Thaddeus*, 1768; who was a tanner; lived at the foot of the Meeting-house Hill; left Leicester, 1800; went to Watertown, and d. there 1814. *Sarah*, 1776; m. Daniel Works, 1794.

UPHAM, NATHANIEL. His wife was Rebekah. They had *Thomas*, 1747; *Mehitabel*, 1750; *Rebekah*, 1753.

UPHAM, JONATHAN, brother of the Ebenezer above; m. Martha Tucker, 1750. Had *Bathsheba*, 1752.

UPHAM, JACOB, brother of the above; m. Sarah Stower, 1751. Had *Phebe*, 1752.

WHITTEMORE, JOHN, is described in early papers as of Rumney Marsh in Boston. His wife's name was Rebekah. He was in Leicester before 1730, and is called "Deacon" in 1735. He had *John*, 1721. *Nathan*, 1723. *Rebekah*, 1725; m. Oliver Witt, 1745. *Phebe*, 1727; m. Ralph Earle, then of Shrewsbury, 1749. *Nathaniel*, 1732. *James*, 1734. Mr. Whittemore owned the farm where his grandson Joseph lived, and recently died.

WHITTEMORE, JOHN, Jun., son of the above; m. Elizabeth Earle, 1749, dau. of Robert; and had *John*, 1750. *Molly*, 1754. *Thomas*, 1755. *Rebekah* and *Phebe*, 1756; d. 1759. *Ruth*, 1766. He lived where Mr. Partridge lives, near the Gage Place.

WHITTEMORE, JAMES, son of John, 1st; m. Dorothy Green, 1761; and had *James*, 1762. *Phebe*, 1765; m. Samuel Waite. *Dolly*, 1767; d. unmarried. *Samuel*, 1769; removed with his family into New York. *Katy*, 1772; d. unmarried. *Clark*, 1776; lived in Worcester. *John*. *Joseph*, 1786; d. 1859.

Mr. Whittemore lived where his son Joseph recently lived and died. He d. 1811, aged seventy-seven. He was always known by the title, "Lieutenant" James.

WHITTEMORE, NATHAN, son of John, 1st; m. Lois Earle, dau. of William, 2d, 1763. They had *Nathan*, 1764; *Lucretia*, 1766; *Joseph*, 1768.

WHITTEMORE, ASA; lived in the south part of the town. His wife's name was Lucy. They had *Lucy*, 1775; *Asa*, 1777; *Amos*, 1779; *Polly*, 1780; *Nabby*, 1782; *Amasa*, 1784; *Jonas*, 1786; *Charles*, 1790; *John S.*, 1794.

He d. 1821, aged seventy-one: his wife d. 1822, aged sixty-five.

WICKER, WILLIAM, was here before 1720. His wife's name was Rebekah. They had *Rebekah*, 1720; *Jacob*, 1723; *John*, 1726; *James*, 1729; *Mercy*, 1740.

Jacob m. Abiah Washburn, sister of Col. Seth, 1747; and moved to Hardwick. He lived north of Moose Hill, in what is now Paxton.

WARREN, WILLIAM. His wife was Susannah. They had

Thomas, 1736; *Susannah*, 1728; *William*, 1732; *Thomas*, 1736; *Hannah*, 1739.

WARREN, EBENEZER; lived in the west part of the town, where Joseph, his grandson, now lives. His wife's name was Lydia. They had *Jonathan*, 1750; who was a tanner, and lived in the south-west part of the town, where his son Jonathan died. *Lydia*, 1752; m. Abner Dunbar, 1774. *Ebenezer*, 1754. *Elijah*, 1759.

WARREN, ELIJAH, son of the above; m. Elizabeth Wheeler, 1781. Had *Amos*, 1782; lives in Woodstock, Vt. *Joseph*, 1784. *Betsey*, 1785; m. Jonathan Bond. *Lydia*, 1788. *Mary W.*, 1790. *Charlotte*, 1792. He m. Mary Belcher Wheeler, 1801; and had *Sarah H.*, 1802. *Katherine H.*, 1804; d. 1828. *Louisa A.*, 1807; m. Rev. Amos D. Wheeler, now of Topsham, Me., 1830. *Henry E.*, 1809. Mr. Warren d. 1843.

WITT, JONATHAN; came from Southborough. His wife's name was Dinah. They had *Lydia*, 1745. He lived in what is now Paxton.

WITT, OLIVER; m. Rebekah Whittemore; and had *Sarah*, 1746; *Jonathan*, 1751; *Phebe*, 1748.

WILSON, JAMES; came from Lexington, and settled on Lot No. 10, on the Charlton Road, about half a mile from the Meeting-house. He was there in 1714; and was probably the first settler, or among the very first, in the town. In 1758, he removed to Stockbridge; having resided a few years previously in Spencer. His wife's name was Mehitabel. They had *Amy*, 1725; m. Thomas Tolman. *James*, jun., 1727. *William*, 1729. *John*, 1730. *Azariah*, 1731.

WARD, HEZEKIAH; came from Grafton in 1768. He owned the farm now belonging to the town; which, after the war, he sold to Timothy Sprague, and removed to Paxton. He was a magistrate and a leading citizen while in town. He m. Martha Earle, dau. of Robert; and had *Hezekiah*, 1771.

His first wife was Sarah, dau. of William Green, 1st, of Leicester. He was then called of New Medfield.

WAITE, NATHANIEL, the first of the name who came to Leicester, was b. in Malden, 1701. He settled upon the farm on which his son Samuel lived and died; the road to which, when he came there, was indicated by marked trees in the primitive forest. His first wife was Mary Richardson, m. 1735; but she died in a few months, and he m. Hannah, dau. of Richard Southgate. She was b. in Coombs, England, 1709; and d. 1754. They had *Nathaniel*, jun., 1738; lived in Hubbardston; d. 1815. *Hannah*, 1740; m. Thomas Earle. *Nathan*, 1742. *David*, 1744; removed to New Braintree; d. 1815. *Phinehas*, 1746; m. Patty Forbes; lived where Deacon Murdoch lived; d. 1810. *Jonathan*, 1748; lived in Woodstock, Vt.; d. 1810. *Samuel*, 1750. *William*, 1751; m. Hannah, dau. of Joseph Sargent; lived in New Braintree; d. 1837. *Mary*, 1753; m. Nathan Sargent, 2d; lived in New Braintree; d. 1816. *Phebe*, 1857; m. Nathaniel Whittemore of Peterborough; d. 1835. *Asa*, 1759. *Elizabeth;* m. Potter Cole; removed, when a widow, to Ohio; d. 1845.

Mr. Waite m. a third wife (Phebe Read) in 1756.

Mr. Waite d. 1791, at the age of ninety, never having been sick a day in his life; and was followed to his grave by all the above-named twelve children.

WAITE, NATHAN, son of the above, owned, and for many years kept as a tavern, the house (now removed) opposite the Catholic Church. He d. 1818, aged seventy-four. He m., first, Joana Tucker, 1765; and had *Joana*, 1766; m. Dr. Otis Gould of Dartmouth. *Nathan*, jun., 1768; m. Martha Bruce in 1792, and removed to Sterling. *Sally*, 1770; m. Capt. Darius Cutting, 1789.

Mrs. Waite d. 1771. Mr. Waite m., second, Hannah Parks of Shrewsbury; and had *Nahum*, 1775; m. Olive Lynde; d. 1816. *Hannah*, 1778; m. Samuel Southgate, 1801. *Alice*, 1782. *Joseph*, 1784; d., unmarried, 1815.

WAITE, SAMUEL, son of Nathaniel, m. Phebe, dau. of James Whittemore, 1792; and had *Lyman*, 1793. *Samuel*, 1795.

William, 1797. *Edwin*, 1798. *Emeline*, 1802; m. Cyrus Underwood of Auburn, N.Y., 1824. *Laura Alma*, 1803. *Phinehas*, 1805. *Charles*, 1808.

Mr. Waite d. 1847, aged ninety-seven: his wife d. 1819. He built the house in which he lived, where his son Lyman now lives.

WAITE, ASA, known as "Major Waite," was brother of the above. He m. Rebekah, dau. of Samuel Works; and had *Elmer*, 1789. *Lucretia*, 1796; d. 1826. Mrs. Waite d. 1843. Mr. Waite is mentioned elsewhere as having been in the Revolutionary War. He d. 1814.

WATSON, SAMUEL. His wife was Margaret. Their children: *Elizabeth*, 1723; m. Robert Paul. *William*, 1724. *Samuel*, 1728. *John*, 1730. *Daniel*, 1732.

WATSON, JOHN. There was a John Watson here before 1722; but whether father of this one, I cannot ascertain. The name of the wife of the one noticed here was Mary. Their children: *Patrick*, 1745. *John*, 1747. *Samuel*, 1749. *Dorothy*, 1754; m. James Smith. *Sarah*, 1757; m. Nathan Kingsley. *Molly*, 1759; m. Isaac Prouty. *Elizabeth*, 1762; m. Elijah Washburn. *Hannah*, 1764. *Lydia*, 1766; m. John Read, Rutland.

Mr. Watson lived in the west part of the town. He d. 1795, aged eighty; his wife, the same year, aged seventy.

WATSON, JOHNSON, m. Lydia Sargent, 1764. Had *Mary*, 1765; *Joseph*, 1767; *Sarah*, 1769.

WATSON, WILLIAM, lived on the Charlton Road, about a mile south of the Meeting-house. He m. Susannah Bulloch of Rehoboth, 1769; and had *Susannah*, 1769. *Anna*, 1773; m. Moses Hammond. *William*, 1775. *Abigail*, 1779; m. Rev. William Mason of Castine. *Samuel* (afterwards *Samuel D.*), 1781; who, at one time, commanded the regiment to which Leicester belonged; was extensively engaged in business, and a popular citizen; he removed to Amherst, and d. there in reduced circumstances.

Mr. Watson was known as "Capt. Watson." He d. 1828, aged eighty-four: his wife d. 1804, aged fifty-eight.

WATSON, SAMUEL, son of John, m. Ruth Baldwin, 1772; and lived in the west part of the town, about half a mile north of the Great Road. His children were *Nabby*, 1774. *Chloe*, 1775. *Polly*, 1777. *Ruth*, 1781. *Lucy*, 1783. *Samuel*, 1785; d. 1818. *Asa B.*, 1793.

Mr. Watson d. 1818, aged sixty-nine: Mrs. Watson d. 1849, aged ninety-eight. Lucy m. Hon. James Draper of Spencer, 1805. Ruth m. Daniel Kent, 1805.

WATSON, BENJAMIN. His father was Samuel. He lived in the south-east part of the town, on the road leading from Cherry Valley to Auburn, near the Turnpike. He m. Ruth Bancroft, 1778; and had *Eunice*, 1779. *Samuel*, 1782; who has been a leading citizen of the town; represented it in the General Court; and is noticed in other parts of this work. *Ruth*, 1784. *Benjamin*, 1785; removed to Mercer, Me. Mrs. Watson d. 1834; Mr. Watson, in 1831, aged eighty-five.

WATSON, MATTHEW, brother of the above, lived in Cherry Valley, where Nathan Holman lives. He m. Mary Taylor, 1762; both of Leicester. They had *Nancy*, 1763; m. Daniel Denny, son of Samuel; and d., 1852, in Worcester. *Peggy*, 1786; m. Edmund Snow; d. 1859. *Polly*, 1768. *Matthew*, 1770; d. unmarried.

Mr. Watson built the house on the Old Road, opposite the Southgate Place, in Cherry Valley.

WHEATON, BENJAMIN. His wife's name was Abigail, dau. of John Lynde, 1744; and had *John*, 1745; *Sarah*, 1747; *Christopher*, 1748; *Pliny*, 1751; *Dan*, 1753. He lived in the north-west part of the town.

WHEATON, JOHN, son of the above, m. Phebe Hubbard of Holden, 1770; and had *Phebe; Sarah*, 1775; *Pliny*, 1778; *Joseph* and *Benjamin*, 1783.

WASHBURN, JOSEPH, b. in Bridgewater; m. Hannah Johnson, b. in Hingham; went to Middletown, Conn.; and came to

Leicester before 1745. His children were born in Bridgewater; and the following named came with him, or previously, to Leicester: *Seth*, 1723. *Elijah*. *Ebenezer*, 1734. *Abiah*, m. Jacob Wicker, 1747. *Sarah*, m. Joseph Cerley; went to Whitingham, Vt.; d. 1817. *Mary*, m. —— Clough of Stafford, Conn.

Mr. Washburn was a blacksmith; lived in a house, where there is now a cellar, on the right-hand side of the road leading to William Silvester's, about a quarter of a mile from the Great Road. He d. in 1759; his widow, in 1780, aged eighty-seven.

Elijah m. Hannah Taylor, 1746; and went to Natick, and afterwards to New Hampshire. Ebenezer m. Dorothy, dau. of Jonathan Newhall, 1757; and removed to Hardwick. While he lived in Leicester, he was employed to teach school. He was father of Dr. Cyrus Washburn of Vernon, Vt.

WASHBURN, SETH, is noticed elsewhere. He was son of the above; was born, 1723, in Bridgewater; went to Middletown, and then came to Leicester before 1745; m. Mary Harrod, 1750; and had *Seth*, 1751. *Joseph*, 1755. *Asa*, 1757. *Mary*, 1759; m. Samuel Sargent, 1781; d. 1849. *Hannah*, 1762; long a popular school-teacher in Leicester; m. Jonathan A. Phippin, Westminster, Vt.; d., 1850. *Sarah*, 1764; m. John Hodgkin, 1789; d. 1850. *Amity*, 1767; m. John Hayward, 1793; d., without children, 1794. *Lucy*, 1769; m. Josiah Woodward of Millbury, 1794; d. 1796. *Elizabeth*, 1774, d. 1777.

Col. Washburn m. Sarah Sargent, 1788, for a second wife. His first wife d. Sept. 16, 1787: he d. Feb. 20, 1794, aged seventy.

WASHBURN, SETH, Jun., son of the above, m. Susannah Rood of Sturbridge, 1772. He lived in the north-west part of the town, near the George Bond Place, where there is a cellar: the house disappeared many years since. He had *Nathaniel* 1773. After this, he removed to Wilbraham; and died in the army, during the Revolution, at Governor's Island, N.Y., 1776.

WASHBURN, ASA, son of Seth, 1st, m. Sarah Upham of Spencer; and had *Reuben*, 1781, who was graduated at Dartmouth; studied and practised law; has been a Judge of the County Court in Vermont; and lives in Ludlow. *Levi*, 1783.

Not long after this, Mr. Washburn removed to Putney, Vt.; where he raised a large family of sons and daughters. He became an acting magistrate and a leading and influential citizen in the town where he resided. He d. Oct. 6, 1834.

WASHBURN, JOSEPH, son of Seth, 1st, is noticed in the work. He m. Ruth Davis, dau. of Ebenezer Davis of Charlton, 1787; and had *Ebenezer D.*, Oct. 26, 1788; settled in Alabama; was a lawyer, a Judge of the Court, there; and d. 1838, leaving a family there. *Seth*, Sept. 30, 1790; was a physician, and eminent in his profession; settled in Greenfield, where he d. January, 1838, leaving a family. *Lucinda A.*, Dec. 23, 1792; m. John Wilder, then of Leicester, 1815; d. in Providence, R.I., Nov. 1, 1843, leaving a family of children. *Joseph*, Sept. 8, 1795; a merchant; now lives in Savannah, Ga. *Abigail D.*, Sept. 22, 1797; d. unmarried, March 11, 1816. *Emory*, Feb. 14, 1800; removed to Worcester, 1828; is mentioned elsewhere. *Ruth*, May 8, 1802; m. Rev. Joseph Muenscher, D.D., now of Mount Vernon, O., 1825.

Mr. Washburn died March 27, 1807, aged fifty-two: Mrs. Washburn died March 22, 1827, aged sixty-one. At the time of his death, he lived, and owned the farm, where Mrs. Newhall lives, half a mile north of the Meeting-house.

WASHBURN, GIDEON, was cousin to Joseph, 1st; b. in Bridgewater, 1704; m. Mary Perkins of Bridgewater, and had four sons, and, with two of them (*Abraham* and *Jacob*), removed to Leicester, and settled in the north part of the town. He died 1794, aged ninety-one; never having had a physician in his life.

WASHBURN, JACOB, son of the above, was b. 1733. He had *Sally*, 1779; *Jacob;* and *Francis*.

He lived in the north part of the town; and d. 1818, aged eighty-five. He was a lieutenant of a company in the French War.

The children of Abram, son of Gideon, were *James*, *Eliab*, *Luke*. He lived in the north part of the town.

WASHBURN, JACOB, son of Jacob, m. Achsa Johnson, 1789; and had *Cephas*, 1792; *Jacob*, 3d, 1793.

Mr. Washburn died 1818, aged eighty-five.

WASHBURN, FRANCIS, son of Jacob, 1st, m. Catherine Earle, 1796; and had *Welcome*, 1797; *John*, 1801. He then m. Polly Watson, 1806; and had *Delphos*, 1808. *Catherine E.*, 1813; m. Ezekiel Bellows.

APPENDIX.

APPENDIX.

No. 1.—*Indian Deed of the Township.*

KNOW all men by these presents, that the heirs of Oraskaso, Sachem of a place called Towtaid, situate and lying near the new town of the English called Worcester, with all others which may, under them, belong unto the same place aforesaid, Towtaid,—these heirs being two women, with their husbands, newly married; which being by name called Philip Tray, with his wife Momokhue; and John Wampscon, with Waiwaynom his wife,—for divers good causes and considerations us thereunto moving; and more especially for and in consideration of the sum of *fifteen pounds*, current money of New England, to us in hand paid by Joshua Lamb, Nathaniel Page, Andrew Gardner, Benjamin Gamblin, Benjamin Tucker, John Curtice, Richard Draper, and Samuel Ruggles, with Ralph Bradhurst of Roxbury, in the County of Suffolk in New England, the receipt of which we do fully acknowledge ourselves to be fully satisfied and paid,—have given, granted, bargained, sold, alienated, infeoffed, and confirmed, and by these presents do fully and absolutely give, grant, bargain, sell, alienate, infeoff, and confirm, unto the said Lamb, Page, Gardner, Gamblin, Tucker, Curtice, Draper, Ruggles, and Bradhurst, their heirs and assigns, a certain tract of land,—containing, by estimation, eight miles square,—situate, lying, and being near Worcester aforesaid; abutting, southerly, on the lands of Joseph Dudley, Esq., lately purchased of the Indians; and, westerly, the most southernmost corner upon a little pond called Paupakquamcock, then to a hill called Wikapokotownow, and from thence to a little hill called Mossonachud, and unto a great hill called Aspomsok; and so then, easterly, upon a line until it comes against Worcester bounds, and joins unto their bounds; or howsoever otherwise butted and bounded: together with all and singular the rights, commodities, liberties, privileges, and appurtenances whatsoever to the same belonging, or however otherwise appertaining: To have and to hold the said tract or parcel of land — situating, containing, and bounding as aforesaid — to the said Lamb, &c., their heirs and assigns, in common tenancy, to their only proper use, sake of, and benefit, for ever. And the said Philip Tray and Momokhue, and John Wampscon and Waiwaynow, their wives, with all others under them as aforesaid, do covenant, promise, and grant, for themselves, their heirs, executors, and administrators, to and with the said Joshua Lamb, &c., their heirs and assigns, that they will the above-granted and bargained lands, and every part and parcel thereof, with their and every of their appurtenances, warrant and defend from all and every person and persons whatsoever claiming any right or title thereunto, or interest therein, from, by, or under us.

In witness whereof, the said Philip Tray and Momokhue, and John Wampscon, with Waiwaynow, being their wives, have hereunto set their hands and seals, this twenty-seventh day of January, *anno Domini* one thousand six hundred and eighty-six.

Signed, sealed, and delivered
in presence of us:

	PHILIP TRAY, ⊙ his mark.	[Seal.]
TOM TRAY, ⊙ his mark.	MOMOKHUE TRAY, T her mark.	„
NONAWANO, ∽ his mark.	JOHN WAMSCON.	„
CAPT. & MOOGUS, his mark.	WAIWAYNOW WAMSCON, + her mark.	„
ANDREW 8 PITTEME, — his mark.	WANDWOAMAG § (*the deacon*), his mark.	„
	JONAS, his O wife's mark.	„

Philip Tray, Monokhue (his wife), Waiwaynow, and Wandowamag, all personally appearing before me, underwritten, one of his Majesty's Council of his territory and dominions of New England, June 1, 1687, did acknowledge this instrument to be their act and deed.

WILLIAM STOUGHTON.

Recorded March 8, 1713–14.

No. 2. — *Extracts from Deed from the Proprietors of the Town to the Settlers of the Eastern Half.*

It bears date Jan. 11, 1724; and is recorded Nov. 29, 1729. The names of the committee are stated in the deed, — William Dudley and Joshua Lamb of Roxbury, Nathaniel Kanney, of Boston (victualler), and Samuel Green of Leicester. The deed is to the settlers (naming them) "who have built or settled fifty families thereon."

No.	Acres	Name
No. 1.	30 A.	John Stebbins.
2.	,, ,,	Joseph Stebbins.
3.	40 ,,	James Wilson.
4.	,, ,,	Samuel Green.
5.	,, ,,	Arthur Carey.
6.	,, ,,	Ministry.
7.	,, ,,	Moses Stockbridge.
8.	,, ,,	Hezekiah Russ.
9.	30 ,,	John Peters.
10.	,, ,,	William Brown.
11.	,, ,,	Thomas Hopkins.
12.	,, ,,	Daniel Denny.
13.	40 ,,	John Smith.
14.	50 ,,	Ralph Earle.
15.	,, ,,	Nathaniel Kanney.
16.	40 ,,	Samuel Stimpson.
17.	,, ,,	Benjamin Woodbridge.
18.	,, ,,	John Lynde.
19.	,, ,,	Josiah Winslow.
20.	,, ,,	Josiah Winslow.
21.	,, ,,	Josiah Langdon.
22.	,, ,,	Joshua Henshaw.
23.	,, ,,	Joseph Parsons.
24.	30 ,,	Nathaniel Richardson.
25.	40 ,,	John Menzies.
No. 26.	30 A.	Nathaniel Richardson.
27.	40 ,,	Joseph Sargent.
28.	,, ,,	Samuel Green.
29.	50 ,,	Daniel Livermore.
30.	40 ,,	James Southgate.
31.	,, ,,	Samuel Green.
32.	,, ,,	Daniel Parker.
33.	50 ,,	William Brown.
34.	40 ,,	Thomas Baker.
35.	,, ,,	Richard Southgate.
36.	,, ,,	William Green.
37.	,, ,,	Samuel Prince.
38.	,, ,,	Nathaniel Kanney.
39.	,, ,,	Dorothy Friar.
40.	,, ,,	Thomas Dexter.
41.	,, ,,	Richard Southgate.
42.	,, ,,	Richard Southgate.
43.	,, ,,	Daniel Denny.
44.	,, ,,	William Kean.
45.	,, ,,	James Winslow.
46.	,, ,,	Daniel Denny.
47.	,, ,,	John Smith.
48.	,, ,,	Stephen Winchester.
49.	30 ,,	Paul Dudley.
50.	40 ,,	John King.

Two thirty-acre lots, called the Mill Lots, to Samuel Green; and one thirty-acre lot, called the Mill Lot, to Thomas Richardson: they performing the conditions mentioned in a grant of the said mill-lots to them.

Of the foregoing, Thomas Baker of Brookfield never came to Leicester. He sold Lot 34 to Judge Menzies.

Joseph Parsons never came to the town.

No. 3.—*An Account of Bounties paid by the Town of Leicester, and by Individuals of said Town, to Soldiers who engaged to serve in the Army at different Periods from* 1775 *to the End of the War.*

1. 1775, May. To thirty-seven non-commissioned and privates, each of which received of the town 28s., and of individuals 30s., each, for eight months . . . . £51. 16s. and £55. 10s.

2. Dec. 1. Sixteen men at Dorchester, two months each, received of the officers of the militia 30s. . . . . £24.

3. 1776, Jan. 20. Sixteen men at Roxbury and Dorchester two months, each of which received of individuals and militia-officers 30s. . . . . £24.

4. To eight men one year at New York, from January, 1776, at £12 each . . . . £96.

5. June 24. Nineteen men to New York five months at £9 each, paid by individuals and militia-officers . . . . £171.

6. Six men to Ticonderoga at £15 each, paid by individuals and militia-officers . . . . £90.

7. Sept. 10. Twelve men to New York two months, at £4. 10s. each, paid by individuals and the militia-officers . . . . £54.

8. Nov. 20 and 30. Four men to New York, at £12 each, paid by individuals and the militia-officers . . . . £48.

9. 1777, April 12. Seven men to Rhode Island, two months, at £4 each . . . . £28.

10. April 30. Six men to complete the State's quota of the Continental Army, for eight months, at £18 on an average . . £108.

11. July 11. Two men, £4. 10s. each . . . . £9.

12. Aug. 9. Twenty-one men to the northward, at £24 each, paid by individuals and militia-officers for three months . . . £504.

13. Dec. 27. Three men, two at £30 each, and one at £15 . £75.

14. 1778, Feb. 7. Ten men to guard at Boston under Gen. Heath, at £18 per man . . . . £180.

15. April 18. Six men to re-enforce the Continental Army, nine months, at £130 each . . . . £780.

16. Five men, eight months, at £80 . . . . £400.

17. June 12. Four men for defence of Rhode Island, at £18 each, paid by officers and individuals . . . . £72.

18. June 23. Four men to guard Convention troops, at £15 each, paid by officers and others . . . . £60.

19. July 27. Ten men to re-enforce Gen. Sullivan at Rhode Island, at £18 each, paid by officers and others . . . . . £180.

20. 1778, Sept. 6. Four men to re-enforce the army at Providence in Rhode Island, £30 each . . . . £120.

21. 1779, June 8. Two men to Providence, R.I., paid by the selectmen, £200 each . . . . £400.

22. June 23. Six men to join the Continental Army, at £600 each, paid by selectmen . . . . £3,600.

23. July 5. Four men, three at £45 each, and one at £30 . £165.

24. Sept. 20. Six men at Rhode Island; four men at £80 each, and two at £70 each . . . . £460.

25. Oct. 10. Nine men to Claverack in New York, at £170 each . . . . £1,530.

26. 1780, April 19. To three men to guard at Rutland for eight months, at £16 hard silver money each, paid by selectmen . £48.

27. June 28. To seventeen men six months, to join the Continental Army, at £30 each, in silver money, paid by selectmen . £510.

Leicester, April 16, 1784. — These may certify that the above is a true account of the number of men hired, and the sums of money paid them by the inhabitants of the town of Leicester; and though we cannot produce all the receipts from the individuals who received the money, by reason of deaths, removals, &c.

JOSEPH SARGENT,
SAMUEL DENNY,
SAMUEL GREEN,
WILLIAM HENSHAW, } *Selectmen of Leicester.*

No. 4. — *Scale of Depreciation of "Continental Money."*

In Mr. Felt's work on the Massachusetts currency, I find two tables of depreciation. One appears to be based upon assumed and arbitrary prices of sundry leading articles of consumption, which are thus made a standard of value; and I copy from his work the average rates of depreciation calculated upon all those compared with silver.

He also gives the Massachusetts scale of depreciation agreeable to a law of the Commonwealth, fixing the rates at which public and private contracts made since the 1st January, 1777, were to be settled.

In the computations I have made, and embodied in this work, I have adopted the Massachusetts standard, as the town would be more likely to refer to that than any other scale; making a silver dollar the par or standard of comparison.

	1777.	1778.	1779.	1780.
Jan. . . .	1.16 for 1	4.50 for 1	8.38 for 1	32.50 for 1
Feb. . . .	1.03 „ „	4.64 „ „	9.34 „ „	
March .	1.03 „ „	4.80 „ „	10.87 „ „	
April . .	1.28 „ „	5.19 „ „	12.35 „ „	
May . . .	1.57 „ „	5.80 „ „	14.14 „ „	
June . .	1.60 „ „	5.91 „ „	16.02 „ „	
July . . .	1.82 „ „	6.34 „ „	22.57 „ „	
Aug. . .	2.38 „ „	6.30 „ „	20.38 „ „	
Sept. . .	2.50 „ „	6.90 „ „	16.95 „ „	
Oct. . . .	3.82 „ „	6.90 „ „	17.14 „ „	
Nov. . .	3.82 „ „	6.97 „ „	23.37 „ „	
Dec. . . .	4.34 „ „	7.47 „ „	30.25 „ „	

MASSACHUSETTS SCALE.

	1777.	1778.	1779.	1780.
Jan. . . .	1.05 for 1	3.25 for 1	7.42 for 1	29.34 for 1
Feb. . . .	1.07 „ „	3.50 „ „	8.68 „ „	33.22 „ „
March .	1.09 „ „	3.75 „ „	10.00 „ „	37.36 „ „
April . .	1.12 „ „	4.00 „ „	11.04 „ „	40.00 „ „
May . . .	1.15 „ „	4.00 „ „	11.25 „ „	
June . .	1.20 „ „	4.00 „ „	13.42 „ „	
July . . .	1.25 „ „	4.25 „ „	14.77 „ „	
Aug. . .	1.50 „ „	4.50 „ „	16.30 „ „	
Sept. . .	1.75 „ „	4.75 „ „	18.00 „ „	
Oct. . . .	2.75 „ „	5.00 „ „	20.00 „ „	
Nov. . .	3.00 „ „	5.43 „ „	23.08 „ „	
Dec. . . .	3.10 „ „	6.34 „ „	25.93 „ „	

From April 1, 1780, the depreciation was so rapid that it was rated more frequently than once a month. Thus:—

April 25	$42.00	June 10	$64.00
„ 30	44.00	„ 15	68.00
May 5	46.00	„ 20	69.00
„ 10	47.00	Aug. 15	70.00
„ 15	49.00	Sept. 10	71.00
„ 20	54.00	Oct. 15	72.00
„ 27	60.00	Nov. 30	74.00
„ 30	62.00	Feb. 27, 1781	75.00

Felt's History, &c., pp. 186, 196; *Lincoln's Hist. of Worcester*, p. 125.

No. 5. — *Schools.*

The following historical sketch is extracted from the Report of the Committee of 1848–9, drawn up by Mr. Denny: —

When we compare our own advantages with the situation of our ancestors only three generations before us, in regard to education, although we may well feel grateful for our privileges, we shall find no great cause to boast of our improvement of them.

In examining the early records of Leicester, and especially the public documents connected with our Revolutionary history, emanating from our forefathers, — whose education, in many cases, was wholly obtained at the district schools in this town, — we cannot but be surprised at the general intelligence, and strength of intellect, developed there, and oftentimes combined with a highly cultivated mind and superior education.

If the community now improved the advantages which they enjoy, as our fathers did theirs, we could not fail of having some intellectual giants in these days.

As an evidence of their estimation of the importance of education, we find the first settlers in this town — after having, by great sacrifices, provided for the spiritual wants of themselves and their posterity by the erection of a meeting-house and the settlement of a minister — next turning their attention to the support of a schoolmaster to instruct in reading and writing, — the first and most important branches of education.

The first vote on record respecting schools, after the settlement of the town, was on the last day of the year 1731; about twelve years after the erection of their meeting-house, and ten years after the settlement of their minister. The record informs us that "it was voted to choose a committee of three to provide a schoolmaster; and that the said committee agree with a man to keep school for three months, and no longer; and that the school be kept in three parts of the town, so as may be most for the conveniency of the inhabitants' children going to school." The sum of £10. 10s. was raised for this purpose; equal to $8.75 lawful money.* Mr. John Lynd, jun., was the first teacher of a public school in this town.

When it is considered, that the population to be accommodated by this three months' schooling was scattered over a territory of sixty-four

* See Town Record, Book No. 1, p. 138.

square miles, — comprising the whole of the present limits of Leicester and Spencer, and a part of the towns of Paxton and Auburn, — the "conveniency of the inhabitants' children" could not have been very great.

The following year, no school was provided; and the town was presented before the Quarter Sessions for this neglect.

The succeeding winter, the town voted to raise just double the amount before appropriated, to pay the schoolmaster for his winter's services; and the selectmen were empowered to hire a schoolmaster. Nothing, however, was done by them until about a year afterwards; when Mr. John Lynd, jun., was again hired to keep a writing and reading school, at the house of Mr. Jonathan Sargent (then living opposite the Catholic Church), three months, at the rate of £4. 10s., or $3.75, per month; "and for so much more of the year as the town shall employ him, at the same lay."

The school was not, however, continued beyond the three months agreed upon: but, during the next winter, the same person was engaged, at about the same salary, to keep the school in three different places, one month in each place; with the understanding, that, "if the town employed him any more, they was to come on new tarms."

This nine months of schooling was all the privilege for a public education which the town enjoyed for the seventeen years of its settlement previous to 1736; for, although the town was laid out in 1714, it was not much settled until five years afterwards.

In 1736, we find an article in the warrant to see what the town will do about a schoolmaster; and another, "to see if the town will build a schoolhouse, and appoint a place to put it."

In the transactions of the town at their next meeting, we find that they "voted to build a schoolhouse, 16 feet in width, 20 feet in length, and 6½ feet between joynts; and that it be set the north side of the Meeting-house, about ten rods, in the most convenantest place."

The location of this building, where the young ideas of many of our venerable forefathers were first taught to shoot, must have been a little north-west of the spot where the present Town Hall now stands;* and

---

* There is reason to believe that this schoolhouse was not placed where the town located it, or that it was afterwards moved; as the venerable Mrs. Hannah Phippin — now living, at the age of eighty-eight, in Westminster, Vt. — says, in a recent letter to her nephew (Judge Washburn), she remembers that it was "an old shell of a building," and stood on the corner of the Common, a little east of the Meeting-house, on the north side of the Country Road.

The next schoolhouse in this district was opposite the house of Edward Rawson

the wonder is, how their ideas could shoot so high as they did, when confined within the walls of a building only six and a half feet between joints.

In looking back to this model schoolhouse, — erected before the community was blessed with such a multiplicity of lectures upon ventilation, and the thousand other topics of the day we live in, — and comparing the size and height of that structure with some of the buildings erected in modern times for a similar use, we have no great cause to boast of our improvement in this respect.

During this year, the town was again presented for want of a schoolmaster; but, when we compare the amount of money required to be raised at that time with the very limited means of the population, we may well charge their neglect in this matter rather to their destitution than to their want of interest in the subject of education.

They raised, during the following winter, nine pounds, to pay Mr. Joshua Nichols for keeping a school in two different places, for one month each: but, for some cause, the selectmen did not see fit to employ him for more than one month in all; perhaps owing, in part, to their having to pay the sum of £4. 12s. for expenses incurred at the Quarter Sessions for want of a schoolmaster the previous year.

The year 1737 brought with it, to the inhabitants of this town, an uncommon amount of taxes; partly on account of having built galleries and made general repairs on their Meeting-house, and settled a new minister, the year previous. It was probably on this account that the schoolhouse was not built this year, as was contemplated.

The sum of eighteen pounds was voted to pay a schoolmaster; but only a part of it was expended. The matter being left to the selectmen, a master was engaged. But it appears that, after about six weeks, the school was discontinued: as we find, among the expenses of the town, five pounds paid to John Lynde, jun., for schooling one month; and £2. 11s. 8d. allowed to Joshua Nichols "for keeping school ten days, and for answering as schoolmaster the last summer."

So it appears, that, by voting to have the school kept at the house of Joshua Nichols, they contrived to have a nominal schoolmaster a part of the time, to satisfy the law, and keep clear of the Quarter Sessions.

Esq., on the spot where the brick card factory now stands, belonging to the estate of the late Col. Joseph D. Sargent.

The third was built about two rods west of the present dwelling-house of Cheney Hatch, Esq.; and was demolished in 1828, when the present building was erected on the the Clappville Road.

It is probable that the schoolhouse was built during the summer of 1738, as the last we hear about providing a place for the school was for the previous winter. When the town first voted the money to build this house, they raised only forty pounds, with the proviso, that, "if there be an overplus, it was to lay in the treasury, and be disposed of by the town."

We find, by the account of the treasurer afterwards, that the whole cost of the building was nearly fifty per cent more than had been anticipated, or £57. 8s. 2d., old tenor; equal to $47.84. During that year, they had about three months' schooling.

As soon as the new schoolhouse was erected, we find the town providing with greater liberality for the education of their children, not only in reading and writing, but also in some of the higher branches.

In 1739, Mr. Samuel Coolidge was paid thirty-eight pounds for teaching a grammar school six months. This sum, although an advance upon former wages of school-teachers, was only $1.32 per week; but, as the town provided board in addition, it might be considered a fair compensation, when a laboring-man was allowed thirty-three cents per day for himself, and half that sum for a yoke of oxen, on the highway. The salary of their minister, at this time, was £150 (old tenor), or $125.

For a few years previous to this time, the population had increased very much; and the portion of the town which is now Spencer had been settled by a large number of families, who were beginning to feel dissatisfied with paying taxes for the support of the ministry and school, which were of comparatively little advantage to them. In 1741, an article was inserted in the warrant, "to see if the town will allow the school to be moved from place to place, as may be thought proper;" and another, "to see if the town will excuse those persons who are settled in that part of the said town, called the proprietors' part, from being taxed, for the future, to the minister and school in said town."

The town voted to remove the school from place to place, "as shall be thought proper by the selectmen;" but not to release any portion of the inhabitants from their taxes.

The school was not, however, removed this year; and the same request was made in the spring of 1742; and the town voted to remove the school into the four quarters of the town, "so as to have the remote ends of the town have some benefit of the same;" and the selectmen hired Mr. John Gibbons for eighty-nine pounds to keep school through the whole year.

In 1743, the town voted to keep the school in six places in the town, — two months in a place; and raised one hundred pounds, old tenor, for the purpose.

In that and the following year, Mr. Adam Bullard was employed as teacher; and, for the last three months, his salary was £18. 10s. (old tenor), "and the keeping his horse in the bargain."

From this time onward, for the next twenty years, no great change was made in the schools in this town. Each year, about the same amount of schooling was enjoyed; and the schools were moved into different parts of the town to accommodate all its inhabitants. The average amount expended yearly was about forty pounds (lawful money), or $133.33. After the district of Spencer was set off in 1753, about the same amount was expended as before; and, of course, the remaining inhabitants had a better opportunity.

About ten years before the commencement of the Revolutionary War, quite a revolution took place in the school system here. A committee, chosen by the town in March, 1765, reported in favor of dividing the town into school districts; and each district, or "quarter," was to build their own schoolhouse.

There was, however, found to be difficulty in some of the districts about locating their schoolhouses; and, at the town-meeting in the fall of the same year, the whole subject was again brought up, and a different arrangement was made. The town voted to raise £120 to build five schoolhouses, to be located in the East, South-east, West, North-west, and North-east Districts.

In the East, South-east, and West Districts, the inhabitants were divided as to the location of the building; and the town chose a committee of three men, who were not residents in the district, to locate each of these schoolhouses, in case the inhabitants of the district did not generally agree among themselves. They also voted that the money assessed in each district should be expended on the schoolhouse in that district; thus throwing the expense of building upon the districts, as at first, but taking the management into the hands of the town.

A committee was then chosen in each district to estimate the cost of their building, and receive subscriptions — either in money, materials, or labor — for each man's assessment, to be provided, under the direction of the committee, at a stated time; and all the schoolhouses were to be completed by the first day of October, 1767.

The Centre District was not included in this arrangement, as they had already a schoolhouse belonging to the town within their limits. The town, however, at this time, chose a committee to sell this house to the best advantage.

At the next March meeting, it was voted that the assessments of all persons who had not furnished materials, &c., as proposed, be committed to the constable for collection in money, to be paid to the several districts where it belonged. So much dissatisfaction was manifested, in some of the districts, about the location of their schoolhouses, that they were not all completed until about five years after this plan was adopted.

In the year 1766, the first female teacher was employed in our public schools. In that year, the town appropriated seventy pounds, lawful money, for schools; and voted to have eighteen months' schooling in all, which was three months in each district. The selectmen were "desired to appropriate one-third part of this money in hiring schooling mistresses in each quarter;" and, if any of the districts were dissatisfied with this arrangement, they had the privilege of taking their portion in money.

In 1774, the town voted to accept the report of a committee, recommending a new schoolhouse in the South-west District; one, near Mr. Nathan Snow's, in the North District; and one, near Mr. Nathan Hersey's, in the West District: and, when these were completed, the town was in possession of nine schoolhouses; and no great change has been made in their location from that time to the present.

In 1776, a revision of the school districts was made, and the names of the several heads of families in each district recorded on the town-books.

For about fifteen years from this time, the town raised, annually, an amount about equal to $133 for the support of common schools; besides a donation of £500, in 1783, to the Academy.

In the year 1789, the town agreed to make a general and thorough reformation among the old schoolhouses; and raised the sum of £400, to be expended in building and repairing schoolhouses. Each district was to furnish their own funds, and to build a new house, or repair the old one, to the acceptance of a committee of eight persons, chosen by the town; and, if the districts neglected to do it, the committee were to do it for them.

Great opposition was manifested to this measure, and the town was much excited on the subject. For the next two years, they held frequent meetings; but at length all things settled down quietly. It was about this time that the schoolhouses in the South and Centre Districts were built; both of which are now demolished, and others built in their stead.

At this time, the Academy was struggling for existence, and was at times forced to give up its school for want of funds. The town, feeling deeply interested in its success, generously appropriated fifty pounds for the support of a preceptor in 1789; which, with many individual donations from the inhabitants of this and other places, enabled it to survive these early struggles; and it has since continued to flourish, with increasing popularity, until the present time, — a blessing, not only to our youth, but to thousands from every portion of our country.

In 1794, the town sold at auction, to Pliny Earle, twenty acres of land adjoining the farm of Capt. Daniel Kent, and known by the name of the School Lot; which was laid out by the original proprietors of the town, as required by their charter, for the benefit of schools; and had been kept by the town about seventy-five years.

It is unnecessary to follow up the particular history of our schools through the last fifty years, as many of those now present have taken an active part in their management; and others, who are younger, have received much of their education in them during that time.

Suffice it to say, that the town has continued to raise its annual appropriation, and increased it from year to year, as its population and wealth have increased, until the present time; and it is much to the credit of this community, that ever since the erection of the first schoolhouse, one hundred and ten years ago, it has never, for a single year, neglected this duty.

Even during the Revolutionary struggle, — when the currency, at one time, was so much depreciated in value, that it required an appropriation of £1,710 (Continental money) to support the schools for one year, the nominal value of which was $5,700, — the schools were continued as usual.

During the last year, in addition to the fifteen hundred dollars raised by the town, the amount paid for tuition by its citizens, at the Academy, was $560.54; which, with the amount received from the School Fund of the State, makes a total of about $2,140 expended for education.

In thus reviewing the past history of our schools, the reflection is forced upon our minds, that, with the improvements of modern times, many of the good old fashions of former days are passing away. All changes are not improvements, and all improvements are not without their evils.

In the current which is sweeping down with resistless force into the sea of oblivion the manners and customs, the habits and practices, of our early fathers, we have reason to fear, that, amidst the rubbish and useless things which give way for real improvements, some of their more solid and valuable qualities have been succeeded by modern experiments of doubtful value. The alterations in our schoolhouses, by adding somewhat to their height, so that they measure a few more inches "between joynts," and the substitution of stoves for the old-fashioned fireplaces, and a few other changes in the construction of our buildings, may be considered improvements. But even these improvements are not unmixed with evils. We do not now see how we could live comfortably, or even afford to live at all, if the old, wide-mouthed schoolhouse chimney was consuming its half a cord of wood per day; but then it was not so much of an evil, when wood was contributed freely and without measure by the farmers in the district, and was chopped by the schoolboys at noontime, instead of wrestling, for exercise. With such a ventilator to our schoolrooms, we need not understand any thing about oxygen or nitrogen; and the ruddy cheeks and bright countenances of the young, in those days, would compare favorably with the pale faces of our school-children, who are compelled to breathe the close and unwholesome air of some of our schoolrooms for six hours in the day, through one-half the days of their childhood. But we trust this evil will be temporary, and that our schoolrooms will soon be ventilated as well as warmed.

In the cultivation of the manners of our youth, in the present day, the field seems to have been entirely changed from the schoolroom to the ballroom; and, in outward appearances at least, a stranger would not notice a great increase of politeness, in these days, over olden times. There are even now some old-fashioned people, who would rather see the respect and deference which was once paid to the committee-man or the minister, — when, on entering and leaving the village school, there was a voluntary uprising of its members; or the respectful bow and courtesy of the school-children in the street, while passing their superiors in age, — than to see the whole subject of the cultivation of the manners of our youth banished from the school-room.

The improvements in school-books is another invention of modern times, not unmixed with evil. Though it might have been some objection to the good old days of "Dilworth's Spelling-book" and the "Only Sure Guide to the English Tongue," that the scholar would, after a while, get them all by heart; yet this objection would at length be removed by their advancement to a higher class in the "Understanding Reader," and then to the "Scott's Lessons;" which, to be sure, would sometimes be rather familiar before the large scholars became one and twenty. But even this objection is by some thought to be a less evil than the continual change which is going on in our schools, and the great inconvenience and expense to which parents are now subjected, by the variety of books in our different districts, and the introduction of new books in the various branches of education, before a single copy of the old ones has been worn out.

We would not be understood to condemn the practice of exchanging school-books, when evident improvements are made in them; but we do consider the great multiplication of these books, and the frequent changes made in our schools, to be productive of much evil as well as some good. At the present day, when so many school-books are urged by their respective authors upon teachers and school-committees, we think the good of the community would be promoted by great caution on their part, and a determination to make no changes without strong evidence that the public good requires it.

The present is truly an age of invention. While great improvements have been made in the mechanic arts by labor-saving machinery, and the intercourse among men has been increased, by more rapid and commodious modes of travel, a hundred-fold; and, in the conveyance of intelligence from one part of the world to another, distance has almost been annihilated by the magnetic telegraph, — the community are inclined to become restless under the old order of things, and desire to see the world making progress in every thing with railroad speed, if not with lightning velocity.

But, in the process of education, we have yet discovered no method so safe and sure to make ripe scholars and sound and sensible men and women as the good old way of hard study, close application, and patient drilling in the solid branches of education which are taught in our district schools. There has never yet been, and we have no reason to suppose there ever will be, discovered any royal road to learning.

JOHN NELSON,
MOSES HARRINGTON,
JOSEPH A. DENNY, } *School Committee.*

The following is a Statement of the Amount raised for Schooling: —

Year	Amount	Year	Amount	Year	Amount
1745 .	£100 old tenor.	1780 .	£1710 lawful money.	1815 . .	$600 federal money.
1746 . .	100 " "	1781 . .	40 silver money.	1816 . .	600 " "
1747 . .	120 " "	1782 . .	40 " "	1817 . .	600 " "
1748 . .	160 " "	1783 . .	40 " "	1818 . .	600 " "
1749 . .	200 " "	1784 . .	40 " "	1819 . .	600 " "
1750 . .	30 lawful money.	1785 . .	40 " "	1820 . .	600 " "
1751 . .	30 " "	1786 . .	40 " "	1821 . .	600 " "
1752 . .	35 " "	1787 . .	40 " "	1822 . .	600 " "
1753 . .	40 " "	1788 . .	40 " "	1823 . .	600 " "
1754 . .	40 " "	1789 . .	40 " "	1824 . .	600 " "
1755 . .	40 " "	1790 . .	40 " "	1825 . .	600 " "
1756 . .	28 " "	1791 . .	40 " "	1826 . .	600 " "
1757 . .	20 " "	1792 . .	60 " "	1827 . .	800 " "
1758 . .	35 " "	1793 . .	60 " "	1828 . .	800 " "
1759 . .	45 " "	1794 . .	60 " "	1829 . .	800 " "
1760 . .	40 " "	1795 . .	80 " "	1830 . .	800 " "
1761 . .	48 " "	1796 . .	80 " "	1831 . .	800 " "
1762 . .	50 " "	1797 . .	80 " "	1832 . .	800 " "
1763 . .	50 " "	1798 . .	$300 federal money.	1833 . .	800 " "
1764 . .	50 " "	1799 . .	300 " "	1834 . .	800 " "
1765 . .	70 " "	1800 . .	300 " "	1835 . .	1000 " "
1766 . .	70 " "	1801 . .	333.33 " "	1836 . .	1000 " "
1767 . .	70 " "	1802 . .	400 " "	1837 . .	1000 " "
1768 . .	50 " "	1803 . .	400 " "	1838 . .	1000 " "
1769 . .	70 " "	1804 . .	400 " "	1839 . .	1200 " "
1770 . .	70 " "	1805 . .	400 " "	1840 . .	1200 " "
1771 . .	70 " "	1806 . .	400 " "	1841 . .	1200 " "
1772 . .	70 " "	1807 . .	400 " "	1842 . .	1200 " "
1773 . .	70 " "	1808 . .	400 " "	1843 . .	1200 " "
1774 . .	70 " } for Schooling and support of Poor.	1809 . .	400 " "	1844 . .	1200 " "
1775 . .	70 "	1810 . .	400 " "	1845 . .	1200 " "
1776 . .	70 "	1811 . .	400 " "	1846 . .	1200 " "
1777 . .	90 "	1812 . .	400 " "	1847 . .	1200 " "
1778 . .	108 " "	1813 . .	600 " "	1848 . .	1500 " "
1779 . .	216 " "	1814 . .	600 " "	1849 . .	1500 " "

No. 6. — *Instructions, &c., of the Town.*

No. 1. Oct. 17, 1765. — At a meeting, regularly warned and assembled, of the inhabitants of the town of Leicester, and districts of Spencer and Paxton, — *Voted* to give instructions to their representative; and that Daniel Henshaw, Esq., Thomas Denny, and Jonathan Newhall of Leicester, Capt. Benjamin Johnson and Joshua Lamb of Spencer, Capt. Samuel Brown and Jonathan Knights of Paxton, be the committee to draw up the instructions. *Voted*, That the instructions drawn up by the committee be accepted and recorded; which are as follows: —

To Capt. JOHN BROWN, Representative for the Town of Leicester, and Districts of Spencer and Paxton.

SIR, — Your being chosen by the inhabitants of the aforesaid town and districts to represent them in General Assembly is a strong testimony of the confidence they place in your ability and integrity. By this choice, they have put you in power to act in their public concerns in general, as your own reason shall dictate. We, your constituents, now in general meeting assembled, notwithstanding, esteem it our right, and, at this critical juncture of time and affairs, our duty, to give you our instructions in some important matters which may come before you within the remaining part of the year. And, sir, we expect of you that you will, with decent firmness and unshaken resolution, use your power and influence to assert and maintain our natural rights, — our rights as Englishmen, which derive to us as subjects of Great Britain, and those granted to us by charter. You are sensible, sir, that this Province have been at a very great expense in carrying on the late war, which hath involved them in a very great burthen of debt, under which they are now laboring; and how exceeding difficult it is for your constituents to pay the part thereof that is annually assessed on them.

We expect, therefore, that you be very frugal in your grants of the government's money: and we must recommend to you the strictest care that the money be drawn out of the treasury according to the appropriation thereof by the General Assembly; and that, with the utmost firmness, you remonstrate against its being drawn out for any other end, as virtually taxing the people contrary to the Constitution, and subversive of one of their darling rights.

We cannot help reminding you of some recent as well as former instances hereof, which we esteem truly grievous; and as we are thus laboring under such a grievous burthen of debt, which we cheerfully brought on ourselves in largely contributing to the assistance of Great Britain, our mother-country, against her and our enemies, in the late war, — which, under the favorable smiles and directions of Heaven, made such glorious acquisition to her kingdom and revenue, —

It is, therefore, with inexpressible grief and concern we have had repeated taxes levied on us by the Parliament of Great Britain since the conclusion of the peace; more especially an act levying certain stamps and duties on the Colonies and Plantations in America. With great respect and deference to that august assembly, we cannot but think that the said act is contrary to the rights of mankind, and subversive of the English Constitution, and hath a direct tendency to bring us into a state of abject slavery and vassalage. We look on ourselves — though settled at a thousand leagues' distance from Great Britain, and subject to them in all constitutional measures — yet to be a part of the British Empire; that we have the same rights especially inherent in us with the inhabitants of the land; that our predecessors purchased their lands here of the natives, and settled themselves thereon, and maintained almost a continual war with the neighboring savages, without any charge to Great Britain: yet, notwithstanding, we have always looked on her interest ours, and have always cheerfully contributed to her assistance against her enemies, and are still willing to do it according to our ability. And, as we thus expect to bear part of the burthens with them, so we expect to share in the privileges which so happily adorn and distinguish the English Government.

We esteem it an essential privilege of Britons to be taxed by their own representatives; and as we understand it a maxim of the English Constitution, that no man can be separated from his property but by his own consent or fault, the same rights we claim and have internally enjoyed ever since the settling of this land. And now, sir, you are sensible that we had no voice in Parliament in making the Stamp Act, which levies such a heavy tax on us, and is especially burthensome on the widow and fatherless: yea, we understand we could not be heard by petition when said act was pending in Parliament, owing, as we apprehend, to some fault in our agency.

We not only complain of the unconstitutional manner of making said law, but the grievous burthen laid on us thereby; and, if it should be executed, will prove ruinous to us, and bring us into a state of beggary, and greatly detrimental, if not ruinous, to Great Britain. But, besides, what alarms us most of all is the unparalleled stretch given to admiralty jurisdiction; by which every man, at the option of a malicious informer, is liable to be carried a thousand miles before a Court of Admiralty, — from where he is known, and from all his friends, — and there tried without jury, and amerced by an arbitrary judge of that court, and taxed with cost, as he pleaseth; and, if the party have not wherewith to satisfy the same, to die in prison in an unknown land, without friends to bury him. This we apprehend to be truly deplorable, and directly repugnant to Magna Charta, by which no freeman shall be taken and imprisoned, or disseized of his freehold or liberties or free customs, nor passed upon nor condemned, but by the lawful judgment of his peers, or by the law of the land; and if the judge of said court should, either through weakness or wickedness, or wickedness of the informer or evidences, — who to him may be unknown, — condemn the innocent, there is no appeal but to the Parliament of Great Britain, which not one of your constituents will be able to prosecute.

Never was this country brought into such a strait before. Such is our loyalty to the king, — whom we revere next under God, — our veneration for the Parliament of Great Britain, whom we esteem as the most august assembly of men on earth, and to whose constitutional laws we owe all obedience; and it is contrary even to our desires to disobey either, but would sacrifice our lives and fortunes in their defence: yet such is our love to the English Constitution of government, — the best calculated on earth, both for the honor of the prince and the freedom and happiness of the subject, — in which, we apprehend, we have a right and share. The love we have to our fellow-subjects of Great Britain, the love and duty we owe to ourselves and posterity, yea, the first instinct in nature, — the great law of self-preservation, — all appear contrary to said act.

In this dilemma we are brought; and how to extricate ourselves we know not. To disobey any just and equitable law of Parliament, we have no inclination; to obey the law, we must sacrifice our liberty and every earthly thing that is dear to us, and bring ourselves and posterity into slavery and beggary, and open a door for vice and villany, and to be the final ruin of the whole English continent.

We lament the convulsions we are already thrown into, and we detest and abhor some late tumultuous ravages that have been committed, especially on the 26th of August last, wherein his Honor our Lieutenant-Governor suffered; which, we apprehend, was perpetrated by foreigners and ruffians taking occasion by the present commotions. As these, sir, are the present sentiments of said act, and the consequent of the execution, we must enjoin it upon you by no means to give your consent to any measures whatever that may imply our willingness to submit to it, or to be any ways aiding or assisting in putting the same in execution; but, in every proper measure, we expect you appear against it: and, as the stamp-officer in this as well as the neighboring governments have declined executing their respective offices, we recommend it to you to use your influence, that the business of the government be carried on as usual, until the resolution of Parliament upon our dutiful and humble petition be known.

Voted, That the following additional instructions be given to Capt. Brown; viz.: —

We cannot at this time help expressing our surprise, that his Excellency the Governor, in his speech to the General Assembly on the twenty-fifth day of September last, should intimate as though the Province was concerned in the late tumults at Boston, and thereby represent us an undutiful and disloyal people. We take it exceeding hard that such intimations should come from that chair; which may have a tendency to set us in a bad and false light at home.

We expect, therefore, that you take all proper measures to set our innocency in a proper and clear light, and the abhorrence we have of such outrages, when not one-thousandth part of the Province knew any thing of it: and, as we have an abhorrence of such outrages, so we expect that you by no means consent to have the damages to the sufferers made up to them out of the public treasury, but that you use your influence to the contrary, lest it become a bad precedent, and prove an encouragement to such riotous practices for the future; and we think, though recommended as a piece of justice, yet cannot be done by the government on any other footing but as a deed of mercy; which, if the perpetrators are not able, might more properly be recommended to those who are able by contribution.

No. 2. Sept. 19, 1768.—The town of Leicester in town-meeting assembled Sept. 19, 1768, in consequence of the alarming crisis of affairs; and on motion from the town of Boston, after choosing Capt. Brown, moderator, entered into the following resolves:—

Principally, and first of all, *Resolved*, That his most gracious Majesty King George the Third is our most rightful liege lord and sovereign, to whom we owe all obedience as our king; and that, with our lives and fortunes, we will defend him and the Protestant succession in his royal house, which we heartily wish may last as long as the sun and moon endure, and for which we will not cease to offer up our hearty prayers to Almighty God, and that he would bring to nought and confusion all his majesty's secret as well as more open enemies.

Resolved, That we esteem the English Constitution of government well calculated both for the dignity of the king and the freedom of the subject, as founded in nature, and asserted in the great charter of England called Magna Charta, in the Bill of Rights, and other charters of royal authority.

Resolved, That we esteem rights belong to us as free-born subjects of his royal Majesty the King of Great Britain.

Resolved, That we will at all times grant such aid to his Majesty, even to the sacrificing of our lives, as the necessity of the case may require.

Resolved, That it is far from our desire to object against any act of Parliament but such as infringe upon our rights.

Resolved, That we look upon the late dissolution of the General Court of the Province, and the delaying to call another, as a real grievance; as they are the assembly of the estates of the Province, and guardians of the people's rights, to whom we might apply, and on whom we might depend, for redress of all wrongs here, and to consult measures to avoid difficulties that might be coming upon us from abroad.

Being deprived of such a court, — so especial in our Constitution, — on a motion made from the town of Boston to hold a convention at Boston on the 22d current, —

Voted, That we will choose a man to go to Boston, to join those that may meet there at the time aforesaid, to consult such measures (without any authority) as may come before them.

Then, by vote, chose Capt. John Brown for the purpose aforesaid.

Then voted to give instructions to Capt. Brown to give his advice and use his influence that all rash measures be prevented, and every mild one may be adopted that may be consistent with Englishmen claiming their rights.

DANIEL HENSHAW, *Moderator*.

No. 3. Jan. 4, 1773. — On the second article — a letter from the town of Boston, and a pamphlet, wherein the rights of the colonists, and the infringements thereof, are set forth — being read, —

Voted, That the rights, as there stated, do belong to the inhabitants of this Province.

Voted, That they will choose a committee of nine persons to take the matter into consideration, and report, as soon as may be, what they think proper for this town to do thereon.

Then voted Capt. Brown, of Leicester; Capt. Witt and Capt. Brown, of Paxton; Mr. Moses Livermore and Joshua Lamb, of Spencer; William Henshaw and Hezekiah Ward, of Leicester; and Willard Mower, of Paxton, — be the committee for the above purpose.

The committee, as appointed on the second article, reported several resolves, and instructions to the representative; which, after several amendments, were accepted unanimously; and are as follows: —

1st, *Resolved*, That we do bear true allegiance to our rightful sovereign King George the Third, of Great Britain, &c.; and are, and always have been, ready to hazard our lives in defence of his person, crown, and dignity.

2d, *Resolved*, That we have a right to all the liberties and privileges of subjects born within the realm of England; and that we esteem and prize them so highly, that we think it our duty to risk our lives and fortunes in defence thereof.

3d, *Resolved*, That the Parliament of Great Britain has enacted laws subversive of our rights and privileges, in a particular manner, in raising a revenue in the Colonies, without their consent; thereby depriving us of that right of keeping our own money until we think fit personally, or by our representative, to dispose of the whole, or any part thereof.

4th, *Resolved*, That neither the British Parliament, nor any other power on earth, has a right to dispose of one farthing of our money, or any of our property, without our consent in person or by our representative.

5th, *Resolved*, That the carrying any person or persons out of this Province, beyond the seas or elsewhere, for any supposed or real crime committed here, is against Magna Charta, and unconstitutional.

To Mr. Thomas Denny, Representative of the Town of Leicester, and the Districts of Spencer and Paxton.

We, the freeholders and other inhabitants of the town and districts aforesaid, legally assembled in town-meeting, after having taken into serious consideration the almost insupportable hardships this people have been long laboring under by a constant and uniform plan of oppression, — whereby many of our natural and constitutional rights are wrested from us, — think it our duty to communicate to you our sentiments thereon, not doubting but you will heartily concur with us therein.

It is needless, at this time, to recapitulate all our rights, and the infringements thereof, seeing they are so fairly set forth by the inhabitants of the town of Boston; to whom we return our sincere thanks for the care they have ever shown of preserving our rights and privileges, of which their late circular-letter is a recent instance.

When we consider that our property is taken from us by the

British Parliament without our consent, our Governor rendered independent of the grants of the General Assembly of this Province, and the Judges of the Superior Court made wholly dependent on the crown for their support (whereas they ought to be as independent as possible of prince and people, in order to an impartial administration of justice), what have we not to fear? The evils arising from this last innovation are so plain and obvious, even to a common capacity, that we shall forbear dwelling upon them, and only give you the opinion of a patriotic writer: "What must be our chance, when the laws of life and death are to be spoken by judges totally dependent on the crown; sent, perhaps, from Great Britain; filled with British prejudices, and backed by a standing army?" And again: "If we reflect that the judges of these courts are to be during pleasure; that they are to have adequate provision made for them, which is to continue during their complaisant behavior; and that they may be strangers to these Colonies, — what an engine of oppression may this authority be in such hands!"

It has been said in behalf of the judges of the Superior Court, that the annual grants made them have not been adequate to their services, and the expenses attending them.

We are of the same opinion; and, as their time is mostly spent in the service of this Province, they ought to receive therefrom an honorable support during their good behavior.

These, sir, are a few of the many grievances we complain of; and, as you are sufficiently acquainted with the rest, we need not enumerate them. We think it advisable, and would have you use your interest, that the Honorable House of Representatives send a dutiful and loyal petition to the King, and a remonstrance to the Commons, of Great Britain; hoping they may succeed, as the Earl of Hillsborough is removed from his office, and succeeded by a nobleman who has hitherto appeared friendly to the rights of the Colonies.* We would also recommend to you to promote, as far as in you lies, an intercourse with the sister Colonies on this continent on these matters, as we are all embarked in one common cause, that the joint wisdom of the whole be exerted in removing the grievances so justly complained of.

In fine, when we reflect on the toils our forefathers underwent in the settlement of this country, the dangers to which they stood continually exposed from an insidious and bloodthirsty enemy, and the blood and

---

* Lord Dartmouth.

treasures they expended, we think ourselves justly entitled to all the calamities an envious despot can heap upon us, should we tamely and pusillanimously suffer the execution of them. It would be despising the bounties of our Creator, an infamous prostitution of ourselves, and a total disregard of posterity.

Thus we have briefly given you our sentiments, and trust you will use your utmost efforts for a speedy redress of our grievances; and may the Almighty crown them with abundant success!

No. 4. May 19, 1773. — At a meeting of the inhabitants of Leicester, and the districts of Spencer and Paxton, made choice of Mr. Thomas Denny to represent them in the Great and General Court the year ensuing, and gave him the following instructions: —

Mr. Thomas Denny.

Sir, — You have, for several years past, successively received the almost unanimous voice of us, your constituents, to represent us in the Great and General Court, or Assembly, of this Province. And it is because we have found you faithful in our service, willing to receive our instructions, and gladly to execute our commands, that we have now given you a fresh testimony of the confidence we repose in you by once more electing you our representative; whereby we have intrusted you with the preservation of all our rights and privileges, which we hold as dear as our lives.

As we have lately given you instructions on many points, it is needless to repeat them; and shall only remind you of a few things which now occur to our minds.

The choosing a Standing Committee of Correspondence and Inquiry, agreeable to the request of the worthy and respectable House of Burgesses of Virginia, we think highly commendable; and desire that you use your interest therefor in the General Assembly, hoping the example will be followed by all the other Assemblies on the continent; well knowing, that, by a firm union alone, we shall be able to render abortive the machinations of our enemies, and establish our liberties on a solid foundation.

And, as we have the highest regard for (so as even to revere the name of) liberty, we cannot behold but with the greatest abhorrence any of our fellow-creatures in a state of slavery.

Therefore we strictly enjoin you to use your utmost influence that a stop may be put to the slave-trade by the inhabitants of this Province; which, we apprehend, may be effected by one of these two ways: either by laying a heavy duty on every negro imported or brought from Africa or elsewhere into this Province; or by making a law, that every negro brought or imported as aforesaid should be a free man or woman as soon as they come within the jurisdiction of it; and that every negro child that shall be born in said government after the enacting such law should be free at the same age that the children of white people are; and, from the time of their birth till they are capable of earning their living, to be maintained by the town in which they are born, or at the expense of the Province, as shall appear most reasonable.

Thus, by enacting such a law, in process of time will the blacks become free; or, if the Honorable House of Representatives shall think of a more eligible method, we shall be heartily glad of it. But whether you can justly take away or free a negro from his master, who fairly purchased him, and (although illegally; for such is the purchase of any person against their consent, unless it be for a capital offence) which the custom of this country has justified him in, we shall not determine; but hope that unerring Wisdom will direct you in this and all your other important undertakings.

No. 5. Dec. 27, 1773.— At a meeting of the town of Leicester, and the districts of Spencer and Paxton, legally convened at Leicester aforesaid on the twenty-seventh day of December, 1773, the following resolves were unanimously passed:—

1st, *Resolved*, That we bear a due allegiance to his Majesty King George the Third; and are ready at all times, at the hazard of our lives and interests, to defend his person, crown, and dignity.

2d, *Resolved*, That the inhabitants of this Province have, and ever had, the sole right of disposing of their persons and estates as they might think proper.

3d, *Resolved*, That the British Parliament, in an act passed soon after the repeal of the Stamp Act, claiming a right over the properties of his majesty's subjects in America, is a usurpation of authority to which no power on earth is entitled, and contrary to the fundamental principles of our happy Constitution.

4th, *Resolved*, That the laying a duty on any article imported into this Province from Great Britain is an exercise of that unjustly assumed prerogative, and loudly calls upon every friend to his country to oppose so destructive a measure; and that we will oppose to the utmost of our power, at the hazard of our lives and fortunes, any impositions unconstitutionally laid upon us.

5th, *Resolved*, That we will not use any tea in our families, or suffer any to be consumed therein, while loaded with a tribute contrary to our consent; and that whoever shall sell any of that destructive herb shall be deemed by us inimical to the rights of his country, as endeavoring to counteract the designs of those who are zealous for its true interests.

6th, *Resolved*, That we highly approve of the measures entered into by our brethren in Boston and the towns adjacent at their late meetings, and return them our hearty thanks for the firmness and intrepidity so conspicuous in them, when, despising the insolence of office, they discovered to the world a true sense of the blessings which our Constitution affords, and a noble resolution to defend them.

After which, it was *Voted*, That a committee of fourteen persons be appointed for the inspecting any teas that may be sold or consumed in the town and districts aforesaid, and report at the annual meeting in May the names of the persons so offending; and a committee was accordingly chosen.

Ordered, That the proceedings of this town be recorded by the town-clerk, and forwarded by the Committee of Correspondence to the committee in Boston.

No. 6. May 19, 1774. — At the adjournment of the annual May meeting, it was *Voted*, That the letter prepared by the Committee of Correspondence be forthwith transmitted by the clerk of this town to the town-clerk of Boston; and is as follows: —

LEICESTER, May 19, 1774.

GENTLEMEN, — Yours of the 12th instant has come safe to hand; which informs us of an act of the British Parliament for blocking up the harbor of Boston with a fleet of ships of war; prohibiting the entrance or exportation of any sort of merchandise, on penalty of forfeiture of such goods and vessels which carry the same, so long as said act shall continue, or, in other words, until the Province of Massachusetts Bay shall acknowledge the right of the British Parliament to tax them in all cases whatsoever; which, we hope, will never be complied with while there is an American living.

The act referred to we have seen, and think it the most arbitrary of any that has been passed since the Revolution, — an act replete with spite and malice, and vesting his majesty with a right to the soil of America; for if the said Parliament have power to invest his majesty with a right to dispose of private property, or can assign and appoint any particular quays or wharves for the landing or discharging, lading and shipping, of goods, as his majesty shall think proper, they may, with the same propriety, pass an act prohibiting any town or husbandman from sowing grain, mowing grass, and feeding his pastures, so long as his majesty thinks proper.

And the penalty is, that if any person offends in landing of goods or merchandise, or in the lading or putting them off at any other quay or wharf so appointed, they are to be forfeited, together with the ships, boats, cattle, and carriages which are used to convey the same. In like manner may they make a forfeiture of our houses, lands, cattle, &c., if we offer to improve them, without his majesty's special license.

We hope, gentlemen, you will not be intimidated by this arbitrary act, although your town may suffer greatly in its trade, and your poor — who maintained themselves by their daily labor — should be unemployed. We doubt not a kind Providence will find out a way for their support, and that the other Colonies will stand by you; and we hope there is no town in this Province will be so ungrateful as to forsake you.

The cause is interesting to all America; and all America must be convinced of this great truth, "By uniting, we shall stand."

We hope and believe that Great Britain will be soon convinced that the Americans can live as long without their trade as they can without ours.

You will see the instructions given to the representative of this town and districts, which will show the abhorrence they have of the forementioned act; and we believe they will give you all the support in their power.

We are, gentlemen, with esteem,

Your friends and fellow-countrymen,

WM. HENSHAW, per order.

No. 7. July 6, 1774. — At a town-meeting legally warned and assembled, —

Voted, That there be a committee appointed to draw up resolves, formed on the sentiments of the town and districts, on the present melancholy situation of this country; and that the following persons be a committee for that purpose: viz., Thomas Denny, Joseph Henshaw, and Joseph Allen, of Leicester; James Draper and Joseph Wilson, of Spencer; Oliver Witt and Ralph Earle, of Paxton.

Voted, That the report of the committee for draughting the resolves be accepted; which is as follows: —

At a meeting of the freeholders and other inhabitants of the town of Leicester and districts of Spencer and Paxton, on the sixth day of July, 1774, — not tumultuously, riotously, or seditiously, but soberly and seriously, as men, as freemen, and as Christians, — to take into our consideration the present distressed state of our affairs: the harbor of our metropolis blockaded with an armed force, whereby no trade or commerce is suffered to be carried on, and they, with us, prevented the common means of procuring support; great numbers in the town of Boston suffering by this means for their daily bread; our General Assembly dissolved for resolving upon a method to reconcile the difference between Great Britain and the Colonies, so earnestly desired by every good man.

We are threatened with acts of Parliament to overturn our Constitution, to destroy the Democratic part thereof, and to establish absolute monarchy, — which threatens tyranny, and the inhabitants of this Province with slavery. After seriously debating and considering the deplorable circumstances we are in, and threatened to be brought into, by an act of the British Parliament for blocking up the harbor of Boston, which is repugnant to every idea of justice; is putting themselves into a state of war with said town; depriving its inhabitants, with every other part of the Province who are inclined to use trade in said port, of those privileges, for the support and convenience of their families, which God and nature hath given them; and hath a direct tendency to alienate the affections of the people of this Province and the other Colonies on the continent from the mother-country, and to create discord and confusion: —

Under these embarrassments, we think it our duty to take into consideration the constitution of government we are under, and recognize those rights and privileges which we do or ought to enjoy, that posterity may know what our claims are, and to what struggles we are called in defence of them.

Our forefathers came into this land when it was a howling wilderness, inhabited only by savages, of whom they purchased the soil without the assistance of any other power or state. They took the King of Great

Britain, or whoever should be King of England, to be their king, under such limitations, restrictions, and regulations as by a charter, under the Great Seal granted by King Charles II., was stipulated and agreed; which charter, in the arbitrary reign of King James, was forcibly and wrongfully wrested from the Colony: and afterwards another was granted by King William and Queen Mary of glorious memory, which charter laid the foundation of the present constitution of government in this Province; wherein it is granted and confirmed under the Great Seal, that the King shall appoint the Governor, Lieutenant-Governor, and Secretary; and that there shall be held and kept by the Governor a General Court, or Assembly, on the last Wednesday of May, for ever; which General Court, or Assembly, shall consist of the Governor, Council, and such freeholders as shall be from time to time elected and deputed by the several towns in the Province; which Assembly shall choose twenty-eight councillors yearly, and every year for ever thereafter.

And it is further ordained by said Royal Charter, that the General Court shall have full power and authority to erect and constitute judicatories, and courts of records, to be held in the name of the king, for the hearing, trying, and determining all manner of crimes, offences, pleas, processes, plaints, actions, causes, and things whatsoever, arising or happening within the Province; and also with full power and authority, from time to time, to make, ordain, and establish all manner of wholesome and reasonable orders, laws, statutes, directions, and instructions, either with penalties or without (so as the same be not repugnant or contrary to the laws of the realm of England), as they shall judge to be for the good and welfare of the Province, and for the governing and ordering thereof, and of the people inhabiting or who may inhabit the same, and for the necessary support and government thereof.

And, further, it is granted and ordained, that the Great and General Court shall impose and levy proportionate rates and taxes upon the estates and persons of all and every of the inhabitants of the Province, to be issued and disposed of for the necessary defence and support of the government of the Province. And therein it is further ordained, that the Governor, with the advice and consent of the Council, shall from time to time appoint judges, sheriffs, justices of the peace, and other officers belonging to the King's Court. And further, that all and every of the subjects of the king, which go to inhabit said Province, or be born there, shall have and enjoy all the liberties and immunities of free and natural subjects, to all intents, constructions, and purposes whatsoever, as if they and every of them were born within the realm of England.

As the charter aforesaid is the basis of the civil constitution of government in this Province, we hold the same as sacred, and that no power on earth whatsoever hath right or authority to disannul or revoke said charter or any of it, or abridge the inhabitants of the Province of any of the powers, privileges, or immunities, therein stipulated or agreed to be holden by every person inhabiting said Province; and therefore we, the inhabitants of the town of Leicester and districts of Spencer and Paxton, in town-meeting assembled, do now, both in our corporate and separate capacities, claim, assert, and demand the said powers, privileges, and immunities as our indefeasible rights; and, therefore, —

Voted and Resolved, That any person, power, or state, that shall attempt or endeavor, by any means whatsoever, to destroy or nullify said charter, either in whole or in part, and, to effect such design, shall attempt to deprive the people of this Province, or any of them, of said powers and privileges stipulated and granted in the charter, is an enemy to the Province, and thereby puts him, her, or them, into a state of war with the Province and every inhabitant thereof; and ought to be so esteemed, and treated accordingly.

Voted and Resolved, That no power, state, or potentate, have right to make laws, orders, statutes, or ordinances, for the internal police of this his majesty's Province, but the Legislature established within the same, as set forth and ordained in the charter; or to repeal, nullify, or make void, any law or laws already made by the Legislature thereof (excepting the king, as stipulated in said charter, in a limited time), but the same Legislature which made them: and, therefore, any law made for that purpose by any other power, state, or potentate, is, *ipso facto*, null and void, and ought to be esteemed so by every inhabitant in the Province.

Resolved, That every court or judicatory set up for the hearing and determining of any crimes, offences, actions, causes, or things whatsoever, that may arise within this Province, other than such as have been or may be established by the charter or by the laws of the Province, is, in our opinion, unconstitutional and illegal; and every judgment, decree, or determination, entered up or made by such court, is void: and that the inhabitants of this Province ought not to submit to, or pay any regard to, such judgment or determination; and that every officer, endeavoring to put into execution any judgment or determination so entered up by such court, ought to be resisted by every inhabitant of the Province, and treated as a person endeavoring to subvert the Constitution of this Province, and the order of judicial proceedings therein established.

Resolved, That as the trial by juries is a grand barrier against arbitrary power, and is the right of every subject of the King of Great Britain (being granted by Magna Charta), which right belongs to the inhabitants of this Province; and that such jurors be appointed and chosen, summoned, and impanelled, according to the laws of this Province, and the usual custom and practice therein; and that a jury summoned, called, and impanelled by any other method, or by virtue of any other edict or law whatsoever, is illegal; and it is the duty of every person, who may be summoned as a juror by any other way than the laws of this Province, to refuse to obey such summons, or to refuse being impanelled. And, further,—

Resolved, That any verdict entered up by a jury summoned and impanelled in any other way than by the laws of this Province, and the ancient usage and custom of the executive courts, is, in our opinion, null and void.

Resolved, That we will, to the utmost of our power, maintain and support the king's authority in this Province, according to the charter aforesaid; and that we will to the utmost of our power, even to the risk of our lives and fortunes, support and maintain the execution of the laws of this Province, as established by the charter and the Legislature thereof.

Resolved, That all persons pretending to be officers, who were not appointed according to charter or the laws of this Province, have no right to exercise such office; and, therefore, any person pretending to officiate therein ought to be resisted.

Resolved, That we will not by ourselves, or any for, by, or under us, directly or indirectly, purchase any goods that may be imported from Great Britain after the thirty-first day of August next; and that we will break off all commercial connections with any merchant, trader, or factor, who shall import goods from Great Britain into this Province after said time; and that we will not purchase any goods of such trader who shall purchase such goods, or offer or expose them for sale, until the harbor of Boston be opened, and the tea-duty taken off, unless other measures for our redress be recommended by General Congress.

57

Resolved, That it is the duty of every person whatever, arrived to age of discretion, as much as may be consistent with their business and occupation for the support of their families, to associate together, and discourse and inform themselves of their rights and privileges as men, as members of society and the English Constitution; that they may not be imposed upon by those men who look upon them with envy, and are using every art to deprive the laborious part of mankind of the fruits of their own labor, and wish to live in luxury on that of others.

No. 8. Sept. 29, 1774. — At a meeting of the inhabitants of Leicester, and the districts of Spencer and Paxton, Mr. Thomas Denny was chosen to represent them in the Great and General Court to be convened at Salem, in the county of Essex, on the fifth day of October next.

Voted, That instructions be given to the representative, and that the following persons be a committee for draughting them; viz.: Capt. Joseph Henshaw, Capt. John Brown, Joseph Allen, Deacon Muzzy, Dr. Ormes, Phinehas Moore, and Capt. Willard Moore.

Voted, That the following instructions, after being read paragraph by paragraph, be given to the representative; viz.: —

To Mr. THOMAS DENNY.

SIR, — Your constituents cannot give you a greater testimony of their confidence in your integrity and resolution than by re-electing you their representative at the ensuing Great and General Court, or Assembly, to be convened at Salem on Wednesday, the fifth day of October next, — a time which requires the greatest prudence, on the one hand, to guard against any unavailing obstinacy; and, on the other hand, the utmost firmness to avoid falling into any supine acquiescence derogatory of the rights to which the inhabitants of this Province are justly entitled. They think proper to give you the following instructions; viz.: —

In the first place, — agreeable to the recommendation of the Worcester Convention, — we instruct and strictly enjoin you that you refuse to be sworn by any person except such as may be appointed agreeable to the charter of this Province; and likewise refuse to be sworn by the Lieutenant-Governor, who has taken the oaths as a councillor by mandamus from the king.

2. That you by no means act in conjunction with the Council ap-

pointed by mandamus from the king, or such of the councillors elected in May last who have since been sworn into said council.

3. That you absolutely refuse to be adjourned to Boston, while that town is garrisoned with troops and surrounded with ships of war; and, should any thing impede your acting as a House at Salem, that you immediately repair to Concord, and join the Provincial Congress to be convened at said place on the second Tuesday in October next, and there to observe the instructions which may be given by us, from time to time, for the rule of your conduct in that assembly.

We would recommend that you join with those members which may be present at Salem in a body, to consult and determine upon some proper plan of conduct, before you offer yourself to be sworn; that so every member may regulate his behavior accordingly.

No. 9. Oct. 10, 1774. — At a meeting of the town of Leicester, and the districts of Spencer and Paxton, —

Voted, That Mr. Thomas Denny be the only person to represent this town at the ensuing Provincial Convention to be holden at Concord.

The following instructions, drawn up by the committee chosen on the 29th September last, were separately read, and accepted by said town and districts: —

To Col. THOMAS DENNY.

SIR, — You are delegated by the town of Leicester, and districts of Spencer and Paxton, to represent them at the ensuing General Convention, — an assembly in which, at this dark and difficult day, perhaps the most important business will come before you that was ever transacted since the settlement of North America. No period since the Revolution has worn a more gloomy and alarming aspect.

A series of occurrences and events afford great reason to believe that a deep and desperate plan of despotism has been laid for the extinction of civil liberty, and which threatens universal havoc. Every thing now conspires to prompt the full exertion of true policy, valor, and intrepidity. The choice your constituents have made in this day of trial, as it manifests their affection and confidence, so they doubt not it will excite your warmest attachment and closest attention to the common cause; and therefore communicate their sentiments to you in a few following particulars: —

1st, That you keep those invaluable rights and liberties, which have been handed down to us by our ancestors, ever near your heart. Charters have become bubbles, — empty shadows, without any certain stability or security: therefore we instruct that you oppose any motions which may be made for patching up that under King William and Queen Mary. As the British Parliament have, by some late edicts, declared the most essential parts thereof null and void, and are, *vi et armis*, forcing their decrees, it behooves us to stand on the defensive: and as we are without form, and void, and darkness seems to cover the face of the land, we direct that your influence be employed, in the first place, towards establishing some form of government, courts of judicature, &c., as may be best adapted to our present circumstances; remembering, in this and every other transaction, to keep close to the advice you may, from time to time, receive from the Continental Congress, and avoid every act which may militate with their general plan.

2d, That you endeavor to have the militia of the Province put on the most respectable footing, and that every town be supplied with one or more field-pieces, properly mounted, and furnished with ammunition. A militia, composed of the yeomanry and proprietors of the country, is its surest defence: therefore we esteem it a matter of the last necessity that they be properly disciplined, and taught the art of war, with all expedition, as we know not how soon we may be called to action.

3d, As we esteem the Province treasury to be unsafe in the town of Boston while in its present disordered state, we instruct that you endeavor for its removal to some place of safety remote from the capital; and that the treasurer be directed to exhibit his accounts of the treasury to be audited, and, in case of deficiency, that sufficient security be obtained therefor.

4th, That you inquire by what authority the Lieutenant-General has taken possession of the Common-land within the limits of Boston, — being the property of that town, — and require the intrenchments there made to be demolished, and the fortification at the entrance of the town to be dismantled. Also by what authority the powder in the Arsenal at Charlestown was removed, the carriages belonging to the train of artillery in Boston seized and detained, with many other acts of rapine and violence, which it is probable may be laid before you; and make restitution therefor.

5th, That you cause a just estimate to be made of the daily loss accruing to the town of Boston and the Province from the stoppage of their trade, prohibition of water-carriage, and all other loss and damage of every kind, resulting in consequence of the operation of an act of the British Parliament for blockading the harbor of Boston, and one other act for subverting the civil government of this Province.

6th, That you use all suitable means to encourage arts and manufactures among us by granting premiums, or any other ways which may be most conducive to this end, — one of which, we apprehend, to be by devising some effectual method for the strict and religious observance of the non-consumption agreement so generally entered into through this Province; and also by promoting the continental plan for the entire prevention of all imports and exports to and from Great Britain, and, should it be judged necessary, the English West-India Islands.

7th, That you promote a friendly and intimate correspondence with our sister Colonies of Canada, Nova Scotia, &c.; that so the whole continent of North America, as they have one common cause and interest, may thereby unite in the same measures. We are not in doubt, at this day, how essential a point our enemies esteem it to divide us, that we may fall an easy prey; and surely our solicitude for a strict union ought to be proportionate to their opposition, especially when we consider how difficult large bodies are brought to unite in one and the same sentiments, while our enemies, with a single *fiat*, are ready with their whole force to rush upon us.

8th, That those contumacious persons, who, in defiance of the groans and entreaties of their fellow-countrymen, have obstinately persisted in their resolutions to endeavor, so far as in them lay, the destruction of that civil government under which they have been protected (and many of whom have been cherished and grown wanton with its smiles), by being sworn and acting as councillors by mandamus from the king, in direct violation of the charter, together with such others who have proved themselves notoriously inimical to their country, be apprehended, and secured for trial.

9th, That, as amidst all the trouble and difficulties from the hands of wicked men under which we groan, we have experienced many and great favors from the hand of God, in the course of the year past, by discovering the machinations of our enemies, whereby we have in some measure frustrated their designs; by permitting no epidemical disease to pass through the land; by giving a suitable seedtime, a plenteous harvest, and crowning the year with His goodness.

These and many other instances of the divine favor demand our most grateful recognition; and we should be still more unworthy of them, should we, by too close an attachment to our present difficulties, neglect to offer our tribute of praise and thanksgiving therefor to that Being from whom alone must come all our help. We instruct that you endeavor that a day may be set apart for this religious purpose.

10th, There is no doubt but many other matters than what are above enumerated will come under your consideration. As they do not at present occur, we must leave them to your judgment.

Confiding in your prudence and unshaken resolution, we commend you, and the concerns you are intrusted with, to the divine protection and blessing.

No. 10. Jan. 9, 1775. — At a meeting of the town and districts aforesaid, *Voted*, That Joseph Allen, Capt. Washburn, Deacon Muzzy, Dr. Frink, and Capt. Samuel Green, be a committee to draw instructions for the member chosen.

Voted, That the instructions be accepted; which are as follows: —

To Col. JOSEPH HENSHAW.

SIR, — You are delegated this day, by the town of Leicester and district of Spencer, to represent them at the ensuing Provincial Congress. The distress of the country, arising from the ruinous system of Colony administration adopted ten or twelve years past, has got to that height as will require the whole united wisdom and firmness of the Congress to remove.

We, your constituents, instruct and require that you promote with all your influence any plan for the common good which may be generally adopted by the Congress; and, considering the present situation of the Province, — its defenceless, loose, disjointed state, and the apparent danger of its sinking into anarchy and confusion, — do particularly instruct that you urge an immediate assumption of government, as the only means by which we may be reduced to order, and the laws of the Province have their usual and uninterrupted course; remembering in this to keep as near the charter as the perplexed state of the Province will admit, and to have the measures of the American Congress in constant view, so that both may co-operate for the general good.

Particular matters will no doubt turn up in the course of the session, which as we, your constituents, are not now apprised of, so cannot particularly instruct; but, confiding in your integrity and resolution, we commend you and the concerns you are intrusted with to the divine blessing.

No. 11. July 13, 1775. — At a meeting of the inhabitants of the town of Leicester, *Voted* to give instructions to their representative.

Voted, That Joseph Allen, William Green, Capt. Samuel Green, Joseph Henshaw, and Joseph Sargent, be a committee to frame the instructions.

Voted, That the following instructions be accepted: —

To Mr. HEZEKIAH WARD, Representative of the Town of Leicester.

SIR, — At this most critical and important period, on which are suspended the happiness or ruin of British America, you are called by the suffrages of your townsmen to represent them in the ensuing General Assembly of this Province.

To this important *now*, posterity will look back either with joy and admiration, secure in the possession of their inestimable liberties; or with the keenest sensations of grief, while they drag the galling chain of servitude.

Since the settlement of America, no period has been so replete with great and interesting events as the present; and it will require the utmost exertions of the human mind to counteract the designs of our enemies.

On these considerations, we think proper to give you the following instructions; viz.: —

1st, It is our will, and we do instruct you, that you govern yourself by resolves and orders of the Continental Congress in all matters for which that honorable body shall give directions.

2d, That, in the establishment of government, you use your influence, in the most open and unreserved manner, that such persons be excluded from any share therein who have shown themselves inimical to the rights of their country; and likewise those far more dangerous still, and more to be despised, who, waiting the tide of events, have, with a modesty peculiar to themselves, declined to support the just claims of their country in opposition to the tyrants who would enslave it: but that you exert your utmost abilities that such persons be appointed to offices of trust as have discovered themselves to be men of religion and virtue, and at the same time of penetration, genius, and knowledge; who have uniformly stood forth the resolute defenders of the rights of their country.

3d, That you view with a jealous yet candid eye the disposition and motions of the American Army; always remembering the importance of preserving the superiority of the civil power over that of the military; as an inattention to this might possibly involve us in still greater and more complicated calamities than we have yet experienced.

4th, That you endeavor, so far as in you lies, that the laws of this Province for suppressing vice and immoralities of all kinds be religiously put into execution, and that the hands of the civil officers be strengthened by all the aid and countenance that may be necessary to afford them.

5th, We instruct that you use your influence to obtain a just estimate of the loss and damage sustained by this Colony through the operation of several late acts of the British Parliament, from the commencement of the Boston Port Bill; that such estimate may remain on file, and, if no other compensation can be obtained, it may hereafter be brought into an average loss on the whole continent.

(There was a committee appointed by a late Congress for this purpose, which reported the loss until toward the close of the last year; which report was ordered to lie on the table. Should you obtain a vote to have this matter committed, that report may serve as a guide.)

6th, That, as in our opinion the Fee Bill is very unequal, we instruct that you use your endeavors that such fees as are too low may be raised, and those which are too high may be reduced.

As your proceedings will be generally under the direction of the American Congress, so we cannot be more particular in giving you instructions; but, praying for the favor of Heaven on the measures of the General Assembly, we commend you to the divine blessing.

No. 12. May 22, 1776. — At a meeting of the town of Leicester, *Voted*, That Col. Joseph Henshaw, Joseph Allen, Richard Southgate, Capt. Samuel Green, and Capt. Jonathan Newhall, be a committee to prepare instructions to their representative. The instructions are as follows: —

To Capt. SETH WASHBURN.

SIR, — The town of Leicester having made choice of you to represent it at the General Court the ensuing year (in the course of which, 'tis more than probable, the most resolute exertions of the court may be called forth to defend the Colony against the force of the British king and ministry), your constituents are of opinion that temporary appointments, sufficient for the peace, order, and defence of the Colony during the present contest, would have answered more valuable; as, should the Honorable Congress declare an independence on the kingdom of Great Britain, and form a system of government which may be adopted by the continent, some future court might be under the necessity of undoing most or all the last has done.

When measures are hastily adopted, and as often revoked, it discovers that stability to be wanting which alone can confer dignity or secure authority. Therefore your constituents, to prevent, as much as they may, such mistakes taking place again, instruct you that you pay the strictest attention to every question which may be agitated in the House, and digest it well in your own mind before you give your vote.

That you use your utmost endeavor to obtain a repeal of the act providing for more equal representation in the General Court.

Your constituents view this act as having a manifest tendency to create a jealousy and opposition between the trading and landed interest of the Colony, at a time when it is universally confessed that unanimity (under God) is what we must depend on for safety.

Your constituents flatter themselves, that the good people of the Colony will not generally increase their number of representatives; which would be, moreover, a great additional charge to that which is now and will be necessarily incurred for the defence of the Colony; and therefore the strictest economy, consistent with our safety, ought to be observed.

That you endeavor to have the form prescribed in the Test Act for subscription explained or altered. You are sensible, sir, what universal uneasiness the clause for complying with such requirements and directions of the laws of this Colony as now are, or may hereafter be, provided for the regulation of the militia, occasioned in your town.

Your constituents esteem it as unadvised and ill-timed. They know it of themselves, and think the same of others, that no people have paid a more strict or cheerful obedience to the laws of the land than the people of this Colony; and are truly sorry that the late court should, by the forementioned clause, discover a jealousy and distrust of their fidelity. Your constituents are willing to believe it was principally designed as a test for those, the general tenor of whose conduct denominated them Tories, or enemies to their country. Moreover, they view it as a precedent which may be attended with very pernicious consequences; and are of opinion, that the form in the Test Act, without the forementioned clause, would have answered all the ends and purposes of the test.

You are likewise instructed to bear your testimony against the same persons filling places of great importance in the legislative and executive departments, the incongruity of which needs no comment.

Your constituents understand from report, that the late court had in contemplation the stopping-up the harbor of Boston, by sinking hulks in the channel to prevent the enemies' ships passing to the town. Should such motion be acted on, you are instructed to oppose it. We can think of one case only, which, in our opinion, would justify the measure; viz., when there is *sudden* danger of a sudden attack, and no time to make a regular defence.

Stopping the harbor of Boston your constituents consider as an effectual method to ruin the trade, sink the value of estates, and depopulate the town, as if the enemy had reduced it to ashes before their departure; and, the town being depopulated, it is not material whether it was accomplished by fire or water. When trade has once forsook its old course, and forced a new channel, its recovery may be despaired of.

Therefore, considering the loss this Colony in particular has sustained by the loss of the trade of its capital, and the consequent reduction of estates, your constituents cannot consent that their representatives should be aiding in a measure, which, in our opinion, would further greatly injure that town, and the Colony in general.

As America is threatened, and we may soon expect a formidable force will be employed to accomplish our ruin, we are alarmed at the apprehensions, since the enemy have evacuated the metropolis and the Continental Army removed to the southward, that so few forces have been raised to secure and defend that important place; for, should the enemy return to repossess themselves of the town, its last state, in which the Colony is deeply involved, would be infinitely worse than the former.

Wherefore we strictly enjoin it on and instruct you, that you move for a re-enforcement of troops, to be immediately raised, sufficient to complete the fortifications and defend the town, should an attack be made thereon, till relief could be had from the standing militia of the Colony.

May 22, 1776. — At a meeting of the freeholders and other inhabitants of Leicester, duly warned, it was *Voted* by the inhabitants then present, *unanimously*, That, in case the Honorable the Continental Congress should declare these Colonies independent of Great Britain, they would support said Congress in effectuating such a measure, *at the risk of their lives and fortunes.*

A true entry. Attest,

JOS. ALLEN, *Town Clerk.*

No. 7. — *Town-Clerks, and Selectmen before* 1821.

1. TOWN-CLERKS.

Nathaniel Richardson, 1722.
John Potter, 1723.
Daniel Denny, 1724–1726.
Joshua Nichols, 1727–1732.
Josiah Converse, 1733–1736.
John Whittemore, 1737–1749.
John Whittemore, 1751–1761.
David Henshaw, 1750.
Thomas Steele, 1762–1769.
William Henshaw, 1770–1771 and 1773.
Thomas Denny, 1772.
Thomas Denny, 1784–1786.
Joseph Allen, 1774–1777.
John Southgate, 1778–1779.
John Lyon, 1780.
Hezekiah Ward, 1781–1783.
Austin Flint, 1786–1800.
Nathaniel P. Denny, 1801–1813.
John Wilder, 1814.
Joseph Denny, 1815.
Edward Flint, 1816–1825.
Emory Washburn, 1826.
Joseph A. Denny, 1827.
John Sargent, 1828–1849.
Joseph A. Denny, 1850–1860.

2. SELECTMEN.

Those marked with an asterisk (*) were at some time chairmen.

*Samuel Green, 1722–1724, 1727–1729, 1731.
*John Smith, 1722, 1724, 1726, 1729–1730.
*Nathaniel Richardson, 1722, 1724.
*John Lynde, 1722–1723, 1732, 1734–1736, 1742.
James Southgate, 1722–1726, 1734–1736, 1739.
*John Menzies, 1723–1724.
John Potter, 1723, 1727.
*Richard Southgate, 1725–1731, 1736.
Thomas Newhall, 1725–1726, 1731.
Benjamin Johnson, 1725, 1733, 1738–1739, 1743, 1749.
*Daniel Denny, 1725–1726, 1728–1731, 1734–1735, 1737–1739, 1741, 1743, 1748, 1750–1751, 1756.
Thomas Richardson, 1727–1731, 1735–1736, 1741.
Joshua Nichols, 1727, 1742, 1744.
James Wilson, 1730, 1746–1748, 1751.
William Brown, 1728, 1736.
John Saunderson, 1732, 1740.
*John Whittemore, 1732–1734, 1739, 1742–1745, 1747–1749, 1751.
*Josiah Converse, 1733–1735.
Nathaniel Green, 1737–1738, 1744.
Samuel Capen, 1737–1738.
*Benjamin Tucker, 1737–1739, 1742–1744, 1746–1751, 1758, 1760–1763.
Peter Sylvester, 1737.
*Christopher J. Lawton, 1740–1741.
Jonathan Witt, 1740.
Samuel Brown, 1740–1741.
Jonathan Sargent, 1740.
*Thomas Steele, 1741, 1752–1755, 1758–1759, 1761–1764, 1767–1768.
Luke Lincoln, 1742–1744, 1746–1747.
Samuel Garfield, 1745.
John Smith, jun., 1745.

Moses Smith, 1745, 1750, 1752–1753.
*Nathaniel Goodspeed, 1745–1748, 1755, 1758–1759, 1764–1766.
John Brown, 1746, 1749–1750, 1754, 1756–1757, 1759–1760, 1763, 1766.
Nathaniel Waite, 1749, 1752–1755, 1759.
*Daniel Henshaw, 1750–1751, 1755–1757, 1760–1762, 1764–1766.
Samuel Stower, 1752–1753.
William Green, jun., 1752–1754, 1763, 1766–1768, 1775–1777.
John Fletcher, 1754, 1767–1768.
Oliver Witt, 1755–1757, 1760–1762, 1764.
John Lynde, jun., 1756.
*Benjamin Earle, 1757.
*Jonathan Newhall, 1757–1759, 1761–1765, 1774.
*Thomas Denny, 1765–1766, 1769–1772.
John Dunbar, 1767.
*William Henshaw, 1767–1772, 1779, 1782, 1784–1786.
Ephraim Mower, 1768.
*Seth Washburn, 1769–1773, 1775, 1792.
*Samuel Denny, 1769, 1773, 1775–1777, 1779–1780, 1782–1786, 1787.
Robert Craig, 1769, 1771, 1775.
*Samuel Green, 1770, 1772, 1774, 1776–1777, 1780, 1782–1786, 1788–1792, 1794, 1796, 1798.
Nathan Sargent, 1770–1771.
Edward Bond, 1772.
James Baldwin, 1773–1775.
*Thomas Newhall, 1773, 1778–1781, 1783, 1785–1786, 1789–1792, 1797–1798.
Isaac Choate, 1774.
*Joseph Sargent, 1774, 1776, 1781–1784, 1787–1788.
*Hezekiah Ward, 1774, 1778–1779, 1781–1782, 1784.
William Watson, 1776, 1786–1788, 1790–1792, 1799, 1800–1801, 1803.
Loring Lincoln, 1777.
Joseph Allen, 1777.
*Henry King, 1778, 1791–1794, 1798.
John Southgate, 1778–1779, 1783, 1793.
James Baldwin, jun., 1778.
John Lyon, 1780.
Dr. Isaac Green, 1780.
Peter Taft, 1781.
Ebenezer Upham, 1781.
*Edward Rawson, 1784–1785, 1787–1790.
Jonathan Sargent, 1787–1788.
*David Henshaw, 1789, 1793–1796, 1798–1799, 1802, 1806–1807.
*Thomas Denny, 1789–1791, 1793–1794, 1796, 1799–1801, 1803, 1811–1812.
Timothy Sprague, 1793, 1795–1797, 1799–1801.
Knight Sprague, 1795, 1797.
Benjamin Watson, 1795.
Thomas Parker, 1795.
Richard Bond, 1796–1797.
Nathan Waite, 1797.
William Sprague, 1798.
Samuel Trask, 1799–1800.
*John Sargent, 1800–1806, 1811–1816, 1820.
*Austin Flint, 1801–1805, 1813–1820.
Joseph Washburn, 1802–1807.
John Hobart, 1802, 1809, 1810–1811, 1819.
*Samuel Waite, 1804–1810.
Andrew Scott, 1804–1805.
Daniel Hubard, 1806–1810.
Jonathan Earle, 1807–1808.
Darius Cutting, 1808–1810.
*Nathaniel P. Denny, 1808–1814.
Samuel D. Watson, 1812, 1815–1820.
Daniel McFarland, 1812–1813.
John King, 1813–1820.
Henry Sargent, 1814, 1817–1820.
Jonah Earle, 1815–1818.

No. 8. — *Location of Roads.*

I have selected a few of the roads early laid out, as the readiest way of presenting to the reader, whose curiosity may lead him to the inquiry, the condition at the time, and the geographical appearance, of the town, by the objects referred to in making these locations.

The earliest of these is the one leading north from the Meeting-house, laid out May 3, 1721. "Beginning from the Common-land, behind the Meeting-house, at a black-birch, striped, and standing by a great red oak; from thence straight down to a great black oak, standing a little from the swamp; from thence to a black oak in the swamp; from thence to a black oak by the side of the hill, two standing together; from thence to a double oak upon the rise of the hill; and from thence to an oak-stump upon the ledge above *Carie's* Swamp; from thence to a great black oak; and from thence to an oak sapling near against Arthur *Carie's* rise; all striped: and the road to go on the west side of them all." By this it appears that it must have been a forest from the Meeting-house to the top of Carey's Hill. Carey's Swamp is just east of Mrs. Newhall's.

The "Country Road," from Worcester to Spencer, was laid out by the town, Oct. 5, 1723. "From Chestnut Hill to the Meeting-house shall be four rods in breadth, as it is now marked on both sides of the way; with and under this alteration, — that that part of the aforesaid road below Mr. Denny's house, towards the brook, shall be measured from his fence on the south side of his house, four rods wide, all along southward of said fence until it comes to the brook at the bridge; and then the road is to run as marked out from that bridge, all along to Richard Southgate's, of the above-mentioned width, and Daniel Denny is to alter his fence where it encroaches thereupon; and, from Richard Southgate's house, along in that way which was formerly in use *when the town was laid out*, and hath now trees marked on the north and north-east sides thereof all along, and which, in like manner, is to be four rods wide, and Mr. Southgate's fence is to be altered, and the road, as now designated, to be cleared for the convenience of better passing with horse and teams; and so to Nathaniel Richardson's house; and from that to the said Meeting-house, by the old road up the hill, as now in use, without taking any notice of the trees within John Smith's fence, though formerly marked; and from the Meeting-house along by Judge Menzies' fence, as Deacon Southgate shall think fit; and from that fence to William Brown's house, as it is, all along, marked upon trees on the same, on the north and north-west side of the road; and from said William Brown's house to Oliver Watson's, as marked: all which roads are to be at least four rods wide."

The houses referred to in the above, as then standing, were Daniel Denny's, where Rufus Upham lately lived; Richard Southgate's, north-west from where John Southgate lived, — the house now gone; Nathaniel Richardson's, the house opposite to the present Catholic Church. John Smith's land was on the east side of Meeting-house Hill. William Brown's was on Mount Pleasant, lately belonging to Col. Henry Sargent, known as the Mower House.

The "Oxford Road," from the Great Road to the Capt. Gleason Place, was laid out July 20, 1724. "Began at a heap of stones, and a birch stake there erected by said selectmen, at the corner on the east side of said road, just over a *slow*, westerly of the Pound; the said course being there marked also with a birch stake in said heap of stones, with three chops in said stake on the west side, and then running from thence southerly to a black-oak tree, seven *foot* to the east of said tree, and making it up three rods wide west of said tree, which tree is marked with three chops on the west and south, — said tree was about six or seven rods from the abovesaid corner; and from thence to another black-oak tree, three rods east of said tree, which tree stands *betwixt* the aforesaid tree and the house where John Armstrong now lives; and from thence to Benjamin Johnson's fence, on the east side of the road, three rods from said fence, near by the said Johnson's house; and so along by the west end of said house to a young chestnut-tree, betwixt the house where the said Johnson now lives and the house where John Peters formerly lived, three rods to the east of said tree, being marked with a spot above said chops upon the east side of said tree; and from thence to a large chestnut-tree standing westerly by the house of Thomas Pierce, three rods westerly of said tree, being marked on the westward side; and from thence southerly to a black-oak tree, near by the house of Thomas Hopkins, three rods to the west of said tree."

The Charlton Road, from Capt. Gleason's to Green's Mill, was laid out November, 1724. Begins at a black oak near the house of Thomas Hopkins; thence to three chestnuts; thence to a red oak; thence to a clump of red oaks; thence to a red oak; thence to a black oak; thence to a gray oak; thence to a large black oak; thence to another large black oak, near a *slow*, westerly of the Widow Watson's house; thence to a young red oak; thence to another red-oak tree; thence to a black oak; thence to another black oak; and so on to a small white oak; a black oak; a black oak, "just up the pitch of the Livermore Hill;" a black oak; "thence to a pitch-pine on the top of the hill;" and so on, from one tree to another, "until it comes to two pines," — "the said pines standing near said Livermore's house;" then by trees, &c., "to William Green's orchard fence, three rods to the eastward of said fence; and so along by said Green's fence, as it now stands, on the westerly side of said road, to a black-oak tree;" thence to other trees, "to a black oak almost at the entering of Thomas Richardson's; and from thence to a black oak; and from thence to a black oak; and so including the causeway that is by Thomas Richardson's fence;" thence by a succession of trees described; "and so along to Capt. Samuel Green's cornmill." The road was laid out three rods wide.

By this description, it will appear that the road was laid, all the way, through the primitive forest, except near Mrs. Watson's (whose house was about twenty rods north-east of the house formerly of Capt. William Watson), at Jonas Livermore's at the foot of Livermore Hill, at William Green's orchard, where Amos Whittemore lately lived, and at Thomas Richardson's (afterwards the Baptist Parsonage); and that these were the only inhabitants, at that time, between Thomas Hopkins's (Capt. Gleason's) and Green's Mills.

The road from Green's Mills to Charlton line was laid out in February, 1745. "Began at Leicester south line, adjoining land of Thomas Parker, near about the way which is used for a cart-way, where we marked a black-oak tree, on the west side of said way, with two *chops* facing said way, and supposed to be in the land of Mr. *Bodwin* (Bowdoin). We ran along northerly till we came on the land of Mr. *Boarns* (Bourne); and so along till we came to Dr. Green's land; and, on the eighteenth day of February current, met again, and marked the way through Dr. Green's land. We began *to* near said Green's *wolf-pit*, a little south of said pit; and so along north a few rods east of said pit; and so along; and then easterly through said Green's improvements; and came into the way formerly laid out, at the south-east corner of Dr. Green's garden."

The road from the Southgate Place to the John King Place was laid out December, 1739. Beginning at the Country Road by Richard Southgate's; then by the house (against the house to be two rods, all the rest of the way three rods, wide), by marked trees, to Thomas Steel's, across his pasture, to the northerly end of the stone wall by his garden; and so by said wall; and, easterly, by side of said Steel's barn, extending southerly through said Steel's land by marked trees, through Bethune's land, across the way that leads to Oxford, to William Green's.

Steel's was the Henshaw Place; Green's, the John King Place.

INDEX.